The Marines Take Anbar

PUBLISHED WITH THE MARINE CORPS ASSOCIATION

The Marines Take Anbar

The Four-Year Fight
Against Al Qaeda

RICHARD H. SHULTZ JR.

Foreword by Maj. Gen. Donald R. Gardner, USMC (Ret.)

Naval Institute Press
Annapolis, Maryland

© 2013 by Richard Shultz
All rights reserved. No part of this book may be reproduced or utilized in any form or by any means, electronic or mechanical, including photocopying and recording, or by any information storage and retrieval system, without permission in writing from the publisher.

First Naval Institute Press paperback edition published in 2024.
ISBN: 978-1-68247-208-8 (paperback)
ISBN: 978-1-61251-141-2 (eBook)

The Library of Congress has cataloged the hardcover edition as follows:
Shultz, Richard H., author
   The Marines take Anbar : the four-year fight to defeat al Qaeda in Iraq / Richard Shultz.
     pages cm
   Includes bibliographical references and index.
    ISBN 978-1-61251-140-5 (hbk. : alk. paper)—ISBN 978-1-61251-141-2 (ebook) 1. Iraq War, 2003–2011—Campaigns—Iraq—Anbar (Province) 2. United States. Marine Corps—History—Iraq War, 2003– 3. Counterinsurgency—Iraq—Anbar (Province) 4. Qaida (Organization) 5. Anbar (Iraq : Province)—Politics and government—2003– I. Title.
   DS79.764.A63S38 2012
   956.7044'345—dc23

                                                                      2012046621

∞ Print editions meet the requirements of ANSI/NISO z39.48-1992 (Permanence of Paper).
Printed in the United States of America.

9 8 7 6 5 4 3 2 1

Contents

List of Illustrations — vii
Foreword — ix
Acknowledgments — xi

Introduction — 1

CHAPTER 1. This Is Al Anbar — 5

CHAPTER 2. 2003: All the Wrong Moves — 33

CHAPTER 3. 2004: Ugly Surprises — 58

CHAPTER 4. 2005: Stalemate — 104

CHAPTER 5. 2006: The Tipping Point — 144

CHAPTER 6. 2007: Cashing In — 184

CHAPTER 7. Conclusion — 231

Notes — 245
Index — 279

Illustrations

MAPS

1.1	Map of modern-day Iraq	23
1.2	Major population locations in Iraq based on ethnicity and religion	27
4.1	Iraq map of provincial stability	108
4.2	The location of named II MEF clearing operations in 2005	120

GRAPH

4.1	Enemy-initiated attacks	107

PHOTOS

Sheikh Ali Hatim Abd al-Razzaq Ali al-Sulayman	5
Fallujah city council members	21
General Tommy Franks and Secretary of Defense Donald Rumsfeld	36
L. Paul Bremer departing Iraq	44
Lt. Gen. James T. Conway and Maj. Gen. James N. Mattis	60
Lt. Gen. James T. Conway discusses the end of major combat operations	61
Col. Joe Dunford, RCT-5 commander, with Maj. Gen. James Mattis	67
Col. John Toolan, the commander of RCT-1	72
A typical IED roadside bomb attack in Anbar	88
Marine and Army battalions attacked the city of Fallujah from north to south	96
Marines fighting inside "the House from Hell"	101
Col. Stephen Davis, commander of RCT-2, examines weapons	121
Marines from 3/2 in action at al-Ubaydi during Operation Matador in May 2005	123

Marines from 1/6 in action during Operation Khanjar at Lake Tharthar in June 2005	127
An aerial view of Anbar's capital, Ramadi	129
The governor of Anbar Province, Mamoon Sami Rashid al-Alwani	137
Brig. Gen. James William	138
Iraqi citizens voting in Husaybah during the December 15, 2005 election	142
Runners prepare for the start of the Ramadi 5K race in September 2006	146
Maj. Gen. Tariq Yusif Mohammad al-Thiyabi, Anbar's Provincial Director of Police	149
Maj. Gen. Richard Zilmer, Governor Mamoon Sami Rashid al-Alwani, and Col. Sean MacFarland	155
Col. Lawrence Nicholson	161
Sheikh Aifan Sadun al-Issawi	165
Sheikh Abdul Sittar Albu-Risha and Col. Sean MacFarland	166
Sheikh Wissam Abd al-Ibrahim al-Hardan al-Aethawi, with Brig. Gen. John Allen	168
A combat patrol in Ramadi in 2006	172
Lt. Col. William Jurney, commander of 1/6 in Ramadi in 2006	173
Maj. Gen. Walter Gaskin	185
Brig. Gen. John Allen with Sheikh Ahmed Bezia Fteikhan al-Risha	187
An IED removal unit in Anbar	192
Iraqi police and Marines on a training exercise in Fallujah in 2007	206
A school renovation project takes place outside al-Karmah in 2007	225
Maj. Gen. John F. Kelly	231

Foreword

THE UNITED STATES MARINES ARE WARFIGHTERS! Our legacy includes Guadalcanal, Iwo Jima, the "Frozen Chosin," and Hue City. The Anbar campaign adds Fallujah to those epic battles. As time passes and the events of the Iraq War come into sharper focus, it is certain that scholars will consider the successful campaign to secure and stabilize the country's Anbar Province as an important turning point in that conflict. As Iraq's largest province and a center of Iraq's Sunni population, the vast region served as a major base of the anti-Coalition insurgency that gripped the country following the collapse of Saddam Hussein's Ba'athist regime in 2003. From 2004 to 2008 the Marines of the 1st Marine Expeditionary Force and 2nd Marine Expeditionary Force, with supporting units from the U.S. Army, U.S. Navy, U.S. Air Force, Iraqi military, and other Coalition countries, conducted a vigorous, hard-fought counterinsurgency campaign to defeat the al Qaeda–dominated insurgency throughout the province. During 2003 serious policy mistakes were made in Iraq, and the Marines, in early 2004, were deployed to Anbar Province and ordered to gain control and clean it up!

Richard Shultz's *The Marines Take Anbar* demonstrates how the Corps' nature as a versatile, tough-as-nails fighting organization allowed it to achieve success in Anbar. Throughout the campaign, Marines drew upon their long history of fighting small wars and insurrections to adjust and adapt to the province's complex environment and devise novel and effective counterinsurgency tactics. The foundation for this success was a fundamental shift by the 1st Marine Expeditionary Force to a counterinsurgency doctrine and realization that you could not win this war with kinetic operations. The resulting cooperation between the Coalition and Anbar's tribes evolved into the Anbar Awakening. As Dr. Shultz's account reveals, the Marines had little understanding of tribal engagement or the social and cultural organization of Anbar Province when first deployed to the troubled region. However, over the course of the campaign the Marines quickly began to comprehend the critical role tribes played in the everyday lives of Iraqi citizens in Anbar Province. Using this knowledge, general officers and small-unit leaders alike were able to exploit divisions in the tenuous alliances formed between the tribes and insurgent organizations, like Salafi Jihadists and al Qaeda, to convince these tribes to fight alongside the Coalition. The tribes from the districts of Anbar Province subsequently provided the Coalition with valuable intelligence, and more than four thousand Iraqis joined police and security forces. The sheikhs were supporting the Awakening, and were making a difference.

Throughout the Anbar campaign, reservists from the Marine Corps History Division's Field History Branch deployed to Iraq and collected interviews from participants. These interviews were collected in the field, often shortly after important operations. Thus, they serve as a valuable source of information on Marine Corps operations in the field, their deployments, and the Anbar campaign. These important, timely interviews reveal not only the perspectives of commanders and senior leadership, but also thoughts and observations of aviation, civil affairs, infantry, and logistics Marines serving multiple tours in Iraq. Additionally, the Field History Branch interviewed key Iraqis, gaining an even better understanding of operations during the Anbar campaign.

Dr. Shultz is one of the first historians to utilize these interviews to assist in documenting the Marines' war in Anbar Province. *The Marines Take Anbar* provides important insights and vivid descriptions of one of the most successful counterinsurgency campaigns conducted by Coalition forces during the Iraq War and provides numerous lessons that will be of interest to Marines, soldiers, sailors, fliers, and indeed all who in the future will engage in counterinsurgencies or other threats to the vital interests of the United States.

This exceptional work by Dr. Shultz represents a valuable resource on the Anbar campaign, ranking with our earlier epic battles and the several small wars of the Marine Corps.

Maj. Gen. Donald R. Gardner, USMC (Ret.)
President Emeritus
Marine Corps University

Acknowledgments

THIS BOOK COULD NEVER HAVE BEEN RESEARCHED and written without the encouragement and support of Maj. Gen. Don Gardner. The idea for a study on the Marine Corps' four-year campaign in the Anbar Province of Iraq has its origins in the early fall of 2007, when I was having lunch with General Gardner, who at the time was the president of the Marine Corps University.

During lunch the issue of Anbar came up in relation to the U.S. Surge in Iraq, which had been initiated in the spring of 2007. Based on the application of new counterinsurgency (COIN) strategy, by the fall of 2007 the Surge was beginning to show signs of success in the greater Baghdad region. This was receiving a great deal of fanfare in the media. But what the COIN strategy and Surge were achieving at that time, the Marine Corps had first initiated in Anbar in early 2006. And by late 2007 they had defeated the al Qaeda–led insurgency in the heart of the Sunni triangle. But there was no media attention to this four-year campaign. It was the best-kept secret of the Iraq war.

General Gardner proposed that the Anbar story needed to be told and offered me the opportunity to tell it. He asked that I prepare a proposal that he would review and then have me submit to the Marine Corp Heritage Foundation for research support. The Foundation directors graciously decided to support the request, and research began in the spring of 2008. Because of my teaching schedule at the Fletcher School, where I am the director of the International Security Studies Program, it was agreed that a book-length manuscript would be delivered by the end of 2010. I came close, but it took a few more months, and the manuscript was finished in March 2011. I want to thank the Marine Corps Heritage Foundation for its valuable assistance.

In addition to his role at the inception of this volume, General Gardner, as president of the Marine Corps University, opened the door for me to conduct a major part of my research under the auspices of the History Division of the U.S. Marine Corps. In doing so, General Gardner put me in contact with the second individual without whose support and encouragement this book would never have been completed. The director of the History Division, Dr. Charles Niemeyer, guided me through the primary sources that constitute the bulk of the evidence used in this study. This included the vast body of end-of-tour oral history interviews conducted with Marine officers who served in Anbar during 2004–2008. It is an amazing primary source that the History Division has completed under Dr. Niemeyer's outstanding leadership. I also had access to an array of other primary sources such as command histories thanks to Dr. Niemeyer. Along with General Gardner, I owe him a great debt.

In conducting the research I also had access to several of the Marine Corps leaders who directed the campaign in Anbar. I want to thank Gen. Joseph Dunford, Lt. Gen. John Kelly, Lt. Gen. Richard Zilmer, and Maj. Gen. Lawrence Nicholson for coming to Fletcher and sharing with me their insights and experiences in Anbar. And I especially want to thank Gen. John Allen, who not only gave me valuable interviews both at Fletcher and in Washington but also read and commented on the manuscript. In all of my interactions with these Marine Corps commanders and others not mentioned here, I count myself extremely fortunate.

At the Fletcher School I was privileged to have the help of a brilliant research assistant, Lauren Dorgan. At the time, Lauren was completing her graduate studies at Fletcher before joining the U. S. government. While she also read and commented on the manuscript as a whole, she was instrumental in researching and drafting chapter 2, "All the Wrong Moves." Her work on that chapter was of the highest quality, and I want to thank her for her outstanding assistance. I also want to thank all those talented Fletcher students with whom I was able to discuss Anbar within the context of my seminar "Internal Conflict and War."

The research for this book also greatly benefited from my involvement with the Armed Groups Intelligence Project and the Adapting America's Security Paradigm Project of the National Strategy Information Center (NSIC) in Washington. NSIC's president, Dr. Roy Godson, was one of the first in the 1990s to identify the rise of armed groups as a major security challenge. His insights guided my thinking and understanding of nonstate challenges. He has also been instrumental in helping me grasp the systemic implications of these developments by involving me in these NSIC's projects. Without Roy Godson's intellectual guidance and friendship, I would never have completed either this volume or my earlier 2006 study *Insurgents, Terrorists and Militias: The Warriors of Contemporary Combat*.

The production of a manuscript like this one requires a manager who has a number of special skills ranging from editing and proofreading various different versions of the manuscript, to making the manuscript conform with the publisher's format requirements, to preparing all of the photos, maps, and graphs for insertion into the manuscript. I have been so very fortunate that Freda Kilgallen, program manager of the International Security Studies Program at the Fletcher School, carried out these tasks for me. In fact, this is the third major volume she has helped me with, and I have greatly benefited from her professionalism, laser-like attention to detail, and exceptional thoroughness. Like with those other books, as well as with numerous articles, Freda made this book better, and I want to thank her for all she has done for me.

At the Naval Institute Press I want to thank Tom Cutler, director of professional publishing, and the members of his able staff for all of their assistance in shepherding my manuscript through the production process. It was a pleasure to work with them, and I am deeply grateful for all their efforts.

Finally, I would like to thank my wife, Casey, and my son, Nicholas, for all their love and unwavering support. They are the centers of my universe, and I am delighted to dedicate this book to them. They are the best and I love them dearly.

Introduction

IN MARCH 2004 THE MARINE CORPS deployed elements of the 1st Marine Expeditionary Force (I MEF) back to Iraq, this time to Anbar Province in the heart of the Sunni Triangle. The campaign plan I MEF drew up for Anbar left little doubt that its leadership believed they were embarking on a stability operation. While they were likely to face some local hostility, there was no consideration of the possibility that they would confront an organized resistance or insurgency. Then-Col. Joe Dunford, the chief of staff, recalled that during the planning for the Anbar deployment "we were not talking about an insurgency at this point. . . . The word 'insurgency' wasn't used in the early part of 2004."[1]

However, once on the ground I MEF quickly found itself locked in a bloody test of wills with al Qaeda in Iraq (AQI) and other resistance forces. Anbar rapidly turned into ground zero for a burgeoning and bloody insurgency. AQI made Iraq the forward edge of its global battle with the United States. In doing so, it pulled out all the stops in an effort to inflict a defeat of strategic proportions on America. Iraq would become for the United States what Afghanistan had turned into for the Soviet Union.

By the summer of 2006 the Marines fighting in Anbar were said to be losing, and there was almost nothing they could do to turn around that situation. This was the overwhelming conventional wisdom at the time. Enemy violence was skyrocketing, while almost every prediction for any U.S. success in Anbar was plummeting.

But one year later, in the fall of 2007, the situation on the ground in Anbar had been transformed. Violence was declining precipitously as the Marines cleared out the insurgents and took control of the ground. And by the time I MEF returned to Anbar in early 2008 for its third tour in the Sunni heartland of Iraq, its commander, Maj. Gen. John Kelly, was taken aback by the dramatic changes he found. The province was remarkably different from the one he left after his initial deployment in 2004. At that time, Marines were embroiled in a rapidly escalating and bloody fight.

Kelly recalled that in early 2005, as he prepared to depart, "there were roughly four hundred violent events a week in Anbar." But "when I returned in February 2008 that number was down to fifty attacks per week." And by the summer violent actions "were down to eight or nine a week." And that number "held for the last five–six months" of the year. "As a result," the general noted, "AQI had to commute into Anbar to blow something up. . . . If they tried to stay in a city the people very quickly would identify them."[2] The fight was over in Anbar.

How did the Marines do it? How were they able to learn and adapt in the midst of war? And how were they able to do so one year before the successful execution of the Surge in Iraq and the counterinsurgency (COIN) strategy on which it was based?

A common theme running through the texts on military learning and innovation is the axiom that learning and innovation come hard to large organizations in general and to military organizations at war in particular.[3] There are considerable barriers that make change in those military organizations problematic.

For example, in a recent study—*Lifting the Fog of Peace*—Janine Davidson identified three reasons why this is so difficult.[4] The first two reasons are drawn from organizational and bureaucratic theory.[5] Those utilizing the former to assess military institutions find innate rigidity and strong resistance to change. This is attributed to the formalized norms, standard operating procedures (SOP), and routine ways that large organizations do things. Those processes often serve as barriers to change. They throw up Chinese walls that constitute acute obstructions, seriously hindering adaptation.[6]

Bureaucratic politics specialists find yet other impediments to change. Davidson notes that "military leaders, like the leaders of other large organizations, seek to promote the importance of their organization and to preserve the organization's distinct organization essence" or central mission. Challenges to that central mission are likely to be resisted unless the leadership comes to believe that change will "enhance the importance and influence of the organization."[7] More Chinese walls!

Finally, there are the constraints imposed by organizational culture. Specialists on the topic such as Richard Downie find that institutional memory and history, key factors that shape organizational culture, frequently impede the organization's capacity to innovate and change. "When the norms, SOPs, and doctrines" of an organization "become widely accepted and practiced" they will "form . . . the organization's institutional memory." That memory is then socialized into its members making the organization "normally resistant to change."[8] Yet more Chinese walls!

In spite of these impediments, large organizations, even military organizations, can learn to, and do, change. Davidson finds militaries "change in response to three catalysts: (1) external pressure; (2) the opportunity or need to grow and/or survive, and (3) failure." But innovation does not "happen easily or automatically," she adds, because "militaries tie their cultural identities to specific roles or have career structures that fail to reward (or even punish) new ways of thinking."[9]

In Anbar, the Marines bucked these impediments to change. Why were they able to do so? Because the Marine Corps is steeped in tradition and over time has developed an idiosyncratic culture that fosters change rather than the opposition to it. A mainstay among the Corps traditions is the premium placed on learning as a core competency. It shapes and facilitates the way Marines think and operate.

In *First to Fight: An Inside View of the U.S. Marine Corps*, Victor Krulak underscored this commitment to learning. He did so through a number of historical vignettes that run the gamut from imaginative changes in strategy and operational concepts to the development of inventive weaponry and equipment. What stands out in each example is learning.[10] Krulak identifies several attributes "that constitute the identity of the Marine Corps."[11] Three of these—the capacity to think and reflect, to innovate, and to improvise—reflect the tenets of organizational learning, as described in the leading texts.[12]

Moreover, because Marines expect to be first in the fight, Krulak explains, they assume they will find themselves initially engaged without a clear understanding of the context or the enemy. The "war you prepare for," writes Krulak, "is rarely the war you get."[13] As a result, Marines learn roles, methods, and modes of behavior to respond to situations marked by ambiguity, uncertainty, and unforeseen challenges.

This approach is infused into training and professional education. James Warren observes in his U.S. Marine Corps combat history how, beginning at the Basic School for Officers, "training exercises" foster "adaptability, boldness, and self-criticism."[14] And through formal and informal study of their history, Marines learn that these core principles have served them well. The Marine Corps is "history-dependent" and consistent with Barbara Levitt and James March's observation that a key part of learning involves "encoding inferences from history into routines that guide behavior."[15]

Davidson outlines the following steps in the process through which learning is possible. It begins with members of the organization recognizing that there are performance gaps that can only be redressed through change. To make those changes, the organization has to acquire and process information in order to pinpoint alternatives.[16] Based on these developments, the "organization assesses and interprets the discoveries or evaluations made by individual members, and if deemed valid through consensus, explores options to resolve the anomalous situation." Resolution of those anomalies will take the form of actions that "adapt organizational behavior" through changes in organizational "norms, doctrine, or SOPs."[17]

The Marine Corps' organizational culture seeks to emulate this learning process and embed lessons from its experiences into the Corps memory. Its history is rife with examples of at first being caught in the fog of war but then, having learned from knowledge gained in the fight, being flexible enough to make adjustments, overcome gaps in performance, and turn misfortune into triumph.

The narrative that follows tells the story of how the Marine Corps was able to successfully adapt and change by tracing the steps through which its campaign in Anbar unfolded between 2004 and 2008. The study highlights those key junctures where learning took place and change followed.

The narrative opens with an overview of Anbar. To fight successfully in such irregular warfare situations, Marines needed a cultural understanding of the local population. But those deploying there in March 2004 were not equipped with such an appreciation. However, over the next four years they were able to gain an on-the-job understanding of Anbar and how to put it to good use. To appreciate what they learned to turn the situation around the culture and traditions of the people who live there—the Iraqi Sunni Arabs—are highlighted.

Next, the narrative turns to the period between the fall of Saddam's regime and the arrival of I MEF in Anbar. Ill-conceived postconflict decisions during those months, described in chapter 2, threw fuel on a budding resistance to U.S. occupation. Marine Lt. Gen. John Allen, who played a key role in the campaign in Anbar in 2007, described those policies as having created in 2004 "a perfect storm across Anbar," providing "the perfect opportunity for AQ [al Qaeda]."[18] Washington made all the wrong moves in 2003, and it was left to the Marines to pick up the pieces.

The heart of the narrative is the story of how the Marine Corps between March 2004 and September 2007 was able to successfully pick up those pieces. In 2004 I MEF found itself in the fog of war, not ready for the kind of insurgency emerging in Anbar; subsequently, it suffered ugly surprises. In 2005 the situation became increasingly worse. But the Marines were learning and gaining ground knowledge from the fight. That knowledge was plowed into the development of I MEF's 2006 campaign plan.

This narrative presents the decisive details of how I MEF designed a counterinsurgency strategy contextualized for Anbar. That strategy, which consisted of the COIN phases of "clear, hold, build" tribal engagement to expand the operating force available to the MEFs to ensure local security, and targeted counterterrorism aimed at degrading al Qaeda's clandestine apparatus, was all critical to the Marine success in Anbar. Implemented in 2006–2007 by I MEF and II MEF, it culminated in the situation General Kelly found when he returned to Iraq in early 2008.

The Marines had once more adapted and improvised. And in doing so they will have added a new entry—Anbar—to the long list of the Corps' other well-known historical triumphs at Belleau Woods, Guadalcanal, Tarawa, Peleliu, Iwo Jima, Okinawa, Inchon, Chosin, Khe Sanh, and Hue City. The narrative that follows tells the story of the successful four-year campaign to defeat al Qaeda in Iraq's Anbar Province.

CHAPTER 1

This Is Al Anbar

Sheikh Ali Hatim Abd al-Razzaq Ali al-Sulayman, the heir apparent to the Paramount Sheikh of the Dulaym Tribal Federation.
MONTGOMERY AND MCWILLIAMS, EDS., AL-ANBAR AWAKENING, VOL. 2, 106

MAKING HISTORY

THE UNITED STATES MARINE CORPS has a long, storied, and battle-ribboned history of more than two hundred years of waging war against America's enemies. The Corps' record has been chronicled in many excellent books that describe its legendary fights from the early days of the Continental Marines through all those engagements that followed.

That combat history is important to all Marines, each of whom will come to know it and believe he or she will be there when new history is made. The author of one recent volume on the Corps put it this way: "Marines are more conscious of their role in famous battles . . . than any other branch of the armed services."[1]

Indeed, Marines not only read about their history but also learn about it through the oral tradition of the cadences of their drill instructors (DI). The DI runs and trains Marines, employing a distinct style and lyrics, the content of which often constitutes a short course in Marine exploits. Consider the following verse taken from "Run to the Cadence with the U.S. Marine Corps," an oral collection of couplets recorded with DIs at Parris Island, the place where new enlistees learn to adapt to and embrace the Marine lifestyle and culture:

> 1, 2, 3, 4
> Marine Corps
> Listen up, I'm going to sing it some more
> Marine Corps

| 5

> *Tun Tavern to the Belleau Woods*
> *Marine Corps*
> *Making history so it's understood.*
> *Marine Corps*
> *Iwo Jima from a Guadalcanal*
> *Marine Corps*
> *Kicking butt just a everywhere*
> *Marine Corps*
> *Frozen Chosin to the Ho Chi Minh*
> *Marine Corps*
> *I think it's time that we do it again*
> *Marine Corps*
> *Beirut, Lebanon*
> *Marine Corps*
> *I think it's time that we get it done*
> *Marine Corps*
> *1, 2, 3, 4*
> *Tell me now what you're waiting for*

Since the terrorist attacks of September 11, the Marine Corps has deployed globally for major fights in Afghanistan and Iraq, as well as for lesser fights in other parts of the world. Those battles, no doubt, will prompt Marine DIs to revise their cadences, adding new entries from "the long war." Of these battles, none will be more momentous than the four-year test of wills in the Al Anbar governorate of Iraq. What follows is the story of that campaign.

KNOWING THE BATTLEFIELD

To fight successfully in the irregular warfare setting occupied by Iraq's Al Anbar governorate, Marines needed a cultural understanding of the local population, the way the inhabitants perceived and thought about their world, and the ways in which they organized social and political relations to survive in it.

Today, the notion that culture matters has become a mantra for the U.S. military.[2] New doctrine and professional publications are rife with the exhortation to know about the local way of life and to make use of that understanding to shape how you approach it. That local knowledge will tell you what you can and cannot do once deployed, and how you will be received or resisted by those people who live there. But that's today. Marines setting out for Iraq in March 2004 were not equipped with such an appreciation of Anbar.

And if that were not bad enough, the situation on the ground in Anbar had turned deadly. It was turning into ground zero for an increasingly violent and bloody resistance. The largely Sunni population there regarded Operation Iraqi Freedom (OIF) as an invasion and the continuing American military presence as an occupation that was empowering the Shia. In the towns and cities of the Euphrates River valley extending from Al Qa'im near the Syrian border through Haditha, Haqlaniyah, Rawah, Hit, Ramadi, and Fallujah, the armed resistance had rapidly burgeoned into what the Pentagon came to call an insurgency.

But over the next four years the Marines were able to gain an on-the-job understanding of Anbar and put it to good use. The result, according to Maj. Gen. John R. Allen (USMC), who served as deputy commanding general of 2nd Marine Expeditionary Force (II MEF) in Anbar from February 2007 to February 2008, was that "the world in Anbar Province changed." When he arrived, the situation on the ground "was by and large dominated by kinetic, security-based operations—shooting and moving and killing." But when General Allen and the Marines that he commanded departed, the Al Anbar situation was "oriented more along the lines of reconstruction, restoration, and support to law enforcement."[3] This was reflected in the dramatic drop of insurgent attacks, according to General Allen:

> By the time we left in 2008, you would have to look hard at a bar graph for direct fire attacks. Well, we had 432 incidents per week when we arrived. When we left, there were barely thirty-five incidents a week. We were experiencing three to five incidents a day—going from sixty to three to five per day—and you would have to look hard at that bar in February 2008 to find the color for direct fire on there. The vast majority of enemy incidents in the province, by the end of our deployment, were our discovery of IEDs [improvised explosive devices]—not even IED attacks—but, our discovery of IEDs. So the environment changed dramatically and it changed within the first three months.[4]

This narrative tells the story of how the Marines were able to defeat the insurgency in Anbar, a fight that as late as mid-2006 was characterized in a classified Marine intelligence report as not winnable. Marines, that assessment pronounced, were "no longer able to defeat the bloody insurgency in western Iraq or counter al-Qaeda's rising popularity there. . . . [The] social and political situation [had] deteriorated to a point" where U.S. and Iraqi forces were "no longer capable of militarily defeating the insurgency in al-Anbar."[5]

But in order to appreciate the story, which Marine DIs will surely extol in their cadences at Parris Island as they train future Marines, one must become familiar with Al Anbar. The Marines have developed a framework, described below, for decoding complex traditional cultures to assist Marine forces deploying to future Anbars. This framework is used here to impart the local knowledge necessary to understand the Marines' campaign at Anbar.

ANTHROPOLOGY FOR MARINES

When asked how the Marines turned the situation around in Anbar, General Allen was unequivocal:

> Without tribal engagement, almost nothing else was going to be possible in Anbar Province, which was very much a tribal society. . . . Tribal engagement was the facilitator, a means to an end. It not only facilitated force generation and recruitment for the Iraqi security forces in a very big way—when the tribes came over through our aggressive tribal engagement, it denied the tribal lands to the enemy. It also gave us the opportunity to build credible government at a provincial and local level . . . [and] provided ultimately for the environment of security in which economic development could occur.[6]

While General Allen is spot on, learning about tribal societies and how to operate effectively in their midst was a pretty tall order for the Marines arriving in Anbar in early 2004. After all, anthropologists can spend many years trying to understand the idiosyncratic characteristics of a particular tribe and its social setting. But the Marine forces of the I MEF were not equipped with the capacity to decipher a complex traditional society. They were going back to Iraq on relatively short notice.

The cultural challenges the Marines had to overcome in the four-year-long Anbar campaign have led the Corps to develop new operational concepts and approaches for future fights in similar circumstances. At the Marine Corps' Center for Advanced Operational Culture, specialists have developed a user-friendly framework that Marines can employ to become knowledgeable about "the cultural principles for any region [or foreign environment] to which they may be deployed."[7] For the architects of this approach, culture is understood as the shared way members of a particular group of people—such as a tribe—perceive and think about their world and how they organize social relationships to survive in it. Culture constitutes the communal worldview and social structure through which indigenous people make choices and take actions.

The framework, which is drawn from various schools of anthropological analysis, consists of "five dimensions of culture that are specifically relevant to

Marine operations."[8] For each dimension, the authors propose a series of questions, the answers to which provide the local knowledge needed by Marines: a familiarity with the physical environment, beliefs and values, social organization, political structure, and economy. The framework can be used both analytically and operationally. In other words, it is a method that can help Marines gain an understanding—a profile—of a traditional culture and then put that understanding to operational use in planning how they will carry out their mission in that culture. Here is a brief depiction of what each dimension encompasses:

- Physical environment. Relationships between people and their geographical location. The physical setting can possess great symbolic significance. For example, it may have been the center of past resistance or the place that produced great leaders or the home of an elite class.
- Beliefs and value system. The shared beliefs and values that unite people and serve as the enduring basis for their worldview. These beliefs form the prism through which events are interpreted. Beliefs and values are based on past events, remembrances, stories, symbols, rules of behavior, and the actions of heroic personalities. They are passed from one generation to the next.
- Social organization. Societies consist of social organizations that designate individuals and groups by their status, positions, and roles in the social order. Kinship, tribe, religion, and ethnic identity determine group status in traditional societies, as well as shape the degree of cooperation, competition, and conflict among them.
- Political structure. Social organization, in turn, determines who exercises political power. In traditional cultures, authority is not located in and generated through centralized leadership and modern political structures. Rather, cultural forms of leadership predominate and political power is exercised through a small core of leaders drawn from local identity groups such as tribes.
- Economy. In traditional cultures economic interaction—production and distribution of goods and services—is determined by the social relationships and power distribution among local ethnic, religious, tribal, or other communal groups.

In the discussion that follows, this framework is adapted to produce a profile of the people of Al Anbar. The goal is to help the reader become familiar with and grasp the identity of the people who live there—the Iraqi Sunni Arabs. Their persona is based on "ethnicity and language, religion, tribal roots and membership, and historical experience. Sunni Arabs [in Anbar] feel that they are part of a community that shares a set of similar characteristics, values, and experiences."[9]

WEST FROM BAGHDAD

Historians call Iraq the cradle of civilization for good reason. The story of the human presence there is a long one, dating back to the Paleolithic or Old Stone Age of 25,000 to 5,000 BC. Later, humanity's greatest early kingdoms rose and fell there—Sumer, Akkad, Babylon, and Assyria.

Many of humanity's momentous achievements and enduring assets have their origins in Mesopotamia. The Sumerians developed the first system of irrigation, the iron plow, cuneiform writing, and square and cube roots. The Babylonians devised the Hammurabi Code, the first elaborate system of law. And the Neo-Babylonians are credited with astrology, algebra and theorems, and the division of the day into twenty-four hours and a sphere into 360 degrees.

Then in AD 661 the conquest of the Muslim armies ushered in the nearly 1,300-year domination of Iraq by three successive empires: the Umayyads, the Abbasids, and the Ottomans. The Umayyads put an end to Persian rule and brought Mesopotamia—modern-day Iraq—into the Islamic world. Under the Abbasids, the Islamic world reached its pinnacle of greatness, covering practically all of western Asia and northern Africa. At the center of their empire was Mesopotamia.

Underscoring the centrality of Mesopotamia was Caliph Mansour's decision in AD 762 to establish a new capital there—Baghdad. He was captivated by the site's strategic position and wealth of natural resources. The new capital was at the crossroads of important caravan routes and had a healthy climate and plenty of water. Baghdad emerged as the Arab and Islamic worlds' center of learning and commerce. Many of the tales told in *The Thousand and One Nights* are set in the Baghdad of the Abbasid period.

History and Geography

Why did all of these momentous events take place in this part of the ancient world? The answers are twofold: geography and resources.

The physical setting—past and present—has been dominated by two powerful rivers, the Tigris and the Euphrates. Indeed, the ancient name for modern-day Iraq—Mesopotamia—is Greek for the "land between the two rivers." Surging out of Turkey's Taurus Mountains, the Tigris and Euphrates Rivers travel south and southeast through Iraq (Mesopotamia). In the north the two are separated by as much as 250 miles of open plains, but by the time the rivers reach Baghdad that space narrows to twenty miles. Eventually they empty into the Persian Gulf.

The silt from these two rivers, since ancient times, has turned the valleys through which they flow into highly desirable farmlands where agriculture thrives. The Sumerians were the first to understand this phenomenon, and they developed an irrigation system to capitalize on it. Others followed suit, building increasingly complex irrigation networks to yield substantial amounts of wheat and barley, along with many kinds of fruit.

It is within this lush farm country, on the eastern bank of the Upper Euphrates valley, that Al Anbar sits. Those who live there say their roots go back to the region's ancient time of greatness. This history contributes to their view of themselves as culturally superior to those who live elsewhere in today's Iraq. Geography is the starting point for understanding how and why they see themselves as such.

Located in central Iraq, Anbar Province has Baghdad to its east and Syria, Jordan, and Saudi Arabia on its western border. It is the largest of Iraq's eighteen governorates. During the early days of the monarchy in the 1930s, it was known as Dulaym Liwa, named after the Dulaym tribal confederation, the governorate's largest and most powerful social grouping. Later the name changed to Ramadi Liwa, for the governorate's main city, which today serves as the capital.

In the 1960s the name changed once more, this time to Anbar. This name was taken from an old historic town, the ruins of which can be found a few kilometers north of Fallujah. In the third century AD the Persian conqueror Shapur I built a citadel there to ensure control over the irrigation system that made this area an agricultural treasure trove. In AD 634 the citadel was seized by Muslim troops. By that time the area had become known as Al Anbar, which translates as "the depot" or "the warehouse." This refers to the large grain storehouses that were part of the Persian citadel. Mesopotamia's third mosque was built at Al Anbar. And Caliph Mansour, while waiting for his new capital to be completed at Baghdad, made Al Anbar his temporary headquarters.

Today, no one really knows how many people reside in Anbar. There are no precise statistics because the province has been a volatile place, not easily presided over. For example, in the mid-1990s there was serious antigovernment violence in parts of the province, and thousands were imprisoned. Saddam's regime estimated the total population at 3.5 million. Today, the estimates vary between 2 million and 6 million.

Whatever the exact number, the population is concentrated in seven of Anbar's eight districts: Abu Gharaib, Fallujah, Ramadi, Hit, Haditha, Anah, and Al Qa'im. Within these territories the majority of the residents live in either the cities and towns that dot the Euphrates River, which runs along Anbar's northern border, or in the rural farmlands to the south of this historic waterway.

Many of these population centers have their roots in the three empires that dominated Iraq (Mesopotamia) from the seventh to the twentieth century. For example, during the Middle Ages Hit produced cereal and fruits that were praised in the poetry of that time. Haditha's origins lie in Caliph Omar's decision to build a fortress there. Later, waterwheels were built to supply the water of the Euphrates to a vast system of irrigation canals that fed lush fruit orchards and date plantations. And the city of Anah was the summer residence of Harun al-Rashid, the fifth caliph of the Abbasid dynasty. During his reign the caliphate reached the zenith of its power and splendor.

Other parts of Anbar have their roots in the long period of Ottoman rule. For example, Midhat Pasha built Anbar's present-day capital of Ramadi in 1869 to gain control over the nomadic tribes of the Dulaym confederation. But Ramadi's environs quickly came to be laced with canals that turned the area into rich farmland. It also became the chief customs port of entry from Syria on the Euphrates road.

The largest part of the governorate—the Ar Rutba district—includes the sizeable Al-Hijarah Desert region in the southwest. Its main town, Rutba, lies well to the north on the road used by those entering Iraq from Jordan and Syria. In earlier times its drinking wells made Rutba the first stop for caravans en route to Baghdad.

The geography and resources of the Anbar region are inexorably tied to its history, which in turn serves as the foundation for the shared beliefs and values that unite the Sunni Arab tribes that dominate the governorate.

Decoding Beliefs and Values

In the summer of 2006 a highly credentialed team of Middle East military and civilian specialists delivered to the Pentagon a three hundred–page tome titled *Iraq Tribal Study: Al-Anbar Governorate*.[10] Produced under contract for the Defense Intelligence Agency, the study is a tour de force on how to understand and engage the Sunni tribes found in this part of Iraq. But as we shall see later, by the summer of 2006 the Marines were already on their way to doing exactly that. The *Iraq Tribal Study* was the kind of analytic exercise the Defense Intelligence Agency (DIA) or Central Intelligence Agency (CIA) should have produced in late 2003 as the situation in Anbar was rapidly disintegrating, or, better yet, before the United States intervened, to provide the knowledge needed to keep resistance within manageable limits.

Although not classified, the final product had stamped on every page "For Official Use Only." That did not prevent it from finding its way onto the Internet and into a summer 2007 column by Walter Pincus in the *Washington Post*. Pincus concentrated on the study's key recommendation, which "proposed changing how the United States interacts with Sunni tribal leaders . . . to [win] their support in fighting al-Qaeda in Iraq. The *Iraq Tribal Study* provided a handbook on how to gain that support."[11]

The starting point for winning their support was to come to know the long-standing beliefs and values that unite the Sunni Arabs of Al Anbar and shape the worldview through which they interpret events and take actions. Those beliefs and values are derived from three sources: Bedouin tribal traditions, Islam, and Arab culture. Each of these sources of identity, in conjunction with historical experiences, has created for the Sunni Arab population of Al Anbar the following self-perception: "[They] feel that they are part of a community that shares a set of similar characteristics, values and experiences. . . . [They] are proud of their religious and political history. They tend to regard themselves as the descendents and heirs to a long and great history of intellectual development, wealth, and political rule over the massive Islamic empire. They regard themselves as a group apart from other ethnic and religious groups, who they see as less worthy of political power and cultural-religious legitimacy."[12]

Understanding these elements of identity, the way they interact with each other, and the worldview they facilitate is the starting point for operating in Al Anbar.

Bedouin Traditions

In general terms, a tribe is defined as a traditional social group made up of several families, clans, or other elements who share a real or perceived ancestry and culture. But not all tribes are the same. Al Anbar's Dulaym tribal confederation's communal rules and ethos are rooted deep in its Bedouin past. They trace their lineage to the Bedouin tribes that populated the Arabian Peninsula in the pre-Islamic age. In AD 634, an army of 18,000 of these Arab tribesmen pushed their way into Mesopotamia, which at the time was ruled by the Sassanids, Persians who had taken control of Mesopotamia in AD 227. These Arab Muslim warriors soundly defeated the Sassanids. Arabic replaced the Persian language, and gradually the territory was converted to Islam. A large Arab migration to Mesopotamia followed, and with these immigrants came the culture and ideals of the Bedouin, including their martial prowess and warrior traditions.

These traditions took root in Anbar and have persisted, even among those parts of the population that cannot claim Bedouin roots. They nevertheless have adopted the Bedouins' moral code. One specialist explains, "Many Arabs, in both the villages and the cities . . . [consider] the Bedouin ethos as an ideal to which, in theory at least, they would like to measure up." Bedouins are looked upon as representing "the ancient glory of the heroic age."[13]

But what did those Marines deploying to Anbar in March 2004 need to know about that ethos? A starting point is the individual's loyalty to the tribe. The roots of that commitment can be traced back to the austere conditions the original Bedouins had to endure. The *Iraq Tribal Study* explains, "The Bedouins were nomads who lived together in tribes to survive in the harsh desert environment." Because of that "harshness and lack of resources of the desert . . . the tribe's first and foremost critical function was to provide protection from attacks from other competing tribes." The tribal members "pool[ed] resources to improve their chances of survival."[14]

Loyalty to the tribe was upheld by a stringent code of behavior that all members followed, beginning with personal and group honor. Honor, according to Bedouin expert Shelagh Weir, was central to their value system. For the individual, a strong code of honor extended to the family, clan, and tribe, creating a deep sense of responsibility to those social units.[15] This sense of responsibility extended to a willingness to risk one's life for the honor of the tribe.[16] "Honor necessitated acting in a manly manner that brings dignity to all tribesmen."[17]

Men demonstrated their commitment to honor through courage and bravery in battle or personal sacrifice for the good of the tribe. For women, "honor meant acting modestly, protecting her sexuality from all but her husband, and defending that which belongs to her family against all who wish to take it."[18]

Solidarity, loyalty, and honor are keystones of the Bedouin tribal value system. Long ago these principles took root in Anbar and were still deeply important to the people who lived there in March 2004. From them flow other principles of that code of behavior, all of which remain part of the character of present-day Anbar tribes. Among the most enduring are hospitality, generosity, careful etiquette, and civility. Indeed, the modern-day adherents of these precepts often follow rather exacting conventions. For the individual, this creates a deep sense of responsibility to the tribe.

For example, bringing to justice anyone who violates individual or group honor is central to this ethos. Revenge, blood feuds, and even war can serve as the means for addressing such transgressions. Often, revenge is formally prescribed as the duty of all of the tribes' men. This includes a readiness to risk life and limb to defend the honor of the tribe.[19] Nonviolent means can also be employed to settle disputes. These require mediation by tribal elders, and honor is restored not through bloodletting, but through other forms of recompense. These tenets of revenge and mediation are Bedouin customs that remain part of contemporary life in both rural and urban Anbar.

Among other Bedouin traditions maintained by the tribes of Al Anbar is respect for martial feats, military achievement, and a readiness to resort to the use of force. Fighting prowess was their raison d'être. This is captured in the well-mounted Bedouin fighter, at the ready to carry out a surprise attack against an enemy tribe. Fighting skills were born of necessity. The rigors of life demanded communal cooperation, social discipline, and security in order to survive. Men of the tribe were expected to demonstrate mental and physical toughness in the face of unremitting dangers. This was the duty of all able-bodied men. Images of these early fighters have endured and are still embraced in today's Anbar.

Islamic Principles

In conjunction with their Bedouin traditions, the people of Anbar view themselves within the context of an Arab culture and Islamic principles that produced one of the world's greatest civilizations. Islamic values have had an influence on Iraqi (Mesopotamian) tribes dating back to the Arab-Muslim conquest of the seventh century. At that time Islam served as a unifying creed that "was able to effectively organize and dominate the different tribal groups of the Arabian Peninsula . . . replacing the extreme political fragmentation that had formerly existed in Arabia, with various tribal groups vying with one another for local dominance. It was the integration of the Arabian tribes . . . that set the stage for the Arab Islamic conquests."[20] This included taking control of Mesopotamia, but that was not easy. The locals put up stiff resistance, and the territory of modern-day Iraq proved difficult to suborn and convert to Islam.

According to Phebe Marr, "During much of the first Islamic century, Iraq remained in turmoil."[21] Entrenched tribalism and Islamic factionalism caused violent discord. Many of Islam's early political struggles were fought in Mesopotamia, and it was there that its greatest schism occurred.

The details of that seventh-century rupture are too complex to cover here; it suffices to say that it grew out of a dispute over who should replace the third caliphate, the civil and religious potentate of the Muslim world. The impact of that clash cannot be overstated. Islam split into two great divisions: the Shia and the Sunnis.

The Muslim population in today's Iraq remains divided along these sectarian lines. In Al Anbar, the Sunni wing took root; it still predominates there and in adjacent governorates. But it is not the majority sect in the Arab parts of the country—the Shia are. However, the Sunnis in Anbar see themselves as part of a worldwide Islamic community that not only constitutes 90 percent of all Muslims but also is intellectually and theologically superior to the Shia.

That said, to fully understand the Islamic element of identity in Anbar and its impact on the worldview of those who live there, the Marines deploying in 2004 needed to drill down deep into Sunni theology. What they would have found is that no single interpretation of Islam exists. Rather, most Sunnis subscribe to one of four main schools of thought—Hanbali, Hanafi, Maliki, and Shafi'i. Knowing which of these schools dominates in Anbar is crucial.

The differences among these four perspectives turn on how more or less stringently Islamic principles are interpreted and practiced. The two main sources for each are the same—the Quran and the Sunna. The former is Islam's holy book, the latter the record of how the Prophet Mohammad led his life and what he approved of and did not approve of with respect to lifestyle and behavior.

The strictest of the four is the Hanbali school, established by Ahmed Hanbal in the ninth century. Its adherents can be characterized as doctrinaire. In other words, they believe in a strict interpretation of and adherence to the Quran and Sunna. The Hanbali school leaves no room to reinterpret and bend these principles to the contemporary world. Hanbali scholars oppose innovative interpretations that modify the literal meaning of Islam. One would be safe in calling this school dogmatic in outlook. The popularity of the Hanbali school has fluctuated since its founding. In modern times it reemerged first in the nineteenth century with the appearance of the Wahhabis and then in the twentieth century in the guise of the Salafi Islamic revival.

The Wahhabi offshoot of the Hanbali school was founded in the mid-eighteenth century by an Arabian cleric who believed Islam had been deeply corrupted. It is beyond the scope of this book to examine the roots of the Wahhab movement in Arabia.[22] Wahhabism is associated with the Hanbali school because both advance puritanical visions of faith and religious practice. The Hanbali school is recognized in Saudi Arabia as authoritative, and the Wahhabi interpretation of Islam has been practiced there since the al-Saud dynasty founded the contemporary Saudi state in 1932.[23]

Salafis also seek to return Islam to its roots through a literal interpretation of the Quran and the Sunna. The term "Salafi" is commonly used to describe perhaps the most doctrinaire form of Islamic thought. The Salafi movement is made up of Sunni Muslims drawn mainly (but not exclusively) from the Hanbali school. Many of the most puritanical groups found in the Muslim world are Salafis. They reject all reinterpretations and revisions of Islamic law that have transpired since the time of the prophet. Salafis seek to reestablish the purity of Islam and to resist deviant and corrupt practices.

It is important to note that many Salafi Islamists are nonviolent. While they believe in a strict adherence to the rules and guidance found in the Quran and the Sunna, they do not advocate the use of force against those who do not accept their beliefs. Rather, they advocate peaceful preaching and proselytizing. They use organizational and educational activities to expand the ranks of true Muslims and deepen their Islamic education and conviction along Salafi lines.[24]

But there are Salafists who do advocate the use of violence. Their roots lie in the Muslim Brotherhood, founded in 1928. The Brotherhood, as it evolved, saw itself as a vanguard party for political change and social justice in the Muslim world. Elements of it became increasingly militant, and the call for jihad—holy war—entered their political vocabulary.

By the 1950s a Salafi jihad ideology had taken shape. Its ideological guru was Sayyid Qutb, a member of the extremist wing of Egypt's Muslim Brotherhood. He proclaimed that nearly all Islam had fallen into a state of moral ignorance (*jahiliyya*). Islam was being subverted from the outside by the influence of Western decadence, materialism, and faithlessness, and from the inside by Muslim regimes in the hands of dictators who denigrated religious values. Qutb labeled these rulers heretics and apostates. He declared they had no legitimacy and called for jihad to overthrow them. In doing so, Qutb coupled a Salafist interpretation of Islam with a violent political ideology that fostered armed revolution.

Qutb and those who followed in his footsteps elevated the use of force—holy war—to such a position of importance that they came to view it as equal with Islam's five key principles, or pillars.[25] Once a regime's leaders were labeled infidels, armed violence became a justifiable means of dealing with them. And those leaders could be killed by whatever means were available.[26]

In Egypt this led Qutb and his followers into a confrontation with Gamal Abd al Nasser. In 1954 there was an attempt to kill Nasser. He was an apostate, in their view, and therefore should be executed. As a result of these actions, the Egyptian government declared the Brotherhood illegal. A wave of repression ensued, with the imprisonment and torture of thousands of Muslim Brotherhood members. Qutb was arrested, found guilty of plotting to overthrow the state, and hanged in August 1966.

However, by then a Salafi jihad ideology had taken root. It exposed those depraved social and political conditions requiring jihad, proposed a new idealized system to replace them, and identified steps to bring it to fruition. But it took the Soviet invasion of Afghanistan to give this fledgling movement a sacred cause behind which to mobilize beyond the national level, a cause to liberate a part of the Muslim community—the Ummah—from foreign infidel invaders.

Those who came from around the Muslim world to resist Moscow's aggression against the house of Islam (*dar al-Islam*) became the first generation of transnational jihadi warriors, and from their ranks would emerge the leadership of al Qaeda. Afghanistan was the starting point for what turned into the global Salafi jihad movement. By March 2004 its central front was in Anbar.

Al Qaeda and many of its associated groups quickly came to see the conflict in Iraq within the context of the "long jihad." Indeed, they anointed Iraq as the forward edge of the global battle against the United States. Victory there would have enormous strategic consequences. Additionally, Iraq afforded the opportunity to spawn a new corps of fighters—holy warriors—who after Iraq could put their skills to good use fighting in their native lands or elsewhere. In other words, in the first decades of the twenty-first century these new jihadis would serve the same purpose as was served by those holy warriors who after their self-proclaimed victory over Moscow took the jihad global.[27]

But Anbar was not a natural fit for them. The tribes that make up the Dulaym confederation are not Salafists and are far from the Hanbali school. Their practice of Islam is neither puritanical nor dogmatic. According to Iraqi and Islamic scholars, the Sunni Arabs in Iraq, including those in Anbar, are largely Hanafis, the most moderate of the four schools noted earlier.[28]

The Hanafi school is the oldest and has the most followers worldwide. Its origins lie in Mesopotamia, having been founded in Kufa by Nu'man Abu Hanifa in AD 767. What makes the Hanafi different from the Hanbali school is an emphasis on interpreting the Quran and Sunna in a manner that nurtures new ways of applying Islamic norms to daily life as it evolves over time. Hanafi scholars employ personal judgment to relate Islamic tenets to present-day circumstances. They are generally known to be more tolerant and moderate in their Islamic orientation. Hanafis are said to be flexible when it comes to differences within the Muslim community; this school is considered to be the one most receptive to modern ideas.[29]

While this moderate interpretation of Islam constitutes the mainstream approach in Anbar, it does not mean that there were no homegrown Salafi jihadists to be found there. They were present as well, the noted Iraqi historian Amatzi Baram observed in 2005. He explained that during the 1990s Saddam loosened up his approach to Sunni Islam, initiating in 1993 the Return to Faith campaign. "This granted Sunni clerics and mosques more freedom to practice religious rites and ceremonies, which reduced opposition to the regime from amongst the Sunni Arab religious community." Moreover, "the regime actively encouraged piety and made great efforts to present itself as being pious." Saddam had taken these steps out of necessity, as the 1991 Gulf War and the international sanctions that followed it had severely weakened his grip on the country. As a result, Baram writes, "many young Iraqi men turned to Islam," and "the mosques, indeed, served as focal points for religiously inclined young men interested in more than just Friday prayer." Of these, "a minority even moved toward the more extreme Salafi . . . interpretation of Islam."[30]

Out of these developments arose homegrown Salafi jihadis in Anbar. Following the U.S. intervention, they joined with their international brethren who began flocking to Iraq. In April 2003 Iraq became the central front in the Salafi global holy war when bin Laden called for Salafi warriors to join the fight there. Over the next several months they started arriving on their own or, more important, through an underground network that Abu Mussab al-Zarqawi established with his indigenous counterparts inside Iraq.

While all of this background information may seem arcane, it had real operational significance for Marines deploying to Anbar in 2004, as well as for those units of the Corps that followed.

Arab Culture

Finally, Arab culture is the third piece of the identity puzzle that shapes the worldview of the inhabitants of Anbar. They feel their Arab identity deeply. But what does it entail, and what did Marines need to know about it in 2004?

The historical roots of Arab identity lie in the nomadic tribes of the greater Arabian peninsula and the once brilliant empire that emerged out of that region with its capital in Baghdad. But all of that greatness receded into the backdrop of history when Ottoman Turks conquered the Arab empire and held that area for four centuries. The Arabs were eclipsed and subjugated, as greatness shifted to the Ottomans.

But in the nineteenth century things started to change with the revival of classic Arabic and the study of Arabic literature. The historian Philip Hitti noted that at that time "a consciousness of the past glory of the Arab empire and the cultural achievements and contributions of its citizens began to dawn," and with it "the urge for a resuscitated, reunited Arab society began to be strongly and widely felt. Political passivity gave way to political activity."[31]

What emerged from that renaissance is today's modern Arab ethnonationalist identity. However, this new identity was not fully formed until yet another round of fragmentation and domination of the Arabs following World War I had taken place, this time at the hands of the Europeans. But because of that misfortune, Arab ethnonationalism grew stronger, becoming a common identity based on a shared past, on the uniqueness of its people, and on what they saw as historical injustices imposed on them by the West.

Following World War II, Arab ethnonationalism finally blossomed. And the identity of the Sunni Arabs of Iraq (including those in Anbar) was deeply influenced by the narrative of modern Arab ethnonationalism. They had lived for centuries under Ottoman domination and, following World War I, within a British-imposed state legitimized by the League of Nations.

London had promised to help establish an independent Arab state if the Arabs joined them in expelling the Ottomans from Mesopotamia during World War I. The Great Arab Revolt ensued, and as World War I ended British forces finally gained control of Mesopotamia. It had been a tough fight. Upon taking control of Baghdad, the commander of British forces, Lieutenant General Maude, declared that London intended to set Mesopotamia free from four hundred years of alien rule. He and his army had come as liberators, not conquerors.[32] But it did not work out that way. What resulted was the League of Nation's mandate system. This amounted to occupation. Iraq was made a Class A mandate, with Britain in charge. Over an ill-defined period, London would groom the Iraqis for self-rule.

The mandate system was seen as a great humiliation by the Arabs, and resistance resulted. Resistance became an important part of the ethnonational narrative of the Arabs. In Iraq the mandate system sparked a countrywide rebellion. London prevailed after several months of bloody fighting. The 1920 revolt left a deep scar that became embedded in Iraq's national narrative. Resistance to foreign domination became the duty of every Iraqi and a part of modern Iraqi identity. In the aftermath of their defeat at the hands of the British, that resistance took the form of political and social opposition.

Iraq achieved its independence in 1932. The state that emerged was dominated by Arab Sunni elites. The details of how this came about have been the subject of many books and need not be recounted here. We need only note that from the time that the mandate ended in 1932 until 2003 the Sunnis ruled Iraq. The Iraq that emerged was a nation based on an identity that featured modern Arab nationalist themes and highlighted Iraq's place within the larger family of Arab nations. This includes a fierce sense of independence and resistance to outside interference.

Shaped over many years, the three enduring elements of identity discussed above—Bedouin tribal traditions, Islam, and Arab culture—have reinforced a self-perception of Anbar's Sunni Arabs as an elite community superior to Iraq's other ethnic and religious groups. And that self-perception was reinforced by the fact that Sunnis dominated Iraq's social and political order during the decades of Ba'athist rule and before. They were Iraq's elite class in their own minds and in social and political reality. Consequently, it should have come as no surprise that a sudden loss of this status could quickly translate into armed resistance in Al Anbar and elsewhere in the Sunni Triangle, if actions were not taken to forestall it.

Deciphering these elements of identity, the way they interact with each other, the beliefs and perceptions they generate, and the rules of behavior they foster was the starting point for Marines deploying to Anbar in March 2004. Without this decoding, engagement was going to be problematic. But no such decoding was provided to I MEF.

Social Organization and Political Power

In the Middle East of the nineteenth and twentieth centuries, imperial powers and indigenous strongmen regularly sought to consolidate state power. Equally often they encountered stiff tribal resistance to their centralizing schemes. To be sure, the ability of tribes to resist depended on the strength of their own solidarity, the political landscape of the day, the power of occupiers and national authorities,

A key center of gravity in Anbar was the traditional tribal leaders—the sheikhs. Fallujah city council members discuss business at the Fallujah Civil-Military Operations Center.
LT. COL. DAVID A. BENHOFF, AMONG THE PEOPLE, 6

and the harshness of the times. Tribal defiance has been a longstanding feature of the Iraqi landscape. More often than not, tribes have been able to turn back these assaults on their autonomy, as even Saddam and his Ba'athist cronies found out.[33]

After seizing power in 1966, the Ba'athist Party immediately denigrated "sheikhs and tribalism . . . as the epitome of backwardness." Both stood in the way of "building a new society" and "creating a [new] Arab man." As a result, sheikhs were gunned down or jailed in large numbers and tens of thousands of tribal people were forced to relocate to cities. Using tribal names was forbidden.[34]

In spite of these brutal measures, tribalism remained the core around which local Iraqi society revolved. Then, out of necessity, Saddam not only had to accept this reality but also depend on it to survive two disastrous wars of his own making.

First there was the eight-year bloodbath with Iran, from 1980 to 1988. Given the need for soldiers—and lots of them—to stop Iran's advance into Iraqi territory, Saddam was compelled to encourage tribalism. He had no choice but to make peace with many tribes and their sheikhs in order to expand the army. From the Sunni Triangle the Ba'athists recruited men to fill the leadership ranks of the Republican Guards, the Special Republican Guards, and the various other intelligence and security units. Tribes of the Dulaymi confederation of Anbar provided more than their share of men.

A second disastrous war, this time against the United States–led Coalition in 1991, resulted in the further empowerment of certain Iraqi tribes, in particular those in the Sunni Triangle. Defeat in Kuwait, Shia and Kurdish uprisings, and UN sanctions forced Saddam to subcontract security to local tribal sheikhs. He bought their allegiance by offering cash, other resources, and the opportunity to exercise local power. Tribes "received a large number of light arms and sometimes even rocket launchers, mortars, and howitzers. The intention was to enable the sheikhs to build a private army [or militia] among his tribesmen."[35] These local forces then served as a substitute for an army and other security forces unable to cover all of Iraq.

These blunders by Saddam brought many advantages to the tribes of the Dulaym confederation, and they did well under Saddam's regime, for the most part. However, gaining status and power had its downside, for Saddam's paranoid mind automatically saw the confederation as posing a threat. Living in constant fear of losing control to the same kind of cabal he had helped orchestrate in the past, Saddam inflicted periodic bloodlettings on the Dulaymis to prevent such subterfuge, real or imagined. Many prominent figures "were purged, jailed and murdered by [his] security forces due to suspicions of coup plots and disloyalty."[36] One of these bloodbaths, a particularly vicious one in the mid-1990s, did cause elements of the Dulaymi to rebel. Further carnage followed as Saddam took his revenge.

OIF swept Saddam from power in the spring of 2003, but the Sunni tribes and sheikhs to the west and north of Baghdad were still standing. They retained their local authority, power, and guns. Their militias not only remained intact but also were strengthened by returning cashiered Iraqi army vets.

This was the case in Al Anbar, where the Dulaymi tribes continued to predominate. But they had lost the resources provided by Saddam. How were they going to react to regime change and occupation, especially if it meant the loss of power and status to the Shia? Would the Sunnis of Anbar take up arms and rebel?

The Dulaym confederation is the largest and most powerful social organization in Anbar. It has a long history of maintaining that position. According to the *Iraq Tribal Study*, "The Dulayms trace their ancestry to the Zubaydi Tribal Confederation, one of the original tribes to migrate from Yemen to the Arabian Peninsula and Iraq."[37] The confederation appears to be made up of approximately fifteen to twenty separate tribes, although that is only a guess. The last detailed genealogical survey was conducted by the British at the end of World War I. The tribal structure in Anbar begins at the level of the extended family and proceeds outward, following a sequence going from groups of extended families or clans, to subtribes, and then to tribes. Finally, several tribes can come together to form a confederation (*qabila*).

Both historically and in contemporary times power at each level of tribal organization was concentrated in the hands of its leading sheikh or sheikhs. From very early times he was the father of the tribe—its leader—and had responsibility for tribal well-being. Sheikhs have traditionally had as a core obligation the protection and security of their people. During periods of conflict, the sheikh led tribal militia forces, with his sons serving as his lieutenants. In addition to security, the sheikh provides for his tribe's social and economic well-being.

A sheikh can come to lead the tribe by acceding to the role as the eldest son of the prior sheikh. But this is not automatic: there may be an unwritten custom

MAP 1.1 Map of modern-day Iraq

that the son be worthy. A second path is through achievement. The sheikh earns the position based on martial prowess, bravery, good judgment, or capacity to provide for the tribe. Finally, he may become sheikh by outwitting or otherwise wresting power from his competitors. A sheikh's power is not without limits. A tribal council generally exists, made up of elders with whom the sheikh confers when dealing with important tribal matters. Only after doing so are decisions made.

Finally, at the level of the tribal confederation is a council of the leading sheikhs of the tribes that make up the alliance. A paramount sheikh heads the confederation, or *qabila*, but in reality the *qabila* is loosely organized and directed by a council of sheikhs from each of its member tribes.

Confederations have traditionally dealt with those security needs that their constituent sheikhs could not provide to their individual tribes. Among the most important is local defense. Montgomery McFate, a noted anthropologist who specializes in these matters, describes this function as "cooperative self-defense among tribal groups." She goes on to explain that "the Dulaymi . . . traditionally have been responsible for security in the Al-Anbar province."[38]

To provide security during times of conflict, sheikhs mobilized forces from within their tribes. These confederations proved to be formidable fighting units and often were able to defy imperial governments and their armies. Tribal sheikhs relied on tribesmen steeped in the Bedouin martial skills that had become important attributes of tribal and Arab culture. These were passed on from one generation to the next and are still important in the twenty-first century.

Depending on the context, sheikhs and their tribes can exercise considerable political power at the regional level. This is the case particularly when central authority is not strong. As noted earlier, this was the case in the Sunni Triangle once Saddam had managed to lose two wars. He had to delegate political power and give autonomy to the tribes located there, and he had to openly support their sheikhs. This was nothing new. The British had done the same thing, as had the Ottomans at various times.

So, with the ouster of Saddam's Ba'athist regime, political power at the provincial level devolved to the tribes and sheikhs. Their social structure was intact and resilient. This was true in both the rural areas and the cities of Al Anbar. Tribalism remained the basis of social organization and political power—and traditional tribal values were still very important.

WHEN IN ANBAR: OPERATIONAL DO'S AND DON'TS

When I MEF returned to Iraq in March 2004, a full-blown insurgency was emerging in Al Anbar, the Marines' new area of operations (AO). The situation was going from bad to worse in a hurry. Fallujah was illustrative of what the Marines were going to have to deal with. The city was riddled with jihadis who were aligned with Abu Mussab al-Zarqawi, the former Afghan mujahideen who had fought in the 1980s anti-Soviet jihad. By the late 1990s he was back in Afghanistan, running a jihadi training camp with bin Laden's help. He created Tawhid al-Jihad, an al Qaeda clone, which focused on attacking Jordan, Israel, and Turkey before 9/11. The U.S. invasion of Iraq changed Tawhid al-Jihad's primary AO to Iraq.

By July 2003 al-Zarqawi's fighters had kicked off a campaign of murderous attacks inside Iraq. A car bomb was detonated with devastating effect against the Jordanian embassy. A suicide attacker was sent to UN headquarters in Baghdad to kill its top envoy, Sergio Vieira de Mello. And that was followed by the murder of Shiite leader Muhammed Baqr al-Hakim. The murder of al-Hakim was al-Zarqawi's first move in inciting a civil war between Shia and Sunnis.

These horrendous killings were a prelude to a relentless campaign of deadly mass attacks and beheadings that catapulted Zarqawi into international infamy as the mastermind of al Qaeda's savage war in Iraq. Within Al Anbar's principal cities and towns, his organization had a strong presence.

Consider Fallujah. Tawhid al-Jihad fighters were working with a local Salafi jihad unit run by Umar Husayn Hadid, an electrician by trade who during the 1990s established his credentials in Fallujah as a malevolent jihadi. Baram reports that during that time Hadid ran a "campaign against 'sins' in . . . Fallujah, threatening the owners of beauty parlors and music stores. In the mid-1990s, Hadid terrified the townspeople by blowing up Fallujah's only cinema." After Ba'ath Party security forces killed one of Hadid's top henchmen, he retaliated with the "murder of a senior official of Saddam's Ba'ath Party in Fallujah." A trial in absentia followed and Hadid was "sentenced to death by hanging."[39] He disappeared but resurfaced in Fallujah after the fall of Saddam's regime.

By 2004 Hadid was commanding "a Tawhid al-Jihad offshoot of about 1,500 men known as the Black Banners Brigade." Having established a close relationship with Zarqawi, he "assumed control of Jolan, [which was] known as the district in Fallujah where the most radical insurgents and terrorists, many of them non-Iraqis, took shelter."[40] During 2004 the Marines considered the Jolan district the most deadly sector of a very dangerous city. As the local Zarqawi look-alike, Hadid used bloody methods that were similar to those of his jihadi compatriot, as the following vignette illustrates: "'I asked Omar once how he could bear to do it, how he could hold himself together when he slaughtered another human being,' said one of Hadid's cousins, a 28-year-old man who gave his name only as Abu Nour. 'He laughed and swore he'd never personally beheaded a hostage. He said he chose men who don't have hearts to do the actual killing. He said it's a battle, so everything is permissible.'"[41]

How did this situation come to pass in such a short period of time? After all, it was less than a year since the official end of combat operations and the departure of the Marines from Iraq. The short answer is that the United States facilitated this debacle by making all the wrong moves in the aftermath of OIF, as chapter 2 underscores. But the point to be made here is that Anbar did not have to descend into the violent state of affairs that awaited the Marines. While some degree of armed resistance in the Sunni Triangle was surely inevitable, the potency of the fight I MEF had to take on was not.

A social and political understanding of the governorate would have provided early warning signals that could have helped shape a strategy aimed at keeping armed resistance at a much lower level of intensity. Those guidelines can be deduced from the above profile of Anbar.

The starting point for developing the guidelines would have been to identify the social and political center of gravity in Anbar. The great Prussian philosopher of war Carl von Clausewitz employed the term "center of gravity" to refer to an enemy's "hub of all power and movement, on which everything depends."[42] Clausewitz believed that a commander who was able to identify and disrupt the center of gravity could undermine his enemy's ability to wage war.

But for Clausewitz, while an enemy's center of gravity could include a country's capital, its military, a particular leader, or the strength of a coalition, the path to each nonetheless always was through major battle. Battle dominated his thinking about the conduct of war. However, it is important to note that Clausewitz understood war as a conventional fight: army versus army on battlefields.[43]

In Iraq Clausewitz's way of war was OIF, the conventional fight that was over within a few weeks. It was not the "long war" that followed. OIF was consistent with the way in which the United States military thought about and prepared for war during most of the twentieth century. The "long war" differed markedly. According to former deputy supreme Allied commander Europe Gen. Rupert Smith, that prolonged conflict—the war that followed OIF—was unconventional and irregular, and took place not on a traditional battlefield, but amongst the people.

General Smith sees such conflicts as adversarial struggles for the loyalty of or control over a population wherever they live and work, irrespective of state boundaries. Often they are battles over who has or can gain legitimacy or control of that population.[44]

In Anbar the center of gravity was the Sunni Arab tribes of the Dulaymi confederation. They were the central social and political unit in the governorate long before and during Ba'athist rule. And they remained pivotal in the power vacuum

THIS IS AL ANBAR | 27

that followed Saddam's demise. Thus, the central U.S. goal should have been to keep them out of the hands of both the former regime elements and the Salafi jihadis, each of whom intended to take up arms against U.S. forces. If either armed group was to turn its resistance into a robust and protracted struggle, it needed the help of the tribes of the Dulaymi confederation. That was essential if a dogged fight against U.S. occupation was to be waged.

MAP 1.2 Major population locations in Iraq based on ethnicity and religion

CONNABLE, *U.S. MARINES IN IRAQ, 2004–2008*, XI

However, it was not written in the stars that they would form up into a viable coalition. Just the opposite. The Sunni Arab tribes of Anbar were not the natural allies of either the former regime elements or al Qaeda and its local look-alikes. But to be able to prevent this kind of alliance from taking place, the United States had to engage the tribes on their terms. That required developing a strategy of engagement that reflected an understanding of their Bedouin tribal traditions, Islamic principles, and Arab cultural values.

Based on that knowledge the following operational do's and don'ts constituted the sine qua non—the indispensable starting point—on which to build a tribal engagement strategy.

First, know the tribes' history and how important that history is to the Sunni Arab tribes of Anbar. Do not ignore or downplay it. The past is not really the past but merely prologue. They live in the shadow of their history and legends. And that past makes those tribes see themselves as part of a special people.

Also recall that the Sunnis have enjoyed a special status in Iraq and benefited from it for a long time. This was true during the occupation of the Ottomans, when the Turks did not have the men necessary to control all parts of their vast empire. In Iraq this meant relying on locals whom they could coopt. They provided political, economic, and educational benefits to Sunni tribal leaders to gain their support and then used these sheikhs and their tribesmen to rule over the territory. The Sunni tribes were empowered and evolved into the dominant class in Iraq. The historical narrative of Iraq, including the Ottoman era, is one of Sunni preeminence.

That ascendancy continued after the Ottomans departed, and the Sunnis flourished in more recent times under Ba'athist rule. Consequently, regime change was bound to hit the Sunnis hard and create a great sense of loss, compounded by fear of a coming night of the long knives.

The overthrow of Saddam constituted more than the loss of special status. It brought to the fore the Sunnis' worst nightmare, fear of a fate much more terrible than the loss of position. Why? The Shia. They were rising in power in Baghdad, thanks to the U.S. occupation. And the Shia would surely take revenge on the Sunnis. After all, it was the Sunni-dominated Ba'athist regime that had slaughtered the Shia in the 1990s. Following the debacle of Saddam's Kuwait invasion, Shiites in southern Iraq rose in revolt. Republican Guard divisions brutally crushed that uprising and the Shia felt the full force of Saddam's retribution. Many thousands were killed in what amounted to a scorched-earth policy of sectarian cleansing.

Fear of a massive Shia revenge campaign was very real to the Sunnis, and it opened the door for the former regime elements and jihadists to exploit. Understanding the origins and the depth of Sunni angst—knowing the tribes' histories—and assuaging the fear was the starting point for tribal engagement in Anbar.

Second, understand that the Sunni tribes of the Dulaymi confederation are made up of proud people who demand respect. Never downplay or give only fleeting attention to that reality. And never disrespect the tribesmen. The importance of respect cannot be overstated, notes Col. W. Patrick Lang USA (Ret.). The good colonel knows what he is talking about, having worked with tribesmen on several continents during his long career. In an insightful essay titled "Understanding How to Live and Work with Tribesmen," he writes, "Whether they are Arab Bedouin, Afghan Pushtuns, Laotian Hmong, or Somali herdsmen, it is always RESPECT that tribesmen look for from outsiders who come to their lands seeking their help and friendship. This is true whether tribesmen are nomads or villagers."[45]

But this was not going to be easy for the Marines to accomplish. After all, the United States was hardly seen by the tribesmen of Anbar as having come seeking their help and friendship. Moreover, some of the military tactics used by American forces in Anbar in 2003 were seen as the antithesis of respect. The way houses were searched in the dead of night with the front door kicked in and the men humiliated in full view of their families is but one example.

From the perspective of those who were on the receiving end of these and other more lethal experiences, the United States was an invader and occupier to fight and resist, and their historical narrative demanded such defiance. Recall that resistance is an important part of Arab ethnonational heritage.

In the period before the Marines moved into Anbar, the message coming from Baghdad, now under the control of Coalition Provisional Authority (CPA), was hardly one of respect for the folkways and traditions of the tribesmen of the Sunni Triangle. The CPA saw them as backward and primitive. Modernity had passed them by. They were not to be engaged but eschewed. They were not going to be part of the CPA's new Iraq. Rather than respect, the tribes of Anbar were witnessing disdain for their traditional way of life.

Third, learn, accept, and—to the extent possible—emulate the code of values and beliefs that guide the tribes' behavior and ways of doing things. Most important to that system of principles is honor.

Throughout the Middle East, writes anthropologist Montgomery McFate, collective honor is the common denominator that can be found in all traditional communities. She explains, "In these societies . . . because honor always derives from the group, an individual's conduct also reflects back on the group and its honor. . . . If an individual acts shamefully, the whole tribe is shamed." Likewise, when an individual's honor is violated "it must be regained. The most expedient means to restore lost . . . honor is through violence."[46] And the whole tribe has a duty to fight to restore honor. It is a collective duty.

The importance of honor is captured in this adage from Arab tribal customary law: "It is better to die with honor than live with humiliation."[47] Colonel Lang places honor at the center of tribal mores: "Among the tribal Arabs, *Urf* consists of the practices and traditions of behavior, ownership, personal status, recompense for an injury done, and most of all HONOR, that have grown up in the tribal group over many years. . . . Because of the central role played in tribal life by *Urf* . . . one must always remember that the traditions of the tribes are always present in the background, and that knowledge of these traditions and respect toward its practitioners will pay rich dividends."[48] To do the opposite will demand retribution to restore honor. McFate gives the following example, which reveals how complex the algebra of honor is in Iraq:

> In Ramadi a U.S. soldier who frequently urinated from the top of his Bradley offended the citizens' honor so deeply that local insurgents twice tried to destroy the vehicle, first with a rocket-propelled grenade and then with a Russian C5K missile. After their attacks failed, they requested the services of an insurgent sniper for hire, who described the assassination as follows: "[T]he Bradley stopped and the soldier stood on it ready to relieve himself. He was relaxed. He put his hand on his trousers. I took aim and fired one shot and saw him drop dead." As one insurgent in Fallujah observed, "America has invaded us and insulted us and so it is legitimate for us to fight. It is our honor and our duty and we know that it will be a long fight."[49]

Fourth, understand the system of prescribed methods used to bring to justice those who violate honor. This tenet is directly related to individual and group honor and is equally important to grasp. McFate's example reveals the deadly way in which it can be played out. Knowing the intricacies of these conventions is essential. They include revenge, blood feuds, and even war as the means for resolving such offenses. Revenge is the duty of all of the tribes' men, and each must be willing to risk his life to defend the honor of the tribe by exacting revenge on those who violate tribal honor.

American soldiers in Iraq came to refer to such actions as bloodline attacks, which were based on the Arabic rule of five. It was their version of an eye for an eye: "If you do something to someone, then five of his bloodline will try to attack you." This was the "vengeance of brothers, sons, cousins and nephews."[50] An eye for an eye and a tooth.

Fifth, know that this is a male-dominated society and that demonstrating manliness is another one of those enduring aspects of the tribes' code of values. It is an essential requirement that men demonstrate courage and fighting prowess in defense of the tribe. Maintaining the safety and security of the tribe is a core duty. This ethic of manliness has existed since the first Bedouin appeared in Arabia and remains an underlying principle in the tribal culture of Anbar.

Other principles are also important to know, and understanding how to respond to them is essential. These principles include hospitality, generosity, careful etiquette, and civility. Each will be graciously extended to the outsider who shows respect and understands how important maintaining one's honor is to those welcoming the stranger into their midst.

Sixth, know that religion is likewise very salient to the Sunni tribesmen of Anbar. They truly believe in God. And they follow a vision of the universe and how to live righteously in it taught to them through the practices of Prophet Mohammad. However, do not assume that all Sunni Muslims are the same with respect to how they approach Islam. To be sure, they all follow the same two primary sources, the Quran and the Sunna. But beyond that, important differences exist that affect their behavior and lifestyle. Even though it is complicated, know that there are four main schools of Sunni thought. And also know how they differ and which one dominates in Anbar. That is crucial and has important operational implications.

Seventh, know that the tribes of the Dulaym confederation are not just a local social club. Rather, they are political actors and have a strong political identity. At different times, they have wielded considerable power and political clout. This has especially been the case when the central authority in Baghdad was weak and unable to extend authority.

But understanding the inner workings of this amalgam of tribes is a major challenge. Who are the key sheikhs? How are decisions reached? What are the resources that the confederation members need? How do they get them? These are only the most obvious details that have to be sorted out if engagement is to stand a chance.

Eighth, understand that a core principle of these confederation affiliates is group solidarity. It starts at the family level, and moves up through the clan and tribes to the confederation. And when threats and dangers from outside appear, collective security and self-defense demands that all pull together. Men are expected to demonstrate mental and physical toughness in the face of danger and to fight in defense of the tribe. It is the duty of all able-bodied men.

Throughout their history, the tribes of the Dulaymi confederation have been the primary guarantors of local security. Alliances were formed among its members to accomplish security. Attack one of them and here is what you can expect back: "Anyone who commits an act of aggression against any one of us must expect retaliation from us all."[51] This is no empty adage from a long-forgotten past. Rather, there is a lengthy ledger of well-documented cases of collective defense to resist external intruders. Today we would describe the methods of defense as irregular warfare.

Traditional Bedouin ways of fighting became important attributes of tribal and Arab culture that were passed on from one generation to the next. And they were still important at the dawn of the twentieth century, a fact that T. E. Lawrence understood and on which he capitalized during World War I. Knowledge of Arab warfighting traditions led him to conclude that raiding could be employed effectively against the Turks. And it was. Raiding became the key operational concept of the Great Arab Revolt in Mesopotamia.[52]

Nearly a century later, revolt and raiding remained deep-seated parts of the narrative of the Sunnis of Al Anbar. The fighting methods and traditions found in that narrative still shaped attitudes about such matters. And following OIF they were on display in the violent and brutal insurgency that awaited the Marines in March 2004.

Ninth, be open to working with tribal leaders, even though they will not conform to modern conceptions of leadership as understood in organizations like the U.S. Marine Corps. Colonel Lang, drawing on years of experience embedded in traditional societies, explains that "one of the most common errors made by Americans" when attempting to work in traditional societies like that found in Anbar is "to adopt the idea that traditional leaders are 'dinosaurs' who are outdated relics of the past."[53] They see them as corrupt, uninformed about modern ways, primitive, and backward.

Do not take such an approach, cautions the colonel: "In entering into relations with tribesmen, we should understand that one must begin by dealing with their leaders."[54] You will never gain tribal friendship or form alliances without the concurrence of their sheikhs.

Tenth, never think that the tribesmen of the Dulaymi confederation want to adopt our ways and become like us. What all of the above says is that they do not. They are quite comfortable in their own skin. They are living in a tribal society because they want to. They "find it satisfying and protective," explains Colonel Lang. "The important thing that you [must] understand is that they are living in accord with ancestral traditions because they want to."[55]

Unfortunately, these do's and don'ts were not part of the calculus that guided the CPA in the days and months following OIF. Rather, the CPA and its head, Paul Bremer, made all the wrong moves when it came to Al Anbar. It would be left to the Marines to pick up the pieces. But to do so, they had to base their operational plans on an understanding of the cultural context of Anbar and how to work inside the tribal system that dominates the human terrain found there. That proved to be no easy task in 2004 when the Marines returned to Iraq.

CHAPTER 2

2003

All the Wrong Moves

DAY-AFTER ILLUSIONS

JUST BEFORE ROLLING INTO IRAQ as part of the 2003 American intervention to oust Saddam, the Marine wanted to know what would happen to Iraq after the coalition forces beat the Iraqi military and took over the country. As he recounted later, Lt. Gen. John Kelly had a confident response for the young Marine warrior: "Well, we're America, the greatest nation on Earth, there's probably battalions worth of engineers and specialists and all that," Kelly said, "and as we move north and take the regime down, they'll come in behind us and they'll establish democracy and take over the running of the country."[1]

Kelly was not the only one who thought the United States, as a great and mighty power, must have a plan for the day after the war. In a meeting just months before the war, President George Bush asked national security adviser Condoleezza Rice a similar question: "A humanitarian army is going to follow our army into Iraq, right?" Rice told the president that he was right, there would be, and looked away.[2]

But the battalions of specialists never followed, and the humanitarian army never marched in, because no one had planned for it, built it, or called it up. Planning for the Iraq War focused so intensely on taking down Saddam Hussein—regime change—that the administration never developed a clear plan of what should happen the next day. Why? Part of the answer may well lie in the administration's attitudes toward such activities. Entering office with an open disdain for what had been called nation building during the Clinton years, the Bush administration had little interest in conducting anything of the sort in Iraq. One diplomat is said to have called the American plan for Iraq the *Wizard of Oz* concept of regime change: "We go in, we kill the wicked witch, the munchkins jump up, they're grateful, and then we get in the hot-air balloon and we're out of there."[3]

Serious contradictions lay at the core of planning and execution of the Iraq War. Key players in the White House and the Pentagon made their case for war by simultaneously arguing for the worst-case scenario regarding the existential danger Iraq posed for the United States and the need to change the regime and the best-case scenario regarding the ease with which Iraq could be rebuilt.[4] Moreover, there was a deep contradiction in how the United States expected to win the war and then keep the peace, as Lt. Col. Steven Peterson, who worked on war planning, later wrote in a paper that, according to Michael Gordon and Bernard Trainor's *Cobra II*, became the talk of the military war colleges. The war plan was premised on destroying the regime's command-and-control capacity, whereas planning for an easy postwar transition was premised on the idea that Iraq's government would essentially hum along smoothly after the war and make the transition to a democratic order.[5]

In 2003 the ill-planned postconflict decisions, rather than enabling the seamless transition to reconstruction and democratic transformation that Pentagon planners envisioned, actively set that transition back and threw fuel on an emerging violent resistance to U.S. occupation. In 2003 the United States made all the wrong moves.

PLANNING BUT NEVER A PLAN

Various departments and officials did conduct planning for a postwar Iraq before the start of OIF, but a clear and unified plan never materialized. Research was done, debates took place, but the results were ignored. A dysfunctional interagency process meant that when the Department of State, the Department of Defense, and the CIA disagreed on a policy—as they often did—the debate was rarely fleshed out, and a clear decision was rarely reached. When first a retired general and then a retired diplomat were sent in to run postwar Iraq with scant preparation, each man discarded even decisions made at the White House level, although they had received so little guidance they may not have known at the time whose decisions they were rejecting. In the weeks and months leading up to the war, American officials had a shocking lack of certainty about what Iraqi government would look like after Saddam fell. Even major decisions, such as the ill-conceived decision to disband the Iraqi army, came as a surprise to many in the administration, including Secretary of State Colin Powell.[6]

The Department of State conducted the most in-depth and lengthy process of considering Iraq the day after the invasion. The Future of Iraq project brought together exiles and experts to look into many of the issues that would be faced in postinvasion Iraq. But the project reflected the Department of State culture—a consultative, long, extensive process convening seventeen working groups and more than two hundred Iraqis to create a thirteen-volume exploration of a variety of issues related to building a new Iraq. It did not result, however, in a clear and comprehensive plan for postinvasion action.[7]

The Future of Iraq project did foresee and highlight many of the looming dangers and urgent problems that came to pass following regime change. Iraqis warned about the likelihood of revenge taking and looting. Various exiles anticipated disagreements about the role of Islam and federalism in the new Iraq. They argued over the extent to which Iraq should undergo de-Ba'athification and about the role of the UN in the new country. Most clearly, they foresaw problems with a lengthy occupation. One adviser to the project later wrote that Iraqis agreed on one point: "None would tolerate a U.S. military occupation."[8] But rather than opening debate, kick-starting a problem-solving process, and generating an interagency-based action plan for the new regime, the Future of Iraq project became a $5 million dead end.

When the Pentagon gained approval from President Bush to take over the postwar planning, the Future of Iraq project was all but junked. The man appointed to take charge of postwar Iraq just weeks before the invasion—retired lieutenant general Jay Garner—never was briefed on the results of the project, nor was he even informed that it existed. When he found out on his own, he was explicitly prevented by Secretary of Defense Donald Rumsfeld from hiring some of the key Department of State officials involved in the project.[9]

When the Department of Defense took over the planning for postwar Iraq, it was taking on a task unlike any it had seen in many decades. In fact, the department had not led such a major postconflict effort since World War II.[10] But facing a difficult task unlike any it had seen in a half-century, Pentagon officials did not seem to take seriously the challenges of taking over Iraq, a country with a legacy of resistance to occupation, decaying national infrastructure, and profound religious and ethnic splits that had been held together by the brutal strongman dictatorship of Saddam Hussein.

At the helm of the military operation, Gen. Tommy Franks focused on kinetic operations and winning what in military parlance is known as the first three phases of the war, which center on battle and the clash of armies. But he gave little, if any, attention to Phase IV, postwar operations. Asked in a U.S. Central Command (CENTCOM) meeting before the war about the state of Phase IV planning, Franks said, Deputy Secretary of Defense "Wolfowitz is taking care of that."[11] In what may be the ultimate illustration of Franks' perception of his role in postwar Iraq, in May 2003, a month after the fall of Baghdad, he announced his intention to retire after thirty-eight years in the Army. That month, as their boss was phasing out of OIF, Army commanders on the ground realized that their soldiers would, indeed, have to stay and pacify Iraq. They started looking for a Phase IV plan. But what they found, as army major and OIF historian Isaiah Willson III wrote, was that "there was no Phase IV plan."[12]

At the Pentagon the civilian leadership had embarked on a lofty but unrealistic vision of building in Iraq a future Arab ally that would be a democracy. Moreover,

Gen. Tommy Franks and Secretary of Defense Donald Rumsfeld brief Pentagon reporters on the campaign in Iraq.

REYNOLDS, *U.S. MARINES IN IRAQ, 2003: BASRAH, BAGHDAD, AND BEYOND*, 25

they hoped that regime change in Iraq would pave the way for a broader transformation of the entire region. Within the Pentagon, Undersecretary of Defense for Policy Doug Feith took charge of postwar planning within the Office for Special Plans. Along with Deputy Secretary of Defense Paul Wolfowitz, Vice President Dick Cheney, and Rumsfeld himself, Feith is often seen as one of the key officials who took the lead in pushing for war with Iraq. Advocates of the war on both ends of the political spectrum saw Iraq, it is often said, as a blank slate on which they could undertake the creation of a democratic Middle Eastern country.[13]

This kind of thinking was abetted and encouraged by key Iraqi exiles, especially Ahmed Chalabi, who batted aside questions of postwar difficulties by promising that exiles like himself would be ready and willing to lead the new Iraq. This was a promising formulation for a Bush administration eager to take down Saddam but not looking to engage in nation building. Chalabi's Iraqi National Congress (INC) did more than provide a formula for a postwar government: it delivered copious (though questionable) intelligence that made the case for war and regime change. Chalabi, an exile from Iraq's Shiite majority, had spent a decade cultivating relationships with journalists, lawmakers, and key individuals who would hold top positions in President Bush's administration. Despite a lifetime dogged by allegations of financial impropriety, and fleeing indictment in Jordan on embezzlement charges, Chalabi managed to become a key adviser to the administration during the run-up to the war. Indeed, he became a heavy favorite of many in the Pentagon to take charge of Iraq after the United States invaded.[14] Other Iraqi exiles aligned with Chalabi painted rosy pictures of postinvasion Iraq. Consider Kanan Makiya, who told President Bush that Iraqis would meet U.S. troops with "sweets and flowers."[15]

Much of the planning that went on at the Pentagon was in keeping with the transformative spirit of many in the administration and the hopes that they had about the possibilities of reforming Iraq and the whole region.[16] Everything was up for discussion, except nation building. Later, during the occupation, transformative thinking continued to outstrip practical planning; key American officials went to Iraq more concerned with transforming the country than with stabilizing it. For example, key economic advisers wanted to quickly change Iraq's sluggish state-run economy into a capitalist, market-based economy, planning to end subsidies and food rations and open up markets in months.[17]

While defense officials had high hopes and were thinking big about Iraq's democratic emergence, they actively eschewed thinking small, or considering the details of life that would make an occupation acceptable or at least tolerable. They did not intend to occupy, so why plan an occupation? When Ambassador Barbara Bodine briefed Rumsfeld about paying Iraqi civil servants, for example, the secretary of defense is said to have recoiled at the notion of American taxpayers fronting Iraqi paychecks. "They can wait two weeks or two months," Rumsfeld told Bodine.[18]

A wide range of foreseeable problems and issues were not anticipated or planned for, starting with the salaries that were not paid to Iraqi government employees for weeks. Contradictions were allowed to remain inherent in the way such matters were approached. For example, there was the assumption that the Iraqi government would continue to function while nobody paid the employees, and no effective plans were made to secure the ministries where these unpaid Iraqi officials would be working. Most of all, the defense officials failed to come up with a clear course of action—a way forward—for what to do the day after Iraq fell. The man Rumsfeld picked to head the administration of postwar Iraq, retired general Jay Garner, was not even approached about the job until January. The war started in March.

The decision-making process in the administration, led by national security adviser Condoleeza Rice, was marked by fits and starts; significant research and planning sat on the proverbial shelf while the people sent to Iraq with a mission of rebuilding scrambled to invent a plan on the fly. Rice bears significant blame for this, a fact that key players at the Department of State and Department of Defense, who disagreed on so much, do agree on. The national security adviser failed to take charge of the issues and take on the tough work of leading debate between the disagreeing officials and then ultimately directing the process toward a clear decision. Instead of relaying the full extent of an interagency dispute to the president, Rice tended to write a bridging proposal, something that took material from both sides and "tended to paper over, rather than resolve, important differences of opinion. Her pursuit of harmony came, at times, at the expense of coherence."[19]

From his vantage point, Deputy Secretary of State Richard Armitage called Rice's office "dysfunctional."[20]

The way Rice ran the National Security Council (NSC) created a false sense of consensus and, among those responsible for administering policy, a startling lack of certainty about their instructions. In many cases, foreign policy decisions were either never made or made without this debate and consensus.[21] Indeed, when it came to the debate over Iraq, major disputes between State and the Pentagon went unsettled. Such was the case, for example, with the debate over whether Iraqi exiles like Ahmed Chalabi should be put in charge of a postwar Iraq.

Undersecretary of Defense for Policy Doug Feith, for one, was certain that the administration had approved a plan called Iraqi Interim Authority, through which selected Iraqi exiles would be quickly brought in and given a significant share of the power of governance, including control of several ministries, with their control expanding gradually. The exiles would also be charged with bringing aboard nonexile Iraqis as quickly as possible.[22] Bush approved the Iraqi Interim Authority plan, Feith writes in his memoir, but the plan was quickly tossed in the scrap heap. Feith took note of the number of postwar memoirs and books that neglect to even mention the plan. "But the IIA [Iraqi Interim Authority] was the official U.S. policy for post-Saddam governance of Iraq, a plan developed through the interagency process and approved by the president," Feith protests.[23] Indecision and persistent interagency disagreement, along with spreading chaos in Iraq after the invasion, likely sped the demise of Feith's plan.[24]

In part because of the uncertainty at the top, the military officials drawing up plans for war in Iraq at CENTCOM lacked clarity about what to plan for the day after the war. For nearly two years, CENTCOM planned for the war, and Phases I through III of the war were clearly drawn out. But Phase IV—the post-war—remained something of an empty slate. Col. John Agoglia, one of the key planners at CENTCOM, later said that planners knew there was a hole in the plan where the postwar activities were supposed to be.[25] As late as August 2002, the military assumed that State would work on a plan for building an Iraqi postregime government before the war. CENTCOM planners also assumed that Iraqi army units would stay on and work to rebuild the country.[26]

But in August 2002, many months after planning for the actual war began, CENTCOM was informed that postwar administration of the country would be among its responsibilities. At that point, Agoglia recalled, "The ability to focus on it was very difficult at the command perspective. You had a lot of energy focused on the tactical piece, again Phase I through III [warfighting activities]. There wasn't a whole lot of intellectual energy being focused on Phase IV."[27]

In planning the war, attention to governance and reconstruction took a backseat to planning for battle. This was justified on the grounds that fighting the kinetic battle took precedence over securing the peace.

POSTWAR MISSTEPS BEGIN

U.S. troops sped toward Baghdad in March 2003 with a significantly smaller force than the one that had won the First Gulf War. They brilliantly executed a plan to take Iraq and to defeat Saddam's army. Baghdad fell in just three weeks.

Unfortunately, the agile and nimble force that seized Iraq was simply too small to hold and secure territory once conquered. The force was large enough to take down the Iraqi regime, but nowhere close to large enough to secure the peace. Moreover, it had neither the operational plan (OPLAN) nor the training for such a mission. One RAND study found that postwar situations in collapsed states require around twenty troops for a thousand citizens to achieve stability, or about 400,000 or 500,000 for all of Iraq.[28] At the outset of the war, about 145,000 troops carried out the whole ground invasion.[29]

In those early weeks, the American lack of preparedness and the lack of emphasis on securing stability, governance, and reconstruction came into sharp focus. The man supposed to lead the way for postwar Iraq, retired general Jay Garner, was not even allowed into the country for a full month. He and his team, the Office of Humanitarian and Reconstruction Assistance (OHRA), waited and watched from Kuwait. Garner's team members watched on their television sets at the Kuwait Hilton as looters destroyed the ministries OHRA was supposed to be leading.[30]

That looting was the second major indicator that postwar stabilization and governance were hardly a priority in the planning for OIF. Troops had no orders to protect government buildings, and they did not protect them. The result was unmitigated looting. Looters destroyed valuable government property and stripped government buildings of everything down to the plumbing and wiring. Many of those thefts exacerbated the later difficulties in restarting services. In total, the buildings of seventeen of the twenty-three government ministries were destroyed.[31] A CPA calculation later found that the cost of all this looting was $12 billion.[32] Perhaps most important, the postwar chaos took a heavy toll on Iraqi confidence in the invaders.[33]

Even when the OHRA team did enter the country, it lacked the resources necessary to do almost anything. The team lacked translators, military escorts, drivers, phones, even lights, functional toilets, and laundry service. All they had, as one former administration adviser phrased it, was responsibility.[34] As journalist George Packer described them, OHRA was a "skeletal, disorganized, impecunious crew of fewer than two hundred unarmed civilians wandering around in the dust and dark of the Republican Palace searching for colleagues because they didn't have phones to call one another."[35] With ministries in shambles and phone lines down around the country, one ambassador tasked with running the ministry of trade was reduced to wandering the streets of Baghdad, asking people at random through a translator if they knew anyone who had worked there.[36]

One of the most iconic images of that era is the deck of cards given to soldiers, each card emblazoned with the face of a key Ba'athist official, with Saddam Hussein as ace of spades. The cards, envisioned as a way to ensure that card-playing soldiers would get to know the faces of their prime targets, demonstrated the emphasis from on high on Saddam and his Ba'athist cronies. This, in turn, illustrated the vision that U.S. officials had of the war as a classic, state-on-state battle that ended with the defeat of an army and the capture of the former government. As Bremer later wrote, the Ba'ath-centric military strategy, along with the heavy emphasis on finding Iraq's elusive weapons of mass destruction, diverted significant resources and attention from the serious fight at hand, against those who were attacking American troops and sabotaging Iraqi infrastructure.[37]

But there was a deeper problem, and that was with the top-down emphasis on kinetic tactics: the tactics themselves tipped many who were on the fence after the war, people who could choose to either cooperate with the United States or make common cause with those fighting the Americans. And in Anbar Province, the stronghold of a Sunni population that lost its grip on power and privilege with the invasion, many were not naturally predisposed to embrace an American invader, let alone one who was quick to shoot.

Moreover, the units that took the lead in key Sunni strongholds were seen by some as particularly disinclined to putting down their guns and conducting stability operations. The 3rd Armored Cavalry Regiment, which arrived in Iraq after the invasion to take over the key city of Ramadi, was described by one captain in the U.S. Army as unable to make the transition to postwar operations. "They did not appear to be ready for nor understand the urban/peace operations mission they had been assigned. Their attitude in terms of rules of engagement suggested to me that they had not made the change from combat operations to stability operations."[38] Antagonistic tactics were common in those days, like conducting wide sweeps to round up Iraqis for detention and questioning. Such sweeps were in particularly heavy use by the 4th Infantry, based in Tikrit, often called the northern point of the Sunni Triangle; units were known for "grabbing whole villages, because combat soldiers [were] unable to figure out who was of value and who was not," according to a later investigation by the Army inspector general's office.[39]

Tribal sheikhs, who had taken control in Anbar before American soldiers arrived, later said they had been prepared to cooperate if the invasion forces had met them halfway. But instead, they said, American troops swept into the cities. Crowds gathered. Troops fired on them, opening a cycle of blame and retribution in a culture where pride and respect are core values.[40]

"A young man, an 18-year-old youth, threw a rock at an American tank, and the soldiers shot him dead," recounted Dr. Thamer Ibrahim Tahir al-Assafi, a professor at Al Anbar University who is active in politics. "We are a tribal people, we know revenge. If someone gets killed from your family, you have to kill the killer, or at least a relative of his."[41] Sheikhs who later cooperated with the Marines described the shock of the first Americans entering Anbar, whom many described as fast to shoot, fast to arrest, and slow to apologize. From pragmatic tribal leaders, this spurred an antagonistic response. "When they entered as invaders, for sure, it's the right of the people to resist invaders," said Sheikh Sabah al-Sattam Effan Fahran al-Shurji al-Aziz.[42]

The single key event often cited as the trigger for the emerging insurgency began as a protest outside a school in Fallujah. The 82nd Airborne had been in the city for five days and had seized the school as a base. Col. Arnold Bray, the area commander, later said that their intention was to "show presence just so the average citizen would feel safe."[43] But many Iraqis did not see it that way. Nearly everything about the events of April 28, 2003, is contested, starting with the reason for the protests. Some Americans saw the gathering as a celebration of Saddam Hussein's birthday. According to Iraqis, the hundreds had gathered simply to demand that troops stop occupying the school and allow classes to go on. "It was a peaceful demonstration. They did not have any weapons," cleric Kamal Shaker Mahmoud told Reuters. "They were asking the Americans to leave the school so they could use it."[44]

American troops opened fire on the crowd. Iraqis who were there swear that no one in the crowd was armed; they describe the shooting as nothing short of a massacre.[45] Asserting the crowd's innocence later, one Iraqi who had been there said, "if we had had weapons, we would have killed them. . . . We wanted to enter the school and kill them."[46] By contrast, Maj. Gen. Charles Swannack, who commanded the 82nd, has said there were several instigators firing AK-47s at soldiers from nearby rooftops and that AK-47 casings were found in the area.[47] Even the death toll was disputed; the Americans said six Iraqis were killed, while hospital officials claimed thirteen killed and seventy-five wounded. Human Rights Watch concluded that provocateurs might have been among the crowd.[48]

One fact about the shootings is undisputed: they marked the beginning of weeks of violence that fell off only after the Americans pulled out of Fallujah and left the defense of the area to a militia.⁴⁹ The event was an important radicalizing moment for many insurgents. The school itself was later renamed the Martyrs.⁵⁰ For years to come, many Iraqis who joined the insurgency told generals and journalists that what happened that day outside the school is what moved them to pick up arms in the budding insurgency.⁵¹

NO INTERIM GOVERNMENT

Back in Baghdad in the spring of 2003, there was trouble at the top. One of the biggest problems was that while Washington struggled to figure out what its policy was, Iraqis saw there was no real interim government.

At the helm of the postwar operation was Garner, a retired general who was first called about the possibility of taking charge of postwar Iraq in January 2003, just months before the war began. Garner, at the time working for a defense contractor, had a long career with the U.S. military. He had gotten to know Iraq a decade earlier, when he ran a successful humanitarian effort in Iraq's Kurdish north after the First Gulf War.⁵² Renowned for his abilities as a world-class informal leader, Garner brought in some of his buddies to help him out, leading someone to joke that they were a Pentagon version of *Space Cowboys*, the Clint Eastwood flick in which over-the-hill former astronauts reunite to take on one last mission for which they are uniquely suited.⁵³

Garner's organization, the OHRA, was established just eight weeks before the war began, and in those few weeks the planning it did was heavily focused on how to handle humanitarian issues such as mass refugee incidents, and emergencies such as oil-well fires.⁵⁴ One of Garner's biggest fears was that Saddam Hussein would turn chemical weapons on his own people, as he had in the past.⁵⁵ In the limited time he had, Garner struggled to wrangle personnel from various agencies, individuals who then had to be examined and certified to deploy in just weeks.⁵⁶ As he put it to the House International Relations Committee, "This is an ad hoc operation, glued together over about four or five weeks' time." The team, he said, "didn't really have enough time to plan."⁵⁷ Shortly after the invasion, Gen. Tommy Franks recalled, he looked at a report on the state of OHRA and concluded that Garner and his 150-person team lacked adequate money and personnel as well as the necessary clarity of mission for the job ahead.⁵⁸

Like Pentagon planners, Garner had in mind a timeline that proved unrealistic. He told his team that he wanted to reconstruct ministries, get a constitution written and ratified, and hold elections by August, writes George Packer. "There was a stunned silence. Someone at the table said, 'Which August?'"⁵⁹ The timeline was in keeping with Garner's personal plan. He had taken only a four-month leave of absence from his company.[60]

Thrown into a country with little staff and no resources, Garner started, as one reporter put it, "calling audibles in the field."[61] He started talking about putting together elections and touting a plan for running Iraq that matched the hopes of many pivotal players in the Pentagon—to get in and out of the country fast by handing power over to the Iraqis as soon as possible. Garner created a group called the Iraqi Leadership Council, which he envisioned first working under American authority and later taking power on its own.[62] Garner's thinking was influenced by his own experience in Vietnam, he told the *New York Times*. He saw problems for the United States in "telling people what to do," as when the United States military got involved in forcing villages to relocate through South Vietnam's Strategic Hamlet program.[63] Getting out of Iraq fast, he said, could help avoid that kind of perception. In May 2003 Garner announced that within the month there would be in place the start of an Iraqi government. Garner told reporters, "Five opposition leaders have begun having meetings and are going to bring in leaders from the inside of Iraq and see if that can't form a nucleus of leadership as we enter into June. Next week, or by the second weekend in May, you'll see the beginning of a nucleus of a temporary Iraqi government, a government with an Iraqi face on it that is totally dealing with the coalition."[64]

Garner's concept of quickly handing power to a group of Iraqis was different in an important way from that of key Pentagon civilians, which could be summed up with a single name: Ahmed Chalabi. Chalabi had grown so close to major figures at the Pentagon that officials there actually flew Chalabi and his armed supporters into southern Iraq immediately after the war began.[65] But Garner never got on board with the plan, widely said to have been favored by Pentagon civilians like Feith and Wolfowitz, to hand Chalabi the keys to the country. "That wasn't going to happen on my watch," Garner later told *Frontline*, saying he never liked Chalabi and suspects him of double-timing the Americans by working with the Iranians, too.[66] Before the war, Feith dressed down Garner for saying he had not hired anyone from the INC. Garner came back with a clear response: "So fire me."[67]

Almost as soon as he arrived in Baghdad, with chaos spreading in the country, Garner was, indeed, fired. On April 24 he took a call from Rumsfeld telling him the news that his replacement would be coming early. And his replacement, Paul Bremer, had no intention of following through on Garner's promise of a temporary Iraqi government. In fact, Bremer wrote in his memoir, he nearly drove off the George Washington Parkway when he heard Garner announce his plan to get a temporary government in place in May.[68] To Bremer, the concept of transferring power early was a "reckless fantasy" that overlooked the importance of building not only democratic institutions but also the institutions of civil society.[69]

L. Paul Bremer III was a Yale- and Harvard-educated career Foreign Service officer who had worked for Henry Kissinger in the 1970s as his executive assistant in the Department of State and later as managing director of the consulting firm Kissinger Associates. Bremer served as ambassador-at-large for counterterrorism during the Reagan administration and chaired the National Commission on Terrorism in 2000.[70] Bremer had a legendary work ethic, credibility at State, and the trust of conservatives, but he lacked two key qualifications that were hard to make up on the fly: he had little knowledge of Iraq and no experience in postconflict reconstruction situations.[71] Like Garner, he had scant opportunity to prepare for the job: Bremer, who had never before been to Iraq, got the call in mid-April, asking him to take over in May.[72] Moreover, Bremer, a strong believer in the importance of unity of command, was not looking to keep on senior people with more experience than he had. While the White House had originally wanted him to split responsibilities with Zalmay Khalilzad, an experienced Middle East hand who had been working with Iraqi leaders for months, Bremer vetoed that idea, sidelining Khalilzad.[73]

Almost as soon as Bremer arrived in Iraq on May 12, 2003, he put on ice any plans to give Iraqis major roles in the government. The American occupation took hold. Under Bremer, the OHRA became the CPA. To Bremer's thinking, the exter-

L. Paul Bremer is seen here departing Iraq on June 28, 2004, at the end of his year as U.S. ambassador and head of the Coalition Provisional Authority.

ESTES, INTO THE FRAY, 39

nals who had spent decades in exile from Iraq lacked legitimacy in the country and simply were not ready for prime time. There was something to this belief: one poll showed that Chalabi was actually less popular than Saddam.[74] But Bremer's CPA alternative meant running a full-fledged occupation. Bremer did, of course, keep some Iraqi faces, creating a twenty-five–member group called the Iraqi Governing Council. But he declined advice to give them more actual power, and they had low visibility in Iraq anyway.[75] The Council had low standing with Iraqis, who regarded it as a rubber stamp for the CPA.[76]

Thousands of pages have been written about Bremer's tenure at the CPA, the sprawling growth of the Green Zone, and the detachment of the Americans inside the compound from Iraqis outside it. What emerged was a stark picture of the Green Zone as an ideologically run outfit populated with conservative young staffers living in an air-conditioned bubble while Iraq came apart.

One defining characteristic of the CPA was that administrators persistently confused law with order. In other words, they were so focused on getting rules on the books that they overlooked the reality on the ground. With the war over, few Iraqi police were on the job to deal with, among other things, the horrendous traffic that came with a surge of used vehicles entering the country and clogging the roads, a surge that came after the CPA ended Iraq's hefty tax on imports.[77] The number of cars on the streets of Iraq more than doubled in a year. To deal with the traffic chaos, CPA staffers crafted a new Iraqi traffic law that regulated behavior for both drivers and police.[78] But the law was never announced to the public or distributed to the police, and its passage did not fix any of the problems at the root of Iraq's traffic troubles, such as untrained police, broken stoplights, and unregulated imports.[79]

Bremer, who described seeing Baghdad on fire as he flew into the country, was nothing if not decisive. Seeing a country in chaos, he wanted to take charge and demonstrate authority. In what he saw as a sign of respect to Iraqis, Bremer was determined to look and act according to position. Throughout Bremer's time in Iraq, his personal dress code was a dark suit and tan hiking boots.[80] Coming out of the gate, one of the first controversies of his tenure involved his asking about a shoot-first policy. Entering the country as looters were running rampant, he worried that the news coverage of "unchecked looting makes us look powerless."[81] He told at a staff meeting that when occupying Haiti in 1994 the American military's decision to shoot six looters had stopped looting cold, and wondered whether a similar policy in Iraq could do the trick. Parts of the meeting were leaked to the *New York Times* and led to the headline "New Policy in Iraq to Authorize G.I.s to Shoot Looters."[82] In this case, Bremer, who did not oversee the military in Iraq, could not or did not get the rules of engagement changed, and the policy never came to be.[83] Like many at the time, Bremer saw force as an answer to chaos. The shoot-the-looters idea, though it never came to pass, demonstrated something critical about Bremer's attitude in those early days: a certain inclination to decide fast, shoot first, and sort later.

PURGING THE BA'ATHISTS

Bremer's first major decision set the tone. On May 16, 2003, less than a week after he arrived in Baghdad, he released a blanket de-Ba'athification order removing tens of thousands of members of Saddam's Ba'ath Party from government jobs in Iraq. The decision was born in part of Bremer's desire to demonstrate control and to show Iraqis that the era of Saddam was over. It was rooted in a then-popular but selective reading of past postwar efforts to extricate a totalitarian party from society. Unfortunately, the decision was not based on a thorough understanding of exactly who would be affected. As it turned out, everyone from actual Saddam cronies to provincial schoolteachers to a veterinarian at the Baghdad zoo were ousted.[84] The message that this sent to a Sunni population who had already lost so much in the invasion was unambiguous: your time is over. De-Ba'athification eviscerated the government and created a huge time sink, as officials spent countless hours figuring out who was and was not affected by the blanket order. Finally, the administration of the law, taken over by Chalabi, was pitiless and political. Exemptions, even for the truly and obviously innocent, were hard to come by.

The de-Ba'athification order, just six paragraphs long, dissolved the Ba'ath Party, removed the four most senior ranks of Ba'athists from their jobs, and banned them from working for the government in the future; it also forbade all former Ba'athists, even junior members, from serving in the top three levels of government jobs, including in hospitals and universities.[85] The order also outlawed public displays of Saddam Hussein and his top deputies and offered rewards for information on leading Ba'athists. Finally, the order allowed Bremer and those designated by him to grant exception "on a case-by-case basis."[86] To do this right, Bremer later wrote, he needed Iraqis to take charge of the exemption process, as they would best understand the intricacies of the Ba'athist system. The party itself had 2 million members; Bremer said the intelligence he had seen held that this order would only affect 20,000 of them, most of them Sunni. Other estimates held that, in fact, 40,000 or 50,000 Ba'ath Party members would lose their jobs; given the impact of unemployment on families, the number of Iraqis affected would be several times that estimate. As analyst Anthony Cordesman later said, "I think, frankly, there wasn't a single person in the CPA who understood what Order 1 meant. Nobody made any effort to survey how many people would be excluded or affected by issuing the order in that form, and it went down to far too low a level, in far too many areas."[87]

De-Ba'athification was a case of decision by analogy, not based on facts on the ground. One of the key analogies of that time was that of post–World War II Germany, an analogy heavily pushed by Chalabi's INC. Before the war, Chalabi wrote in an op-ed for the *Wall Street Journal*, "Iraq needs a comprehensive program of de-Ba'athification even more extensive than the de-Nazification effort in Germany after World War II. You cannot cut off the viper's head and leave the body festering."[88] Bremer himself later wrote, "The model for the de-Ba'athification was to look back at that de-Nazification."[89] There was a certain logic to the comparison. Like Nazism, Saddam's Ba'athism was a totalitarian system that ran on incredible violence, aggressive wars, leader-worship, and paranoia. And while the Ba'ath Party at its formation was influenced by Nazism, Saddam's personal hero was actually Stalin.[90]

But in terms of implementation there were significant differences between de-Nazification and de-Ba'athification. For one, in American-controlled parts of Germany, American troops had a heavy presence, with about one soldier for every nine Germans. It was, noted RAND's James Dobbins, a "very obtrusive presence, which preempted any thought of resistance."[91] By May 2003 there were about 150,000 American troops in Iraq for a population of 25 million people, or a ratio of roughly one service person for every 167 Iraqis, far from the situation in postwar Germany. Moreover, though it encountered significant problems and included heavier penalties for senior party members, the process of de-Nazification in Western-occupied Germany was implemented person by person, village by village, with every adult over the age of eighteen required to fill out a lengthy questionnaire about Nazi party activities. Some were exonerated, while others were tried and convicted of belonging to one of four categories, ranging from follower to major offender.[92] In other words, de-Nazification was different from de-Ba'athification in both its recognition of degrees of involvement and in its detailed process.

In plotting de-Ba'athification, key Bush administration officials who had lived through the end of communism seemed to have forgotten the essential lesson of that era: in a party-ruled, authoritarian system, many party members are careerists or simply survivors, not true ideologues. They saw firsthand that yesterday's card-carrying communists are tomorrow's democratic reformers.

Bremer's decision seemed to come from nowhere and, in fact, appeared to directly contradict the plan approved by President Bush. The Department of State had pushed something called de-Saddamification, a limited plan that would involve removing two classes of the party from power: those who had committed crimes and those at the top level of party leadership. Feith's office, and the Pentagon more broadly, pushed a far more sweeping version of de-Ba'athification, as well as a ban on any Ba'ath Party member holding a senior position.[93] The debate reportedly followed by now familiar lines: State and the CIA advocated a more limited policy, while the Pentagon backed a more sweeping one.

In March President Bush granted approval to a compromise policy, in which 1 percent of Ba'athists would lose their government jobs and others would go through a South Africa–style truth and reconciliation process.[94] When he went to Baghdad, Garner planned to use a light hand with de-Ba'athification at the outset, figuring that locals themselves would either kill or turn in the worst of the offenders. His de-Ba'athification plan was to remove only two people from each ministry as a start.[95] But even as all these other plans were made, Feith printed up a draft de-Ba'athification order along the lines of what the Pentagon had pushed all along and showed it to Bremer before he went to Iraq. According to his memoir, Bremer seized on it as something he wanted to issue in his first days in Iraq.[96] The final version was printed up at the Department of Defense and carried into Iraq by a Bremer aide.[97] In the vacuum of decision making in postwar Iraq, the president's new proconsul was able to issue a decision that directly contradicted the president's decision.

According to Garner, he and other Iraq hands, including the CIA station chief, saw Bremer's order only shortly before it was released and immediately worked to convince Bremer that the order would have tremendous negative consequences. Garner recalls the CIA chief telling Bremer, "Well, if you do this, you're going to drive 40,000 to 50,000 Ba'athists underground by nightfall. The number is closer to 50,000 than it is [to] 30,000." For Garner's part, he was worried that with so many senior people fired at once, the functioning capacity of the government would be destroyed. But, according to Garner, Bremer brushed aside these concerns saying, "I understand what you're saying. I understand that's your opinion, but I have my directions."[98]

There was, indeed, a heavy toll on governance. Two-thirds of the top people at the ministry of health were gone. One-quarter of the directors of various state-owned companies were sacked. Tim Carney, the American advising the ministry of industry, described spending hours in meetings and searching records to find the names of Ba'athists in the top four ranks. "It was a terrible waste of time," he said. "There were so many important things we should have been doing, like starting factories and paying salaries."[99] Thousands of schoolteachers were unceremoniously fired, leaving schools in some Sunni regions with decimated faculties. In the Saddam era, teachers had a hefty incentive to join the party, as they received a bonus that multiplied their paychecks.[100] At least 1,700 staffers and professors in Iraq's university system were fired.[101] The inspectors general of the Pentagon and Department of State later concluded that the CPA decision to cleanse the political system of Hussein sympathizers through the de-Ba'athification effort effectively decapitated the Iraqi police services.[102]

Finally, the part that was supposed to soften the blow of de-Ba'athification, the clause that allowed Bremer to grant exemptions on a case-by-case basis, brought little relief. Early on, implementation varied by region. One of Bremer's first moves was to rescind exemptions given by civilian and military leaders.[103] Even Bremer, who stands by the de-Ba'athification policy, says he regrets the way the policy played out, telling *Frontline*, "The implementation is where I went wrong."[104] Believing that outsiders lacked the deep knowledge needed to separate out the true believers, Bremer turned the exemption process over to the Governing Council, which had put Chalabi in charge. That Council, Bremer later said, started "implementing the policy much more broadly, and we had to walk the cat back in the spring of 2004."[105] But according to a Sunni tribal leader in 2005, the process of getting an exemption even then required so much paperwork and took so much time that he estimated it would take thirteen years to process it all.[106] In the earlier days, even an extraordinary case that won the attention of CPA authorities did not win speedy reversal: Two men came to Carney, the ministry of industry adviser, and introduced themselves as former Iraqi soldiers who had been captured by Iran during the Iran-Iraq War and held for seventeen years. After their release they were granted honorary titles in the Ba'ath Party, which gave them a bonus at the fertilizer plant where they worked. Carney petitioned for an appeal for them, and Bremer granted an appeal, though it was six months in coming.[107]

Defending the decision, Bremer notes the widely favorable reaction to de-Ba'athification he received from many Iraqis, calling the decision the most popular one he made during his time in Iraq. The only problem with that, as one adviser notes, was "the people it was popular with were already on our side."[108] The biggest losers in this, of course, were the Sunnis, a group that lost its grip on power with the invasion. Now, many more Sunnis lost their jobs, their family incomes, their children's schoolteachers, and their role in national governance. This decision sent a cold message to Anbar Province and the Sunni Triangle. The postwar order was not just about removing Saddam, but about removing Sunnis from national life. Moreover, as they looked to Baghdad they saw the Americans initiating a process by which the Shia would come to replace them.

CASHIERING THE ARMY

As with the de-Ba'athification order, Bremer's order disbanding the Iraqi army directly contradicted a plan previously approved by the president. President Bush had approved a plan to disband only Iraq's Republican Guard while keeping the regular army intact. One key point in the presentation made to the president on this issue said specifically that the United States "cannot immediately demobilize

250k–350k personnel and put them on the street."[109] But CPA Order 2, disbanding the army and the Iraqi intelligence services, did just that, spurring massive protests in which many former army officers point-blank told reporters and anyone else who would listen that they felt humiliated and would resist the Americans with force. Disbanding the Iraqi army threw the American military into a ringer, because CENTCOM had counted on the immediate availability of a substantial Iraqi military force in planning for postwar security and rebuilding operations. Finally, the decision sent another dark message to the Sunnis of the country, many of whom unceremoniously lost paychecks and prestige after decades of serving their country in the army.

The Iraqi army, Bremer noted in his memoir, was a lopsided institution with a large Sunni officer corps that commanded largely Shia rank-and-file draftees. To Bremer's thinking, recalling the army would mean recalling the officer corps, as "few draftees of any description and virtually none of the Shia would return to the military voluntarily."[110] It is unclear how Bremer could be certain in his prediction that Shia would not return to their prewar jobs in the military, particularly in an Iraqi economy where joblessness topped 50 percent.[111] But his thinking on Shia soldiers refusing to return to a military system that he believed had abused them led him to the natural conclusion that a recalled all-Sunni Iraqi army would "surely be rejected by the Kurds and Shia who made up 80 percent of Iraq's population." Finally, Bremer argues that in disbanding the army he formalized a situation already in place on the ground. Many of the soldiers had either stayed home during the war or gone home after it. The army was effectively gone already, he explained.[112]

One counterargument to Bremer's perspective is that the military disappeared during the war not just because of festering religious tensions or because they simply wanted to go home, but because, in going home, they were doing exactly what the United States had urged them to do. At the outset of the war, the American military dropped many thousands of leaflets asking Iraqi soldiers to stay home and not to fight. Many complied.[113] Those leaflets were part of a long line of efforts to separate the Iraqi army from the regime. As retired general Anthony Zinni, the former commander of CENTCOM, put it, "We had spent a decade psyopsing the Iraqi army, telling them we would take care of those who didn't fight."[114] Later, when they examined military records, American officials discovered that the army was not nearly as Ba'athist as many Americans had thought.[115] Saddam Hussein himself doubted the loyalty of the army, which he would not allow to enter Baghdad. Only the Special Republican Guard was permitted to enter the capital city. These were the troops in charge of defending Baghdad during the invasion.[116]

By 2003 a well-developed, standard procedure was in place for handling combatants in postconflict areas that was the precise opposite of what Bremer did in disbanding the army. The RAND Corporation's Dobbins explains the steps: register the soldiers, pay them, reassure them that they will continue to be employed, and then, eventually, retrain them for work in the army or police, or in other jobs. This program, says Dobbins, who has led postconflict reconstruction in five countries, is "absolutely standard." By registering and paying former soldiers, he told *Frontline*, "you keep these people off the street. You keep them out of trouble. You know who they are; you know where they are; you know what they're doing. They show up every month until you decide what you want to do with them.... Now, it's a little expensive, but it does mean that you haven't put thousands or hundreds of thousands of armed, hostile people out there and given them an incentive to undermine your operation." Dobbins' words echo the presentation given to President Bush before the war.[117]

In fact, before Bremer came to Iraq officials had begun following something like this standard protocol. Col. Paul Hughes had started working with generals who wanted to cooperate and had collected the names of 100,000 soldiers, and was sorting out how to get the rank-and-file paid. Hughes described the thinking behind the effort this way: "Anyone who's done post-conflict work says do not get rid of the military. You've got to control them. If you don't control them, you don't know what they're going to do."[118]

With Bremer's announcement, all that effort to get the military paid and working shut down. Instead, in one fell swoop the United States sent into the streets of Iraq 400,000 unemployed armed men. Massive protests followed. Officers told media outlets that they would take up arms against the Americans. On June 18, 2003, two thousand soldiers massed in a protest outside the Green Zone. Tahseen Ali Hussein put the consequences in stark terms in a speech to the crowd quoted by Agence France-Presse: "We are all very well-trained soldiers and we are armed. We will start ambushes, bombings and even suicide bombings. We will not let the Americans rule us in such a humiliating way."[119] Then–Maj. Gen. David Petraeus, who commanded the 101st Airborne in Mosul, told a Bremer adviser unequivocally that the decision to leave hundreds of thousands of Iraqi soldiers without a living put Americans at risk.[120] A month after disbanding the Iraqi army, Bremer announced a plan to pay stipends to out-of-work soldiers, but by that time the damage had been done.[121]

The toll for the decision fell on both American and Iraqi soldiers. CENTCOM planners had relied on the idea of tapping a reconstituted army to secure the borders, rebuild infrastructure, and help with a half-dozen other manpower-intensive tasks. As Franks wrote in his memoir, war planning assumed that the United States could work with Iraqi leaders to build a military "drawn from the better units of the defeated regular army," a force that would work with Coalition troops to "restore order and prevent clashes among the religious and ethnic factions."[122]

In sum, the dissolution of the Iraqi army sent yet another strong message about the intention of the Americans to the Sunnis of Anbar and beyond, who already felt marginalized. Sunnis had led the army, and Bremer's decision deprived them of their pensions, jobs, and self-image.

MISMANAGING THE CONSTITUTION

Months after arriving in Baghdad, Bremer reached a decision for how the CPA should proceed toward an Iraqi government. Having made up his mind, he did not take his plan to Rumsfeld or even to the president—he took it to the *Washington Post* editorial page, which published a piece called "Iraq's Path to Sovereignty" in September 2003. The piece started with a premise that elections are the way to give true sovereignty to Iraqis, but that without a new constitution, written by Iraqis, elections cannot be held. He outlined a lengthy process wherein a constitution would be written and ratified by the Iraqi public before elections to choose a new government were held. All of that, in Bremer's plan, would happen before the CPA was dissolved.[123] The plan did not include a precise timeline, but the common assumption was that Bremer's plan of constitution-then-elections would require two years of American occupation.[124]

The plan came as a cold shock both to many Iraqis, who saw sovereignty receding before them, and to key players in Washington, because the piece had not been cleared at the Pentagon with the secretary of defense or with Rice at the NSC.[125] The response was sharp. By November the Bush administration flew Bremer back to Washington to rein him in. The CPA had to wind down within a year.

Meanwhile, the CPA came under pressure from Iraq. Some on the Governing Council were pushing for more power.[126] Even more unexpectedly, Grand Ayatollah Ali Al-Sistani, one of the most respected figures in Shia Islam, was sending messages from the holy city of Najaf, insisting on elections as soon as possible. He issued a fatwa calling for a constitution to be written by an elected—not American-appointed—group.[127] Though Sistani issued his proclamation in June 2003, CPA officials were slow to grasp the weight of such a pronouncement from the seventy-three-year-old cleric who was one of the most trusted figures in the country.[128] Shia in Iraq had a long history of being kept from power by leaders who appointed representatives. Sistani had no interest in seeing that happen again.

Out of the pressures from Washington, Baghdad, and Najaf was born a new plan: The Americans would help create an interim constitution, but it would not be called that. Instead, it would be called a "transitional administrative law" and would include clear requirements for future elections and a permanent constitution. A transitional assembly would be selected in a complicated series of caucuses around the country, which would in turn create an interim government that would assume power in June 2004.[129]

Holding caucuses in occupied Iraq made little sense. In the first place, there was not even an Arabic word for "caucus."[130] The Governing Council, under heavy pressure from Bremer, approved the plan, but then Sistani came out against caucuses. This was pressure the CPA was inclined to resist; in a memo to Bremer, a staffer framed the issue as "whether the CPA and the GC [Governing Council] will allow Iraqi clerics to overrule and nullify decisions made by Iraq's legitimate political authorities." Of course, as a RAND report later noted, the issue of legitimacy is at the heart of the matter: "To many Iraqis, Sistani and the Shi'ite religious hierarchy were far more legitimate than either the GC or the CPA."[131]

Eventually, with the help of UN officials, Sistani was persuaded that elections were not feasible for more than a year, an argument he eventually accepted.[132] But this lengthy and arduous process of debating the way forward demonstrated the toll on the CPA in not taking Iraq's traditional authorities seriously. This was a lesson not learned fast enough to help in the CPA's dealing with another traditional authority, Iraqi tribal leaders.

WRITING OFF THE TRIBES

Bremer wrote in his memoir that he knew from his diplomatic service in Afghanistan and Malawi how important tribes are in some countries. During his time in Iraq, he added, he came to see how important tribal ancestry is to many Iraqis. But he seems to have believed that the tribal leaders would not or could not pose a challenge to a central authority ruling from Baghdad. As he wrote in his memoir, "The tribes also had a reputation for respecting power and had always been acutely aware of who was up and who was down. They were likely to support whoever exercised authority in Baghdad, until someone stronger came along."[133] Bremer visited with tribal leaders, took pictures, drank tea, exchanged pleasantries, and even pushed to have tribal representatives included on the twenty-five-member Governing Council. But Bremer did not regard the tribal leaders as crucial partners in keeping the peace in a new Iraq.

The attitude at the CPA was that empowered tribal leaders would take Iraq backward, that they were the antithesis of the modern regime Americans wanted to build. Noah Feldman, a law professor who had advised the CPA in 2003, later recounted that tribal leaders had come to Bremer offering to work with the CPA to pacify the country. "We told them, 'No, we're not going to take Iraq back to the

Middle Ages,'" Feldman later told *Newsweek*.[134] When military intelligence officers suggested that the Americans make a cash-for-security deal with one of the major tribes of Anbar, the CPA rejected the plan. "The standard answer we got from Bremer's people was that tribes are a vestige of the past, that they have no place in the new democratic Iraq," one officer later told *Time* magazine. "Eventually they paid some lip service and set up a tribal office, but it was grudging."[135]

Instead of working with the tribal leaders, Americans instead in 2003 followed policies that seemed perfectly crafted to alienate them. The CPA's man in Al Anbar, Keith Mines, arrived in the summer of 2003. In September he wrote a memo reporting back to Baghdad that the sheikhs were not happy with their treatment by the CPA or the military: "Al Anbar's sheikhs are expressing increasing resentment over what they perceive as a lack of respect for them by the coalition. Between detentions, arbitrary and often destructive house searches, and the recent killing of coalition-sanctioned police officers by coalition forces, the Anbar sheikhs say they are tired of not receiving the respect that their traditional position should convey."[136]

There was something of a zero-sum attitude about power and authority in the CPA in those days. In the spring of 2004 a sheikh from the Sunni Triangle city of Samarra told officials that Americans' excessive use of force had sparked the city's problems. CPA officials, Ricks wrote, read this analysis in a particular way, that sheikhs were actually concerned that the military was "eroding their authority" and could put at risk the sheikhs' traditional power.[137] The idea that the traditional power of the sheikhs could be aligned to work with the CPA simply did not resonate with the powers that were in Baghdad. Just the opposite was the case. This was made unambiguously clear in Bremer's 2003 CPA-issued statement that "tribes are a part of the past" and "have no place in the new democratic Iraq."[138]

LIMITING ANBAR RESOURCES

While Anbaris were being swept up in mass arrests and the military focus on kinetic tactics was inspiring anger around the province, what people did not see early on were the basic bread-and-butter services that build goodwill and form the core of any postconflict program: jobs, electricity, government services, and more. The CPA's Keith Mines wrote in a letter home, "Police, [electric] power and political process. That is what will fix this place, and if we give them those three, we can get the heck out of here."[139]

At first, reconstruction help was slow in coming because the American government had approved almost no money with which to conduct it. Garner's organization, OHRA, was cash-starved, with teams at first given $25,000 to rebuild government ministries—and even that did not come in the form of hard cash but rather required paperwork and a grant process before it was dispensed.[140] In March 2003 President Bush requested $2.4 billion for Iraq reconstruction, to add to the $1.1 billion Congress had already approved.[141] But that was a small fraction of the need: studies by the World Bank and the Congressional Budget Office showed that Iraq needed upwards of $50 billion, and perhaps as much as $100 billion, for medium-term reconstruction.[142] By the fall of 2003 Washington was sending more help, in the form of an $18.4 billion supplemental for reconstructing Iraq. But even that, a fraction of what had been calculated as Iraq's needs, did little good on the ground in Iraq in 2003—only 2 percent of that money had actually been spent by the end of Bremer's tenure in June 2004.[143]

Coalition efforts to be even-handed with services meant that regions favored by Saddam got far less under the Coalition than they were used to. Electricity was one of the biggest problems in Anbar and throughout Iraq in 2003. Iraq's power system had been inadequate long before the war, a decline dating back to the First Gulf War, when American strikes damaged three-quarters of the country's electrical plants. During economic sanctions in the 1990s, when new equipment was hard to come by, aging plants were patched back together. But annual maintenance schedules were scrapped when the country's power needs were so desperate that plants could not be taken offline even briefly.[144] Meanwhile, the transmission system was so weak it was prone to collapse.[145]

But restoring the status quo antebellum was not Bremer's plan. Before the war, Saddam had distributed electrical power much as he distributed political power. Baghdad, Tikrit, and other cities where Saddam was strong got almost all the power they needed, while the Shiite south was left in the dark.[146] To the Americans in charge at the CPA, that power distribution was unfair. Bremer signed an order requiring the electricity be evenly distributed around Iraq.[147] The result was that the south of Iraq indeed got extra hours of power, but in Baghdad power levels fell to a fraction of prewar levels, with residents getting none some days and a few hours other days, sparking unrest.[148] By March 2004 the provinces in the north and south of the country, according to the CPA, had a power supply that topped prewar levels significantly. But in central Iraq at that time power was at approximately half its prewar levels.[149] From Anbar, Col. David Teeples wrote to Bremer to plead for more electricity, saying the province's electric supply is "our largest concern," citing rolling blackouts and "turbulence within the community." The lack of sufficient electricity in Anbar, Teeples wrote, was preventing factories from opening, spurring unemployment.[150]

The CPA's effort to be even-handed with electricity and other resources meant that some essential programs did not focus on Anbar, where they might have done the most good, until too late. A 2003 program that was originally supposed to create jobs for 300,000, but was scaled down to 150,000 and finally 100,000, did not focus sufficiently on Anbar. At first the jobs were to be evenly divided among governorates. But as the jobs program unfolded, jobs were divided by population, which meant that Anbar Province got even fewer jobs while more placid provinces got larger shares. Later, once the uprising broke in Fallujah, Bremer moved to focus reconstruction efforts on the Sunni Triangle and Baghdad, creating an accelerated Iraqi reconstruction team to pour resources into Anbar. As a RAND study later noted, "However, by this time CPA was fighting a rearguard action against a mutually reinforcing downward spiral of joblessness and anti-coalition violence."[151]

In sum, here then was yet another grim signal to the Sunnis of Anbar. Their fate in the new Iraq would be a dark one.

FAILURE TO MANAGE SUNNI FEARS

When the United States invaded Iraq in 2003, Sunnis comprised just one-fifth of the Iraqi population but had dominated the country's politics for hundreds of years, under the Ottomans, the British, and later the Ba'athists. Sunnis had a lot to lose with the American invasion; in the early months of the occupation, even ordinary Sunnis who had nothing to do with Saddam's rule lost a lot. With de-Ba'athification and the disbanding of the Iraqi army, Sunnis lost their traditional roles in national institutions, their family incomes, community stability, personal self-identity, and more.

In the wake of the invasion, Sunnis saw Shia not only taking control of Baghdad's power ministries, but also asserting power in those institutions that affect day-to-day life. Shiite clerics, David Phillips wrote, "stepped in to fill the void" in government services postinvasion in a wide-sweeping way, partly as a deliberate power grab. In April 2003 Ayatollah al-Haera even issued a fatwa from Iran urging Shia to "seize as many positions as possible to impose a fait accompli for any incoming government."[152] Clerics took over schools and hospitals and, along the way, imposed "their Islamic code on daily life."[153] Even in the earliest days of the occupation, Garner was hearing that fundamentalist Shia were taking over medical facilities, electricity, security, and myriad other services related to quality of life.[154]

One prime example of the rapidly changing atmosphere could be found in Iraq's university system, where puritanical Shia, on a power surge after the war, were taking control of Iraq's campuses and imposing religious rules. They forced women to don headscarves, insisted that religious holidays be observed, and papered school hallways with portraits of the ayatollahs. In keeping with the broad

CPA trend of confusing law and order, as discussed earlier, the university system lacked the personnel and will necessary to maintain secularism, but instead passed a bill of rights banning coercion based on religion.[155] In this case, as in so many others, the reality on paper and the reality on the ground diverged mightily.

For their part, the Bush administration and the CPA in those early days focused on gaining support of Shia and keeping the support of Kurds at the utter expense of managing the fears of Sunnis. Even in their memoirs, Bremer and Feith focus almost exclusively on the reactions and feelings of Shia and Kurds to pivotal decisions like de-Ba'athification and disbanding the Iraqi army.[156] As Chandrasekaran puts it, Bremer's governing team "tried to right Saddam's wrongs by engaging in social engineering, favoring the once-oppressed Shiites and Kurds at the expense of the once-ruling Sunnis."[157] This social engineering was not mitigated by any effort to emphasize Iraqi identity over ethnic or religious affiliations on the part of the CPA. In fact, Bremer's Governing Council had ethnic and religious quotas: thirteen Shiites, five Sunni Kurds, five Sunni Arabs, a Christian, and a Turk. Exacerbating the sudden weakness of the Sunnis in national life was the fact that, with de-Ba'athification in effect, there were no Sunni national leaders who had wide name recognition and credibility, so the representation they did get on the Governing Council was weak.[158] Bremer wrote in his memoir that "identifying responsible Sunni leaders was difficult. Saddam had either co-opted or killed most of them."[159]

In time, the widening alienation of Sunnis did gain the attention of the CPA. The governance team wrote in a memo in the fall of 2003, "Sunni communities throughout Iraq, but especially within the Sunni Triangle, are feeling politically and economically disenfranchised. . . . Sunnis do not feel like they are duly represented at the national level, often complaining that they have no representatives on the Governing Council." In a move aimed at bringing the disenfranchised back into the fold, the CPA opened the Office of Provincial Outreach, largely to work with Sunnis and tribes. But it was too little, too late. Sunnis, "still chafing over their loss of position, privilege, and influence," were largely unmoved by the effort. The insurgency was on.[160] Marine Lt. Gen. John Allen, who played a key role in the 2006–2007 campaign in Anbar that defeated the al Qaeda–dominated insurgency, characterized all of the ill-conceived decisions and policies described here as creating by 2004 "a perfect storm across Anbar," providing "the perfect opportunity for AQ [al Qaeda]."[161] In 2003 the United States made all the wrong moves, and it was left to the Marines, who were assigned to take control of Anbar in March 2004, to pick up the pieces.

CHAPTER 3

2004

Ugly Surprises

WARFIGHTING AND PEACEMAKING IN 2003

UNITED STATES MARINES ARE WARFIGHTERS. That's their history, and in OIF they once more demonstrated their mastery of the art of war. At the center of the fight was the 1st Marine Division—Blue Diamond—the oldest and most decorated division in the Corps, having earned nine Presidential Unit Citations since it was activated in 1941.

A combat-ready force of 20,000 Marines, it provides ground combat power for the I MEF. The latter also includes the 3rd Marine Aircraft Wing and 1st Marine Logistics Group.

On March 20, 2003, I MEF forces crossed the Iraq-Kuwait border as part of the Coalition units under Gen. Tommy Franks' command. I MEF's ground component—Blue Diamond—intended, in conjunction with the United Kingdom's I Armored Division and the 3rd U.S. Army Infantry Division, to carry out a high-speed attack that the Iraqi forces would be unable to comprehend or parry.

Blue Diamond would cross the Euphrates, drive east through the heartland of Iraq, and then cross the Tigris to attack Baghdad from the east. It was a route similar to the one Xenophon successfully travelled in 400 BC when he defeated the much larger forces of the king of Persia. The Army's V Corps, composed of approximately three divisions, would simultaneously drive up from the south to the west of the Euphrates and then turn northeast to attack Baghdad.

The commander of I MEF was one of the Corps' most experienced senior officers, Lt. Gen. James Conway. After finishing college in 1969, at the height of the Vietnam War, he joined the Marine Corps. Over the next thirty years Conway commanded every infantry unit, from a platoon all the way up to Blue Diamond. Well read and well educated, Jim Conway is rightly described as a "model of a Marine with an intimidating handshake and disarming Southern charm." In November 2002, then–Major General Conway was promoted to lieutenant general and assigned command of I MEF, just in time for the next bout with Saddam's Iraq.[1] In the first go-around in 1991, Conway had led Battalion Landing Team 3/2 in its diversionary assault during Operation Desert Storm. Now he would lead I MEF.

Leading the 1st Marine Division, a unit whose past commanders led in such epic fights as Guadalcanal, Peleliu, Okinawa, Inchon, "Frozen Chosin," Hue City, and Desert Storm, was another extraordinary general officer, James N. Mattis. By any standard, Mattis would rank high as a combat leader. A student of war who is widely read in history and military strategy, Jim Mattis leads from the front. His "troops call him 'Mad Dog Mattis,' high praise in Marine culture."[2] There can be little doubt that Mattis welcomes the challenge of "battle or brawling," as he frequently refers to combat.

Mattis has a deep understanding and appreciation of twenty-first-century irregular warfare. He often describes it as "morally bruising," and indeed it can lead to actions that smear the Marine Corps. This understanding of the pitfalls of irregular warfare is evident in how Mattis prepares his Marines to fight in these brutal circumstances while maintaining their honor.

Consider the commander's guidance that he gave to his men on the evening of March 17, 2003, as they prepared to cross the line of departure and "enter the uncertain terrain north" of Kuwait. Here is what they could expect: "When I give the word, together we will cross the Line of Departure, close with those forces that choose to fight, and destroy them. Our fight is not with the Iraqi people.... While we will move swiftly and aggressively against those who resist, we will treat others with decency, demonstrating chivalry and soldierly compassion for people who have endured a lifetime under Saddam's oppression.... Chemical attack, treachery, and use of innocent human shields can be expected, as can other unethical tactics."[3]

But in the face of those deadly prospects, General Mattis reminded his men of their honor to the Corps and to their country: "Engage your brain before you engage your weapon.... For the mission's sake, our country's sake, and the sake of the men who carried the Division's colors in past battles ... carry out your mission and *keep your honor clean*." He then closed with the following directive: "Demonstrate to the world there is 'No Better Friend, No Worse Enemy' than a U.S. Marine."[4]

Mattis is serious about maintaining moral integrity. He told the Marines who returned with him to Iraq in 2004, "How you treat people is very, very important. We're not going to become racists. They [the enemy] want you to hate every Iraqi.... You treat those women and children the way you do your own. You make certain you don't do anything that would smear the Marine Corps." He then told of a Marine who administered electric shock to an Iraqi prisoner. "He thought it was funny. It is, if you like five years in Leavenworth [prison]."[5]

Conway and Mattis. I MEF and Blue Diamond were in good hands. Mattis conducted one of the deepest and swiftest ground operations in the history of the Marine Corps. After crossing the Kuwaiti border, the forces of the 1st Marine

Lt. Gen. James T. Conway, left, and Maj. Gen. James N. Mattis discuss preparations for the final phase of the war.

REYNOLDS, *U.S. MARINES IN IRAQ, 2003: BASRAH, BAGHDAD, AND BEYOND*, 85

Division drove across the Fertile Crescent and into the streets of Baghdad. Elements of the division then went 150 miles farther north. Along the way, they rescued American POWs in Samarra and took control of Tikrit, Saddam's hometown.

On April 19, 2003, on the lavish grounds of the dictator's Tikrit palace, General Conway announced to the Marines who had taken that critical city that full-scale combat operations were over. It had been a remarkable campaign, a fight for which the Marines were well prepared, and it was over.[6] What followed was a mission that I MEF had not planned for: occupation.

Of course, it was not called that. Rather, the official postwar mission was known by the acronym SASO, for security and stability operations. The *Department of Defense Dictionary of Military and Associated Terms* defines it this way: "An overarching term encompassing various military missions, tasks, and activities conducted outside the United States in coordination with other instruments of national power to maintain or reestablish a safe and secure environment, provide essential governmental services, emergency infrastructure reconstruction, and humanitarian relief."[7] Also known as Phase IV operations, this was not a mission I MEF had prepared for. Moreover, it was one that General Conway did not welcome, writes Nicholas Reynolds. "He wanted his Marines to fight the war and then to 're-cock,' to get ready for the next war. This was the pattern that came naturally to him and to many other Marines." He would rather leave "occupation duties to others."[8] But CENTCOM had other ideas.

By the third week of April, elements of Blue Diamond were moving south to take up the SASO mission in the seven provinces of the Shia heartland. What they found was an infrastructure decimated by years of purposeful neglect and corruption. Everything was on the edge of collapse—water, electricity, sanitation, health care, education, law and order, and local governance. But with the exception of

Lt. Gen. James T. Conway discusses the end of major combat operations with Marines from I MEF at Saddam's Tikrit palace.

GROEN, *WITH THE 1ST MARINE DIVISION IN IRAQ, 2003*, 370

north Babil Province, which is on the fault line between the Sunni and Shia populations, the Marines found a permissive environment.

In northern Babil, convoys were increasingly coming under attack in May. In early June the 1st Marine Division organized Task Force Scorpion to deal with the situation. Task Force Scorpion's main operational unit was the 4th Light Armored Reconnaissance Battalion (4th LAR). By the end of June, the attacks were over, Task Force Scorpion having proven to be too mobile and too lethal for the insurgents attacking the convoys.

Elsewhere in Blue Diamond's postconflict AO the situation was passive. An infantry battalion was assigned to each governorate and reinforced by civil affairs, engineers, and other support elements. The story of the SASO period is one where Marine units adapted to a mission they had not prepared for and did not want. But when it was over, those involved were satisfied with the job they had done, believing they had helped the Shia south start on the long road to recovery. They had given the people in those seven governorates, who had suffered Saddam's terrible brutality and repression in the aftermath of their 1991 rebellion, a fresh start.

While the situation in the south was not violent, winning over the population was not easy, according to Brig. Gen. John Kelly, who at the time was Blue Diamond's assistant division commander. That was because there was "a great deal of resentment in the south about the United States not coming to their aid at the end of the Gulf War [in 1991]." These Iraqis said, "we had convinced them that all they needed to do was rise up and we'd come to their aid. They did [rise up] but we didn't come to their aid and consequently . . . between 100,000 and 250,000 were just butchered. There are mass graves all over the south," Kelly noted.[9]

Adding to the challenge, according to Kelly, was that there were no other U.S. government organizations on the ground with a postconflict plan for the Marines to coordinate with. Blue Diamond had to go it alone, he explained. In mid-April, "We thought the division would immediately start to retrograde and go back to Camp Pendleton." However, that "wasn't the case at all." Instead, "We were assigned seven provinces in the south . . . and it quickly became obvious that the division was going to have to take a chunk of Iraq and police it and get it back on its feet."[10]

Furthermore, it was on its own in doing so because, as Kelly remonstrated, while "there may have been a plan for reestablishing Iraq and rebuilding it . . . there sure as hell wasn't anyone on the ground to do it. At the time the organization that was on paper supposed to have that responsibility—OHRA [Office of Humanitarian and Reconstruction Assistance]—was not present [in the south of Iraq]."[11] It was left to the Marines to fill the gap.

So, the 1st Marine Division assigned a battalion to each province, and the battalions' commanding officers had the authority, according to Kelly, to do whatever was needed. They could "hire and fire mayors, organize town councils, select judges and juries. I mean they did everything. . . . We took advantage of the lull and before the people could get angry at us . . . we kind of seized the moment and started working on their behalf." There was no blueprint, and "every battalion commander had a little bit of a different twist in his zone."[12]

Col. Joe Dunford was Blue Diamond's chief of staff at the time. Having commanded the 5th Marines during the ground war, he oversaw the SASO mission from the division's headquarters in the shadow of the ruins of ancient Babylon. The tasking was straightforward: "Battalion commanders would go down [to each of the Shia provinces] and be responsible for the security, for the governance, and for the development of each of those particular areas."[13] Straightforward, but beyond the role of military forces in SASO doctrine.

In effect, while doctrine calls for military forces to execute SASO missions in coordination with other instruments of national power—Pentagon-speak for other civilian agencies of the U.S. government—none of those agencies had any meaningful presence in the Shia heartland. Each Marine battalion had to adapt and carry out security, governance, and development on its own.

But, as Dunford concluded, "It worked pretty well." Like Kelly, Dunford believes that when most of the 1st Marine Division departed in July, "it was with a pretty fair degree of optimism that things were going pretty well. . . . Things were going well in the south. And in each one of those cities . . . [battalion] commanders could point with some pride to the accomplishments and the progress they made, whether it was by restoring basic services . . . or whether it was towards . . . the conduct of local elections and establishing provincial councils."[14]

GOING BACK

The remaining elements of the 1st Marine Division finally returned to California in late September. And on "the last plane with the 1st Battalion, 7th Marines," was Colonel Dunford. But within ten days after returning he "got the word. . . . Okay gang, we're going back for OIF II. So, we immediately went into preparation for it."[15]

That preparation, as we shall see, was greatly influenced by the experience in southern Iraq, according to Col. Jim Howcroft, who was I MEFs intelligence chief—G-2—at the time. He noted that a key planning assumption was that Anbar was going to be "more a situation of lawlessness and people taking advantage of the breakdown of authority rather than any type of organized resistance." Why? Howcroft elaborated, "What we had done and the success we had in southern Iraq definitely colored our approach to going back to Anbar. We thought that what had worked in the south would work in the west as well." As a result, the former G-2 noted, "[We] thought we didn't need artillery, we would not need tanks because we hadn't needed them in southern Iraq."[16]

When asked how he assessed the security environment in Anbar as I MEF prepared to return, Colonel Howcroft said, "At the time it was considered generally permissive except for certain pockets. We knew Fallujah was bad. But you know Fallujah has been bad for a long time."[17]

Col. John Toolan, who had command of Blue Diamond's 1st Regimental Combat Team (RCT-1) in the fall of 2004, said the same thing. Toolan had taken command of the regiment during the 1st Marine Division's drive to Baghdad in OIF I. He replaced Col. Joe Dowdy, who in the midst of the campaign had been relieved of his duties by General Mattis.[18] Toolan had stayed in Iraq until the end of July with a reduced force of one battalion. As he was departing, Mattis told him to expect to be back in Iraq "within six or seven months."[19]

Back at Camp Pendleton Colonel Toolan began to prepare RCT-1 to go back for what they anticipated to be a "fairly benign environment." Shaping this perception was the experience in southern Iraq, says Toolan. "We were successful. . . . So during the interim, between July and February when we left again, you have to keep in mind that our mindset . . . our focus of effort was really on the reconstruction aspects . . . in what we perceived to be a fairly benign environment."[20]

So, when the order came for RCT-1 to return to Iraq as the main element of the 1st Marine Division, this assumption about the security environment in Anbar remained unchanged. As a result, preparation by RCT-1 concentrated, according to Toolan, on "intercultural dealings, intercultural issues, and reconstruction-type civil-military operations. There was to be very little fighting. There was to be very little counterinsurgency-type operations."[21]

PLANNING FOR OIF II: THE FIRST FIFTEEN PLAYS

Gen. Jim Conway was sitting in on a Brigadier General's Promotion Board in early October when Commandant Mike Hagee called. He wanted to know if the I MEF commander was prepared to send three battalions back to Iraq. The response was what the commandant expected: "I said absolutely," recalled Conway. "We had had two battalions who had not had the opportunity to go out with the 1st Marine Division [in OIF I] and I knew we could come up with another one. So I said yes.... Well, three grew to six pretty quickly. Six became nine." When it was all said and done, Conway would take "63 percent of the MEF" back to Iraq in early 2004.[22]

However, in October it was not clear where I MEF would go once it returned to Iraq and which units it would replace. At first the Joint Staff wanted to send them to Mosul to replace the 101st Airborne Division, then they considered having I MEF relieve the 82nd Airborne Division in the provinces of Al Anbar and northern Babil. October ended without a decision. However, the Marines were expected to be on the ground in February. It was not much time to get ready.

Finally, on November 5 Secretary of Defense Rumsfeld made it official. Marine Corps forces from I MEF would be returning to Iraq to replace the 82nd Airborne Division by February 2004. They would stay seven months and would then be replaced by other Marine forces.

With not much time to do so, Conway put the staffs of I MEF and Blue Diamond on to planning the deployment. The issue was more than just substituting I MEF for the 82nd Airborne—Conway wanted a different concept of operations. It should be similar to the one that had worked so well in the Shia south, and different from the 82nd Airborne's approach in Anbar. He put it this way in a 2005 interview: "We have our ways [of conducting operations] that were probably more akin to the British method of operation than the U. S. Army methods.... We went back to the *Small Wars Manual* for our initial doctrinal guidance when we had conducted operations in the south. It seemed pretty valid to us and we thought that we could do a continuation of the same type of thing in Al Anbar Province."[23]

In 2005 a debate took place both in and outside the Pentagon over how best to conduct operations in situations like the one in Iraq. It revolved around the firepower-intensive approach that along with rapid maneuver was at the heart of the American military's way of war. Was that approach doing more harm than good in Iraq? After all, this was a different context, some argued, that really did require a less forceful line of attack. Irregular warfare was poles apart from its conventional counterpart, critics argued.

In 2006, based on its *Quadrennial Defense Review*, the Department of Defense not only would identify irregular warfare as a vital mission area for the U.S. military but also would stress the need to prepare for it in new ways. The "long war," the *Quadrennial Defense Review* would argue, is "irregular in its nature." And enemies in that fight are "not traditional conventional military forces."[24] Irregular warfare favored indirect and asymmetric approaches, was inherently a protracted struggle, and required new U.S. strategies and capabilities.

But that sea change in thinking had to wait until 2006. In 2003, as the Marines prepared for deployment, the conventional tactics carried out by the 82nd were at issue. However, those tactics were a matter to be kept beneath the surface. Criticizing those you are about to replace goes against the culture of the services, as illustrated in General Mattis' message to the 1st Marine Division as they prepared to deploy: "All hands, we are going back into the brawl. We will be relieving the magnificent soldiers fighting under the 82nd Airborne Division, whose hard won successes in the Sunni Triangle have opened opportunities for us to exploit."[25]

But there were news reports at the time suggesting that the Marines were planning to employ a different concept of operations in Iraq, not only because of their experience in the south but also thanks to the Corps' legacy of fighting small wars. The Corps also wanted to put some distance between itself and what its planners saw as a too-kinetic approach taken by the Army. A "kinetic approach" is one more of those cryptic Pentagon euphemisms. What it really means is a combat operation in which a high premium is placed on closing with and killing the enemy. It was central to the modern conventional warfare planned for and practiced in the twentieth century.

In a January 7, 2004, article titled "Marines to Offer New Tactics in Iraq: Reduced Use of Force Planned after Takeover from Army," Tom Ricks, the *Washington Post*'s military correspondent, reported that Marine officers were critical of the Army approach. But only off the record. Here is one example cited by Ricks: "I'm appalled at the current heavy-handed use of air [strikes] and artillery in Iraq. . . . Success in a counterinsurgency environment is based on winning popular support, not blowing up people's houses."[26]

But there were other indicators in addition to anonymous comments reported in the press. Perhaps the most attention-getting of these was that the battle dress uniform (BDU) the Marines considered wearing in Anbar was a different color from the Army's BDU. Normally, in an environment like Iraq's, the standard uniform is desert BDUs. While the color of desert terrain varies depending on the minerals in the soil and the time of day, and while no one color or combination of colors matches all deserts, the desert BDU is the standard issue for all such areas, including Iraq. But the Marines were considering wearing green BDUs, which are not normally worn in a desert setting.

Eventually, the decision was to go with the desert BDU because the leadership of I MEF and Blue Diamond did not want to be seen as critical of the 82nd. But they did want to "advertise ourselves as the new guys coming in, and to establish a new relationship, whether it be with provincial councils or local governance bodies or with the Iraqi security forces. And clearly, as Marines," noted Colonel Dunford, "we wanted to advertise ourselves . . . as different. At the same time, what we didn't want to do was go in and be negative about the Army."[27]

To shape that new approach the staffs of I MEF and Blue Diamond went to school. They collected data, studied history, met with experts, and held workshops, including a two-day SASO symposium in mid-December chaired by General Mattis. From these various endeavors emerged I MEF's concept of operations, which General Mattis later put in a nutshell when he modified Blue Diamond's motto—"No Better Friend, No Worse Enemy"—with the codicil "First, Do No Harm." He told his Marines that when they went to Iraq in 2003 they faced a "government we were trying to tear down. This time we are trying to build one up."[28]

General Conway, in a speech in early January 2004, elaborated. The campaign plan for Anbar would consist of three principle lines of operations:

- Security and stability. Eliminate those causing instability, establish a program to train Iraqi security, concentrate first on stabilizing the urban areas.

- Information operations. Establish an information campaign that through the effective dissemination of its products builds Iraqi confidence in I MEF.

- Civil affairs. Acquire resources to plan for and establish governance teams that design and implement various development projects that have early impact.[29]

These would morph into what was dubbed "the First Fifteen Plays," I MEF's plan for the initial phase—the first sixty days—of the deployment.

Then-Colonel Dunford, Blue Diamond's chief of staff, described the fifteen plays as a fleshing out of Conway's lines of operations: "We were to address all those areas," all with the goal to "diminish the frustrations of people, separate them from those causing instability. And we were not talking about an insurgency at this point but former regime elements, criminals, and terrorists. The word 'insurgency' wasn't used in the early part of 2004. And so, as we prepared for OIF II, we had all these things that we would do to help the people recover and grow the Iraqi security forces, which was a key piece of it."[30]

Col. Joe Dunford, RCT-5 commander, second from left, discusses with Maj. Gen. James Mattis the details of RCT-5's plan for the assault into Baghdad.
GROEN, *WITH THE 1ST MARINE DIVISION IN IRAQ,* 2003, 260

In sum, planning prior to deployment was based on the following assumptions: One, the environment in Anbar was generally permissive and the population *not hostile.* Two, the experience in southern Iraq and general lessons from it would serve as the basis for the new effort. Three, I MEF would build on what was believed to be a successful stability operation carried out by the 82nd Airborne, but would do so in a very different and less kinetic way. And four, although I MEF was likely to face some hostility, it would not be an organized resistance or insurgency. These suppositions were part and parcel of the fifteen plays. An examination of each of the plays leaves little doubt that I MEF believed it was about to embark on a stability operation:

1. Coordinate and disseminate information operation messages to introduce Marines to the local populace and gain information superiority.
2. Interact with local tribal, administrative, and religious leaders.
3. Meet with local governing councils in order to build rapport and gain credibility.
4. Diminish Iraqi population support for or tolerance of anti-Coalition forces.
5. Reduce Iraqi unemployment by creating public sector jobs as rapidly as possible and establish job security.
6. Increase the effectiveness of public services and local governing bodies.

7. Distribute school, medical, and children's recreational supplies.
8. Integrate the stability and support actions of Combined Action Program units in order to enhance Iraqi confidence.
9. Increase effectiveness of Iraqi security forces (ISF) by providing basic and advanced training, and close integration into our formations and supervision.
10. Develop the Sunni advisory program.
11. Conduct patrols to include emphasis on joint patrols with Iraqi forces in order to build confidence and assess their abilities.
12. Initiate former Iraqi military engagement program. Use veteran points to bring former military to the forefront of employment efforts to display respect for former military and reduce adversarial relationships with them.
13. Commence identification of former regime elements and terrorist cells, avoiding any loss of developed human intelligence sources.
14. Defeat anti-Coalition forces in coordination with Iraqi forces.
15. Disrupt enemy infiltration of Iraq through overland movement or movement along waterways. Pay special attention to the border regions to disrupt the introduction of foreign fighters with an initial emphasis on the Syrian border.[31]

While this was taking place on the East Coast, Colonel Toolan was on the West Coast preparing RCT-1 to deploy back to Iraq. Then, in November, General Mattis told Toolan "that RCT-1 would be the main effort for this next deployment and that I would have the region around Fallujah. . . . So when he gave me that particular area I then honed in on what was going on in Fallujah and the surrounding cities. It took a little while for it to really hit me, hit the staff, hit us together, that that AO was . . . different than Hillah and Babylon [in southern Iraq]."[32]

Still, Toolan's "focus was reconstruction," not fighting or combat operations. Then, in December, he happened to see a news report "saying Fallujah was the most dangerous city in the world."[33] In the summer of 2003 several news stories began to appear about the city. Consider the following one from *CBS Evening News* on June 9: "Almost every night in Fallujah, there's another ambush of U.S. soldiers patrolling the town's streets. . . . 'Instead of being the hunter, it's almost as if we're being hunted,' says Pfc. Jeff Sappington of the 315th Battalion, 2nd Brigade, 3rd Infantry Division."[34]

This made an impression on Toolan. "We took that as, okay, things may be a little bit different . . . but I think we still have the right mindset. . . . We will have all this effort going in reconstruction. I think we'll be able to win their hearts and minds. At the very minimum we'll be able to win the respect of the people. . . . We can do that and I think we'll win over people because we'll build hospitals, we'll build schools, and we'll get money flowing in."[35]

THE ENEMY: "WHEN DO A BUNCH OF GUYS TRYING TO KILL YOU TURN INTO AN INSURGENCY?"

At the end of March 2004, Brigadier General Kelly, Blue Diamond's assistant division commander, had a bird's-eye view of the evolving situation in Anbar. But trying to figure out that complex setting was not easy. And, as I will describe shortly, things were heating up very fast in the province and were about to turn ugly in Fallujah.

General Kelly knew what he did not know. As he watched the situation from Ramadi he posed the crucial question, one that would stump U.S. forces deployed to Iraq and their policy-maker masters back in Washington for some time: "When do a bunch of guys that are trying to kill you turn into an insurgency?" In other words, "When do you know you are facing an organized opposition and how do you figure out who makes up its constituent parts?"

In the second half of 2003, there was a consensus in the U.S. government that those doing the shooting could not possibly be characterized as an organized insurgency. Even General Kelly did not think so: "I argued last summer [2003] that it wasn't an insurgency because to me an insurgency has to have some end and it didn't seem to have an end. I thought what we were dealing with primarily at the time was . . . bad guys, Ba'athists, who had no place to go."[36]

And General Kelly was far from alone. Secretary of Defense Rumsfeld could not imagine it either. He frequently referred to "those guys" killing U.S. soldiers and Marines as "pockets of dead-enders." When asked about the opposition in Iraq at a June 2003 press conference in the Pentagon, he downplayed the issue, describing them "as small elements of 10 to 20 people, not large military formations or networks of attackers." General Franks, head of the CENTCOM theater, would soon finish them off, the Pentagon chief confidently forecast.[37]

The reality in the fall of 2003 was that with few exceptions no one at the senior level in Washington or Baghdad—military or civilian—expected a robust and organized resistance. Inside the defense and security institutions of the U.S. government that planned and carried out the war, it was just not imaginable. Indeed, during preparation for OIF, the U.S. intelligence community gave no meaningful consideration to the possibility that in the aftermath of the conventional fight, armed insurgent and terrorist groups would form up and attack U.S. forces. CIA analysts received no prewar tasking from their senior managers at Langley to estimate whether this was even a possibility.[38]

Some former CIA officials after the fact have asserted otherwise. But to date none has identified any serious assessments supporting that claim.[39] What they have offered up is a January 2003 National Intelligence Council assessment titled "Principal Challenges in Post-Saddam Iraq." But nowhere in its thirty-eight pages does the document seriously consider the possible emergence of an organized and complex insurgency like the one the Marines would confront upon putting boots on the ground in Anbar in 2004. Only at the end of that document—the very last paragraph—do we find the briefest hint:

> The ability of al-Qa'ida or other terrorist groups to maintain a presence in northern Iraq (or, more clandestinely, elsewhere) would depend largely on whether a new regime was able to exert effective security control over the entire country. In addition, rogue ex-regime elements could forge an alliance with existing terrorist organizations or act independently to wage guerrilla warfare against the new government or Coalition forces.[40]

There are specialized departments in CIA's analysis division that focus specifically on the issues of insurgency and terrorism; surely they produced detailed supporting studies. They must have been asked by the National Intelligence Council, their own senior managers, or policy makers to examine the sources and conditions of a possible insurgency in Iraq and to estimate how it might emerge. And also, surely they were asked about the possibility that al Qaeda would make Iraq the central front in its global war against what they call "the far enemy," the United States. These specialized departments must have gone beyond this afterthought at the end of "Principal Challenges in Post-Saddam Iraq."

If any such reports existed, Col. Jim Howcroft, the G2—chief of intelligence—for I MEF in the fall of 2003 would have seen them. After all, he had access to all the classified databases, which his staff mined for any and all relevant material. But at the end of the day no such assessment existed. Everything the G2 saw led this career Marine intelligence officer to conclude that Anbar "was generally permissive except for certain pockets." That was his bottom line at the time.[41]

Of course, the G2 knew "Al Anbar was a bad place; a lawless place." He "knew there were bad guys out there who wanted to do us harm, that we would have to fight with and defeat to win the population over to our side. . . . We knew Anbar wasn't going to be easy but I don't believe that we thought we would have to contest it as much as we did." Looking back on it, Howcroft carped that at the end of 2003 the intelligence community lacked information about what was going on in Anbar: "I got nothing of value from DIA and CIA. They didn't have any sources, they didn't know."[42]

What I MEF needed was local knowledge—"who the actors were, and who their leaders were, and what leverages you needed to apply to them"—and they did not have it. Howcroft explained, "We had basic information from cultural studies; books from academics. We understood there were different tribes, and [knew] which ones were more important. We had that. We understood that."[43]

But missing were the details, the nitty-gritty: "We didn't know who was who, and what was what. And again, when we talk about local culture, we knew that culture is more than what hand you shake. It's who are the decision-makers here, who allocates resources, how are decisions made? All of those things you have to learn. There was no book that told you these are the different power brokers, here's how you approach this guy, here's how you approach that one."[44] CIA did not have that information, nor did DIA.

Once in Anbar it did not get appreciably better. The MEF needed to know who the bad guys were, who the good guys were, and how to deal with each. But when asked whether at the end of his tour in the summer of 2004 he had those details—the nitty-gritty—the colonel demurred: "Certainly not while I was there. . . . We were understanding that there were different groups and the nuances involved and that what one group wanted was different from what other groups wanted. . . . But it was being able to understand how they all fit together and who the leaders were and all that. We didn't develop that [during my tour]."[45]

A paucity of local knowledge plagued I MEF. The intelligence community did not have the means of collecting and delivering the information Colonel Howcroft wanted, so the Marines would have to develop their own.

BOOTS ON THE GROUND

On February 14, 2004, the units of I MEF began the long trip from California to Iraq. Their destination once in country—Al Anbar—was designated AO Atlanta. One or more of the Marine and Army combat units configured under the I MEF were assigned to each of the AOs. Colonel Toolan, commanding RCT-1, placed his three battalions in the following areas of AO Raleigh: 2nd Battalion, 1st Marines (2/1) was just east of Fallujah at Camp Baharia. The 1st Battalion, 5th Marines (1/5) was at Camp Abu Gharaib, west of the town that would become an infamous part of the war not long after the Marines arrived in Anbar. Adjacent to Anbar was the province of northern Babil Province. Toolan sent 2nd Battalion, 2nd Marines (2/2) there to help cover it in conjunction with the 10th Mountain Division's 1st Battalion, 32nd Infantry Brigade.

Col. John Toolan, left, the commander of RCT-1, is seen here in Fallujah in 2004.

Estes, *Into the Fray*, 33

Col. Craig Tucker took 7th Regimental Combat Team (RCT-7) out west to AO Denver, which covered a vast swathe of Anbar. It included the Syrian border, which was the main pipeline through which foreign jihadis flowed into Iraq. During the first part of March he assigned 2nd Battalion, 7th Marines (2/7), to Al Asad Air Base. In addition to the town of Al Asad, they had responsibility for the area stretching from Hit to Rutbah to the Jordanian and Syrian borders. The 3rd Battalion, 7th Marines (3/7), along with the 1st Light Armored Reconnaissance Battalion (1st LAR), had responsibility for the area that included Al Qa'im, Rawah, Hadithah, and Husaybah.

Finally, the 1st Brigade, 1st Infantry Division of the U.S. Army, which had the 2nd Battalion, 4th Marines (2/4), embedded within it, was assigned to AO Topeka. It included both Ramadi, the capital of the province, and a significant amount of territory surrounding that city.

These units constituted the main ground combat elements of I MEF. But because the MEF deployed as a Marine Air-Ground Task Force (MAGTF), it could include more than these infantry battalions, which could be supported by armor and artillery, and could also include recon battalions and snipers. Initially, however, I MEF did not take all of these support units. It also had an aviation element consisting of both fixed-wing attack aircraft and helicopters of the 3rd MAW (Marine Aircraft Wing), as well as all of the MAGTF's support units—communications, combat engineers, motor transport, medical, and supply units of its 1st First Service Support Group (1st FSSG).

Because its concept of operations, built around the First Fifteen Plays, was configured for a permissive environment and security and support operations—SASO—the MEF did not take all the combat power of an MAGTF. Dunford explained that at the time they did not think they would need them: "If you look at our artillery . . . if we were going over there to conduct major combat operations, you know, we might see a need for direct support artillery battalions for the regiments. Well, clearly, we didn't bring them over there . . . based on General Mattis' and General Conway's guidance. . . . They made an assessment of what we needed." I MEF did not need artillery. It also would have no need for fixed-wing attack aircraft, said Blue Diamond's chief of staff at the time, "based on what we thought the nature of the fight was going to be."[46]

But the fight the Marines engaged in once on the ground in Anbar was not what they had planned for, said Dunford. That plan—the First Fifteen Plays—"didn't survive first contact."[47] Gen. Jim Conway noted, "We didn't lose a single Marine in southern Iraq in our five and half months there." But "the second night that I was in Camp Fallujah," following the change of command with the 82nd, "we lost five Marines and a corpsman to an indirect fire attack. In fact, there was a lot of indirect fire coming into Fallujah. It made us realize it was going to be a very different place."[48]

Fallujah was at the heart of Colonel Toolan's AO. It did not take the commander of RCT-1 long to realize that what he had read in December—Fallujah was the most dangerous city in the world—was not hyperbole.

> I arrived around March 20th. The transfer of authority was going to go March 28th. On March 26th I went to a meeting in Fallujah with the city council. My convoy was ambushed and we fought through the ambush. We went into the council meeting. We had to provide security around the building. We were in there thirty minutes when we were attacked with mortars and rockets. We had to fight our way back to base. I took eight casualties. It was not a good day. That was on March 26th and I didn't even own the area yet. It was still under the 82nd Airborne.[49]

It was supposed to be a SASO mission. "We trained up for that mission and we were in it for one day," said Toolan. "We were supposed to be helping," but almost immediately "we were killing them. . . . I was in the fight before I took over. . . . I was in a major urban fight."[50]

The day before Toolan shot his way into and out of Fallujah, a Marine service support convoy was struck by an improvised explosive device—an IED—in the vicinity of the Fallujah Cloverleaf, a major intersection in the city. One of the enemy's weapons of choice, it killed one Marine that day. It was one of many IEDs planted each night when anti-Coalition forces, as they were called, maneuvered out to prepare for operations against military convoys.

Things were no calmer in AO Denver. The first of these attacks took place on March 26, only a few days after RCT-7 combat units had arrived in the AO.

According to RCT-7's monthly report, "During the last two weeks of March throughout AO Denver there were daily and nightly IED and ambush attacks against RCT-7 Marines on patrol and in Forward Operating Bases (FOBs). Main and Alternative Supply Routes became contested territory as scores of IEDs and mines were employed against RCT-7 convoys."[51]

It was neither what they planned for nor what they expected to find, recalled Colonel Howcroft: "We had gone in with this sort of subtle, smooth—you know, the military is the last resort, engage local leaders, work with the local authorities. . . . All that kind of stuff." As in General Mattis' codicil to Blue Diamond's motto—"No Better Friend, No Worse Enemy"—I MEF was going to "first do no harm." Reflecting on those initial days in Anbar, the G2 conceded, "Yeah. That was our focus. . . . Maybe we were naive."[52]

So, as the initial days and weeks unfolded in Anbar, one thing was certain. The assessments made in December did not wash once I MEF was on the ground. Dunford explained, "The assessment that was made, prior to deployment, and the assessment that was made when we were conducting the relief in place with the 82nd Airborne [was based on the following] fundamental assumptions. Number one: we would inherit six thousand Iraqi security forces in uniform at various stages of training, they just need some more work—six thousand. Number two: we're not dealing with insurgency, we're dealing with remnants of former regime loyalists, criminals, and terrorists. And number three: in general terms, we had the support of the people."[53] Within days of arriving, the Marines found that each assumption was wrong. And then the Blackwater tragedy occurred in Fallujah.

BLACKWATER

On March 31 four contractors from the private security company Blackwater USA were escorting a food-delivery convoy from Eurest Support Services, a subsidiary of the catering company Compass Group. The horrific particulars of their murder and the grisly actions that followed were captured by Bing West in his book *No True Glory*. Those events would have a profound effect on I MEF for the remainder of 2004 and beyond.

On that day in March 2004, West writes, the Blackwater guards, all "capable men," decided to "take a shortcut through Fallujah. . . . They were driving two Mitsubishi Pajero sport utility vehicles on the main thoroughfare, Highway 10." They did not communicate this decision to local Marine units deployed in the vicinity. No sooner had they passed through the center of the town than "from the doorway of shops, insurgents dashed into the street and sprayed both vehicles." Neither vehicle had armor plating.[54]

And then the situation turned Somalia-esque, resembling the vicious brutality of Mogadishu in October of 1993. Recall those images. The photograph on the front page of the *New York Times* was one you can never forget. It was of a dead U.S. soldier surrounded by raging Somalis kicking and spitting on the corpse.

As the mob closed in on the two SUVs in downtown Fallujah, "an American with bullet wounds in his chest staggered out [of one of the SUVs] and fell to the ground." The mob descended on the fallen Blackwater employee like vultures. "He was kicked, stomped, stabbed, and butchered." And then in a grim flashback to Mogadishu, the bodies of the contractors were burned, dismembered, dragged through the streets, and eventually hung from a bridge crossing the Euphrates. Underneath was the epitaph "Fallujah is the cemetery for Americans."[55]

The events of March 31 in Fallujah put an end to any plans for SASO. The message coming out of the CPA and Washington was that this outrage was going to have to be dealt with. Fallujah could not remain out of control or, as the Marines would later learn, become ground zero for AQI. But the leadership of I MEF wanted to go slowly in responding to the slaughter of the four Americans. West reports, "The MEF had the photos, names and addresses of the perpetrators and was determined to arrest or kill them," but they did not want to do so in a "dramatic or sudden way."[56]

Take no immediate or major military action, counseled General Mattis. "As we review the actions in Fallujah yesterday . . . we are convinced this act was spontaneous mob action. . . . We must avoid the temptation to strike out in retribution. . . . Going overly kinetic at this juncture plays into the hands of the opposition," said the commanding general of Blue Diamond. He believed the enemy "did not plan this crime, it dropped into their lap. . . . We should not fall victim to their hope for a vengeful response."[57]

General Conway concurred. He saw the terrible events of March 31 as "a serious mistake . . . in the first place and one that was very avoidable through some very simple coordination." If only the convoy had notified the Marines of their decision to take that shortcut. Conway and Mattis cautioned the chain of command: "Let's not overreact to the death of the contractors. That was a mistake and one that should not drive our policies or our strategies in and around the city. In the midst of trying to push back against that [kind of overreaction]," recalled the I MEF commanding general, "we got word to attack Fallujah. A division-level attack, whatever amount of force that we thought we needed. But we were ordered to attack Fallujah."[58]

Baghdad and Washington were not interested in military advice that counseled restraint, even when it came from two tough Marine generals who were on the ground in Anbar. They had been stunned by al Jazeera's coverage of the slaughter. Its correspondent, Ahmed Mansur, and his camera operator, Laith Mushtaq, were on the street broadcasting live from inside the city. And their exclusive footage was being picked up and rebroadcast by CNN, BBC, and everyone else. Ambassador Bremer saw the news reports in his Baghdad office and immediately summoned Lieutenant General Sanchez, who at the time was commander of the Combined Joint Task Force 7, the top U.S. military position.

Bremer did not buy Conway's and Mattis' go-slow approach. He told Sanchez that he wanted "a vigorous attack," and "Sanchez agreed." In Washington the reaction was the same. President Bush's and Secretary Rumsfeld's reaction "was emotional and aggressive," and it came without delay. On April 1 General Sanchez's spokesperson, Brig. Gen. Mark Kimmit, announced at a Baghdad press conference, "U.S. troops will go in. . . . It's going to be deliberate; it will be precise; and it will be overwhelming."[59]

Since arriving in Anbar, Colonel Toolan and RCT-1 had experienced one ugly surprise after another. They had prepared for SASO, "but never really had the opportunity to do that." Instead, recall Toolan's earlier retort: "I was in the fight before I took over" from the 82nd. He had to shoot his way in and out of Fallujah just to meet the city council. Then he no sooner "took the transfer of authority for the AO and the next day the contractors from Blackwater came into the city and they were killed, bodies mutilated, hung from the bridge. The following day I got orders to isolate the city and seize key objectives inside the city."[60] In effect, RCT-1 was to take control of Fallujah.

In the mid-1990s, the Marine Corps had begun to focus on urban warfare. The commandant at that time—Gen. Charles C. "Chuck" Krulak—told the Corps that wars in the future would be in cities. It was already happening, he said, pointing to Mogadishu, Sarajevo, and Grozny. So, the Marines began to prepare for what they formalized in doctrine as MOUT—military operations on urban terrain.

All of this made sense given that urbanization was sweeping the world at an accelerating rate. In the Corps' 1998 guidance *Military Operations on Urbanized Terrain*, the following statistics documented that progression: "Forecasts based on population statistics and the worldwide migration trend from agrarian to industrialized societies predict that 85 percent of the world's population will reside in urbanized areas by the year 2025. As the world trend toward urbanization increases, the military significance of cities is likely to increase proportionally."[61]

The Marines built a Mogadishu in the California desert and began learning the tactics, techniques, and procedures to fight successfully on the urban battlefield. They knew that cities could serve as great equalizers between disparate military forces. The fight in Grozny, at the end of the twentieth century, was the most recent illustration.

Before dawn on New Year's Eve 1994, heavy Russian armored columns embarked on what they believed would be a speedy conquest to wrest Grozny from Chechen secessionists. Within hours, the Russian stroll into Grozny turned into a desperate and bloody firefight for survival. It is estimated that "the first Russian assault column to enter Grozny . . . lost 105 of 120 tanks and armored personnel carriers." And overall, "the Russians lost about 70 percent of the tanks committed to the New Year's Eve 1994 assault."[62] One report states that they "lost more tanks in Grozny than they did in the battle for Berlin in 1945."[63]

So, when I MEF was ordered to take Fallujah, "we drew on all we had studied and trained for," since General Krulak told them to get ready for the three-block war in cities, noted Colonel Dunford.[64] "I think, particularly, at the small unit level, that the training that went on in the 1990s, MOUT, the basic urban skills training, and so forth that had gone on in those years prepared us for Fallujah. . . . I don't think you can overestimate what positive impact that had."[65]

THE FIRST BATTLE OF FALLUJAH

Drawing on that MOUT training, Toolan and his staff prepared to carry out Washington's orders. First, they intended to "cordon the city off," recounted the RCT-1 commander. "We cordoned Fallujah off with two battalions—1st Battalion, 5th Marines [1/5], took the southern area and 2nd Battalion, 1st Marines [2/1], took the northern and western approaches. So, we looked at the area and decided that there were nine blocking positions that would basically isolate the city and we went in first and isolated it." But to move into the city itself he would need more forces and General Mattis gave him "three additional battalions."[66]

With those forces, Toolan intended to come from two directions and methodically seize various sectors of the city and specific targets within them. The latter, he said, "included the mayor's compound . . . [and] the Iraqi National Guard facility. There also was a group of stores, one of which was a photo shop. The person who ran the photo shop was the guy responsible for the pictures of the dead contractors hanging from the bridge. [He] made CDs and got it out to all his buds." Toolan labeled that vile venture "a nice information operation by the bad guys." The message was clear: "Hey, look what we did to the Americans. We can do this again."[67]

Once into the city, explained Toolan, they moved toward "two locations to the south of the main supply route [MSR], which we called 'MSR Michigan,' which ran right through the city. Those two areas we knew were where Abu Mussab al-

Zarqawi's . . . folks gathered under his guidance. There were buildings where they were living. So those were going to be our key objectives, but in order to get there we had to go through one of the most populated areas of Fallujah called the Jolan District. . . . Those were our objectives." Toolan wanted to get his hands on Zarqawi and the foreign fighters. The RCT-1 commander hoped to pull off his own "information operation." His men would "capture foreign fighters and let everybody see them." He intended to show the world that "there are foreign fighters in Fallujah."[68]

On April 3 General Sanchez went to I MEF headquarters for a briefing by Toolan on his "concept for seizing the city." Sanchez named the operation Vigilant Resolve. He wanted an end to Fallujah serving as a sanctuary for the likes of Zarqawi and his murderous henchmen. And he wanted those responsible for the Blackwater murders arrested or killed. "That was it," said Toolan. "We were off to the races."[69]

On April 5 the operation began with a cordon of the city, using the two battalions Toolan had designated for that mission. Raids also took place, including one on the photo shop. It was time to put an end to the despicable distribution of the Blackwater pictures. Other high-value targets were also taken out. The assault on Fallujah started the next day, with 2/1 striking into the northwest sector in the area of the Jolan District. From south of the Cloverleaf, 1/5 attacked into the industrial district of the city. The goal was to close in on the enemy from two directions.

RCT-1 proceeded methodically against enemy forces, revealing their locations and eliminating them. On April 7 Toolan ratcheted up the pressure by launching an attack that continued for the next forty-eight hours. The Marines were killing plenty of enemy as they pushed deeper into Fallujah, but it was slow going. The city covers roughly twenty square kilometers and consists of more than 50,000 concrete buildings, most of which were one or two stories high. In some areas the houses had walls around them. In other areas, like the Jolan District, they were bunched in narrow and twisting streets. The average block in Fallujah is one hundred by two hundred meters, and there are approximately one thousand blocks.

RCT-1 was engaged in full-scale urban warfare against an enemy that was surprisingly flexible and adaptive in the use of small-unit tactics. And they knew the battle space of Fallujah. They fought from everywhere, including mosques: snipers aimed from the turrets, and the insurgents used these buildings to store weapons and explosives.

The Marines were also adapting, though, as General Conway recounted, "About three days into the attack, we had taken about a third of the city." When the enemy made a mistake, he noted, his forces made them pay. For instance, when "forty to fifty of their guys . . . were caught walking down the street trying to move into attack positions," RCT-1 called in an AC-130 and wiped them out. "We [also] brought in a lot of snipers," said the I MEF commander, "realizing that they would be a very viable weapon in a built-up area." They were. "The snipers owned the streets."[70]

Things were going well, and intelligence was picking up "intercepts that they were about to run out of ammunition." The enemy's will was running low, too. "We had killed a significant portion of the leadership, and the rest were confused and fighting among themselves . . . arguing among themselves in terms of what they needed to do. They were starting to look at how to slip out of the city."[71]

And then, on April 9, the Marines were ordered to stop the attack. It came from General Sanchez, but the source was Ambassador Bremer. He had prevailed on General Abazaid to order a cease-fire. The Iraqi Governing Council was furious about the attack, claiming that many civilians were intentionally being killed. They characterized the assault as collective punishment against the citizens of Fallujah. Members of the council resigned in protest. There was a growing international uproar as well, and even members of the Coalition were wavering.

Media reports from inside Fallujah were the source of the collective-punishment accusation. Marines were said to be using excessive and indiscriminate force, needlessly killing large numbers of civilians. With the exception of Robert Kaplan of the *Atlantic*, however, no Western journalists were allowed to cover the battle. So the media reports were coming from al Jazeera and other Arab outlets, including Al-Arabiya. These journalists had worked their way into the city, and by their accounts civilian casualties were skyrocketing as desperate residents were fleeing in the wake of relentless U.S. artillery fire and air raids.

Given that the battle was taking place amidst a large civilian population still in the city, there can be little doubt that there were casualties. The Marines had had no time for shaping operations like those employed in the second battle of Fallujah six months later, when they had time to evacuate the population. Bremer's angry demand for the attack to begin immediately had prevented any such preparation, which would have included evacuating the population. So, even as I MEF tried to limit its fire to insurgent locations, the nature of the battlefield made that very challenging to do. And the insurgents made it even more arduous by fighting from the midst of the population.[72]

To make matters worse, the insurgents were manipulating al Jazeera. They invited its reporters to see dead babies at the main hospital, said to have been killed by Coalition air strikes. And that is how al Jazeera reported it. The resistance was stage-managing information. And without other media sources to validate or refute their reports, al Jazeera had a major impact on how the world saw and heard what was happening in Fallujah.

According to Bing West, "Lacking any other source, most major U.S. newspaper and television outlets worldwide repeated the [civilian casualty] estimates cited in the Arab press." These were "based on the allegations of Iraqi and Jordanian doctors in Fallujah," who told al Jazeera there were "six hundred dead and a thousand wounded [civilians]."[73] Those figures were never verified. What's more, it was the insurgents who made the doctors available. Were they really doctors, or were they insurgents masquerading as doctors? Were they speaking freely, or saying what they were ordered to say? There was no way of knowing.

Conway was irate over how the Marines were portrayed: "Al Jazeera and some other Arab media had worked their way into the city and they were reporting that we were killing hundreds of women and children and old people when in fact just the opposite was true." Given the nature of the battle, he conceded that "some women and children did die. We were dropping bombs and shooting artillery, counter battery into Fallujah, no question about it. But we were being very careful. We were checking all of those missions to try to make sure that collateral damage—[civilian casualties]—was absolutely minimized."[74]

As for those doctors, the future commandant added, "There were a couple of doctors at the hospital who were bigger insurgents than the insurgents. So they were only too happy to make comments about how we were filling the hospital with women and children [that we killed]." That they were taken at their word, Conway characterized as "irresponsible reporting of the Arab press." They were lacking in "journalistic integrity."[75]

The stop order turned into a stalemate. On-again off-again fighting continued in and around the city, but the order to take the city down was suspended, and during the weeks that followed pressure built to bring Vigilant Resolve to an end. Conway recalled that even the British charged that the Marines were "being too heavy handed and warned if you [continue to] do that you risk us leaving the Coalition. That was a bucket of cold water in the face," said Conway. "Immediately, the whole thought process changed about going back into Fallujah because that . . . was not worth the breakup of the Coalition to include [loss of] our best ally."[76] Finally, on May 1, the Marines withdrew. Conway announced that the city was being turned over to the newly formed Fallujah Brigade.

During the interim between April 9 and May 1, the insurgents escalated elsewhere in Anbar Province while still attacking Marines at Fallujah. This included major operations in Ramadi, where on one day in April twelve Marines from 2/4 died in combat. It was the same kind of fight as in Fallujah: small enemy units maneuvering on the urban battlefield. And as in Fallujah, they fought from the city's mosques. Beyond the cities and towns, the enemy set up ambushes, placed

IEDs, and fired from concealed positions at convoys as they pushed through the MSRs running through Anbar.

THE INSURGENTS DIG IN

The armed groups in Anbar were proving to be more mobile and better organized than had been thought. Furthermore, with the stand-down at Fallujah, these groups were able to proclaim that they had just defeated the U.S. Marine Corps. The seasoned G2 of I MEF, Colonel Howcroft, summed up how the insurgents were spinning Fallujah: "We have just been able to go toe to toe with the world's only superpower, the guys who had taken down Saddam, and look what we did. We stood up to them and we won. The Marines left. They pulled out. We defended our city and won. . . . Get on board, we're the future here [in Anbar], not these guys. They're going to be leaving."[77]

Colonel Toolan heard the same thing coming from enemy information operations in Anbar: "We beat these guys [the Marines]. We can beat them again. . . . We got them to go into a fight in Fallujah. And we got them to stop and withdraw. . . . They're afraid." This was a very effective message, said Toolan, one that was being replayed throughout the province and beyond. "They had a very tight line of communication between themselves and the people; they were very successful at mentally convincing them."[78]

Dunford added that the fight in Fallujah "was a battle of wills and . . . any time the enemy is successful, and they certainly declared themselves successful . . . that is going to chip away at the willingness of the Iraqi people to cooperate with you and it's going to embolden the insurgents."[79] As we will see, it did just that, as the fight during the summer and fall months in Anbar illustrates. This was much more than a bunch of guys trying to kill Marines.

Moreover, this was not the only payoff that the insurgents and especially AQI accrued from the April battle. They also were handed a sanctuary, and armed groups need sanctuaries. Sanctuaries provide a safe haven in which to establish a secure base for training, planning, and launching operations. Generally, sanctuaries are in remote and ungoverned areas within or across the borders of weak states. In this case, though, it was not remote at all. This sanctuary was a major city smack in the heart of Anbar that was being relinquished to the insurgents.

Maybe Washington did not understand the implications of the decision to stop the attack, but the leadership of I MEF certainly did. General Conway had no illusions of its significance: "Well, what came of it [the decision to halt] is that Fallujah became an enclave. A place where it was realized by the insurgents that we were not going to go. . . . We were not authorized to conduct operations there and they in turn could operate. . . . That was very painful . . . [for them to be] six kilometers from my Command Post."[80]

At the end of the summer, Maj. Gen. Richard Natonski took command of the 1st Marine Division. By then, he observed, Fallujah was offering the insurgents "the ability to rest, rearm, refit, plan, and to go outside the city and launch their attacks and then come back to a secure environment. . . . How could we have control of Anbar when you have this cancer called Fallujah?"[81]

Recognizing its opportunity, AQI moved with alacrity to take control of and build up its operational apparatus in the city. To take charge, it eliminated any challenges to its authority through a brutal murder and intimidation campaign. Natonski explained, "The people in that city lived in great fear. Anyone suspected of collaborating with the Coalition forces could find themselves executed. . . . There were innocent Iraqis that were executed. They lived in fear."[82]

The degree to which this gruesome business took place only came into clear sight after the Marines took Fallujah back, in November. What they found were many videos of executions of those suspected of opposing AQI. These and other horrors had befallen those suspected of collaboration. According to I MEF's assistant chief of staff for operations, "We saw many videos of individuals being driven out of the city—a half a block, a hundred yards—a pistol to the head, right on video and then, boom." And there was no due process here: "The terrorists would kill innocent civilians, or torture innocent civilians, and we have lots of proof of that as we went through some of their torture chambers and slaughterhouses. We found those [places] in the city after the fight, and even during the fight, when we cleared portions of the city."[83] AQI put in place a gory reign of terror.

Having taken control, the insurgents next began to prepare Fallujah for round two with the Marine Corps. They were concentrating forces, building defenses, stockpiling weapons, and setting up elaborate IED traps. RCT-1 was watching these developments in real time. They had live video feeds from unmanned aerial vehicles constantly flying over Fallujah, which "paid big dividends by allowing us to watch enemy defensive fortifications [being built], terrorist training, and weapons stockpiling inside the city," said those RCT-1 Marines watching. "Day by day we saw the enemy strengthen itself inside the city."[84]

Baghdad and the White House had tied the hands of RCT-1 after the May pullout, making these enemy actions off limits, a fact bemoaned in the regiment's October report: "We were prohibited from engaging those targets with direct and indirect fires unless we had approval from the highest levels. The 'approval process' was extremely time consuming. . . . Even if approval finally came hours or days later, in nearly every case, the opportunity to strike had passed."[85]

Beyond defensive preparations, AQI and those aligned with it were moving to establish the means to carry the fight across Anbar and beyond from inside Fallujah. AQI saw the battle there as a central front in the larger global holy war against the West. That was the theme propagated on al Qaeda's Global Islamic Media Front website and its other media outlets. A victory would give the jihadists "an advanced base close to the Land of the Two Holy Places [i.e., Saudi Arabia] and the al-Aqsa Mosque [in Jerusalem]."[86]

To extend the battlefield across Anbar and the Sunni Triangle, the insurgents in Fallujah seemed to be drawing on existing organizational and operational concepts. Were they part of a body of jihadi warfighting principles that al Qaeda and its associated movements had been developing?[87] If so, what were they?

To answer these questions it is necessary to look back to the late 1980s to a small number of articles that began appearing in the *Marine Corps Gazette*. Those pieces put forth what at the time was considered a radical proposition—war was entering its fourth generation.[88] The first generation had been perfected by Napoleon. This was followed by the industrial-age wars of attrition based on massive firepower. This second generation reached its apex in World War I. Maneuver warfare, introduced by the Germans in World War II and refined by the United States in the 1980s, marked the third generation.

Fourth-generation warfare offered a new template. Those who advanced this proposal sought to explain how armed groups, especially terrorist organizations, were adapting and expanding their capacity to fight in irregular, unconventional, and decentralized ways.

Unconventional operations, they explained, will be employed by terrorists and insurgents to bypass the superior military might of nation-states in order to indirectly attack political, economic, population, and symbolic targets. The organization and operations of these fourth-generation warriors will be masked by deception and stealth. There will be no fronts in these fights and no distinctions between civilian and military targets. The laws of war will not prevent attacks on nonmilitary targets. Frequently fighting in the name of religion, fourth-generation warriors will be remorseless enemies seeking to carry out great carnage.

Pentagon and civilian security professionals in the late 1980s and early 1990s were not at all persuaded. But the jihadis were. A study of their publications shows that they examined "information warfare, fourth generation warfare, asymmetric warfare, the Clausewitzian center of gravity versus Al Qaida's decentralized leadership. . . . U.S. warfare doctrines, U.S. fears of weapons of mass destruction . . . as well as lessons learned from specific operations such as the Moscow theatre hostage-taking." Attention was also being paid to the tactical level with assessments of "the use of sniper operations," various kinds of IEDs, and other guerrilla methods.[89] Jihadi websites abounded with handbooks and manuals embracing these concepts. They were developing their own doctrine and principles for the "long jihad."

Between the two battles of Fallujah, the insurgents in the city appear to have been drawing on these organizational principles to develop the means to extend the battlefield across Anbar. The Marines began to grasp what this entailed only after they captured Fallujah in November and were able to eyeball the insurgent infrastructure that had developed since they pulled back in April. General Natonski described some of what was found: "We did find some chemical [warfare] labs. . . . I never imagined the amount of ordnance and weapons that we would find in the city. . . . We also found IED factories and we found propaganda factories. I didn't realize how entrenched the insurgents were in the city."[90] Col. Mike Regner, I MEF's assistant chief of staff for operations, added that 587 caches—storage facilities—were found for IEDs that had been produced in thirty to forty IED factories. Also found were facilities that prepared individuals (*shahids*) for suicide operations.[91]

AQI was also building below ground, as the Marines later discovered. Like Hezbollah in southern Lebanon and Hamas in Gaza, Fallujah had a network of tunnels for the storage of weapons (including antiaircraft artillery guns) and command and control. They also used the tunnels to move units around the city during fighting and as escape routes out of the city. Not surprisingly, the tunnel network included connections to mosques and schools. The MEF's intelligence chief concluded that the insurgents had established an organizational and operational apparatus in Fallujah. They had a model. Between May and November, however, he was "convinced no one in the U.S. forces had a good handle on what was going on in Fallujah." The insurgents there were not just "the locals," said Colonel Howcroft. Many were outsiders who intended to "use Fallujah [as a base] to work out of to conduct operations in other parts of the country. . . . They tied what was going on in Fallujah to the bigger fight."[92]

In summary, then, from Fallujah the insurgents hoped to project power across Anbar, as Washington dithered over what to do about the city. For six months the enemy had a secure sanctuary from which to escalate the fight asymmetrically. They were employing fourth-generation warfare principles at the operational and tactical levels.

THE FIGHT ACROSS ANBAR

From May to November the insurgents in Anbar sought to extend the battlefield across the province. This stretched thin the forces of I MEF, often causing them to find themselves in a reactive mode. It was turning into a deadly version of the arcade game whack-a-mole: hit the insurgents hard in one location and they would withdraw, only to pop up somewhere else. They were using classic protracted irregular warfare tactics.

Compounding the problem for I MEF was the impasse at Fallujah, which was tying down three battalions outside that city. Keeping them there, said General Conway, undermined his capacity to "take care of the rest of the area of responsibility."[93] The reality was that there were not enough Marines or their Army counterparts to go around, according to Joe Dunford, who in July was promoted to brigadier general and became Blue Diamond's assistant division commander. "Through January 2005 we saw the enemy had migrated out towards the west. . . . We knew that the enemy was moving between Al Qa'im, Haditha, and Ramadi, and we knew the routes that he was taking. It's just that we couldn't—we didn't have the forces to deal with that challenge."[94]

This situation presented a significant operational predicament between May and November for the regiments and battalions of Blue Diamond and the 1st Brigade Combat Team (1st BCT) of the Army's 1st Infantry Division. They had to contend with widespread and rising insurgent violence across Anbar.

In AO Topeka the Army's 1st BCT's two battalions (1-16th Infantry, 1-34th Armor) and the Marines of 2/4 had their hands full, especially in Ramadi. The province capital had become increasingly volatile during the April crisis in Fallujah. Army and Marine forces were engaged in a protracted urban firefight against enemy forces that operated in small mobile units.

During that period Army and Marine patrols in and around Ramadi were coming under tough enemy attacks that frequently necessitated the use of quick reaction units to reinforce them. The insurgents were well armed for this urban battle, and as May neared its end, more jihadi fighters were moving into the city. But when I MEF ordered a big push against those areas where the enemy congregated, the insurgents would not stay and fight. After five days of heavy losses, they withdrew to base camps outside the city.

Through 2004, Ramadi was one of three enemy urban centers of gravity in Al Anbar. The other two were Fallujah and Al Qa'im. Of course, Fallujah was the most secure for the insurgents because of the political decision to withdraw the Marines. Ramadi and Al Qa'im were more fluid. MEF forces could push the enemy out of their strongholds. But I MEF did not have the capacity to hold them. And when the insurgents returned they settled the score with any local residents who had helped the Americans in any way. Murder and intimidation were SOP for them.

To put the insurgents on the defensive in AO Topeka, the 1st Brigade and 2/4 employed a full range of tactics including raids, cordons, patrolling, ambushes, and discrete strikes against insurgent leadership targets. It was more whack-a-mole. Bing West summed up the situation when he observed, "Ramadi settled into a routine of short, desultory skirmishes punctuated by IEDs and suicide bombers. The insurgents controlled the population, while the Americans controlled the main streets and highways."[95]

Moving west to AO Denver, RCT-7 had a battalion—3/7—covering Al Qa'im and its environs. For the area encompassing Hadithah, the Marines of 3/4 were deployed, while the Hit region was assigned to 2/7. The 1st LAR was sent to Al Rutbah to disrupt and interdict along the Syrian border. "It was a big area to cover," said Lt. Col. Nick Vukovich, RCT-7's chief operations officer (S-3) in 2004. They had too many tasks and too much territory to cover. "We didn't have the forces there to hold and maintain the initiative everywhere. We could do it in one given place but we couldn't do it across our AO. There was no way."[96]

When asked how the insurgents were arrayed in AO Denver, the S-3 explained, "They used urban sanctuary, they used the open desert as sanctuary, and they operated amongst the populated areas. There was no one place they were at. Were they everywhere? Conceivably they were. They were not static, they were very mobile and very adaptable." Still, there were certain areas where they were more active than others. "Al Qa'im was easily the worst."[97] But at any given time there could be a sharp flare-up in one of AO Denver's other cities, such as Hit, Husaybah, or Hadithah.

The insurgents were also establishing training bases in the AO, including bases north of Al Qa'im and in the Rawah area. Intelligence, surveillance, and reconnaissance (or ISR) was picking up on those activities. "They were training just north of the Euphrates in our AO," said the S-3, but "by the time you would get ground forces up there they had enough early warning to get out of there. We found evidence that was the case."[98]

In the summer, Battalion 1/7 under the command of Lt. Col. Christopher Woodridge relieved 3/7. The battalion had taken part in OIF I, including an assignment in Najaf after the conventional fight. Like the experience of other Marine units that redeployed to the permissive environment of the Shia south, 1/7's experience had been rewarding. In August 2004 they found things were very different in Al Qa'im. According to Woodridge, the "greatest difference in the way we operate now in this environment involves freedom of movement. You simply cannot move forces around the AO without security or without an inherent offensive capability in those formations," regardless of the mission. "Every time you go outside the wire . . . it has to be treated as a combat mission."[99]

Woodridge then compared Najaf with Al Qa'im. "Last year, it was common to take two vehicles and run around the city of Najaf in order to meet with local leadership [or] to assess the effectiveness of civil affairs projects. . . . Here, you simply can't do it like that. If you do, you're gonna lose vehicles, and get Marines killed."[100] Farther west Husaybah was equally volatile for 1/7. On the Syrian border, Husaybah was a hub for smuggling and organized crime and a key entry point for foreign fighters. The Marines tasked with trying to control Husaybah and the area around it found themselves in a "largely reactive fight" against "a very elusive enemy."[101]

The 1/7 engaged in several fierce actions in and around Al Qa'im and Husaybah. The insurgents employed ambushes, security probes, IED strikes against Marine patrols, and even direct attacks. In these latter operations, they were willing to take more than one hundred KIA—killed in action—in order to engage the Marines.

Battalion 1/8 had to cover the Hit, Rawah, and Hadithah regions. Its commander, Lt. Col. Garth Brandl, described the fight there as one against a "faceless enemy; a lot of intimidation of locals . . . improvised explosives, suicide operations, indirect fire. We had very few direct fire engagements there. The enemy was not large enough in force to really affect us with direct fire, but there were quite a few rockets and mortars, IEDs. . . . Our biggest challenge up there was trying to hunt him down. That was a huge challenge."[102]

The hot days of summer did not make much difference in AO Raleigh for RCT-1. Its battalions were arrayed in and around the territory surrounding Fallujah: 2/1 was northwest of the city, 1/5 was due north toward al-Karmah, and 2/2 was south of Fallujah in the vicinity of the Euphrates River. Once established in base camps, the battalions began to mount combat patrols to preempt insurgent operations being directed from its sanctuary inside to points outside the city. It was more whack-a-mole.

The insurgents were operating out of Fallujah with alacrity that summer, launching coordinated attacks against main transportation routes and other targets. To counter these activities, recalled RCT-1 commander Toolan, "We were running air strikes. We were running limited objective attacks on the city against these guys. We were picking up people as they were leaving the city. . . . I believe that we probably killed more bad guys between June and September than we did in April."[103]

But the bad guys kept attacking and, according to RCT-1's command chronology, there was a "surge in enemy activity at the end of July, demonstrat[ing] that there remains a sizeable ACF [anti-Coalition force] that resides in Fallujah." And those forces were operating out of the city against the MSRs. Daily IED and indirect fire attacks meant that for RCT-1 "MSR security continued as an enduring mission." To keep them open, a "sustained presence" by "day and night patrols" was required.[104]

In August it was more of the same in AO Raleigh. In Fallujah the enemy had built an organization that allowed it to "move freely in the city, stockpile weapons, harbor reinforcements, and build fortified defensive positions," said RCT-1's August report. Unmanned aerial vehicle feeds revealed the ways in which "the enemy gets stronger in the city." Their base in Fallujah gave the insurgents the capacity to conduct "significant firefights" with the Marines. To counter these activities, "CAS [close air support] strikes in and around the city became a common place response," and at night the AC-130s took a toll on the insurgents.[105]

By September no convoy moving past Fallujah on any of the MSRs could proceed "without being engaged somewhere along the route." And all critical facilities needed protection. For example, "The pump houses providing water to Camp Fallujah and Camp Baharia required full time on-site security and observation posts to prevent sabotage." The Marines were fighting in a "most non-linear of battle space," and that necessitated constant "situational awareness" against an enemy that was employing irregular warfare methods to prolong the fight.[106]

The MEF's enemies had formed an effective coalition of the like-minded, according to monthly RCT-1 reports. They had "varying backgrounds including former Ba'ath Party officials, foreign fighters, local tribal leaders, and Sunni Muslims, who were the political minority for the first time in thirty years." They were likeminded in that they all had "at least two causes uniting them; the goal

A typical IED roadside bomb attack in Anbar   Estes, *Into the Fray*, 24

of causing the fledging Iraqi democracy to fail, and that of killing Americans," in the hope of driving them out of Iraq. To accomplish these causes, the insurgents intended to fight a protracted war in which they "persisted with adaptive tactics."[107]

To counter this asymmetrical foe, RCT-1 sought to engage them outside Fallujah. The results were mixed. In August RCT-1 moved against al-Karmah, located sixteen miles northeast of Fallujah. Insurgents there carried out attacks on almost a daily basis on Marine patrols, convoys, and the forward operating bases. It was a bad place. During the second battle of Fallujah, the insurgents in al-Karmah proclaimed allegiance with the insurgents in Fallujah and sent weapons and medical supplies. Operation Clean Sweep intended to "interdict IED makers and those placing them." It "did not yield the results hoped for."[108]

At the end of August, RCT-1 initiated Operation Diamond Grind. Its goal was "to deny the enemy initiative outside of Fallujah and cause him to focus on defending himself instead of conducting offensive operations." This had more success.[109]

Nevertheless, as the summer came to an end, it was apparent that the situation in Fallujah had to end. Too much was being conceded to the insurgents, who were growing daily in confidence and capacity. This unacceptable situation was summed up in RCT-1's September report. The insurgents had developed "a sense that they can win. When they operate with near impunity . . . they gain a sense of power and their motivation to continue attacks is increased."[110] Intelligence reports only confirmed that the enemy was emboldened.

In AO Denver the insurgents were "digging in at Hit like at Al Qa'im, where they were embedded . . . [and] had control of the populace." It took a major effort to drive them out. Lieutenant Colonel Vukovich recalled, "We saw things really heating up in Hit and that kind of culminated in October. . . . The insurgents actually took over the town. . . . They took over the police station. They initiated a terror campaign. They actually stood and fought for about two or three days." To retake Hit, RCT-7 brought in two battalions with plenty of fire support. Said Vukovich, it was "a nine-hundred-pound gorilla; the insurgents didn't want to fight that thing and off they went."[111] The Marines knew it was over when "Hit mosques began playing messages that instructed the citizens to stop attacking Coalition forces and repel insurgent attempts to use their homes."[112]

A similar situation was developing at Rawah until 1/8 was sent to drive the insurgents out. While both Hit and Rawah were cleared, what each again revealed, noted RCT-7's monthly report for October, was "the enemy's ability to operate in areas where we did not have a presence."[113] Dealing with these situations while trying to control the rest of the AO was a major challenge for RCT-7. And when it was ordered to send forces to take part in the second battle of Fallujah, the pattern repeated itself.

It should be noted that I MEF forces were also involved in Najaf in August, the result of the decision to use force against the Shia militias of Muqtada al-Sadr there. With Brig. Gen. Dennis Hejlik, I MEF's deputy commander, overseeing the operation, a joint force of Marine and Army battalions, along with special operation forces, crushed the Mehdi militias and returned the Imam Ali Mosque to the proper authorities.[114] The operation in Najaf was a preview of what was in store for Fallujah in November, said Lt. Gen. John Sattler, who took command of I MEF in its immediate aftermath. "A lot of the things we did [in Najaf] . . . we used again in Fallujah. . . . Integration of Army forces; high density, close air support; heavy Army mechanized power; playing the Marine heavy boots on the ground to its strength. All those lessons were taken forward to Fallujah."[115]

GROWING IRAQI SECURITY FORCES

Recall that a key part of General Conway's three principle lines of operations and one of the First Fifteen Plays was to "increase effectiveness of Iraqi security forces." Growing the ISF was a key part of the OPLAN. In conjunction with the forces of I MEF, they would help ensure stability by holding the ground across Anbar. In 2004 that objective proved unattainable—it was a bridge too far.

When I MEF arrived in Anbar, said Brig. Gen. John Kelly, Blue Diamond's assistant division commander, it found little progress had been made in developing local Iraqi forces. There had been many promises by the CPA to provide "equipment for the police, and equipment for the Iraqi Civil Defense Corps, and equipment for the border patrol and cars for the police and radio equipment for the police and on and on and on. And you know we come back here . . . and is there a start on it? Yeah. But is it where it ought to be after a year? No way."[116]

The need to build Iraqi forces was a necessity, explained Colonel Toolan. "From the very beginning we knew it was an essential task and that we had to do it and the plan really was that each Iraqi National Guard battalion that I had, and I had three of them," would be attached to one of RCT-1's battalions. Toolan was working with two of them in the Fallujah area. They were a mixed bag. "The Iraqi National Guard company in Fallujah, the 505th . . . it was always problematic. It just didn't have good leadership and it was very difficult for us to do interactive things because of the challenges that they had. And of course the fighting started pretty quickly and many of them transitioned to the insurgents. And then there was the 506th, which was out on the peninsula where I maintained an excellent relationship with them."[117] This was thanks to its commander, Lieutenant Colonel Suleiman al Marawi, with whom Toolan had formed a special bond.

Following the Marine withdrawal from Fallujah, CENTCOM agreed to turn security of the city over to what was dubbed the Fallujah Brigade. This force grew out of secret meetings between General Conway and former Iraqi generals that were being brokered by Muhammad Latif, a former colonel who had been in Iraqi military intelligence. What emerged was a plan for Latif and one of these ex-generals—Jasim Saleh—to organize a force composed of former soldiers and insurgents living in Fallujah to take over security of the city. No Iraqi National Guard working with Toolan would be included.

In reality, control inside Fallujah was never in the hands of Saleh or Latif. Rather, it was in the hands of two cutthroats. One was Sheikh Abdullah Al Janabi, a radical imam who called for jihad from Fallujah's largest mosque. The other was Umar Husayn Hadid, a malevolent jihadi who had established a close relationship with Zarqawi and controlled the Jolan District of Fallujah. His forces were known as the Black Banner Brigade and included Fallujah's most radical insurgents and terrorists.

The city belonged to the enemy. This fact was driven home to the leadership of I MEF when Janabi and Hadid captured Lieutenant Colonel Suleiman, whom they had characterized as a traitor because he worked closely with Toolan. What followed was his brutal murder at the hands of Hadid, who beheaded him.[118] The message to Colonel Suleiman's 506th Iraqi National Guard battalion and to the 505th was unambiguous: desert or you and your family will suffer the same fate. They deserted.

As for the Fallujah Brigade, it belonged to AQI and the insurgents. As for the plan to build Iraqi force to the point where they could conduct combined operations with the Marines, that was a bust in 2004. Dunford summed it up: "The Iraqi National Guard in Anbar Province didn't want to be seen in public working alongside their counterparts in the United States Marine Corps. What we found was a locally recruited, locally employed Iraqi security forces in Anbar Province that was not effective." When asked why this was the case, he gave two reasons: "I would equate that to Sunni disenfranchisement [and] the murder and intimidation campaign that was clearly evident in Anbar as early as the spring of 2004. That precluded anybody from stepping up and taking responsibility in the Iraqi national security forces."[119] To illustrate the effectiveness of insurgent intimidation Dunford related the following anecdote:

> One day, I went over to visit . . . my counterpart in the 60th Brigade. Typically, when you pulled up to his CP [command post] there would be dozens of soldiers visible in and around the command post. This was less than a mile from the [1st Marine] Division CP. . . . As soon

as we pulled up to the command post, there were no Iraqi security forces visible. So, clearly, your spider senses go up a little bit and you establish a security perimeter. I went into the building and there were no Iraqi soldiers visible inside the building as well. All you could hear is the click-clack of your heels as you walked down the halls. I looked into the general's office and he was sitting there and he was looking fairly distraught. I said, "General where is everyone?" And he relayed to me how, about thirty-six hours earlier, they had one Iraqi soldier sent out to go get some chow . . . and when he left the compound he was followed by some insurgents. The insurgents captured him, they beat him, and they got the names and addresses of the leadership of 60th Brigade. . . . In the intervening hours, the insurgents visited each one of those leaders . . . and told them, "We know where you live and we know where your family is, and if you go back to work, we're gonna kill you and we're gonna kill your family." That was, in effect, the end of the 60th Brigade.[120]

The insurgents used murder and intimidation across Anbar. The governor of Anbar in 2004 suffered the same fate, said Dunford. "His family was attacked in their home, the house set on fire, and three of his sons were kidnapped. Once his sons were returned to him, he disappeared and was never to be seen again serving as the governor of Anbar Province."[121] So when General Natonski took command of Blue Diamond he found that because of the murder and intimidation efforts of AQI he did not have as a counterpart "an effective Iraqi security force. . . . They were really marginalized in terms of effectiveness," he explained in a March 2005 interview.[122] And yet, to cover the vast territory of Anbar, reliable Iraqi counterparts were needed as force multipliers. It was the way to neutralize the protracted, hit-and-run tactics of the insurgents. In 2004 that option, however, was closed off to I MEF.

PREPARING TO TAKE FALLUJAH

"You have got to fix Fallujah," said General Conway to General Sattler during their September change of command. "That authority is coming to do that," the outgoing I MEF commander added. "It was just a matter of getting geared up for it, having the right troops in place and the right support to make it work."[123]

Joe Dunford concurred:

It became increasingly obvious for all of us over the summer that eventually Fallujah was going to have to be dealt with. You could see

over time that the enemy was consolidating his gains in the city. . . .
I think it was pretty clear to us that we would have to go into Fallujah.
The decision . . . was a political decision, and that was only made
just days before we actually went in. . . . But we were making all the
preparations necessary for a long period of time and planning it for a
long period of time.[124]

That political decision had to do with the Iraqi interim government agreeing to call for a joint operation conducted by Coalition forces (to include Iraqi units) to reestablish authority over Fallujah and to free the citizens of the city from the brutal excesses of the insurgents. This took time to decide. UN Secretary General Kofi Annan was putting pressure on Transitional Prime Minister Ayad Allawi of Iraq (as well as on the United States and Britain) not to attack the city.

As a result, Allawi had to make overtures of reconciliation to the insurgents. All avenues of political compromise had to be explored. Of course, it was all posturing and was never going to accomplish anything. The insurgents were full of bravado. They thought they would again prevail, and if not, they were prepared to die in place. Moreover, as Allawi well knew, Fallujah was part of a "rising [tide of] insecurity and instability . . . a region-wide trend." Finally, on October 29 he called a press conference and in a grim tone of voice announced, "If we cannot solve Fallujah peacefully, I have no choice but to take military action. I will do so with a heavy heart."[125]

For several weeks preceding Allawi's press conference, I MEF was preparing to take control of the city. The plan devised by its staff—Phantom Fury—had four phases. This time, unlike in April, they had the time to set themselves up for success.

Phase I entailed an array of shaping activities. These were measures—both nonkinetic and kinetic—that laid the foundation for the assault. Executed in September and October, these measures included operations by Task Force 626. Consisting of highly trained special operations forces like those of the Army's Delta Force, night after night these covert warriors stalked and tracked down high-value targets in and around the city, eliminating noteworthy members of the insurgency, among others. Other Phase I kinetic shaping actions entailed precision artillery and air strikes against key enemy targets such as IED concentrations, cache facilities, and insurgent command and control.

In addition to pinpoint kinetic strikes, shaping involved high-priority information operations, according to Maj. Gen. Richard Natonski, commander of the 1st Marine Division during the assault.[126] These aimed at persuading the population to leave the city before the attack began and involved a massive effort that included dropping leaflets, printing papers, and using radio broadcasts. The citizens of Fallujah were not told the time of the attack, but the information campaign left no doubt that it was in the offing.

Those who did not depart, Natonski explained, were cautioned through information operations that once the Marines were in the city, "any vehicle would be considered hostile because we knew there was going to be a great threat of vehicle-borne improvised explosive devices. We also told them that anyone outside with a weapon would be considered hostile. We told the people to stay in their homes for their own safety." This was the "nonkinetic side of shaping," said Blue Diamond's commanding general.[127] The Marines had learned from the first round in Fallujah. If the city was depopulated, the insurgents would have a harder time manipulating al Jazeera with trumped-up claims of civilian massacres.[128]

Other nonkinetic shaping measures in Phase I involved a program of electronic warfare measures. These used electromagnetic energy and directed energy to attack enemy personnel, facilities, and equipment to degrade, neutralize, and destroy their effectiveness. Also part of shaping was the stockpiling of supplies in and around Fallujah for the coming battle. The importance of building this "iron mountain," as Dunford referred to it, was "to mitigate the risk of indirect fire attacks against the MSRs." By creating an iron mountain of supplies, he added, "we didn't have to use the MSRs and we minimized traffic [supply convoys] on the MSRs."[129]

To degrade the enemy's capacity to carry out asymmetric attacks outside Fallujah once the assault commenced, I MEF initiated Operation Rodeo, a real dragnet affair. I MEF identified those individuals most likely "to be shooting indirect fire and conducting IED attacks against us during that time," Dunford explained. Then "we rounded 'em all up, knowing that the best we could do is keep 'em off the streets for thirty days." So, shortly before the fighting began they were "all off the street, and that was in itself a shaping action."[130]

Finally, deception was an essential element of Phase I shaping. The objective was to persuade the insurgents that the main attack would come through the southeastern side of the city. The idea was to get them to focus their efforts in that direction, to set up the majority of their IEDs and deploy the bulk of their forces in that part of Fallujah. General Natonski explained how this worked: "Ultimately . . . we attacked from the northern side of the city. However, we executed a number of feints [major troop movements] on the southeast side of the city to give them the impression that it would be the direction of attack that we would execute."[131] As we shall see, "The operation had the desired effect."[132]

If Phase I took weeks to execute and involved this array of kinetic and nonkinetic missions, Phase II was to be completed in twenty-four hours and would be highly kinetic, a violent shaping operation over a brief period. Essentially, the goal was to employ U.S. aircraft and artillery to pound critical insurgent targets in the city in preparation for the assault and to cover the movement of Marine and Army forces.

"Sixty preplanned targets" had been marked for Phase II, recalled Natonski. But, he went on to observe, "Because of collateral damage [putting civilians in danger] and positive ID [identification] limitations, we could not hit as many targets as we wanted." Of the sixty targets,

> we were not able to hit, I think, somewhere in the neighborhood of a dozen.... You had to definitely ascertain that there were enemy there. So that really limited what we could hit, even though we knew there were insurgents in there. I think that it was validated that ... targets we had identified before but were limited from attacking ... turned out to be insurgent strongholds which we ended up destroying when troops came in contact. So sometimes the ROE [rules of engagement], in an effort to protect the people, worked against us, and maybe it was good but as we came to find out, the only people in Fallujah when we went in were insurgents. Very, very few civilians [were there].[133]

Phase III called for decisive operations to break the insurgents' hold on the city and take away their sanctuary. Because of political considerations, Blue Diamond commanders emphasized the importance of seizing the city quickly. They did not want a repeat of April when the attacking forces had been ordered to halt as they methodically closed in on the enemy. This time it would be methodically fast.

With speed being of the essence, forces from RCT-1, RCT-7, and the 2nd "Blackjack" Brigade of the 1st Cavalry Division were configured for the attack. Assigned to each were six battalion-size Iraqi units that came from outside Anbar; no forces from the province took part in the assault. The mission of the Blackjack Brigade was to secure the perimeter of the city, sealing off escape routes. The Iraqi battalions, each of which was assigned to a Marine or Army battalion counterpart, were to support their lines of operation.

The assault forces consisted of six Marine and Army battalions assigned to RCT-1 and RCT-7. The latter, under the command of Col. Mark Tucker, included the Marines of 1/8 and 1/3. Joining them was the 2nd Battalion, 2nd Regiment (2-2), of the 1st Infantry Division. The 2-2 had plenty of punch, consisting of armor, mechanized infantry, cavalry, and self-propelled artillery components. RCT-1, now commanded by Col. Michael Shupp, also had a heavy Army battalion assigned to it. The 2nd Battalion, 7th Cavalry Regiment (2-7), from the 1st Cavalry

Division brought heavy armor to the fight. The two Marine battalions in RCT-1 were 3/5 and 3/1.

These six battalions were arrayed north of Fallujah. The assault was essentially a north-to-south sweep through the entire city to clear out all the insurgents. Once through, each battalion would do an about-face and clean up those enemy elements it had missed the first time through. It was the urban battle, said General Natonski, that the Marines had prepared for since the late 1990s, when Commandant Chuck Krulak told the Corps to get ready for the three-block war. Fallujah was a prime example of what Krulak envisioned. Dunford described the scene: "We were fighting house to house, clearing portions, clearing buildings, and all-out combat, probably some of the toughest fighting since Hue City. A few blocks back we had Marines patrolling and clearing buildings. And then a few more blocks back, we had civil affairs Marines delivering humanitarian rations to some of the remaining people that were still in the city."[134]

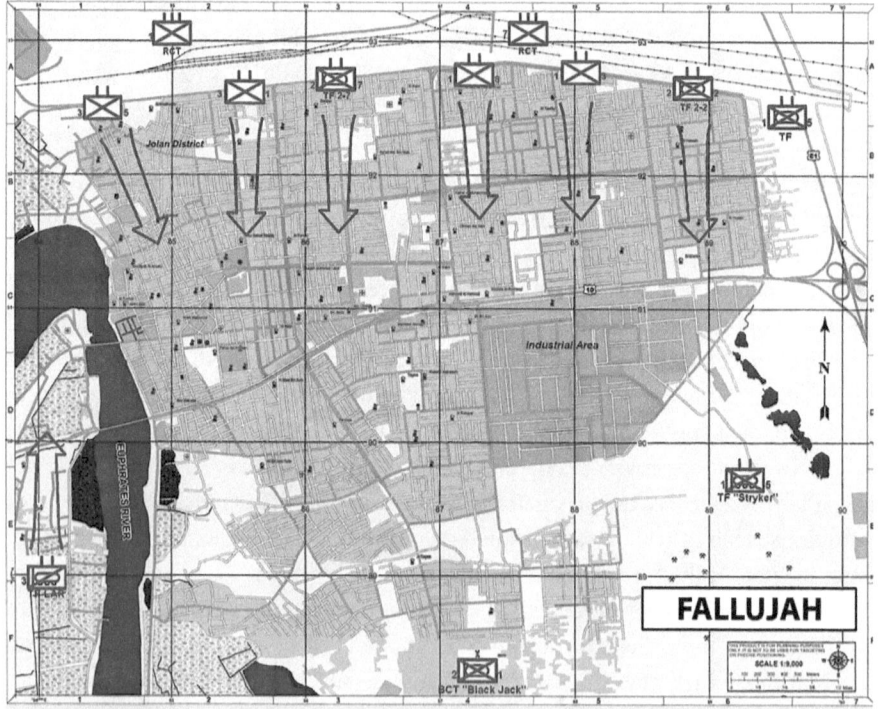

Marine and Army battalions attacked the city of Fallujah from north to south as depicted here.

ESTES, *INTO THE FRAY*, 68

The six battalions, explained Dunford, were effectively integrated: "We were able to seamlessly integrate Bradley Companies with Marine Battalions, Marine Battalions inside of Army Brigades, Army Brigades inside a Marine Division, without a problem. . . . We had two Army Brigades inside the 1st Marine Division during Fallujah II."[135]

Finally, Phase IV of Phantom Fury was the transition to an interim government and the beginning of the reconstruction program. This would include establishing a new local government and police force.

While I MEF was planning for the second battle of Fallujah, the insurgents were not standing still. Even though I MEF had received some reinforcements in the form of the 31st MEU, which consisted of approximately 2,200 Marines, in conjunction with 1/7 it was not adequate to cover AO Denver. The insurgents knew this, and they escalated operations there and elsewhere in Anbar to undermine preparation for Phantom Fury. Consider what they initiated in Husaybah, Al Qa'im, Hit, and Hadithah as RCT-7 redeployed its forces to Fallujah for the coming battle: In Husaybah and Al Qa'im, overt activities by the insurgents, including by foreign jihadi elements, were on the rise because of a reduced Coalition presence. Local government officials were increasingly being targeted for intimidation. Attacks on Iraqi border police increased and, as a result, border forts were destroyed or abandoned. Police stations were also attacked and destroyed. Insurgents were making more use of indirect fire and IEDs against remaining U.S. troops.

Recall that RCT-7 had driven the insurgents out of Hit. But with their redeployment to Fallujah, the insurgents started to return, and there was an influx of foreign jihadi fighters into the town. Attacks increased on the ISF, and it appeared that the insurgents were waiting for the attack on Fallujah to intensify and escalate their activities in Hit.

The situation was likewise heating up in Hadithah. Insurgents were exploiting the reduced presence of Marine forces with escalating intimidation of local officials and attacks on the ISF, including destruction of their checkpoints. The use of IEDs was on the upswing, as was anti-Coalition propaganda.

As the time for attack on Fallujah approached, enemy activities also increased in and around Ramadi. The insurgents had been moving forces and capabilities into AO Topeka as an asymmetrical move to disrupt the preparation for Phantom Fury.

THE ATTACK OF ALL ATTACKS

Interim Prime Minister Ayad Allawi made several more attempts to negotiate with representatives from Fallujah to persuade them to encourage the foreign fighters to leave the city. But his efforts proved fruitless, as the city fathers had no influence over the foreign fighters. Finally, on November 8 Allawi authorized the assault. When briefed on Phantom Fury, the prime minister made only one change. He wanted the operation called Al Fajr, which means New Dawn. The attack would "liberate the people" and "clean Fallujah of the terrorists."[136] Then Fallujah would embark on a new beginning, said Allawi.

Because of the escalation of insurgent violence in anticipation of the assault, Allawi declared a state of emergency across Iraq. In Fallujah an around-the-clock curfew was imposed, and the residents who remained in the city were warned to stay in their homes and not to carry weapons.

As U.S. and Iraqi forces massed north of the city, it was evident from overhead video that RCT-1 and RCT-7 would benefit from the deception operations executed over the previous weeks. Deception worked, declared Dunford: "They fully expected the attack from the southeast, and that misperception . . . had a lot to do with our success."[137]

RCT-1 forces—3/5, 3/1, and 2/7—were poised on the right flank facing north to south. Their main objective in the first phase of Al Fajr was to take control of the Jolan District. That was ground zero for the jihadi forces, and it promised to be a tough fight. On the left flank were the battalions of RCT-7. Their target was the Askari District, also home to a major concentration of insurgents. It would be no cakewalk. On November 8 they would cross the line of departure and rapidly penetrate the city. The attack was intended to be unrelenting, said General Sattler. "I didn't want to let the enemy get any rest." He intended to put the insurgents "on their heels or . . . on their ass."[138]

On the night of November 7, one final step was taken before I MEF launched its full-scale attack. The Fallujah General Hospital on the peninsula to the west of the city and the two bridges that ran across the Euphrates—one going to the hospital, the other connecting to Highway 10—had to be secured. Task Force Wolfpack, which was formed up in late October, was assigned this responsibility; it consisted of elements from the Marines' 3rd Light Armored Reconnaissance Battalion (3rd LAR), 1/23, 1/9, and Iraqi special and regular forces. Together on the night of the November 7 they took control of the hospital and the two bridges. AQI and its allies would be running no propaganda operations from that hospital this time around. And if they tried to escape across those two bridges, they would be cut to ribbons.

If I MEF was ready for a donnybrook, so were the insurgents. According to the G-2 for I MEF, an estimated 3,500 of them were dug into the city. Many of them were considered hardcore fighters, including numerous foreign jihadis who the G-2 later determined came from Syria, Sudan, Jordan, Saudi Arabia, Afghanistan, and Chechnya. He said that many of them had trained for such fights, and they intended to die in place. When asked if there were many cases of surrender, he recalled, "In the first ninety-six hours there were almost none," and, "There was a much higher enemy killed in action than wounded in action because they were fighting until they were dying." It was not until "we finally got into about the fifth and sixth day" that the insurgents "started waving white flags."[139]

At 1900 hours on November 8, the Marines of 3/5 began the assault down their attack lane. After they cleared the first objective, 3/1 crossed the line of departure and secured the train station. The rest of the battalions followed suit. The battle was on, and for the next several days the enemy would get little rest. During the day they faced the combined forces of RCT-1 and RCT-7. At night they were blasted by artillery, air strikes, and AC-130s, or dispatched by the snipers and special operators of Task Force 626.

The two main targets in the first phase of Al Fajr were the Jolan and Askari Districts, both located in the northern half of the city. These two areas were the badlands, major insurgent strongholds. As was expected, the fighting in the Jolan was among the toughest in the city. The district was densely packed and hosted many of the most hardened of the enemy forces. They had prepared those streets and buildings with many ugly surprises. When he was in Fallujah, Zarqawi operated out of the Jolan. So did Janabi, the radical imam, and the deadly Umar Hadid. The Army's 2-7 with its tanks and Bradley fighting vehicles led the way for the Marine battalions of RCT-1, setting up advanced fighting positions that allowed the Marines to start clearing operations that amounted to going from house to house. By the end of the day on November 9, the three battalions of RCT-1 had cleared the Jolan and prepared to complete their move south to the Euphrates River.

Meanwhile, at the same time on November 8, the battalions of RCT-7 pushed through the breach in the enemy's outer defenses and drove on the Askari District. They, too, made rapid gains. The Army's 2-2 armored forces, like those of 2-7, provided essential firepower for the Marines on the ground. By the morning of November 9, RCT-7 was in control of the Askari neighborhoods. In effect, the first phase of Al Fajr had been successfully accomplished, with the insurgents driven from the northern half of Fallujah.

On November 10 the forces of RCT-1 and RCT-7 were poised to continue the attack through to the southern boundary of the city. That day proved to be particularly grueling, as U.S. forces fought to take control of three key mosques in which the insurgents were storing large quantities of weapons and from which they were fighting and initiating attacks. Wresting control of one of these in particular—the Hydra Mosque—was one of the most arduous actions to take place during Al Fajr.

Then, in the aftermath of that brutal day of close-quarters combat, as dusk spread over the city, a most extraordinary event unfolded. As the forces of I MEF settled in for the night, the loudspeakers of B Company, 9th Psychological Operations Battalion, began broadcasting the Marine Corps Hymn across the city.

November 10 was the 229th birthday of the Corps. On that day each year, Marines, no matter where they are, celebrate their legacy, recalling those epic battles—Guadalcanal, Iwo Jima, "Frozen Chosin," Hue City—that fill their history. Even though the Marines hunkered down that night in Fallujah were exhausted from three days of ferocious warfare, they nevertheless intended to hold fast to this long-standing tradition. So, as is their custom, the birthday message of Commandant Hagee was read to all present. One can only imagine what the insurgents must have been thinking as the hymn reverberated through the narrow streets and alleys of Fallujah, punctuated by the hearty shouts of "Semper fi!"

On November 11 the forces of RCT-1 and RCT-7 resumed their drive to the southern boundary of Fallujah, moving across Highway 10, the dividing line between the two phases of the battle. They were now fighting in the southern sectors of the city. By November 13, I MEF was reporting that its forces controlled most of the battle space. But over the next several days Marines engaged in more bloody house-to-house clearing operations. Enemy forces continued to choose to fight and die in place.

On November 16, 2004, the city was officially declared secured, although sporadic outbursts of insurgent violence continued well into December. Marines were still fighting and killing diehard members of AQI in certain parts of the city. During the eight days that the battle for Fallujah lasted, many individual acts of great risk and heroism took place. Indeed, they occurred during almost every hour of the fighting. Those accounts are being captured in many books, articles, websites, and blogs. Below is one account, to give the reader a glimpse of what it was like for the forces of I MEF. The engagement selected is that known as the House from Hell, one of the most fierce and gruesome. The account is by Bing West:

> Toward the end of the savage battle for Fallujah in December of 2004, I met the 3rd Platoon of Kilo Company in the shattered southern remnants of the city. Lieutenant Jesse Grapes was justly proud of his platoon. . . . A few weeks earlier, a half-dozen jihadists barricaded on the second floor of what came to be known as the House From Hell had poured fire on four wounded marines trapped in downstairs rooms. Instead of backing off, Grapes's men rushed the house, smashing at doors and windows and ripping apart metal grates to rescue their comrades. They swarmed into an alcove, dripping red from cuts, gouges, and bullet wounds. Blood flowed across the concrete floor, slippery as

ice. It stuck like gum to their trigger fingers, pulling their aim off target as they ducked grenades that sent shrapnel ricocheting off the walls.

Sergeant Byron Norwood poked his head around a door frame. *Bang.* A round hit him in the head and he fell, mortally wounded. The fight swirled on until Grapes wriggled through a small window and laid down covering fire while the wounded were pulled out. Corporal Richard Gonzalez, the platoon's "mad bomber," rushed forward with a twenty-pound satchel of C4 explosive—enough to demolish two houses. He placed it on the chest of a dead jihadist and ran outside.

The house exploded in a flash, followed by concrete chunks thudding down. A pink mist mixed with the dust and gunpowder in the air. Grapes was happy to see it. He hastily evacuated eleven wounded marines and the body of Sergeant Norwood.[140]

Marines fighting inside "the House from Hell."

BING WEST, "FIVE CORPORALS,"
SMALL UNIT ACTIONS,
MARINE CORPS HISTORY DIVISION, 59

Fallujah will be one more of those epic battles that Marines pay tribute to on their birthday. And there can be little doubt that the exploits in Fallujah have already found their way into the cadences of the DIs at Parris Island. AQI and those who fought with it had convinced themselves that in a head-on fight they could beat the Marines. After all, as they had trumpeted in their information operations over the previous six months, they had done so in April.

It did not turn out that way. This time around the insurgents could have no such illusions about the outcome of the battle. This was vividly illustrated in a conversation between two insurgents, one outside the city (Insurgent A) and one fighting inside Fallujah (Insurgent B). That conversation, picked up by signals intelligence during the height of the battle, reveals just how desperate the situation had become for AQI.

Insurgent A: *Where is this shooting?*
Insurgent B: *Everywhere. In every area.*
Insurgent A: *What was that, artillery?*
Insurgent B: *Artillery, mortars, and tanks everywhere.*
Insurgent A: *Where are you?*
Insurgent B: *The flour mill.*
Insurgent A: *They're attacking the flour mill?*
Insurgent B: *Yes, and they are attacking us too. The artillery is destroying us. All Fallujah is in ruins. What can stand? The tanks come down every street with artillery ahead of them.*
Insurgent A: *Get out of there.*
Insurgent B: *How? If I go into the street I get shot. If I stay inside I get shelled. And let's not forget the mortars, and the aircraft and the snipers.*
Insurgent A: *They said the Americans had withdrawn.*
Insurgent B: *The Americans are everywhere.*
Insurgent A: *They said mujahideen reinforcements were arriving.*
Insurgent B: *Well, they have not arrived yet. Fallujah is finished. It is the attack of all attacks.*
Insurgent A: *Look, call me if anything develops. I don't care what time you call.*
Insurgent B: *I'll do I what can. We did burn one tank.*
Insurgent A: *That's good at least.*
Insurgent B: *But if you burn one tank they send three more. It's useless.*[141]

WINNING THE BATTLE WHILE LOSING GROUND

As 2004 came to an end, the Marines of I MEF faced a situation in Al-Anbar that bore a great resemblance to how Secretary of Defense Rumsfeld had come to describe the fight in Iraq—"a long, hard slog."[142]

During the six months that the bulk of RCT-1 and then RCT-7 forces were bogged down outside Fallujah for political reasons, the insurgency burgeoned elsewhere in Anbar. There just were not enough I MEF forces to go around. As a result, in more instances than not, the Marines were reacting to insurgent moves. They did not have control of the ground throughout the province. And in Fallujah the enemy was given a sanctuary from which to project operation for six months. The fight had settled into the deadly version of whack-a-mole.

It was fourth-generation warfare, asymmetrical and unconventional operations, employed by the terrorists and insurgents to bypass the superior military might of the Marine Corps. There were no fronts in this fight and no distinctions between civilian and military targets. The laws of war were of no concern to AQI as it ruthlessly attacked nonmilitary targets. What's more, AQI justified its remorseless treatment of the people of Fallujah through a perversion of Islam. This was a brutal, no-holds-barred, protracted war, a "test of wills" as Dunford called it, in which the insurgents were counting on Washington to blink.[143]

Col. Jim Howcroft, I MEFs intelligence chief at the time, clearly recognized the reality of this situation. He explained, "Fallujah sort of put us back into our comfort zone and we did that quite well." But he added that in terms of the larger struggle for control of Anbar, "I think it truly, truly hurt us.... We needed time to set the conditions to be successful in Anbar." Fallujah prevented that from happening, and the insurgents capitalized on it. The bottom line for the G-2: "Fallujah took that time away; it set us back a year and a half if not two years."[144] This would become apparent in 2005.

2005

Stalemate

IRAQI NATION BUILDING: JANUARY 2005

As 2005 approached in an Iraq that over the preceding year had been battered by a "23 percent" increase in attacks "against the Coalition, Iraqis, and infrastructure," political transformation was at the top of Washington's agenda.[1] In the midst of an escalating war, Iraq intended to hold three nationwide votes to revamp Iraq's political system. Democracy would replace Saddam's dictatorship. This plan ran counter to conventional wisdom and a substantial body of contemporary evidence, which proposed that security and stability had to be established before initiating development and democratization programs.

The first of these electoral exercises was scheduled to take place on January 30. It would select representatives for a 275-member Iraqi National Assembly. Once elected, the new assembly would first choose a transitional government and then would draft a constitution. The draft constitution would be submitted for approval to a national referendum, planned for the fall of 2005. If the constitution was approved by the Iraqi people, a third vote would be held to select yet another new assembly. Once selected, that assembly would elect the president of the republic who, in turn, would name a prime minister from the majority coalition in the assembly; the prime minister would form a government. All of this would take place in the midst of a burgeoning insurgency.

It was a grand electoral design. And the United States put plenty of military muscle into securing the polls for the initial vote in January, well aware that the insurgents intended to pull out all the stops to derail it. To that end, beginning in November 2004 and continuing well into January, several horrific bombings took place. Then Abu Musab Zarqawi, al Qaeda's top commander in Iraq, declared war on the election itself. In a widely circulated Internet message, he said that all who voted would be "considered enemies of God." Zarqawi proclaimed a "bitter war against democracy and all those who seek to enact it."[2]

To stop Zarqawi and those aligned with him, the Coalition initiated Operation Citadel II, a nationwide effort to secure Baghdad, to neutralize insurgents in key cities, and to facilitate the election process itself. To achieve these ends, soldiers and Marines moved aggressively to counter insurgent activities, to initiate selective offensive actions against known targets, and to set up multiple cordons to secure polling sites.

Operation Citadel II would ensure the emergence of the new Iraq, the grandiose goal of the Bush administration. But in Anbar, Washington's electoral scheme was seen through a very different and foreboding lens. The Sunnis there considered the scheme the latest in a series of body blows aimed at facilitating their demise. The Shia and Kurds were lining up to take power in the new Iraq, and the Sunnis were not about to take part in any electoral ruse that gave a false legitimacy to their subjugation.

The way the Sunnis saw it, a new political narrative was being crafted for Iraq in Washington and brutally imposed by the American army, as manifested in what they considered the sacking of Fallujah. Their reaction to Operation Al Fajr was to unleash the "worst violence to date. Iraqi defenses in Mosul vanished, with police stations ransacked by insurgents who took their equipment and uniforms. All the other cities of northern Iraq [also] saw an increase in violence, perhaps none more than Baghdad. Refugees from Fallujah flooded into the capital, bringing the battle home to Sunni Arabs there."[3] Violence was spiraling out of control.

Then, in late November, U.S. and Iraqi forces struck back, raiding the Abu Hanifa Mosque in north Baghdad. For the growing insurgency, mosques were a part of the battlefield. In Fallujah it was from the mosques that the call to fight the Marines had resounded, and the resistance used those same religious facilities for stockpiling vast quantities of arms and as fighting positions.

Consider these facts. Of the one hundred mosques in the city of Fallujah, sixty were used for those purposes during Operation Al Fajr. According to the international laws governing armed conflict, houses of worship are not to be used for military purposes. They are off limits. If these laws are violated, as in Fallujah, those houses of worship lose the special protection afforded them under the laws of war and can become legitimate targets for military attack.

But was this true for the Abu Hanifa mosque, considered the second-most important Sunni Mosque in the city? Was it being used in these ways, justifying an attack on it? The raid took place during Friday prayers. Reportedly, two thousand people were gathered in the mosque when U.S. soldiers and Iraqi National Guardsmen forcibly entered, intent on apprehending insurgent fighters believed to be hiding there. In the preceding weeks, two U.S. military bases located near the mosque had taken frequent fire from the area. But according to after-action reports, the raid found only "a few guns but nothing more. . . . Three Iraqis were killed."[4] No insurgents were arrested.

The events in Fallujah and Abu Hanifa, on the heels of a multitude of wrong moves made by the United States in 2003 and 2004, ensured that the Sunnis would eschew the January election. And to guarantee it, the major Sunni parties in Iraq, including the Iraqi Islamic Party and the Association of Muslim Scholars, called for a boycott. As a result, the turnout was paltry across the Sunni Triangle.

And nowhere was that boycott more robust than in Anbar, where only 2 percent of the population voted. While many reasons have been proposed to explain this outcome, in reality it was about the legitimacy of the electoral exercise. For most Sunnis who make up the tribes of Anbar, the election was simply not legitimate. They were under occupation and engaged in a war that many supported as justifiable national resistance.

HIGHLY PERSISTENT UNREST

If I MEF's intelligence assessment in 2004 portrayed Anbar as "generally permissive except for certain pockets," a year later the appraisal of what II MEF would confront once on the ground warned to expect just the opposite.[5] The escalating violence the province experienced in 2004 would persist in 2005. And that highly persistent unrest quickly translated into casualties as soon as II MEF set boots on the ground in Anbar.

Consider the situation the 3rd Battalion, 8th Marines (3/8), found itself facing in AO Raleigh in January. It was one of the first units to arrive as part of II MEF's relief in place (RIP) of I MEF. The battalion, which replaced 1/8 on January 20, was immediately engaged in combat in support of Operation Citadel II. It provided forces to secure polling sites, many of which were being targeted by AQI and other armed groups. For 3/8 this resulted in the loss of eleven Marines on the day the election was held, wounded in a rocket attack on an election observation post south of al-Karmah.

As the other battalions of 8th Regimental Combat Team (RCT-8) and 2nd Regimental Combat Team (RCT-2) flowed into the province during the months immediately following the January election, they encountered plenty of the same persistent unrest. The details of the fight these units faced in Anbar's three AOs—Denver, Raleigh, and Topeka—are covered later in this chapter. Suffice it to note at this point that 2005 was going to be a violent and challenging year for II MEF. As was recounted over and over in the monthly reports of its two regiments, the insurgents employed an array of deadly irregular and unconventional warfare tactics and established a clandestine infrastructure in the province to support those actions.

The following statistics of enemy attacks in 2005 provide a macrolevel glimpse of the escalating violence II MEF faced. As noted earlier, enemy strikes against Coalition and Iraqi forces grew significantly in 2004, in spite of U.S. military efforts to contain them. The insurgents continued to "demonstrate the capac-

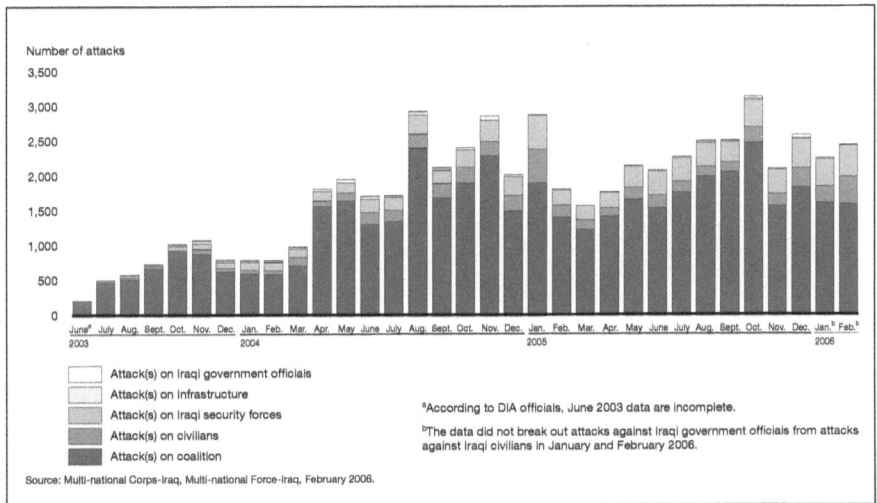

GRAPH 4.1 Enemy-initiated attacks

ity to recruit, supply, and attack."[6] And, as a Government Accountability Office (GAO) report highlights, they accelerated those efforts in 2005, further undermining the security setting: "The insurgency in Iraq intensified from June 2003 through October 2005," at which time it reached the single highest monthly level of attacks. Since then, it has "remained strong and resilient. . . . Insurgents are using increasingly lethal improvised explosive devices and continue to adapt to coalition countermeasures." Graph 4.1 captures these escalating trends.[7]

These statistics covered all of Iraq's provinces. But not all parts of Iraq were experiencing the same degree of violence in 2005. In some provinces, the insurgents were much more entrenched and lethal. Of those, none matched Anbar. This is evident on map 4.1, which assesses governance, security, and economic conditions in Iraq's eighteen provinces in early 2006.[8]

What map 4.1 illustrates is that 2005 was a very violent year in Anbar, the heartland of the Sunnis. In no place was Sunni disaffection greater, and it manifested itself in a very high level of instability and escalating violence. Within this context, AQI sought to exploit the situation and take charge of the insurgency.

AL QAEDA IN IRAQ TAKES CHARGE IN ANBAR

The years 2004 to 2007 in Anbar will long be described in Marine lore as one of the Corps' legendary fights, a four-year bloody test of wills. In the middle of that

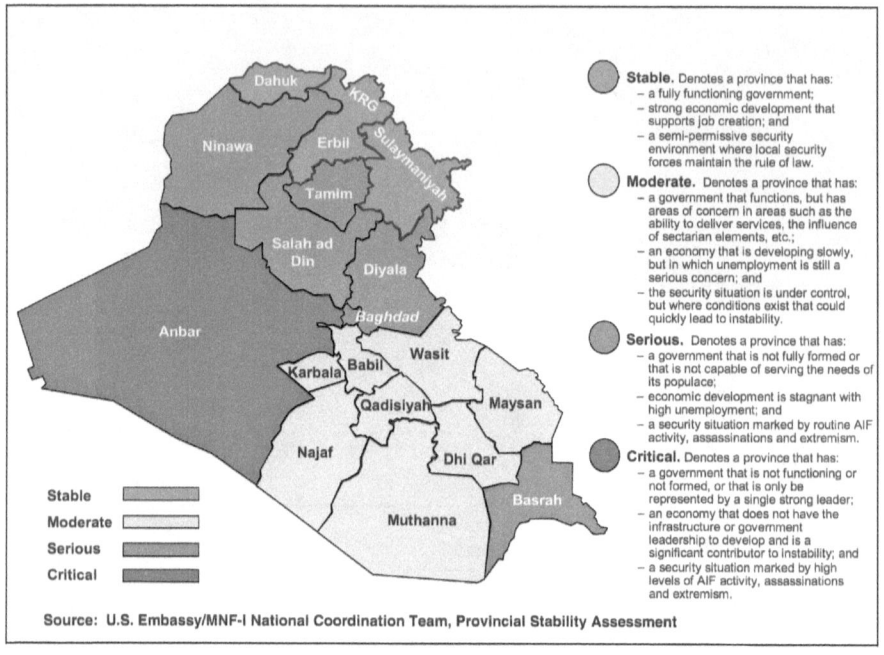

MAP 4.1 Iraq map of provincial stability

fight—in 2005—al Qaeda sought to take charge of the insurgent forces arrayed against the Marines. In 2004 the constituent elements of the insurgency had formed up into an alliance of convenience that was not a natural fit for its members. In fact, in several important respects it was an unnatural partnership.

Locally based groups of Sunnis joined the insurgency in 2004 to fight the American occupation in what they believed was an impending Shia onslaught. From within the Sunni social order, Anbar sheikhs, imams, and former Ba'athist military and civilian officials backed the expanding nationalist resistance groups. Joining them were international and homegrown Salafi jihadists who had designated Iraq as the central front, the forward edge of the global battle on which to engage the far enemy—the United States. They believed that by forcing the Americans to give up the fight in Iraq they could inflict a defeat of enormous consequences on the last remaining superpower.

Al Qaeda saw Iraq as a strategic opportunity, a mirror image of the one it had exploited more than a decade earlier in Afghanistan. At that time, al Qaeda had taken on and defeated another superpower—the Soviet Union—and its vaunted

Red Army. Iraq provided the chance to inflict the same kind of defeat on the United States. Bin Laden, Zawahiri, and Zarqawi all made clear that they viewed Iraq in that way. Consider bin Laden's December 27, 2004, audio message to the "whole of the Islamic nation: I now address my speech to the whole of the Islamic nation: Listen and understand. The issue is big and the misfortune is momentous. The most important and serious issue today for the whole world is this Third World War, which the Crusader–Zionist coalition began against the Islamic nation. It is raging in the land of the two rivers [Iraq]. The world's millstone and pillar is in Baghdad, the capital of the caliphate."[9] This characterization of Iraq was repeated over and over on the many al Qaeda websites and discussed in its chat rooms. Iraq provided a unique and historic opportunity, they proclaimed, to fight and defeat the main enemy of the global Salafi jihad movement.

Consequently, Iraq eclipsed other fights, including Afghanistan, in terms of strategic centrality. It dominated al Qaeda's imagination, who used it to rouse radical Salafi passions and inspire Arab and Muslim youth to see Iraq through the lens of the long jihad. Al Qaeda leaders sought to animate prospective mujahideen to believe they would be fighting in the pivotal battle. Victory in Iraq would be strategic, a major step forward in the restoration of the caliphate.

It was within this context that AQI sought to take control of the insurgency in Anbar. Its goals were different from those of the Sunni nationalists who were fighting against occupation and what they envisioned as looming Shia subjugation. In 2003–2004 those nationalists had aligned with AQI and facilitated the flow of foreign fighters into Iraq, giving them protection within the Sunni social structure. For its part, AQI provided the nationalist resistance factions—the 1920 Brigades, Anuman Brigades, Islamic Mujahideen Army, and several others—with money, resources, and the promise of protection against the Shia. That was 2003–2004.

In 2005 that partnership ended. AQI wanted control, not collaboration, and it intended to take it by marginalizing the sheikhs, imams, and former Ba'athists who led or backed the nationalist resistance in Anbar. They were part of the old Anbar, not part of the new order that AQI intended to establish in Anbar. It sounded as if the CPA had decided to write the tribes and sheikhs out of its own vision of the new Iraq. But the methods AQI intended to use to marginalize these pillars of traditional society in Anbar were very different and far harsher.

Chapter 2 highlighted how in 2003 the United States made all the wrong moves in Anbar, facilitating the insurgency. This chapter illustrates how in 2005 AQI began making its own wrong-headed moves to achieve a takeover, and how, when the Sunnis, disenchanted with the ruthless methods and long-term intentions of their erstwhile partner, began to mount an opposition, AQI moved to viciously cut that opposition off.

Consider the reflections on 2005 of Sheikh Sabah al-Sattam Effan Fahran al-Shurji al-Aziz, the head of the Albu Mahal tribe, which is located in the Al Qa'im area of AO Denver. "At the end of 2004," he explained, "the conflict between us and them [AQI] started. And it continued . . . on a low level up to May 2005." Then al Qaeda escalated "to break the authority of the area. The first thing they did, they assassinated the chief of police, who was a member of our tribe." By August they "entered [and took control] of Al Qa'im, and we had to withdraw."[10]

In the Fallujah area, sheikhs of the Albu Issa tribe—a prominent subtribe of the Dulaym confederation—likewise began objecting to AQI's power play. One of these sheikhs was Sheikh Aifan Sadun al-Issawi, whose father had been the Albu Issa's sheikh general. The consequences of opposing al Qaeda were immediate, he recalled: "During this time, from my cousins, my family, and my tribe's sons, about thirty-seven were killed. Because of this . . . I could not even leave my house. If I wanted to go outside, it meant too much security, and I might have to fight at any second. So I started not to go out much. Even my uncles, who are just across the road from my house, told me, 'Don't come to us, because you are a suspect. They might kill us because we know you.'"[11]

Sheikh Ahmad Bezia Fteikhan al-Rishawi of the Albu Risha tribe tells the same story. The brother of the late Sheikh Abdul Sattar Abu Risha, who was founder of the Anbar Awakening Council, al-Rishawi was elected the tribe's paramount sheikh following his brother's assassination. The Albu Risha tribe is located in the Ramadi area. The sheikh recounted how in 2005 AQI "killed a lot of personnel from the Iraqi police, a lot of Iraqi police. . . . They destroyed the infrastructure. . . . They attacked schools. They attacked university professors. They forbade involvement in any political dialogue. The situation became unbearable. The sheikhs and the brains left the province—professors, teachers, doctors—they all went to Jordan and Syria. Al Qaeda roved the province. We set up security forces around our compounds, and we stayed there. . . . They started lobbing mortar rounds on us, in order to make us run away."[12]

Finally, Dr. Thamer Ibrahim Tahir al-Assafi, a member of Anbar's Muslim Ulema Council (Council of Muslim Scholars) and professor of religious studies at Al Anbar University, provides the following portrayal of al Qaeda's takeover of Ramadi. The city "became so paralyzed that even the employees of the banks could not receive their own salaries. Many fatwas were issued by the terrorists to close the universities. Ramadi became a ghost town. Universities, schools, factories, and institutions were all shut down, so we were oppressed. The government did not pay us our salaries."[13]

This led some in Ramadi, explained Dr. Thamer, "to volunteer for the police." To put a stop to that, AQI reacted brutally and with impunity. "Two terrorists infiltrated the place [the recruitment center] and blew themselves up." And that was just the half of it. He added, "Civilians who aided those wounded, the terrorists would hunt them down on the roads and slaughter them. . . . The terrorists said we deserved death and many among us were killed."[14]

PUSHBACK: EARLY SIGNS OF RESISTANCE TO AL QAEDA IN IRAQ

It is generally not advisable to murder sheikhs, the time-honored chieftains of tribal society, or to massacre those who make up the rank-and-file membership of a tribe. The consequences of doing so can be grave indeed.

Recall that in such traditional cultures, solidarity, loyalty, honor, and protection of the members of the collective serve as the foundations of the tribal value system. Central to this tribal ethos is the duty to bring to justice those who violate these norms, and murder certainly meets that test. Revenge, blood feuds, and even war often ensue as the mandatory means for dealing with such transgressions. In fact, in these situations revenge is formally prescribed—*in perpetuum*—as the duty for all the males of the tribe. This includes risking life and limb to avenge the death of tribal members and most certainly to avenge the murder of a sheikh.

Long ago this way of life took deep root in Anbar, and the people still adhered to it when al Qaeda decided in 2005 to write the sheikhs and tribes out of the future it envisioned for the land between the two rivers. Evidently, AQI either forgot about these tribal norms or, more likely, thought it could simply slash and burn its way through them. A campaign of murder and intimidation would overpower tribal values and duties. That is what AQI seems to have deduced. Instead, what transpired was tribal pushback. Among the first to resist was the Albu Mahal tribe in Al Qa'im.

The situation in Al Qa'im was complex. Following the overthrow of Saddam, the Albu Mahal sat on the fence and did not openly support the emerging insurgency. But by the second half of 2004, the tribal leadership began opposing the Coalition, and men from the tribe joined different insurgent factions, primarily the nationalist ones. The reason for this appears to have been survival. The United States–led Coalition and Baghdad government were ignoring the area, sending few forces for security and offering little aid or reconstruction assistance.

This situation eventually led the Albu Mahal to cooperate with Zarqawi and the al Qaeda foreign fighters operating in the Al Qa'im area. AQI had resources and also facilitated the tribe's smuggling business, which its ancestors had begun long ago. However, early in the spring of 2005 the Albu Mahal–AQI collaboration began to sour. Although AQI facilitated the tribe's illegal crossborder activities, it wanted half the profits for doing so.

AQI was doing other things that did not go down well with the Albu Mahal. These included imposing its fundamentalist social order on the daily life of the tribe, demanding to marry the women of the tribe, and eliminating the authority and power of the sheikhs. Further driving a wedge between the Albu Mahal and AQI was the way AQI fought Marine forces when they initiated sweeps in the area. Suicide operations and other indiscriminate tactics often resulted in killing large numbers of innocent bystanders.

When the sheikhs objected to all of this, as they thought they had the right to do, AQI turned to intimidation and murder, killing respected tribal leaders. The Albu Mahal retaliated and began fighting al Qaeda and other tribes aligned with it. The latter included the Karabila and Salmoni tribes. Finding themselves outgunned, Albu Mahal sheikhs asked the Coalition for help, but they were turned down. According to then-Col. Joe Dunford, "In the spring of 2005, I met with dozens of sheikhs. . . . They said they'd fight on our side, but refused to go through the government in Baghdad. In 2005, we weren't willing to accept that deal."[15]

Cooperation with the tribes was still proscribed. Apparently, L. Paul Bremer's October 2003 CPA injunction that "tribes are part of the past" and "have no place in the new democratic Iraq" was still in effect, thwarting collaboration with these allies in waiting.[16] Moreover, CPA Order 91 had declared that all local or regional militia forces, including those belonging to tribes like those in Anbar, were prohibited from operating independently. Rather, they were directed by this decree to "enter either civilian life or one of the state security services, such as the Iraqi Armed Forces, the Iraqi Police Service, or the Internal Security Services of the Kurdish Regional Government."[17]

For the sheikhs of Anbar, this was a nonstarter. Tribal militias were a long-standing part of the tribal structure. They provided protection and security, and they defended tribal honor. Moreover, the sheikhs were not about to send their men to the Iraqi armed forces or the Iraqi police. Those institutions were in the hands of the Shia.

For the Albu Mahal, the Coalition rebuff had dire consequences on the ground in Al Qa'im. After many weeks of vicious fighting, several thousand Albu Mahal tribesmen and their families were forced out of their traditional homes and had to resettle sixty miles south of their homes. By the summer, Zarqawi and AQI were in control of major parts of Al Qa'im.

The Albu Mahal was not the only tribe in early 2005 pushing back against AQI's power play. The Albu Fahd in the Ramadi region also began resisting. That tribe did so for many of the same reasons as the Albu Mahal. When the insurgency grew in late 2003 in Anbar, the sheikhs of the Albu Fahd began supporting the nationalist factions of the resistance. Those factions were made up of former regime military, intelligence, and political leaders whose tribal family roots were in the Ramadi area. Albu Fahd tribal members joined with them to fight the Coalition occupiers and their Shia clients.

During 2004 those nationalist factions and their Albu Fahd backers aligned with Zarqawi and AQI. AQI had established a considerable presence in the Ramadi region. As elsewhere in Anbar, the Albu Fahd–AQI partnership was an alliance of convenience. The Albu Fahd and other Ramadi area tribes gave AQI local support and allowed them to hide within their extended families. In return, Zarqawi and his commanders provided operational and organizational assistance to the nationalist armed groups in attacking Coalition forces.

However, as the insurgency in Ramadi and its environs grew, differences emerged between the nationalists (and their tribal supporters) and AQI over means and ends. The sheikhs chafed at the violent control AQI sought to impose over Ramadi and its surrounding towns. They also grew tired of the men, women, and children of their tribe paying the human price for Zarqawi's indiscriminate attacks on Coalition forces. Those suicide bombers and IEDs were killing many more Albu Fahd than Coalition forces. Finally, AQI's talk about establishing an Islamic caliphate did not strike a positive chord with the sheikhs. Albu Fahd leader Sheikh Nasser Abd al-Karim Mukhlif al-Fahdawi and his associates had little interest in giving up their authority and returning to the seventh-century lifestyle envisioned by AQI and practiced by the Taliban when they ruled Afghanistan.

Splits among insurgent forces in the Ramadi area began to appear. Local tribal leaders, including Sheikh Nasser and other Albu Fahd chiefs, began to oppose Zarqawi's assertion that he was in charge and justified in killing whomever he identified as the enemy, even local governmental officials and police officers. As we shall see later, by the late fall this opposition had turned to organized resistance and opened the door to cooperation with II MEF.

However, in the spring and summer of 2005, the decision makers in Baghdad and Washington did not grasp the potential strategic opportunity that these splits in the insurgent ranks might offer to the Coalition. Such a sea change in U.S. policy was not in the cards at that time.

But by the late fall months the Marine commanders on the ground in Anbar began to see that the tribal militias that constituted the rank and file of the nationalist factions of the insurgency, and many others who were on the sidelines of the fight, might be retargeted by their sheikhs to fight and kill al Qaeda. What if the sheikhs ordered their men to do so in partnership with the Marine and Army forces in the province? And what if those same sheikhs had every tribal member serve as eyes and ears for those Marines, quietly fingering AQI members and their secret hideaways? Now, *that* would be a real reversal of fortune.

THE EIGHTY-BATTALION SOLUTION: A NEW CAMPAIGN PLAN

In June 2004 Gen. George Casey took command of Multi-National Force–Iraq (MNF-I), replacing the hapless Lt. Gen. Ricardo Sanchez. Casey was part and parcel of the big Army of mechanized infantry and heavy armor. As a general, he served as assistant division commander and then commander of the 1st Armored Division—Old Ironsides. He knew how to fight the big war the Army had been prepared to fight since he was commissioned a first lieutenant in 1970.

But General Casey also knew that Iraq needed a different approach. Mechanized infantry and heavy armor easily swept Saddam's army away, but the irregular war that followed the invasion was different. And Casey was aware of it. He needed a new campaign plan, one that gave him more boots on the ground. He simply did not have enough troops to secure Iraq.

Boots on the ground! That issue had been a volatile one in the run-up to the war. Before the invasion, the chief of staff of the Army, Gen. Eric Shinseki, suggested during a February 2003 session of the Senate's Armed Services Committee that something in the order of several hundred thousand soldiers would probably be required for the occupation of Iraq. Deputy Secretary of Defense Paul Wolfowitz strongly demurred, refuting that estimate as "wildly off the mark."[18] By the time Casey took command of MNF-I, Shinseki was proving to be much closer to the mark than wildly off it. The realities on the ground were quite different from what Wolfowitz and Rumsfeld had envisioned when planning the war.

By early August, Casey's new campaign plan—"Partnership: From Occupation to Constitutional Elections"—was ready. The plan called for the Coalition to carry out "full spectrum counter-insurgency operations to isolate and neutralize former regime extremists and foreign terrorists," in "partnership with the Iraqi government."[19] For that partnership to work, the MNF-I would need to organize, train, and equip a substantial ISF. To carry out a counterinsurgency operation—with its emphasis on clearing insurgents out of populated areas and then holding those areas to provide security and assistance to the people who lived there—a large and effective ISF was indispensable.

Responsibility for organizing, training, and equipping the effort was given to the Multi-National Security Transition Command-Iraq (MNSTC-I), a subordinate element of MNF-I. In 2005 Casey had tasked it to establish and train eighty Iraqi battalions. By year's end he wanted them operationally ready to join the fight by partnering with Coalition battalions. The plan was one the Marine commanders in Anbar could get behind. With some of those Iraqi battalions, they could hold the towns along the Euphrates from Fallujah to Al Qa'im after their forces swept the insurgents out of them.

Consistent with counterinsurgency precepts, a force of eighty ISF battalions—configured into thirty-two brigades—was an important step forward in developing a new strategy to defeat the insurgency. In Anbar the Marines concurred. Their slice of the ISF pie was to be six brigades, consisting of eighteen battalions. Initially, they were to be drawn from the 1st and 7th Divisions of the Iraqi army. As they arrived, II MEF intended to complete their training and, as soon as possible, employ them across the province. ISF was the key to holding the ground and maintaining stability and security at the local level. At least that was what COIN theory promised.

But the reality of ISF was another story. To create eighty effective battalions, MNF-I was going to have to start from scratch. Consequently, reaching General Casey's goal by the end of 2005 was extremely ambitious. That was because of CPA Order 2, which had disbanded the Iraqi military and sent its members packing without pay. A more nuanced approach was needed, one that kept part of the Iraqi military in place, vetted its officers, and trained it to work with Coalition forces to stabilize Iraq. As for the rest of the Iraqi forces, they would be demobilized in a way that helped them transition to civilian life and not to the insurgency. Unfortunately, CPA Order 2 lacked such nuance.

CPA Order 2 made Casey's goal unattainable, at least in 2005. Readiness measures revealed that by the end of the year many of the new Iraqi battalions were not ready for prime time. They could not carry out the mission envisioned in the campaign plan. In fact, Casey himself noted during a news briefing with Secretary Rumsfeld on September 30 that only one battalion had reached a Level-1 proficiency, meaning it was capable of operating on its own. Still, he was upbeat, noting that several units had reached a Level-2 proficiency and could carry out missions with a Coalition counterpart force.[20] Other Department of Defense officials speculated that maybe a third of the units might be in or approaching that status.[21]

Even if an Iraqi battalion reached a Level-2 proficiency and was ready for partnership with a Marine counterpart, it might not be welcomed by the people of Anbar. The reason had to do with the personnel makeup of the eighty battalions. The new army the Americans were raising in Iraq was Shia dominated. The commander of MNSTC-I at that time, Gen. David Petraeus, was quite aware of this and sought to recruit several thousand Sunnis to the ISF with some success.[22]

Nevertheless, the reality was that many of those filling out the ranks of the eighty Iraqi army battalions were Shia. Deploying them to Anbar was problematic. They were likely to be deeply distrusted and not welcomed by the Sunnis who lived there. In fact, in the fall of 2005 when U.S. military commanders began holding town hall meetings in Anbar "to convince tribal leaders to encourage their members to join the ISF" they found strong resistance.[23]

The sheikhs were not about to send their young men out of the province and into the hands of the Shia. Forget it. That could amount to a death sentence. Moreover, they added, any Sunnis joining ISF would be viewed as traitors. And al Qaeda would kill them, if it got the chance.

Furthermore, the sheikhs did not want Shia-dominated battalions in their midst. Their apprehension had some basis in fact. Consider the previously mentioned 7th Division of the Iraq Army. In 2005 its First Brigade, a mostly Shiite outfit, was stationed outside Ramadi. Imagine what local residents must have thought when they saw its soldiers with "posters bearing the image of Shiite cleric Muqtada al-Sadr stuck on their chests or fastened to the end of raised AK-47 assault rifles."[24] More than likely, the Sunnis in Ramadi viewed the First Brigade as a front for Mehdi militia death squads.

However, the sheikhs taking part in those town hall meetings with the Coalition had a solution. They proposed that Coalition forces help them mobilize and arm their tribal militias to provide local security. Given that all counterinsurgency is local, this was a proposition worth exploring. And it may also have been a sign that the sheikhs were looking for a way out of the clutches of AQI. But CPA Order 91 closed that door, at least for the time being.

RELIEF IN PLACE

Between January and March 2005, the Marines carried out a staggered RIP of its forces in Anbar. Maj. Gen. Stephen Johnson, the deputy II MEF commander, led the new contingent to Anbar to relieve Lieutenant General Sattler's I MEF. But General Johnson was going to have to make do with a smaller force under his command to deal with an insurgency that was mushrooming in the heart of the Sunni Triangle. The ground combat strength was less than what Major General Natonski had in the 1st Marine Division. His replacement, Maj. Gen. Richard Huck, commander of the 2nd Marine Division, brought six infantry, one LAR, and one reconnaissance battalion to Iraq for the RIP.

This force had two fewer infantry battalions and no provisional military police battalion. To make up for the shortfall, the Marines were counting on some of those eighty ISF battalions called for in the 2005 campaign plan. It took eleven weeks to replace approximately 25,000 Marines with 22,000. Those forces, in conjunction with the Army regiment in the Ramadi region, had to cover a two-hundred-mile stretch of land starting at the outskirts of Baghdad and ending on the border with Syria. Along this stretch were twelve cities, several of which had substantial enemy presence. This region constituted the badlands of Iraq. As in 2004, a combat regiment was assigned to each of the three AOs in the province: Denver, Raleigh, and

Topeka. In AO Denver RCT-2 replaced RCT-7, in AO Raleigh RCT-8 took over for RCT-1, and in AO Topeka the Army's 2-28 BCT replaced the 2-2 BCT.

To mask the RIP so the insurgents did not have the opportunity to exploit it, I MEF began and II MEF took over Operation River Blitz. This consisted of interdiction operations to disrupt and keep the enemy off balance, including cutting off elements infiltrating east of the Euphrates in the area in and around Hit and Haditha. This was accomplished with small-unit raids and cordon-and-knock and cordon-and-search tactics.

Additionally, counterterrorism teams belonging to the Joint Special Forces Command tracked down and either killed or captured insurgent leaders. They did this every night. To be sure, facing the possibility of one of these special mission units visiting in the middle of the night was a very disquieting prospect for Zarqawi on down through the ranks of AQI and its nationalist allies. General Natonski provided the following account of the effectiveness of these diversionary methods as the RIP was coming to an end in March:

> We continued to keep the enemy disrupted as we prepared for our RIP with 2nd Marine Division. Once again, the effect we wanted was to keep . . . him from executing his planning and execution cycle because if we kept him moving he could not seriously plan attacks on us. We didn't want him to know a RIP was going on, and we wanted to ensure that 2nd Marine Division got spun up as quickly as they could in preparation for assuming the battle space. As you have seen here, we did not receive a single . . . [tactical report] that the enemy knew a RIP was going on, unlike the previous RIP back in September, when the enemy knew exactly what was going on. But because we kept the enemy moving, kept attacking, were aggressive doing raids and vehicle checkpoints, cordons, and searches, the enemy thought that the movement of the RIP forces that were coming in . . . were actually part of the operation. So, they never knew a RIP was going on. And what that had the effect of is it minimized the attacks on convoys of troops moving to their new bases when they were most vulnerable.[25]

SECOND MARINE EXPEDITIONARY FORCE'S CONCEPT OF OPERATIONS

The concept of operations for II MEF grew out of General Casey's campaign plan for 2005. It called for carrying out five lines of operation at the same time. The five taken together were to provide a framework for applying kinetic and nonkinetic actions aimed at gaining control of the ground in Anbar. It sought to separate the insurgents from the people, hold the ground, and then carry out those civil reconstruction activities that win counterinsurgency fights.

The first line focused on security. The goals were to establish safety for the population, isolate the insurgents from the population, and provide civilian agencies with the secure space needed to carry out those activities that make victory attainable. Security was to serve as a table setter that enabled civilian agencies to execute civil activities ranging from humanitarian assistance to economic and political development. Security involved clearing and holding the twelve cities that ran along the Euphrates River in Anbar. Security was the essential starting point. Without it nothing else was possible.

To be successful, the forces of II MEF had to take control of that two-hundred-mile stretch of land starting near Baghdad and ending at the border town of Al Qa'im. In between were the most violent places in Iraq, each with substantial enemy presence. Security was the starting point, and without it the Marines were going to achieve little in Anbar.

The second line of operation—building the ISF—was the essential force multiplier that would allow II MEF to take control of and hold those twelve cities and the areas surrounding them. Once they reached a sufficient level of effectiveness, the ISF could assume a greater role in the counterinsurgency fight. The Marines would clear, but only with the ISF could they hold and secure.

The next two lines of operation—governance and economic development—addressed those aforementioned activities that make victory attainable. The governance line creates a context that allows elected officials to govern in an effective manner, to handle political grievances, and to provide basic services such as electricity, water, and sanitation. The economic development line establishes the critical infrastructure needed to support growth and provide the basics to achieve a decent quality of life.

The final line of operations focused on information and communication. These are of the highest priority within the concept of operations that informed the 2005 campaign plan. Information serves as the basis for developing a convincing narrative, which provides the driving logic for the overall campaign plan. Each operation—civil or military—has an information message that seeks to influence the population, the center of gravity in counterinsurgency.

It was a comprehensive approach, but its starting point was security. Without that secure base, without that separation of the insurgents from the people, those civil reconstruction activities that win internal wars will never get off the ground.

For II MEF, security involved clearing the Euphrates River valley of major insurgent activities. According to the deputy II MEF commander, Major General Johnson, Operation Sayeed intended to do just that. Consisting of "eleven named operations under the Sayeed umbrella . . . the purpose of those operations . . . was to drive al Qaeda from the western Euphrates River Valley, and to eliminate that as a place where they could operate freely." The II MEF deputy commander added, "The operation was also designed . . . to ensure that we had the climate and the environment to conduct the referendum in October, and the national elections in December. The operations under Sayeed were designed to ensure that we had the conditions so that people could vote." Finally, "Operation Sayeed was to restore control of the Iraqi border," closing those ratlines that allowed foreign jihadis to slither into Iraq.[26]

For the forces of II MEF the "eleven named operations" encompassed by Sayeed, as well as those that preceded it, were all about the use of highly lethal force to find and eliminate insurgent presence and activities. In a February 2006 interview, Maj. Gen. James Williams, the assistant commander of the 2nd Marine Division, explained why his battalions were concentrating on kinetic operations in a counterinsurgency fight: "Al Anbar Province was a province that was in essence being inundated by the influx of insurgent and foreign fighter activity." Consequently, "operationally, that led to the kinetic operations that went from April '05 . . . until the most recent operations following the December election."[27]

"In the macro sense," General Williams elaborated, "the operations were fairly simple." In the first phase of Sayeed, the goal was "to basically, kinetically, chase the foreign fighters and the [local] insurgents up the Euphrates River valley. And then Phase II . . . was to close the border off and essentially continue routing the insurgents from the Euphrates River valley and deny them strongholds and destroy or defeat them wherever it was possible."[28]

Following the transfer of authority with I MEF, the battalions of RCT-2, RCT-8, and the Army's 2nd Brigade Combat Team of the 2nd Infantry Division (2-2 BCT) sought to create that situation in each of their AOs, as will be elaborated here. The goal was to deny the insurgents the ability to intimidate, disrupt, and operate with impunity.

In AO Denver the units of RCT-2 pursued this goal by interdicting and stemming the flow of insurgents entering Iraq through western Anbar. This entailed a wide range of combat actions focused on the routes connecting Husaybah, Al Qa'im, Rawah, Haditha, and Hit. It meant sweeping the insurgents out of those cities and destroying enemy networks and infrastructure. This was the "clear" part of "clear and hold," and RCT-2 intended to accomplish that mission.

In AO Topeka the 2-2 BCT set out to find and neutralize the insurgents operating inside the city of Ramadi, as well as in the territory surrounding it. This was an extremely challenging mission, as Ramadi and its environs were teeming with insurgents. It was believed that Zarqawi and his key lieutenants were operating

120 | Chapter 4

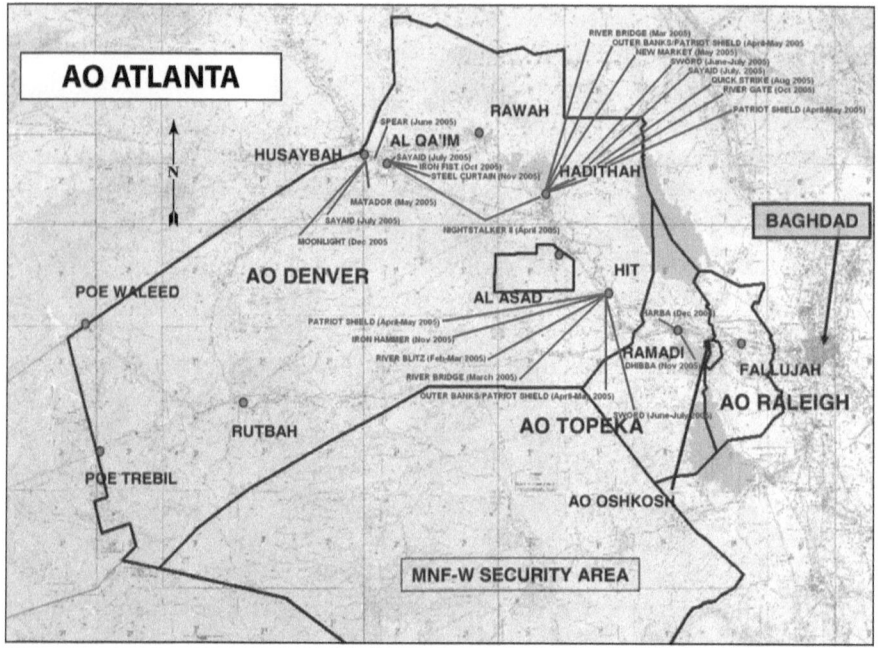

MAP 4.2 The location of named II MEF clearing operations in 2005

ESTES, *INTO THE FRAY*, 96

out of that part of the province. The badlands of Ramadi were considered the most violent and unstable parts of Iraq in 2005.

Finally, in Fallujah the battalions of RCT-8 worked to hold and rebuild the city in the aftermath of Operation Al Fajr. In the rest of AO Raleigh, the regiment planned to quell persistent insurgent activities north of Fallujah to Lake Tharthar and south of the city to Abu Gharaib.

AREA OF OPERATIONS DENVER

"The fight out here is different," said Col. Stephen Davis, four months into his command of RCT-2 in AO Denver. "It's different than the fight in AO Topeka; it's different than in AO Raleigh." What made it different, he explained, was the fact that RCT-2 was "responsible for 30,000 square miles," an area that "encompasses major portions of the border—Iraq's border with Syria—the entire border with Jordan, and a good chunk of the border with Saudi Arabia." To cover it, Davis had "less than 3,400 people in the entirety of the RCT."[29]

Added to this was the fact that AO Denver was the wild, wild West in terms of the fight in the towns that dotted its landscape. Colonel Davis described it this way:

> Life in the Middle East follows water . . . [and] the main line of communication is the Euphrates River out here. Every one of these towns along the Euphrates is different. The fight in each town is different, yet they are all linked. They are all integrated—sometimes intentionally, sometimes unintentionally, depending on . . . the operations that the insurgents want to have going on or the ability the insurgents have to make their presence felt. There are three border points of entry [for the insurgents]. . . . They travel across MSR Mobile and MSR Michigan. You can see they just run right down into Ramadi and then down into Baghdad. . . . That's how the fight sets up.[30]

The mission assigned to RCT-2, the guidance that came from the 2nd Marine Division and II MEF, was to "go out there and disrupt and interdict," said Davis. What that entailed, he added, was, "philosophically, we try to be everywhere and nowhere. We try . . . to out-guerilla the guerilla. . . . Now this is a battle of wills. . . . Everything here is a point/counterpoint game. Point/counterpoint. You think of something; he'll come up with a counter. He thinks up something; you've got to come up with a counter. So it is a thinking man's game. You've got to stay ahead of this curve. You really have to take a lot of time to understand that and accommodate to it in how you think and how you act."[31]

Col. Stephen Davis, commander of RCT-2, examines weapons found during Operation Spear in June 2005.
ESTES, *INTO THE FRAY*, 100

As soon as the battalions of RCT-2 hit the ground in AO Denver, they were involved in disruption and interdiction operations. These continued unabated throughout 2005. As noted above, they began with River Blitz, the operation that II MEF took over to mask the RIP and deny the insurgents the opportunity to exploit it. Once settled in, the regiment, during April and May, initiated a series of clearing actions—Operation Outer Banks—in the Hit–Haditha corridor. The reaction of the insurgents was low level, resisting with IEDs, small engagements, and indirect fire attacks. In the area between Haditha and Al Qa'im, Operation Nightstalker used sniper teams from 3/25's Force Reconnaissance Company to disrupt insurgent movements on the main roads.

During May the regiment swept enemy sanctuaries north of the Euphrates with the execution of Operation Matador. A month earlier, the insurgents had attacked Camp Gannon, a forward operating base located on the Iraq-Syria border at Husbayah. This was considered a key entry point for foreign fighters, referred to by the Marines as "the mouth of the insurgent ratline." The attack on Gannon was a robust one in which the enemy sought to pin down the camp's guards with mortar and rocket fire, while three vehicles driven by suicide bombers attempted to break through and devastate the base. These vehicles included a dump truck and a fire engine. They failed to break through, but the attack illustrated the capacity of the insurgents to execute sophisticated and complex action with approximately one hundred fighters launched from their own operating base.

Operation Matador's goal was to eliminate those bases or sanctuaries north of the Euphrates in the area of Ramana. RCT-2 configured a task force for the operation consisting of several companies from each of its battalions, as well as the Army's 814th Bridge Company. Matador produced fierce fighting as the Marines cleared a zone from Ramana through al-Ubaydi to Ar Rabit. Approximately one hundred fifty insurgents were killed and forty taken prisoner. The forces of RCT-2 disrupted a major insurgent base area, noted Colonel Davis: "We knew they were building a sanctuary north of the river. There was enough sensitive reporting through our ISR [intelligence, surveillance, and reconnaissance] systems." He added that what Matador found was a significant foreign fighter contingent: "There was a mash of foreign fighters. Sudanese, Saudi, many guys from Syria. Some of them had documentation. Some of them had suicide notes on them. . . . North of the river pretty much had become a sanctuary for the bad guys."[32] The Marines found a complex infrastructure that was similar to the one they had uncovered in Fallujah when they took that city.

While Matador was a success—the insurgents were rousted from their nest north of the river—it was only a fleeting victory. As with River Blitz and Outer Banks, Matador resulted in an effective clearing of the insurgents from the area.

Marines from 3/2 in action at al-Ubaydi during Operation Matador in May 2005

ESTES, *INTO THE FRAY*, 98

The operation removed a sanctuary, noted the commander of RCT-2, "for a certain amount of time." But the insurgents would be back as soon as the Marines withdrew. RCT-2 did not have enough forces to establish a lasting presence. The reality, said the RCT-2 commander, was "The enemy will go where we are not, and that's just the hard facts of life. Unless he wants to attack us, and in that case, he will come to where we are. But he's elusive, and we are underresourced [for] this fight out here."[33]

At the end of June and into early July, Operation Sword brought RCT-2 to the town of Hit. The raid was effective, clearing the town and establishing two bases there. Hit became the first town in AO Denver that RCT-2 intended to hold permanently. During July, as RCT-2 rotated forces, Operation Saber aimed at disrupting insurgents and keeping them off balance. It included a multibattalion attack on the right side of the Euphrates River between Al Qa'im and Haditha.

August saw the insurgents strike back. The month began with the ambush of two sniper teams from 3/25 northwest of Haditha. Five members were killed and another went missing. His body was recovered the next day. RCT-2 initiated a rapid response to search for those responsible by a cordon-and-search of Haqlaniyah and Barwanah. On the first day, fourteen Marines died when their assault vehicle hit a massive IED. These events were the beginning of a bloody August for the regiment, particularly for 3/25. The insurgents were demonstrating a resiliency that took advantage of the inability of RCT-2 to hold its territory.

The fall months saw more of the same in AO Denver, as RCT-2 took part in the previously noted Operation Sayeed. The goal was to drive al Qaeda from the western Euphrates River valley, eliminating the area as a place where the insurgents could operate freely. In AO Denver this entailed clearing—again—Hit, Haditha, Husaybah, and Al Qa'im. The goal was to pacify those areas and to gain control of the border, long a haven for al Qaeda and the insurgency.

In early November Colonel Davis assembled two thousand Marines to take this on, under Operation Steel Curtain. Included were forces from the Iraqi army's 1st Brigade, who were to hold the territory after the Marines swept out the insurgents. Steel Curtain also used a local tribal force known as the Desert Protectors. They were from the Albu Mahal, the first tribe that resisted AQI's attempt to take control in Anbar earlier in 2005. By November the Desert Protectors were working hand-in-glove with the Marines in combat, and because of their local knowledge they were able to identify many foreign fighters and local insurgents.

Steel Curtain kicked off on November 3 and lasted for nearly three weeks. It entailed considerable fighting along the Syria-Iraq border and resulted in the elimination of a significant foreign fighting force that was operating throughout the Al Qa'im region. First, Husaybah was cleared from west to east. The next target was western Karabala, which likewise was cleared of local insurgents, foreign fighters, and IEDs. Finally, nearly two weeks into Steel Curtain, the Marines cleared al-Ubaydi. Throughout the fight, Marine operations had continuous air support, including extensive use of precision-guided munitions.

Steel Curtain stirred up animosity among the mix of local tribes, some of whom were sympathetic to al Qaeda and the insurgency. In the aftermath, RCT-2 sought to empower local Iraqis to assume control of local police forces and public services. To facilitate this, the Iraqi army forces assigned to Steel Curtain established a base in Al Qa'im to maintain an ongoing presence.

As explained by Lt. Col. Julian Alford, whose 3/6 was an integral part of the operation, the Marines hoped that this Iraqi army presence would facilitate the perception among the local population that "We're here to stay to help them get back on their feet. The most important thing is getting the power, the water, the sanitation, and the food moving back into this area. . . . When you see the battlefield, it's almost overwhelming, the amount of work that needs to be done at this point. These people, to take the right side, they have to believe that the Iraqi government is going to help them."[34] But this was a hard sell, given the composition of the Iraqi forces deployed to Anbar. They were largely Shia.

During Steel Curtain, the Marine assault forces suffered 10 men killed and another 59 wounded. Insurgent losses were put at 139 killed, and nearly 400 taken prisoner. At the time of Steel Curtain, another event occurred in AO Denver that illustrated the challenge RCT-2 faced in controlling this large area. A four-Humvee-mounted patrol from RCT-2's battalion 1/3, which in the fall of 2005 replaced 3/25, was hit by the insurgents in Haditha on November 19. One Marine was killed—Miguel Terrazas—and two others were badly injured. What ensued was recounted by Bing West in the *Atlantic*:

> The remaining ten men in Terrazas's squad approached a car that had stopped nearby. When the five men inside started to flee, the marines shot and killed them. The platoon leader later reported that his men took fire from a nearby house. They assaulted first one house, and then a second. When the battle was over, fourteen Iraqi men, four women, and six children had been killed.
>
> The tragedy was followed by eight months of investigations. Iraqis claim that enraged marines executed the civilians. Defense lawyers claim the deaths were accidents that occurred while the men were following the Rules of Engagement for clearing rooms when under fire. The ROE stipulate the circumstances under which a soldier may employ deadly force. . . .
>
> A central issue in the Haditha tragedy is whether the marines deliberately shot civilians, or whether they threw grenades into the room first, creating clouds of dust that obscured the presence of civilians. If the latter was the case, a further issue is whether the Rules of Engagement permitted such an action.[35]

An eight-month investigation turned into a much longer legal process in which several Marines were prosecuted; by the fall of 2009 all were exonerated except one, who eventually in 2012 pleaded guilty to one count of negligent dereliction of duty and received no jail time. From the point of view of the fight in Anbar, Haditha illustrated the ongoing problem of fighting with too few forces. The 2005 campaign plan called for full spectrum counterinsurgency operations, but as the year came to a close in AO Denver, that goal remained to be achieved.

AREA OF OPERATIONS RALEIGH

RCT-8 completed its RIP with RCT-1 in March. During that period, it established a twofold OPLAN for AO Raleigh. In Fallujah it would continue to hold the city and prevent AQI from reestablishing a presence there. In addition to maintaining control, RCT-8 would also oversee the rebuilding of Fallujah, which had been seriously damaged during Operation Al Fajr.

The chief of operations—S-3—at that time for RCT-8 was Lt. Col. William Mullen. He managed the drafting of the regiment's OPLAN and in the summer of 2005 described the situation there in the following terms: "Fallujah can be said to have been cleared and we were in the holding process, and to some degree the winning processes with civil affairs moving in, trying to develop the projects" needed to facilitate reconstruction. "Get the people back to some sense of normalcy. The ECPs [entry control points] were established to hold out the insurgents, to keep them out; keep weapons, equipment, and ammunition from getting back into the city. Those have been fairly successful, though I've never seen it completely successful."[36]

However, AO Raleigh encompassed much more than Fallujah. Thus, maintaining the same kind of control elsewhere was not going to be possible given the size of RCT-8. According to Lieutenant Colonel Mullen, it became quickly apparent to the leadership of RCT-8 that "we can go anywhere we want; we just can't stay there and maintain a presence because of the fairly large size" of the AO. While it is not comparable in size "to RCT-2's AO, it is still a fairly large AO and you can't be everywhere."[37]

As a result, the S-3 explained, RCT-8 had to "take risks. . . . We know that the enemy is going to set themselves up in some areas because we can't get to it." But there was no free lunch for the insurgents because they would always have to worry that they could be hit by a "disruption operation." The regiment employed "raids, cordon, and knocks," it sent in "tanks and Army aviation just like a vacuum cleaner, looking for weapons stashes and equipment and ammunition. They've found tons, literally, quite literally tons out there." They also "found command and control centers." The objective was to have a "disrupting effect. . . . So disruption is a constant theme. It is always going on, but we just cannot stay in those areas because the AO is just too big. But we're always out after them."[38]

As in AO Denver, in AO Raleigh the regiment executed several large sweep operations to drive the insurgents out of their redoubts. This began in April when RCT-8's commanding officer, Col. Charles Gurganus, initiated Operation White Feather, which concentrated on stopping insurgent activities directed against the AO's main service roads. At the end of the month, Operation Clear Decision followed, with actions aimed at clearing towns that did not have a Marine presence. Over a seven-day period, elements of 3/8 moved against al-Karmah, which is located sixteen kilometers north and east of Fallujah. Considered one of the most violent cities in Anbar, insurgents moved freely in and out of it and daily attacked

Coalition patrols, convoys, and the forward operating bases. It took a week, but 3/8 finally cleared al-Karmah of insurgents.

Next, RCT-8 moved to sweep a large sector north of Fallujah during mid-May. Dubbed Operation Firm Control, tanks and assault units uncovered an insurgent network of numerous caches of weapons and other support facilities in an area that included Lake Tharthar. This led to the launching of Operation Khanjar, a three-week attack that concentrated on the territory surrounding the lake.

The after-action report from Khanjar characterized the area as having served as a full-service insurgent haven that included a capacity for training, storage of arms and equipment, command and control, and planning. In some cases, the insurgents went to considerable lengths to conceal key parts of their facilities. For example, during the operation the regiment received several tips that a particular house was an enemy command center. But when Marines went to check it out, they found a rundown empty building with no evidence that it had anything to do with the insurgent command and control, so they left. More tips came in about the house. Finally, a unit was sent back to take a second look. Here is what they uncovered:

Marines from 1/6 in action during Operation Khanjar at Lake Tharthar in June 2005
ESTES, *INTO THE FRAY*, 102

They go back and just walk around, and the floor sounded funny. They take a stick and they begin to bang on the floor, and a tile breaks. Actually cement breaks. The insurgents had put a light coat of cement over the floor. And they opened it up and . . . they go down into this command and control center. I mean, it is a real nice one. They had really done it up nice—air conditioning, ventilation, computers, just an amazing amount of stuff. And then, they found weapons caches around the outside of it. . . . They see another little house, and this is even more rundown and smaller than the one before. . . . And so they go in there and do the same thing, bang on the floor, another light coating of cement breaks. They go in there and it's a detention facility for the enemy. They had an Egyptian in there that they had strung up, his arms behind his back. He'd been beaten, tortured. He was in bad shape.[39]

White Feather, Clear Decision, Firm Control, and Khanjar all are illustrative of RCT-8's disruption campaign throughout 2005 and into 2006. Numerous similar operations of varying size were executed through the summer and late into the fall months. But the enemy was resilient and frequently regrouped to continue the fight. RCT-8 kept the insurgents off balance. As the S-3 put it, these operations were key, and as a result the insurgents were hard pressed to muster larger attacks.[40] But as in AO Denver, they were not going away. It was a protracted war—a stalemate—in which time was not on the side of the Marines as 2006 approached.

AREA OF OPERATIONS TOPEKA

"The most dangerous city in Iraq"—that was Fallujah's nom de guerre until Operation Al Fajr cleared the city of insurgents. In 2005 Ramadi, the capital of Anbar Province, earned that bloody moniker. In AO Topeka, Ramadi was ground zero in the fight against the insurgents. The city and its environs were an AQI stronghold; the insurgents intended in 2005 to consolidate their position. U.S. intelligence believed Zarqawi and the AQI leadership had their headquarters north of Ramadi, as evidenced by the fact that Task Force 145 (formerly 626) was looking for him and other high-value targets every night in AO Topeka.

Task Force 145 consisted of forces from the following special mission units: the Army's 1st Special Forces Operational Detachment-Delta, or Delta Force as it is popularly known in the movies; the 75th Ranger Regiment; the 160th Special Operations Aviation Regiment, or Night Stalkers; the Navy's SEAL Team 6; and the Air Force's 24th Special Tactics Squadron. The warriors of Task Force 145 were from the Joint Special Operations Command (JSOC), which has responsibility for counterterrorism worldwide. In 2005 Gen. Stanley A. McChrystal commanded JSOC. Also attached to Task Force 145 were British Special Air Service commandos and members of the CIA's counterterrorism unit, the Special Activities Division.

Task Force 145 was busy hunting high-value targets, and would continue to do so in 2006–2007. But the main effort to stabilize AO Topeka in 2005 was taken up first by the Army's 2nd BCT and, later in the year, by the 2nd BCT of the 28th Infantry Division (2-28 BCT). 2-2 BCT consisted of five battalions—three infantry, one artillery, and one engineers. It was a light regiment.

When 2-28 BCT from the Pennsylvania National Guard replaced 2-2 BCT in August, it came prepared for a heavy fight. It comprised six battalions that included 3-103rd Armor, 1-104th Cavalry, 1-109th Infantry, 1-110th Infantry, 1-172nd Armor, and 876th Engineers. Each was equipped with tanks and Bradley fighting vehicles. Finally, a battalion from the 2nd Marine Division was attached to both the 2-2 BCT and the 2-28 BCT.

Just to maintain a presence in a few parts of Ramadi, 2-2 BCT assigned three battalions. Ramadi and its outskirts were geographically daunting, and were just

An aerial view of Anbar's capital, Ramadi   ESTES, *INTO THE FRAY*, 38

too large to sweep and secure. Its units were largely restricted to a handful of bases, which gave the insurgents plenty of space to hide among Ramadi's 500,000 residents. From there they could fire on the bases with relative ease, generally at will.

Even if the commander of 2-2 BCT, Col. Gray Patton, could have applied all six of his battalions to seizing and holding Ramadi, he probably could not have achieved it. He needed at least three regiments to do that. Consider the difficulty that the Marine battalion, which was assigned to the Army regiment, had holding the Government Center in the heart of Ramadi.

By 2005 the Government Center and the buildings surrounding it for blocks had been riddled with bullet holes from countless firefights between Coalition forces and insurgents. Huge sections of buildings were gone, and others had collapsed in on themselves. Almost on a daily basis, and often half a dozen or more times a day, the Government Center was under small-arms attack. To resupply it, the Marines had to fight their way in and out. And the Government Center was a very small part of Ramadi.

When the Marines ventured out on patrol in the city, it only got worse. They were magnets for unrelenting insurgent small-arms fire and mortars, and ambushes happened all the time. But the Marines were not the only targets for AQI. So was any Iraqi who dared to work with the United States. Take the governor of al Anbar, Mamoon Sami Rashid al-Alwani. He was a top insurgent priority for AQI to kill, and it had made many attempts on his life. Keeping Mamoon and his family alive was the highest priority for II MEF; for one Marine company that was its *sole* mission.

Another priority target for AQI and the insurgents was the Iraqi police. AQI intended to kill as many as it could, with no holds barred. A case in point was a suicide car bomb attack on March 24 at a police checkpoint. The attack killed eleven members of the Iraqi 2nd Special Police Commandos and wounded another fourteen. Two American soldiers were wounded as well.

In April the bodies of eleven Iraqis were discovered in the Ramadi area. They were not police, but ordinary Iraqis trying to make a living. Why murder them? Because they were working at one of the U.S. military bases.

These two examples illustrate a key part of AQI's violent campaign in Ramadi and elsewhere in Anbar, using murder and intimidation to discourage any association with the Coalition and to take control of the insurgency. Hundreds of other Iraqis suffered the same fate in 2005.

In AO Topeka as elsewhere in Anbar, AQI's grisly methods to take charge and establish local dominance met with pushback. In Ramadi tribal sheikhs and nationalist insurgent leaders began rejecting AQI and opened negotiations with the leadership of II MEF. Governor Mamoon would play a key role in brokering those meetings beginning in November.

The late fall of 2005 saw other signs that the citizens of Ramadi and their leaders had had enough of Zarqawi and his vicious crew. Local Ramadi citizens grabbed the number three AQI leader on 2-2 BCT's high-value target list. Known as the "Butcher of Ramadi," Amir Khalaf Fanus was responsible for many murders and kidnappings. His captors turned him over to U.S. officials.

Given the state of the insurgency in AO Topeka, Army and Marine forces were continually on the move, executing sweeps to try to keep the insurgents off balance and on the defensive. In July, 2-2 BCT initiated a route-clearing operation around greater Ramadi to disrupt insurgent units planning and executing attacks against 2-2 BCT. If not attended to, these roads quickly turned into IED- and car bomb–infested gauntlets for any U.S. military convoy attempting to pass over them. In August, 2-28 BCT continued route clearing and terrain denial through cordon-and-search and search-and-attack operations. In October route clearing was focused on the area south of Ramadi, and in November on the north of the city. In the lead-up to the December election, a series of battalion-size operations were executed to secure different parts of Ramadi.

All of these operations and many more like them were making little difference. At the end of 2005, Ramadi remained the most dangerous city in Iraq and a haven for the insurgency.

IRAQI SECURITY FORCES: NO QUICK FIX FOR ANBAR

Of the eighty battalions called for in "Partnership: From Occupation to Constitutional Elections," eighteen were earmarked for Anbar. Initially, they were to come from the 1st and 7th Iraqi army divisions, which were assigned to II MEF. The 1st was to be headquartered at Habbiniyah and was assigned the area from Ramadi east through AO Raleigh. The 7th was to cover the territory west of Ramadi to the Syrian border.

According to the campaign plan, the eighteen battalions in Anbar, as well as those assigned elsewhere, were the key to establishing stability and control of the ground at the local level. Counterinsurgency calls for indigenous forces to hold territory amongst the people. But by the end of 2005, that goal was out of reach in Anbar.

In fact, the overall ratings for the eighty battalions were not encouraging as 2005 came to an end. Fostering the development of a viable ISF—both army and police—that could preserve law and order and maintain local security was proving much more difficult than anticipated.

With respect to the Iraqi army, the level of readiness of the eighty battalions had a long way to go before they reached the Level-1 status of being capable of operating independently in counterinsurgency operations. This lack of readiness was very evident in Anbar. Those Marine battalions that were partnering with units from the 1st and 7th Iraqi army divisions had a less than sanguine view of the situation. For example, according to Lt. Col. William Jurney, who took command of 1/6 in early 2006, the Iraqi battalions he dealt with were undermanned. Each was supposed to have a troop strength of 850 men, but in reality each had only 500. Moreover, a third of those 500 were on leave at any given time during the month. This was because Iraqi soldiers served twenty-one days per month on duty and nine days on leave and travel.[41] Obviously, this undercut training and operational capacity.

Next, as noted earlier, there was the problem of the makeup of the Iraqi battalions in Anbar. They were largely made up of Shiites, with some Kurds. The thinking behind this decision had to do with the failure of the Iraqi National Guard battalions that were active in Anbar in 2004. They had proven to be ineffective because of their local tribal loyalties and because their families were vulnerable to the insurgents' murder and intimidation tactics.

While Iraqi troops from outside Anbar would not be susceptible to these pressures, bringing in outsiders, especially Shia, caused a set of new problems, beginning with the fact that they were persona non grata in the Sunni Triangle. And while some of these battalions may have reached Level-2 status, in Anbar this made little difference. They were not trusted. Given that their mission was counterinsurgency—living with and among the people—being seen as hostile outsiders was an obvious showstopper in terms of their effectiveness.

The notion that battalions largely comprising non-Sunnis were going to live amongst the people of Anbar and provide them with security was a nonstarter in 2005. Furthermore, the Iraqi forces deployed there understood the risks and generally opted to stay in their forward operating bases. They would take part in Marine and Army clearing operations, but they were not willing, with few exceptions, to attempt to hold those areas once the insurgents were swept out.

Establishing local police forces in Anbar in 2005 proved even more challenging. During the year, Maj. David Barnes was the officer in charge of the Police Partnership Program. In November 2004 all the police in the province were fired because of corruption, incompetence, or connections with elements of the insurgency. Consequently, Major Barnes and his unit started from scratch.

By year's end they had had some success in Fallujah, which was under the control of RCT-8 forces. Having established a process for selection, the Police Partnership Program eventually was able to train and certify 1,200 police officers for Fallujah. It took most of the year to accomplish this. And even though the Marines held the ground in Fallujah, the police were still vulnerable to AQI's violent tactics. Major Barnes explained, "Everything we do is still in a combat-type environment." Therefore, the Marines had to provide protection to the police in Fallujah. He added, "I'd like to get to the point where the police chief can come see me whenever he needs to or wants to, and I can go see him in a soft-skinned vehicle whenever I need to, whenever I want to. And I don't have to look for three Humvee and coordinate it. . . . But we are not there yet."[42]

Elsewhere in Anbar, the situation was much worse, especially in Ramadi and cities west of it. "In the western region of Al Anbar, there is not much police development going on," explained Major Barnes. "It is not the right time to introduce the police in those regions. . . . We still have full-blown combat operations going on."[43]

The Police Partnership Program could not come close to recruiting the number of men needed in Anbar. For that to happen, the sheikhs had to tell their tribesmen to join, in many cases by leaving the insurgency. That would certainly change the balance of forces on the ground in Anbar. But that was not happening in 2005.

CHANGING SIDES: AL QAEDA IN IRAQ MISSTEPS

In the spring and summer of 2005, early signs began to surface indicating that the unnatural insurgent alliance in Anbar was fragmenting. Sheikhs and their tribes were beginning to oppose AQI in the face of its missteps. The active and tacit collaboration among the insurgent factions that existed in 2004 was beginning to come apart. Blunders by Zarqawi and his foreign fighters were fostering a local Sunni backlash. Al Qaeda was squandering its opportunity in Anbar and opening one for the Marines of II MEF to exploit.

In AO Denver the Albu Mahal tribe in Al Qa'im was having more than second thoughts about AQI. Remember that the Albu Mahal initially joined the insurgency in 2004, with tribal members fighting for different insurgent factions. According to reports at that time, "The tribe's support for the insurgency was in large part a move motivated by survival rather than ideological support for any particular insurgent group. With limited coalition and Iraqi government presence in the area, members of the Albu Mahal aligned themselves with Zarqawi's AQI foreign insurgents operating in the area" because of the resources AQI could marshal.[44]

Resistance was not new to the Albu Mahal. It was part of its tribal history. During the 1920 revolt against the British, the tribe refused to accept occupation, attacking British supply lines and isolated garrisons by employing tactics long part of the fighting tradition of the Bedouins who migrated to Iraq from the Arabian Peninsula in the period before Islam took root. Today we would call this way of fighting irregular warfare. It entails hit-and-run tactics and surprise attacks by small units. The Albu Mahal used these same tactics against RCT-7 in 2004.

However, by the spring of 2005, the Albu Mahal was at odds with AQI. Several factors contributed to this fissure. First was AQI's demand for half of the tribe's smuggling profits. That was too much. Business was business, but this was extortion, and it did not go down well with the sheikhs. Likewise, they rejected AQI's goal of establishing a rigid Salafi-style social system similar to what had existed in Afghanistan under Taliban rule. The sheikhs had no desire to live under such a puritanical order. The way AQI fought was also unacceptable to them. Sure, it was killing Marines, but many Albu Mahal died as well in the indiscriminate suicide attacks Zarqawi's fighters favored. When the sheikhs implored AQI to desist, they became targets for assassination. These developments drove the Albu Mahal into the hands of RCT-2. During the fall months, they began cooperating in operations against the AQI. Apparently, CPA Order 91 was no longer the modus operandi in AO Denver. The sheikhs formed an independent militia group called the Desert Protectors to patrol the Syrian border with the Marines. These local tribal fighters provided border security and acted as scouts for Marine forces.

It was an opportunity Washington had rejected earlier. But as the end of 2005 approached, cooperation with the tribes could no longer be ruled out. Pragmatism was replacing the ill-conceived strictures laid down by the CPA and Washington in 2003. The tribes were no longer part of the past. And if the Desert Protectors did not want to deploy out of the Al Qa'im region because they would not be able to protect their tribal members and land, well, that was okay too. There were plenty of AQI fighters coming across the border to keep them gainfully occupied.

Helping facilitate these developments in Al Qa'im in the fall of 2005 were members of the 5th Special Forces Group, who had deployed there as Special Forces Operational Detachment A, or "A Detachments," consisting of twelve Special Forces soldiers: two officers and ten sergeants. Members of the 5th Special Forces Group had been there earlier but were pulled out of Al Anbar to support the development of security forces elsewhere in Iraq.

But by the fall a plan was developed to move Special Forces Operational Detachment A and a company headquarters back out to Al Anbar to establish relationships with local tribes. Initially, three Operational Detachment As were sent to operate in Hit, Haditha, and Al Qa'im. They were to engage tribes that either were resisting or had the potential to resist AQI.

As noted above, in Al Qa'im that was the Albu Mahal. They were actively opposing AQI but not faring so well. Some Special Forces soldiers were inserted in Al Qa'im to make linkups with and recruit the first cohort of what became the Desert Protectors, and to get a list of others that were willing to be recruited and trained. These initial recruits were flown back to Fallujah, where Special Forces and SEALs put them through a couple of weeks of training. From there, that initial group was moved back out to Al Qa'im, where they linked up with Special Forces Operational Detachment A and began to operate with RCT-2. Additional tribesmen were sent to Fallujah for training, and then returned back out to the operational area.

What happened in AO Denver with the Albu Mahal was a harbinger of things to come in Anbar in 2006. Armed tribal militia groups were no longer threats. Rather, they presented opportunities. The Albu Mahal provided paramilitary forces willing to fight AQI and those local insurgent groups still aligned with it. The Desert Protectors also helped control and secure territory. And tribal members provided plenty of local intelligence that the Marines put to good use.

Al Qa'im was an important turning point, but it was not the only one. In Ramadi, AQI's center of gravity, the Albu Fahd, one of the most important tribes of the Dulaym confederation in AO Raleigh, was likewise changing sides by the fall of 2005. Initially this tribe opposed cooperating with the Coalition. The sheikhs saw the United States as an occupier, not a liberator, and found the tactics employed by Coalition forces in Ramadi to be abusive. As a result, the Albu Fahd joined the insurgency.

However, during the latter part of 2005 its sheikhs, and in particular Nasser Abdul Kareem al-Mukhlif, an extremely influential figure in the Ramadi area, were having second thoughts. Highly educated, Sheikh Nassar was a physics professor at Al Anbar University. But because he was a Ba'athist official, he lost his university position as a result of the Coalition's de-Ba'athification program. In 2004 Nassar openly supported the nationalist elements of the insurgency, Zarqawi, and AQI.

Consequently, members of the Albu Fahd joined the 1920 Brigades, the Anuman Brigade, and the Islamic Mujahideen Army to fight the Coalition forces. In 2004, when these nationalist elements were forming up, they looked to Zarqawi for assistance. However, as the insurgency evolved in Ramadi the alliance between the nationalists and AQI began to come apart. It did so for many of the same reasons that led the Albu Mahal to change sides in Al Qa'im.

AQI excesses led Sheikh Nassar to support and take part in meetings in the late fall of 2005 with other tribal heads, leaders of the nationalist elements of the insurgency, Iraqi government officials in Anbar, and the senior officers from II MEF. This was the beginning of what would later turn into Sahawat al-Anbar, or the Anbar Awakening, a coalition of local tribes and former insurgents opposed to AQI's attempt to impose its social order on the province.

In 2008 an al Qaeda lessons learned analysis appeared on the Internet, explaining what went wrong in Iraq. In that document, al Qaeda identified several factors that contributed to its demise in Anbar. Some of those factors were in evidence in

2005; others came later and were part of AQI's wrongheaded attempt to roll back the mounting opposition of Anbar tribal groups by killing sheikhs and declaring its intention to establish an Islamic state of Iraq as the country's sole legitimate ruling authority.

First among those missteps identified in the al Qaeda lessons learned was a "failure to understand the people of Iraq." In Anbar that meant knowing the social and political center of gravity, which comprises the tribes of the Dulaym confederation. Those tribes and their sheikhs are the key social and political units in the governorate. According to the author of the lessons learned document, "It's very important to notice that we can't utilize jihadists' work in any country without analyzing the population's structure and looking deep into their social and religious sentiments. . . . It's impossible for any Jama'ah [group of brothers] to continue jihad and rule if they don't analyze the citizens' structure and know if they will be able to accept the Shari'ah for the long term, and live this life and the after life in this manner."[45]

Such an assessment would have told AQI that the tribes and sheikhs of the Dulaymi confederation were not their natural allies and were not interested in living under a Taliban-type social order; to align with them required judicious engagement and thoughtful collaboration. Consequently, in 2006 when AQI announced its intention of establishing an Islamic state of Iraq modeled on the austere tenets of Salafism, few of the Anbar sheikhs were takers.

Moreover, in Anbar the sheikhs had the power, and it was a big mistake to try to subjugate them through brutal acts of intimidation and murder. They had well-armed tribal militia that they were more than willing to employ to fight back against such tactics. And if AQI managed to kill a sheikh, it laid itself open to tribal revenge, the means for responding to such offenses. Recall that revenge is the duty of all tribesmen; each is willing to risk his life to defend the honor of the tribe by exacting revenge on those who violate tribal honor. Kill a tribal member and "the Arabic rule of five" kicks in: "If you do something to someone, then five of his bloodline will try to attack you."[46] Kill a sheikh and the whole tribe will come after you.

A second lesson noted, "Many foreign fighters had unrealistic expectations of the Iraqi jihad and a sense of moral superiority relative to their Iraqi counterparts, who tended to be less ideologically motivated . . . by tribal, nationalistic, and financial objectives. . . . The differences created deep tensions with local fighters frustrated by the imperious foreigners."[47] This behavior on the part of the foreign fighters revealed that they did not understand that the Sunni tribes of the Dulaym confederation are made up of proud men who demand respect. Contempt for the code of beliefs that guide their ways of doing things was another major mistake.

And a willingness to execute suicide operations with little concern for the local tribal members killed only added to the growing fissures in the insurgency.

In sum, the Albu Mahal and the Albu Fahd were the first of the Anbar tribes to split with AQI. AQI missteps exacerbated and deepened its differences with the tribes, opening the door for the Marines to offer the sheikhs an alternative. In the fall of 2005, meetings between II MEF and several tribal chiefs began exploring that opportunity.

NOVEMBER 2005: ORIGINS OF THE ANBAR AWAKENING

As the divide between the tribal leaders and AQI deepened, the former became increasingly receptive to the prospect of working with Coalition forces in Anbar. As a result, groundbreaking meetings took place in November and December in Ramadi to explore the basis for engagement and partnership.

A key figure facilitating these discussions was the governor of Anbar Province, Mamoon Sami Rashid al-Alwani, a member of the al-Alwani tribe and the Iraqi Islamic Party. In 2004 he was elected to the Provincial Council; subsequently the Council selected him to serve as governor. Mamoon replaced Raja Nawaf Farhan Mahalawi, whom AQI had kidnapped and murdered. Mahalawi's predecessor had resigned after his sons were kidnapped and his home set on fire. Mamoon became one of al Qaeda's prime targets. His home and office were under continual attack, and numerous assassination attempts were made on him as well.

The governor of Anbar Province, Mamoon Sami Rashid al-Alwani.

Montgomery and McWilliams, Eds., *Al-Anbar Awakening*, vol. 2, 150

In September 2005 the governor's twelve-year-old son was kidnapped while at school and held for ransom. According to Brig. Gen. James L. Williams, deputy commanding general of the 2nd Marine Division, Mamoon took an advance on his salary to pay off the kidnappers. He refused to accept money from the Coalition. The governor was lucky. Those holding his son were common criminals and not AQI, and they settled for $6,000; they set his son free the day after the ransom was delivered.

Keeping the governor alive became a strategic objective for the Coalition. He had integrity and the potential to be an important player. The Marine battalion assigned to AO Topeka was given the mission. In the first part of 2005, that was 1/5. Later in the year, the mission belonged to 3/7. A company from each of these battalions guarded Mamoon and his family around the clock. II MEF also provided the governor with an armored car, and when he traveled to Baghdad on business, he had VIP status on Marine helicopters.

In 2005 Governor Mamoon began advocating for dialogue between the sheikhs and the Coalition. He contended that the Anbar tribes should enter into the political process and stop backing the insurgency. In a 2009 interview, Mamoon explained how this unfolded. The first development that made engagement possible was his interaction with the 2nd Marine Division and its assistant division commander, Brig. Gen. James Williams. The two men developed a close working relationship, as each came to trust the other.

According to Mamoon, there were "three main elements in Anbar" that he sought to bring together. "The first [was] the civilian government and it basically had no power. . . . The second element [was] . . . the tribes, which did not want to work with the government." Several of the tribes were working with the insurgents, while the others sought to be neutral. "The third element that played a role here [was] the Marines and the American Army." Mamoon wanted to "start a dialogue" and bring them together. "The first people I was able to win over," he explained, "was the Coalition." Next, with backing from the United States, he sought to "hold conferences . . . in order to win over that second element—the tribes," convincing them to take part.[48]

Mamoon was able to enlist the support of some prominent sheikhs. They saw engagement with the Coalition as a way out from under AQI. One of those sheikhs was Albu Fahd leader Nasser al-Mukhlif, who became a key figure in the November and December conferences hosted by Mamoon and General Williams.

A second catalyst for engagement came from two members of the religious establishment in Anbar. Sheikh Abdullah Jallal Mukhif al-Faraji of the Abu Faraj tribe was the deputy head of the Sunni Endowment for al-Anbar and a member

Brig. Gen. James Williams, Assistant Commanding General, 2d Marine Division in 2005.

McWilliams and Wheeler, Eds., *Al-Anbar Awakening*, vol. 1, 112 of the Ramadi City Council. He supported engagement, as did Dr. Thamer Ibrahim Tahir al-Assafi, head of the Sunni Endowment for Anbar. Dr. Thamer recalled in a 2009 interview how life under AQI gave them little alternative: "The Province of Anbar became so paralyzed. . . . Many fatwas were issued by the terrorists to close the universities. Ramadi became a ghost town. Universities, schools, factories, and institutions all were shut down, so we were oppressed. . . . Life became intolerable. So we started looking for salvation, no matter who it was."[49]

Both Sheikh Abdullah Jallal and Dr. Thamer played vital roles in nurturing the November and December meetings. It was risky business to do so, and each was wounded in one of al Qaeda's attempts to kill the governor. This did not stop them from staying committed to engagement and, as Dr. Thamer explained, "When Sheikh Abdul Sattar Abu Risha proposed the Awakening [in 2006], we looked into it deeper, and we found it to be a really good thing to do. I got Sheikh Abdullah Jallal and we said this is the thing to do. We have to do it. And so we carried on . . . to get rid of the terrorists. The religious establishment started working hand-in-hand with the Awakening. When they liberated a street or a town, we used to go in and open the mosques that were closed by the terrorists."[50]

Governor Mamoon orchestrated the first conference that set this process in motion on November 28. According to Brigadier General Williams, "The 28th meeting, which was pulled together very quickly . . . outdid our greatest expectations. The room was filled. . . . You had a huge number of people in the provincial meeting area. Imams and sheikhs, you had people from Fallujah, and from all around the AO. . . . In fact, Sheikh Kamal Shakir al-Nazal was there representing Fallujah." He was the chairperson of the Fallujah City Council.[51]

The turnout reflected the fact that the sheikhs understood they were losing power to AQI, and without help from the Coalition their demise was all but assured. Likewise, the nationalist insurgent leaders understood they were between a rock and a hard place. They were losing control of the insurgency to AQI, and the Marines were inflicting serious losses on their forces. As General Williams put it, each wanted to know "how do we stop your guys from blowing our guys up. . . . So with that as backdrop, the November 28th meeting . . . was pulled together."[52]

It was on that November day in 2005 that the three main elements in Anbar that Governor Mamoon sought to bring together—the civilian government, the tribes that were part of the insurgency and those that were neutral, and the U.S. military (Marines and Army)—began a process that would culminate by the summer of 2007 in the strategic defeat of AQI in Anbar.

November 28 led to another session on December 12. This second session was made up of fourteen individuals selected by the original two hundred sheikhs, imams, and insurgent leaders at the initial session. These individuals became, in effect, a security advisory group to the governor and the Coalition. The focus was on what kind of security force to establish in Anbar and what its relationship to the Coalition would be. As we will see, the key force in that discussion—the police—served as the foundation for taking control of the ground in the province in 2006–2007.

The significance of these early meetings, as well as the decision by tribal and political leaders in Anbar to stipulate that the population vote in the upcoming elections, was not lost on Zarqawi and AQI. These developments could mushroom and turn Anbar into a serious threat to their survival. Without control over the tribes and their leaders, al Qaeda would not be able to operate clandestinely. If the tribes went over to the side of the Coalition, they could send thousands of their militia to fight side by side with Coalition forces. Moreover, every tribal member would become a potential source of intelligence on AQI activities and hiding places. Preventing this from taking place was fundamental to survival. Zarqawi, as one sheikh explained at the time, intended to demonstrate that his "fist is stronger than the Americans'," and that the Coalition could not protect them.[53]

Zarqawi focused his counterattack on the sheikhs and the governor. He intended to kill as many as he could. Brigadier General Williams estimates that there were more than thirty attempts to assassinate Mamoon. In mid-January 2006 Sheikh Nasser al-Mukhlif, shortly after taking part in a tribal leaders' meeting with the Iraqi prime minister and the U.S. ambassador, was murdered by Zarqawi assassins. In early February 2006 Sheikh Kamal Shakir al-Nazal suffered the same fate. Then the chairperson of the Fallujah city council was gunned down by men in two passing cars as he was walking to work. This was only the beginning; several other sheikhs were to follow these men to their deaths.

2005 ELECTIONS

The election on January 30 was the first of two parliamentary elections in Iraq in 2005. A constitutional referendum would also take place, in October. In the first of these three exercises to choose 275 representatives for the transitional Iraqi National Assembly the Sunni population of Anbar stayed home. The major Sunni parties, including the Association of Muslim Scholars and the Iraqi Islamic Party, boycotted the elections, ostensibly because of AQI's threatened violence. Zarqawi declared a "fierce war" against all "apostates" who voted in the election. He labeled candidates running for election "demi-idols," and those planning to vote "infidels." Democracy was nothing short of "heresy" and "against the rule of God."[54] However, this was not the only reason for boycotting, or even the primary reason. The Sunni parties viewed the entire process as biased and against their interest. Why should they encourage voting and give the election credibility? By staying home they were voting against the developing political process.

However, by the fall of 2005, Sunni attitudes in Anbar toward the political process were in transition. On October 15 the Iraqi electorate went to the polls to vote on the new constitution drafted by the 275-member transitional Iraqi National Assembly, as detailed at the beginning of this chapter. That draft document passed by a wide margin—nearly 80 percent were in favor of it. This time more than a quarter of a million Sunnis in Anbar voted, a majority of those who were eligible at the time. Ramadi, however, remained problematic, and the city's main polling areas closed shortly after opening because several voters had been murdered. Of the people voting in Anbar, 96 percent rejected the constitution. It was another strong vote against the political process that was unfolding in Baghdad.

Nevertheless, province leaders agreed to continue discussing whether to encourage Sunni participation in the December election in order to gain representation in the new national assembly. Zarqawi's heinous threats notwithstanding, as the sheikhs moved toward engagement with the Coalition they likewise decided to encourage the population in Anbar to take part in the December election. Change was coming to the province.

To ensure that the people of Anbar had the opportunity to vote in December, Marine and Army forces continued to execute Operation Liberty Express, which the 2nd Marine Division had initiated to provide security for polling sites across Al Anbar during the constitutional referendum. That had worked well, except in Ramadi. This time around, II MEF intended to secure the capital of Anbar as well so that its citizens could vote. To this end, the forces of II MEF carried out a robust and enduring campaign against the insurgents to put them back on their heels. The objective was to cause the insurgents to concentrate on their own security rather than to disrupt the security Marines and soldiers were putting in place so the population of Anbar could vote in safe conditions.

On December 15 general parliamentary elections took place to select a new 275-member Iraqi Council of Representatives that would serve for four years. The turnout countrywide was high, with an estimated 12 million Iraqis—75 percent of the electorate—voting.

In Anbar the Sunnis turned out in such high numbers that additional ballots had to be rushed in by the Coalition. Even in Ramadi, where insurgent violence had kept all but a few from voting in the October referendum, long lines formed outside polling centers this time. According to Brigadier General Williams, "Between Fallujah and Ramadi you had great turnouts, and overall in the western Euphrates you had roughly 80 percent turnout."[55] According to the International Mission for Iraqi Elections, it was higher.[56] Of the 667,321 registered voters in Anbar, 585,429,

142 | CHAPTER 4

Iraqi citizens voting in Husaybah during the December 15, 2005 election

ESTES, *INTO THE FRAY*, 126

or 87.7 percent, voted. This was a dramatic change from the January election, and it exceeded the October vote as well.

The Sunnis ignored Zarqawi's intimidation and violence aimed at them and entered the political process. The Sunni bloc—Iraqi National Accord Front—won approximately 40 seats in the Iraqi Council of Representatives. Three parties composed the National Accord Front: the General Council for the People of Iraq, the Iraqi Islamic Party, and the Iraqi National Dialogue Council. The largest political bloc, with eighty-five seats, was the United Iraq Alliance, which included the Shia Islamic Supreme Council of Iraq and Islamic Dawa Party, and the second largest was the Democratic Patriotic Alliance of Kurdistan, with fifty-three representatives. Still, the Sunnis had managed to come in a respectable third. More important, this was yet another indicator that the political context in Anbar and the Sunni Triangle was changing.

GAINING GROUND

As 2005 came to an end, Al Anbar was in the throes of transition, although many observers of the war at that time were not aware of it or the implications it would have for AQI's hold on the province. Observers viewed Anbar through the lens of escalating violence, and their perceptions were colored by the brutal fighting the Marines had conducted during the year. As depicted here, those engagements were of a considerable number, and the insurgents had responded in kind.

Recall Operation Sayeed. It consisted of eleven named operations that sought to drive al Qaeda from the western Euphrates River valley, eliminating that region as a place where they could hole up and operate freely. During the second half of 2005, Sayeed encompassed three thousand individual actions initiated either by II MEF or by the insurgents. As was the case during 2004 for I MEF, the forces of II MEF could clear the insurgents out of one area after another, but once they had done so, they did not have the number of forces necessary to hold that ground. They were still locked in whack-a-mole.

Like its predecessor, II MEF needed more forces—more boots on the ground. But where was it going to find them? They were not likely to come from the eighteen battalions of the 1st and 7th divisions of the Iraqi army, which General Casey's 2005 campaign plan—"Partnership: From Occupation to Constitutional Elections"—had earmarked for Anbar. Deploying them to Anbar was problematic because they were largely Shia. Those Iraqi army units were deeply distrusted, and were persona non grata in the heartland of the Sunnis.

The sheikhs were not about to put their security or that of their tribes in the hands of Shia-dominated battalions. However, those engaged in the talks brokered by Governor Mamoon in November and December had an alternative in mind—grassroots Sunni security forces drawn from the tribes of the Dulaym tribal confederation. This was an opportunity that I MEF would exploit in 2006.

CHAPTER 5

2006

The Tipping Point

SITUATION REPORT SPRING 2006: SURGING VIOLENCE AND GRIM PROGNOSES

A SITREP, or SITUATION REPORT, for Anbar Province as 2006 devolved from the spring into the early summer months would have had the following bottom line: surging violence and grim prognoses. At least that was the overwhelming conventional wisdom at the time. Enemy violence was skyrocketing, while almost every prediction for any U.S. success in Anbar was spiraling downward. An account is given later in this chapter of how even I MEF's most senior intelligence officer bleakly concluded in August and again in November that Anbar was near to being lost. And worse, there was little I MEF could do to reverse that decline.

At the epicenter of this deteriorating state of affairs was Ramadi, the capital of Anbar. By 2006 it had assumed the moniker "the most dangerous city in Iraq." And with good reason. AQI had taken charge of Anbar's first city. Having been driven from its Fallujah stronghold in November–December 2004 by Operation Al Fajr, it relocated to Ramadi. By 2006 AQI had taken over the city, declaring Ramadi the capital of its new Islamic caliphate. For all intents and purposes, the only ground the Marines held there was the Government Center, and that was under enemy attack day and night. The rest of Ramadi belonged to AQI.

Consider how one embedded reporter from *Time* magazine, Michael Ware, described the perils Marines faced in May 2006 as they ventured into the city on combat patrols. Ware went outside the wire on a "sweltering afternoon" with one of the platoons of Kilo Company, 3/8. As the patrol moved out, 1st Lt. Grier Jones "splits his 30-odd-man platoon into two squads and sets them loose on the streets of Ramadi. They run block to block, covering one another as they sprint across intersections." At one such junction, "the Marines duck into a house. Suddenly a machine gun lets rip, spewing bullets around them." It became very intense very fast as Jones sent "his men to the roof to repel the two-sided attack." Once on top he directed them to fire an AT4 rocket at one of the two enemy positions, and the shooting from that area abruptly stopped.[1]

Then, as Lieutenant Jones "peers over a cement wall to locate the second ambush position a 7.62-mm round whizzes by. 'Whoa, that went right over my head,' he says, smiling. As the Marines on the roof fire at the insurgents, Jones orders a squad to push toward the enemy position." They quickly do so, and "the enemy weapons go quiet; the insurgents are apparently withdrawing to conserve their energy."[2]

For Ware it was a harrowing experience. But for the Marines of Kilo Company, said Lieutenant Jones, "This is every day in Ramadi." Having spent a week with them, the embedded reporter from *Time* concluded, "There's no reason to believe that the Americans' battle against Iraqi insurgents is going to get better [in Ramadi]."[3]

In fact, the intensity of the fight in Anbar's capital was only going to get worse. By summer the number of attacks there was higher than in any other place in Iraq, including Baghdad. AQI exercised its authority with great brutality and ruthlessness.

Moreover, Ramadi was not the only place that AQI redeployed to following Al Fajr. Five other major towns up the Euphrates corridor—Hit, Haditha, Anah, Rawah, and Al Qa'im—likewise had a robust AQI presence. Each of these places "witnessed particularly heavy clashes resulting in the deaths of hundreds of local citizens and the destruction of thousands of shops, schools, houses and government buildings." At least that's what the UN Office for the Coordination of Humanitarian Affairs reported in IRIN, its humanitarian news service.[4]

Titled "Iraq: Anbar Province Plagued by Violence," the IRIN report provided the following particulars: Anbar "has witnessed more fighting and killing than any of Iraq's 18 provinces. . . . While US forces flushed out . . . insurgent groups there in military operations in 2004 and 2005, [they] have returned and escalating violence has prevented NGOs and aid agencies from reaching people who desperately need food and medical supplies."[5] Moreover, as Muhammad Rabia'a, media officer for Anbar Province Council in Ramadi, put it, "the return of insurgents" resulted in an "increase in the number of [people internally] displaced as a result of sectarian violence."[6]

Those who collect statistics added further confirmation of this gloomy state of affairs. In January 2006 there were approximately 2,000 insurgent attacks per month in Iraq's eighteen provinces. In October that number was nearly 5,500.[7] Anbar, one of those eighteen provinces, accounted for nearly 1,400 of those 5,500 acts of violence. This was higher than in Baghdad, which has a population five to six times bigger.[8]

That was the situation in October 2006. But on September 6, 2007, an event occurred in Ramadi that would have been beyond the wildest of imaginations a year earlier. The mayor of the capital, Latif Obaid, gave the signal for the start of what had been up to 2002 the city's annual five-kilometer (5K) road race. Runners were going to compete once more on a course that winds through the streets of Ramadi, ending at the Government Center. In less than twelve months, Ramadi had transformed from being the most dangerous city in Iraq to one safe enough for its city fathers to sponsor a 5K race.

How did such a transformation take place? What happened? The runners for that 5K race in the photo are seen gathering for the start of the September 2007 event. If they had done so a year earlier those runners would have been lucky to make it off the starting line before AQI shot many of them dead. And to be sure, the mayor would have suffered the same fate.

Runners prepare for the start of the Ramadi 5K race in September 2007.

HTTP://EN.WIKIPEDIA.ORG/WIKI/FILE:RAMADI_5K_RUN.JPG, BLUEMARINE 2007

This remarkable turn of events came about because of the course of action initiated by I MEF as it took over the Anbar AO. In the spring of 2006, it changed the concept of operations for the fight against AQI and the insurgency.

MURDER AND INTIMIDATION: THE WINTER OF 2006

It was not going to be easy to reestablish security to levels where events such as the 5K race in Ramadi would once again be feasible. Opportunities for doing so were not always discernible to U.S. military commanders and civilian leaders, and even when they were perceivable, it was not always possible to exploit them.

The situation in Anbar was highly fluid. As chapter 4 made clear, the insurgent alliance was fragmenting. Tribal sheikhs who had either been part of the insurgency or given tacit support to it began changing sides, in a process that came to be referred to as "flipping" by the Marines and soldiers who observed it up close in late 2005 and 2006. As became clear over the course of 2006, flipping had strategic implications for the fight in Anbar.

One of the Marines in Anbar during this time was Maj. Alfred B. Connable. He arrived in Anbar in December 2005 and was assigned to the MEF's intelligence shop as a senior analyst and fusion officer. Connable recalled, "At the end of 2005 . . . you had a very senior, a very well-respected tribal leader who had insurgent credentials . . . [who] had gotten sick of all the violence, and I think he saw that we weren't going to be making any progress on our own." That sheikh was Nasser Abd al-Karim Mukhlif al-Fahdawi of the Albu Fahd tribe, and "he had decided it was time to fight al Qaeda." The sheikh's tribesmen live throughout the Ramadi area.[9]

According to Connable, Sheikh Nasser "was in direct contact with a senior insurgent leader with the 1920 Revolution Brigade." In fact, said the major, he may well have been a "leader of the 1920 Revolution Brigade [himself] . . . the most effective, most well known nationalist insurgent organization operating out of Anbar Province."[10] Recall that in November 2005 Sheikh Nasser and other sheikhs met with Marine officers to explore the conditions for cooperation. As a result, Nasser backed both Sunni participation in the December 2005 elections and formation of the Anbar People's Committee. The Albu Fahd chief also sent his tribal militiamen to join the Ramadi police.

Al Qaeda was well aware of the dangers these developments posed for its survival. If the ranks of the police came to be filled with local tribesmen, its fighters would no longer be able to hide in plain sight. The local population knew who they were and where they were holing up. If the locals started fingering them, feeding that information to the police and U.S. military, AQI would quickly find itself out of business in Ramadi. To stop that from happening, AQI head Abu Mus'ab al-Zarqawi sent a suicide bomber into the midst of a police recruiting drive at the Ramadi Glass Factory on January 5, 2006. Sixty recruits from the Albu Fahd were blown to pieces on that day.

Sheikh Nasser was furious and in response organized a meeting (*majlis*) with Prime Minister Ibrahim al-Jafari and U.S. Ambassador Zalmay Khalilzad in Baghdad. Jafari was not keen on the idea of recruiting Sunni tribesmen into local police forces that Baghdad did not control. For him this amounted to reconstituting Ba'athist security forces. But Khalilzad had a different view of Sunni tribal engagement: it was an opportunity, if managed properly.

After he left government, Khalilzad wrote about what he had in mind for situations like Anbar in a paper, "Political Capabilities to Stabilize Fragile or Post-Conflict States." In it Khalilzad argued that in such settings U.S. political and military advisers must be able to "take a 'hands-on' approach in shaping the local political context. This mediation and shaping role should seek *not* to impose American-made solutions but rather to use U.S. influence to help local leaders agree on local solutions to local challenges." In Anbar this meant tribal engagement. The ambassador added that the United States "must develop cadres of officials and officers with deep area expertise and a talent for political action to shape the orientation and conduct of local leaders and communities."[11]

This is what Khalilzad was trying to do with Jafari, Nasser, and the other sheikhs assembled in the prime minister's office on January 15, 2006. And this time Jafari budged and agreed that local tribesmen could be recruited into the

Ramadi police to help U.S. forces drive al Qaeda out of Anbar's capital. Nasser and his associates were ready to do this, recalled Connable: "The fact that a guy like [the paramount sheikh] of the Albu Fahad [*sic*] is going to turn against AQI reflects . . . that there was a broader grassroots discontent with al Qaeda. . . . So, if you're an Anbari at the end of 2005 and you're being intimidated by these guys, robbed blind by them, and you don't see . . . any value in their message, you don't have much motivation to support them or at some point to even put up with them."[12]

The very next day Sheikh Nasser and his brother were gunned down by al Qaeda assassins. A source inside the Albu Fahd, who also was said to be "a member of al Qaeda," said the sheikh had become "too sympathetic towards the United States." Therefore, "he was a traitor who deserved to be killed."[13] This was the start of a fierce counterattack by AQI to stop tribal engagement in its tracks.

According to Major Connable, "Very quickly . . . the attack levels started to rise and within weeks I think 50 percent of the Anbar People's Committee leaders had been assassinated. . . . That was the point where it all started to fall apart, and by the middle of February, early March, attack levels had risen dramatically."[14]

The chief of the MEF's intelligence shop and Connable's boss in 2006 was Col. Pete Devlin. Al Qaeda was not about to let these sheikhs get in its way, he explained in January 2007. It intended to "stop at nothing . . . absolutely nothing, including violating well-accepted tenets of Islam." Al Qaeda saw itself "above . . . these restrictions," said Devlin, "to save the faith." In this way, he explained, the members were "rationalizing away their horrific behavior. How else can you live with yourself after you sawed a guy's head off?"[15]

According to Maj. Gen. Tariq Yusif Mohammad al-Thiyabi, who would become the provincial director of the police in Anbar, the level of violence unleashed by Zarqawi was ferocious. As a result, in 2006 he aligned with those opposing al Qaeda in Anbar and started to help reestablish the police.

Looking back on those violent days when that opposition began surfacing, General Tariq recalled the bloody particulars of how al Qaeda used terror to keep an iron grip on the province. "To exercise control even further, they started beheading and slaughtering and killing people. For them, to kill a person with a pistol is normal. But to slaughter someone, to behead someone in front of other people—it's a monstrous scene that is supposed to terrorize people. . . . [al Qaeda] started killing officers—high-level officers—tribal leaders, former police officers. Any person that was part of establishing the police was killed. If they didn't find the police officer, they killed his relatives—his father or his brother or his next of kin. That's why they were able to control all the areas [of Anbar]. It reached a level where they were able to walk down the streets in the neighborhoods without even being armed."[16]

Al Qaeda "overstepped all the red lines," said General Tariq. And it was effective. "There was a sense of revolt, but because of fear people could not revolt. It got to the point where three or four or five people could not gather together and talk against these so-called mujahideen, because you're exposing yourself to death if you did that. . . . They were able to control all the areas. Nobody could open his mouth."[17]

In the spring months of 2006 Zarqawi's bloody rampage of murder and intimidation was achieving its desired end. In the capital, AQI was in control, enforcing its code of austere social conduct with a vengeance. The university was shut down, and Internet cafés and other businesses were branded as heretical and were closed. Consequently, cooperation between the tribal sheikhs and U.S. forces in Anbar declined precipitously. Terror was working.

Maj. Gen. Tariq Yusif Mohammad al-Thiyabi, Anbar's Provincial Director of Police

MONTGOMERY AND MCWILLIAMS, EDS., AL-ANBAR AWAKENING, VOL. 2, 178

WAR AMONG THE PEOPLE

Gen. Rupert Smith, former deputy supreme Allied commander Europe (deputy Supreme Allied Commander Europe [SACEUR]), spent forty years in the British Army, retiring in 2002. Nearly three decades of that service was during the Cold War, focused on preparing to fight twentieth-century interstate industrialized war. But in its aftermath, he dealt with conflicts that diverged considerably from that twentieth-century standard—in Northern Ireland, Bosnia, and Kosovo. And in retirement the general watched men he had commanded go off to fight irregular wars in Iraq and Afghanistan. These likewise were very different.

In 2007, to capture those differences, Gen. Rupert Smith wrote *The Utility of Force: The Art of War in the Modern Age*. In this book he asserted, "It is now time to recognize that a paradigm shift in war has undoubtedly occurred: from armies with comparable forces doing battle to a strategic confrontation between a range of combatants . . . using different types of weapons, often improvised. The old paradigm was that of interstate industrialized war. The new one is the paradigm of war amongst the people. . . . [It] can take place anywhere: in the presence of civilians, against civilians, in defense of civilians."[18]

Driving that change was the post–Cold War context in which conflict was taking place. It was marked by a proliferation of weak and failing states that increasingly were unable to control all their territory, maintain a monopoly over the instruments of force, and perform core functions of government, beginning with providing security to their people.

Various kinds of armed groups often spring from weak and failing states, including insurgents, terrorists, militias, and criminal organizations, which exploit the many opportunities created by the chaotic circumstances.[19] When armed groups become empowered, they are able to influence the security and stability of a state in fundamental ways.

To achieve their objectives, armed groups wage irregular warfare, or war amongst the people. There is no official beginning or end of such war. It is not fought on battlefields between armies. It uses nontraditional tactics—from assassinations and roadside bombs and suicide attacks to bribery and propaganda in the media—to slowly gain power over territory and populations. War amongst the people takes place in diverse locations including streets, neighborhoods, villages, websites, schools, and on television.

The interplay between weak states and armed groups can be seen in many parts of the world, including post-Saddam Iraq. Following the March 2003 invasion of Iraq, these actors came together to foster a complex, protracted, irregular war that, as highlighted earlier, the United States neither anticipated nor was prepared to fight.[20]

The regime under Saddam was a police state. With its demise Iraq quickly devolved into a weak state where the central government in Baghdad had neither the legitimacy nor the power to control the state's diverse regions. And the United States had too few troops and the wrong doctrine to step into the vacuum. Chaos, internal conflict, and societal breakdown ensued, as armed groups proliferated. Recall that this was the situation I MEF encountered when it arrived in Anbar in March 2004.[21]

According to General Smith, how states fight war amongst the people, or irregular war, has to be different, and in fundamental ways. This is population-centric warfare, and mastering it will necessitate institutional change in the military's conventional approach to operations. Killing insurgent fighters until there were no more left to kill was not the solution. You cannot kill your way out of such wars. New operational concepts and military means for carrying them out are needed to manage irregular conflicts. That said, explained the general, new concepts of operations will, in one form or another, have as their core element establishing stability and security for the population.

The bottom line for the former deputy SACEUR was providing security to the population and protecting it from armed groups; this is the first order of business in war amongst the people. Military forces create the conditions—they set the table—so that civil tasks can be carried out. Much of what Rupert Smith wrote about in his 2006 book, *The Utility of Force*, I MEF implemented in Anbar in 2006. Anbar was population-centric warfare—war amongst the people—and the operational concepts for it are anchored in counterinsurgency doctrine.

COUNTERINSURGENCY RENAISSANCE

Military failure in war has a long history. Clausewitz, in his classic *On War*, said to expect it. Ugly surprises and awful miscalculations are common occurrences running through the annals of wartime calamity.[22] Some armies learn, adapt, and reverse misfortune. However, in war's chronicles, those that do so are more often the exception than the norm. The U.S. Army and Marine Corps in Iraq in the period 2006–2008 are two of those exceptions. In each case soldiers and Marines learned, retooled, and overcame the grim setbacks of 2004–2005. The first to do so was I MEF in Anbar, followed by the Army in greater Baghdad. They altered, in fundamental ways, how they were fighting. And at the center of that sea change was counterinsurgency doctrine.

Counterinsurgency (COIN) doctrine had been out of favor in the U.S. military since the Vietnam War ended. This was certainly true for the Army, wrote John Nagl, one of a handful of Army officers in the decade preceding OIF who paid attention to it. But the Army was not interested in COIN in those years. It "goes back to the Army's unwillingness to internalize and build on the lessons of Vietnam," said then–Lieutenant Colonel Nagl.[23] The Army's mantra once it was extricated from that disastrous war by the Nixon administration was, "No more Vietnams." Consequently, no lessons were deduced from the Vietnam experience.[24]

In the late 1970s the Army concentrated on its long-standing mission—state-centric conventional war with the Soviet Union. And conventional war preparation continued to predominate even after that country disappeared. Operation Desert Storm confirmed the centrality of conventional warfare, and the Army spent the remainder of the 1990s straight through to the execution of OIF in 2003 priming itself for future Desert Storms. Consequently, writes Nagl, the "American Army of 2003 [found itself] unprepared for an enemy who . . . chose to wage war against America in the shadows."[25]

The Marine Corps of the 1990s had a different view, at least in part. The Corps' commandant in the last years of the twentieth century, Gen. Chuck Krulak, argued that war in the future would be very different from Desert Storm. In an often repeated speech entitled "Not Like Yesterday," Krulak warned that such conventional thinking could lead to military misfortunes for the United States.[26]

War was changing. The sources of conflict, wrote General Krulak, were the result of "the disintegration of the Soviet republics and Yugoslavia, the tragedies in Somalia and Rwanda, and the conflict in Liberia." Those and other similar clashes all pointed to a recurring trend.[27]

Conflicts the United States would fight in the years ahead would not be the "son of Desert Storm," warned the commandant. Rather, they would be "the stepchild of Chechnya. Our most dangerous enemy will . . . challenge us asymmetrically in ways against which we are least able to bring strength to bear—as we witnessed in the slums of Mogadishu. Moreover, as demonstrated in the recent bombing of our east African embassies [in Kenya and Tanzania], they will not limit aggression to our military."[28] The commandant proved prescient. But he was out of step with the conventional mindset of the other Joint Chiefs of Staff (JCS) and their services. Krulak said the United States had to get ready to fight three-block wars against armed groups who would use unconventional and irregular means to attack. His JCS counterparts did not concur.

The conflicts foreseen by General Krulak ballooned following 9/11, and the Marine Corps found itself mired in one of them in bloody Anbar. Elsewhere in Iraq the Army was likewise jammed up in nasty irregular fights. A new approach—a new doctrine—was badly needed. To meet that urgent requirement, Army Gen. David Petraeus, with the help of his Marine Corps counterpart, Gen. Jim Mattis, initiated a counterinsurgency renaissance. It would culminate in the much-extolled field manual *The U.S. Army/Marine Corps Counterinsurgency Field Manual* (or *FM 3-24*).[29]

The story of how General Petraeus shouldered that effort is well known.[30] A warrior and an intellectual with a doctorate in international relations, Petraeus took command of the Army's Combined Arms Center in late 2005; the Center plays a key role in the Army's doctrinal development. When Petraeus arrived he put counterinsurgency "front and center" for the Center. "The Army had not published a field manual on the subject . . . for more than twenty years." Petraeus intended to remedy that quickly so the new field manual could be used in Iraq. To do so, he "called on the expertise of both academics and Army and Marine Corps veterans of the conflicts in Afghanistan and Iraq." In December 2005 they outlined "the manual as a whole and the principles, imperatives, and paradoxes of counterinsurgency" that would frame the new doctrine.[31]

This was followed by revision after revision, stretching from the spring into the late fall months. During the summer Petraeus lost his Marine partner, Jim Mattis. He was replaced by Lt. Gen. James Amos. Mattis took charge of I MEF, a major element of which was already deployed in Anbar. Under the command of Maj. Gen. Richard Zilmer, I MEF (Forward) had arrived back in the Sunni heartland in March.

In preparing *FM 3-24* the Petraeus team returned to the COIN classics of the 1960s for key precepts. What they found was Rupert Smith's bottom line—providing security to the population and protecting it from armed groups is the first order of operational business in counterinsurgency warfare. You will accomplish nothing else if you do not achieve this first. Kalev Sepp, senior lecturer in defense analysis at the U.S. Naval Postgraduate School in Monterey, California, studied more than fifty twentieth-century insurgencies. He found the same thing. COIN's best practices start with population security. Only after government forces "secure a neighborhood, village, township, or infrastructure facility from terrorist insurgent activity" can the government "apply resources to expand the secure area" and establish its legitimacy with the population.[32]

The COIN legends from the 1960s all said the same thing. In preparing *FM 3-24,* Petraeus' team paid close attention to one of these legends—David Galula. A French military officer, he had learned his Mao Tse-tung up close. Serving as an assistant military attaché in China from 1945 to 1948, he watched as the Chinese Communists employed protracted insurgent strategy to sweep the nationalists from power in 1949. Galula then learned the art of counterinsurgency on the ground in Algeria in the late 1950s.

These experiences were captured in his 1964 book, *Counterinsurgency Warfare: Theory and Practice.*[33] In it, he concluded that securing and gaining support of the populace was the primary goal of any COIN campaign. But to have a shot at that goal, you first had to detach the people from the insurgents. Only then can a government carry out those social and political programs that win it legitimacy. The French were not the only COIN experts in the 1960s to discover this central premise: the British did so as well.[34] Americans likewise produced important treatises similar to that of Galula.[35]

Petraeus' team had *FM 3-24* completed and ready for release on December 15, 2006. "It was downloaded more than 1.5 million times in the first month after its posting," according to Nagl. And, he added, it was "widely reviewed, including by several Jihadi Web sites."[36] There is no question that it is a highly sophisticated piece of work. No other field manual is comparable. It was even published by the University of Chicago Press.[37]

In February 2007 Petraeus succeeded Gen. George Casey as commanding general of MNF-I. He announced that his new strategy would be drawn from the recently completed *FM 3-24*. But I MEF had started employing counterinsurgency principles well before the manual had reached completion. As General Zilmer was taking I MEF (Forward) back to Anbar in March, his staff was devising an OPLAN based on COIN precepts. And by the time Petraeus took command in February, the execution of that plan was making a big difference on the ground in Anbar.

A COUNTERINSURGENCY-BASED OPERATIONAL PLAN

When Major General Zilmer took I MEF back to Iraq, changing command with II MEF on February 28, 2006, it was I MEF's third deployment in support of OIF. Combat losses for I and II MEF since the first deployment of Marines to Anbar in March 2004 "now totaled 5,541 (500 killed in action and 5,041 wounded)."[38] Zilmer had no reason to believe Anbar was going to be any less violent this time around.

However, he intended to take a different approach to that violent province, one that if successful could drive those casualty rates down. I MEF (Forward), said its commanding general, was going to "lead in the counterinsurgency fight in Anbar."[39]

What that meant, said his deputy, Brig. Gen. Robert Neller, was focusing on population control and population security. "One could make the argument that . . . this fight is for population control, and that we want to have control so that we can provide security for the population." We intended to "keep the insurgents out, keep the good people in, and be able to provide them with a secure environment so that they're confident in the security forces, and [will] tell us when the bad guys move in on them."[40]

A year earlier II MEF also had planned to carry out a COIN effort. But a shortage of forces undermined that endeavor. It could clear the insurgents from area after area, and did. But it could not hold, let alone build.

I MEF was going to do all three. "Clear, hold, build," said Neller. And I MEF was going to do so methodically, using the oil spot approach, another one of those COIN tenets from the 1960s. The counterinsurgent forces concentrate on a specific area, take control of it, secure the population, and then expand that secured zone outward. It is not a complicated concept. But implementing it is another matter. How Zilmer and Neller intended to carry it off was spelled out in I MEF's OPLAN for 2006.[41]

To begin, recalled Zilmer, the OPLAN called for I MEF "to make as many police as we could possibly make, to train them properly . . . and [also] to increase the size and the capability of the Iraqi army."[42] Neller added that before I MEF deployed to Anbar, its planning staff produced a "mission statement that said our task was to focus on development of the Iraqi security forces and conduct counterinsurgency operations. We felt that our success was going to be our ability to develop Iraqi security forces." Having done so, I MEF would "transfer increasing levels of responsibility to them and that would permit us to reposition our forces into those areas where we had not yet been able to hold ground."[43]

Those 1960s counterinsurgency classics all stressed the critical importance of recruiting and employing local police. And in the fifty-odd cases Sepp reviewed,

Maj. Gen. Richard Zilmer, Governor Mamoon Sami Rashid al-Alwani, and Col. Sean MacFarland are pictured at the Government Center in Ramadi in 2006.
COURTESY OF SEAN MACFARLAND

he likewise found that police were a key element in successful COIN campaigns. Here's why. Police "intelligence operations that help detect terrorist insurgents for arrest and prosecution are the single most important practice to protect a population from threats to its security." And "honest, trained, robust police forces . . . can gather that intelligence at the community level," if the people trust them.[44]

But II MEF had tried this in 2005 and was able to recruit only a handful of police. And those they recruited could hardly protect themselves, let alone the population. Recruiting Anbari citizens into the ranks of local police forces had been an exercise in futility. Clearing an area of insurgents, reestablishing a police force, and then moving on had not worked for II MEF. As soon as the Marines left, the insurgents returned and made short work of the local police. Zilmer, Neller, and their planning staff knew they had to make adjustments.

To successfully recruit local police it is necessary to both clear and hold the areas that they are expected to oversee. Once this has been taken care of, those local police elements can be protected from major insurgent counterattacks. This provides them with the security they need to carry out their local policing mission. I MEF's planning staff, said Major Connable, understood the logic of this basic COIN sequence. And they picked Anbar's most dangerous city—Ramadi—as the place to start implementing it.

"Zilmer realized that we needed to secure Ramadi," recounted Connable. At the "end of March, early April he organized an operational planning team . . . to come up with a plan. . . . For about a month, a group of us put together a . . . very detailed plan to secure the provincial capital." That design called for securing parts of the city before seeking to engage the tribes in the COIN process. Connable explained why:

"We realized at that point in time the tribes were not ready. . . . The Ramadi Glass Factory bombing on January 5th set the tone for recruiting." The message from AQI was unambiguous to any aspiring recruits. As for the sheikhs, the message was the same. The murder and intimidation campaign set the tone for them as well.[45]

Zilmer's planning team surveyed the city with overhead imagery to determine where to put each check point, each police station, and, most important, each combat outpost (COP) that would station I MEF forces in Ramadi on a 24/7 basis. That is how they would start to secure the ground in the city, and from there to spread outward. "We had a . . . very methodical plan to build oil spot zones of security and build out from there," summed up Connable.[46]

This was the starting point, and it had to precede tribal engagement. Take the ground and demonstrate to the sheikhs and tribes that you intended to stay on it. That was the signal they were looking for. The sheikhs would work against AQI, as some of them had already demonstrated. But they needed I MEF to secure their flanks and cover their backs. According to Neller, "There is much talk about 'clear, hold, and build' as a methodology for COIN operations. You cannot perform these tasks if you don't stay in an area and establish a presence and, more importantly, a relationship with the people."[47]

Establishing security for the population was the table setter for COIN operations in Anbar. It "creates the opportunities," said General Neller, "for real progress in the critical economic and governance lines of operations."[48] This was the foundation of the OPLAN that I MEF's planning staff devised in the spring of 2006. Establish and maintain presence among the people of Anbar, be they in Ramadi, in other cities and towns running along the Euphrates all the way up to Al Qa'im, or in less-populated villages. Do that and the door to tribal engagement with the sheikhs will swing wide open.

And if those sheikhs gave a nod and a wink, men from their tribal militias could easily fill the ranks of the local police. Reviving the police required "a strong buy-in from the tribal sheikhs," explained Zilmer in early 2007. "The most important social custom . . . for the Anbar people is that tribal-sheikh relationship. . . . We had to learn that."[49]

And to learn how it worked meant following the kinds of culturally based operational do's and don'ts described earlier. They constituted the indispensable starting point from which to build a tribal engagement strategy. I MEF had to be able to work with those tribal leaders—the sheikhs—even though they did not conform to modern Western conceptions of leadership as manifested in the U.S. Marine Corps.

To effectively engage the sheikhs meant learning, accepting, and, to the extent possible, embracing the code of values and beliefs that guide their behavior and ways of doing things. In effect, Marines and soldiers had to shift their way of doing business, said the commanding general of I MEF (Forward). "We recognized that dealing in a counterinsurgency in the Middle East or in the Arab world requires a fundamental understanding of their culture.... We spent a lot of effort to get our Marines sensitive to that." General Zilmer elaborated that there is "a certain style and methodology that is unique to their culture, and we ignore that at our own peril, and we set ourselves up for frustration." I MEF had to get the fact that it was "walking into a new culture" with a different set of norms to which it had to adapt.[50]

All of that makes sense—in theory. But carrying out tribal engagement on the ground in Anbar tested the extent to which I MEF could adhere to that long-standing Marine mantra—improvise, adapt, overcome. Consider the experience of Lt. Col. Scott Shuster, the commanding officer of Marine Combat Battalion 3/4 in AO Denver.

In discussing how tribal engagement necessitated becoming "comfortable with cultural norms," the battalion commander pulled out a photograph of himself "walking down the street [in Al Qa'im] holding hands with the mayor.... Here in Iraq," he said, "in this culture, walking hand in hand down the street says we are friends, we trust each other, I will do things for him, he will do things for me, this is my brother. It is a sign of respect and it is a sign of acceptance." Now that's adaptation. Of course, Lieutenant Colonel Shuster quickly added, "I wouldn't do that in the United States."[51]

TOPEKA, DENVER, AND RALEIGH

2005 was a bad year for U.S. forces in Iraq, and not just in Anbar. But there were a few bright spots. One of those was in the city of Tal Afar. That AO was the responsibility of the 3rd Armored Cavalry Regiment (3rd ACR), which had arrived there in the spring of 2005 under the command of Col. H. R. McMaster.

Located near the Syrian border in Ninewa Province, the Army had played whack-a-mole with insurgents there in 2004. It would sweep in and sweep the insurgents out. But with too few forces to hold the city, the Army would withdraw to hit another hot spot and AQI forces would pop back up in Tal Afar and terrorize the city. "The life was literally choked out of the city. The terrorists had everyone living in abject fear," said Colonel McMaster.[52] A student of counterinsurgency, he intended to have the 3rd ACR take root in Tal Afar.

What that entailed, in the first place, was to "separate the terrorists and insurgents from the population." Clearing. That meant, explained McMaster, showing the people of Tal Afar that "we were a force to be reckoned with ... that we had the capability and the determination to defeat these terrorists, because they wouldn't throw their lot in with us . . . if we didn't demonstrate that commitment to win the fight." How did the 3rd ACR do that? Holding. "We established permanent security in the city."[53]

What that meant was moving units into the city and establishing—one by one, following that oil spot approach—a series of COPs. Manned by 3rd ACR and Iraqi forces, these outposts put increasing pressure on al Qaeda and other insurgent groups seeking to come back into the city. This was precisely what the population in Tal Afar wanted to see, said McMaster, and they reciprocated. "Intelligence came in at a much higher rate. . . . With the intelligence we were receiving we could conduct very precise offensive operations to capture them. We had people who were willing to come forward and tell us exactly what these people [AQI] did and to testify against them in court, because people were really desperate to return to normalcy and [for us] to bring security to the city and to their children."[54]

The final step: building. In other words, "It was important for us to address some of the local grievances" of the people of Tal Afar.[55] But this was done jointly through engagement. The population had to play its part, which it did by sending its men into the police units that the 3rd ACR was rebuilding.

Tal Afar became a cause célèbre. H. R. McMaster was successfully implementing those COIN principles found in *FM 3-24* before the schedule to produce the new manual hit the drawing board at the Army's Combined Arms Center. "State Department officials heard about it and briefed Secretary of State Condoleezza Rice. . . . She mentioned it in her congressional testimony" in the fall of 2005.[56]

It was to this AO that Col. Sean MacFarland and the 1st Brigade Combat Team, 1st Armored Division—the Ready First—deployed in February 2006. While AQI was still around, recalled the colonel, "the city had been taken away from them. So, our mission was to maintain and improve the security there; introduce Iraqi Police, which, when we got there, there weren't too many, since they were still coming in from Jordan from their training; and then to begin the stabilization process and build up governance and the economy and services in that area."[57] In COIN lingo, the mission for the Ready First was to continue to hold and build.

And that is what they did. MacFarland elaborated:

> I replaced [Col.] H. R. [McMaster] and he had a number of combat outposts out in the city of Tal Afar and we fell in on those. . . . We were able to occupy all his COPs and, in fact, we ended up establishing a couple more because I saw the merit in that, in taking away those enemy safe havens, because there were still a couple parts of the city that we didn't have full control over. . . . So, we established a couple

new combat outposts, which was great training for us before we got to Ramadi.[58]

The Ready First learned in May that it would deploy to Anbar's capital to replace the 2nd Brigade of the 28th Infantry Division. Actually, the AO included more than Ramadi, noted MacFarland: "It started up around Lake Tharthar and continued down around the south of Lake Habbaniyah. It was roughly the size of . . . the state of New Hampshire. It was called AO Topeka and they figured about 600,000 or so people lived there, of whom almost 400,000 to 450,000 lived in Ramadi proper."[59] But the capital would be ground zero for the fight with AQI.

Moreover, Ramadi was going to be a very different scene from what the Ready First had experienced in Tal Afar. "It was a pretty dire situation," recalled MacFarland. "Ramadi was essentially under enemy control." AQI "had freedom of movement throughout most of the city. . . . If we tried to get close to the center of the city . . . we would come into heavy contact. . . . Al Qaeda dominated the insurgency . . . [and] Zarqawi was known to be out there." And he had plenty of fighters with him.[60]

Upon arriving in the AO, Colonel MacFarland was told by I MEF's General Zilmer, who had been told by General Casey, to "fix Ramadi but don't do a Fallujah."[61] That meant taking a COIN approach. Well, MacFarland was ready for that, having employed COIN up in Tal Afar. And Zilmer had embedded COIN in his OPLAN for the theater. It was just the right confluence of thinking and planning, recalled MacFarland in a 2010 interview.[62] He intended to use his Ready First units to clear and hold Ramadi. And Zilmer assigned Marine Battalion 1/6 to give MacFarland a little extra oomph.

According to the Ready First commanding officer, step one was the "isolation of the city." The days of AQI moving in and out at will had to end. Next, MacFarland intended to establish COPs in Ramadi "to take the city and its environs back [from AQI] one neighborhood at a time." And once the first COP owned that first piece of ground in the capital they would engage the local sheikhs, convincing them "we intended to stay." And then they would encourage the sheikhs to partner up and send their tribesmen to join the local police force in "the secured neighborhood."[63] It was Tal Afar redux.

Out in AO Denver, RCT-7 arrived on the heels of Operation Steel Curtain. Recall that the previous November RCT-2 had assembled more than two thousand Marines to sweep the insurgents out of Hit, Haditha, Husaybah, and Al Qa'im. The goal was to pacify those areas and to gain control of the border, long a haven for al Qaeda and the insurgency. The commanding officer of RCT-7, Col. Bill Crowe, intended to build on Steel Curtain by "spreading that oil spot."[64]

160 | CHAPTER 5

What the colonel had in mind was the taking and holding of Al Qa'im. That had been "very successful," he explained. "It was a model for all Iraq to emulate." Why? Because having swept AQI out, RCT-2 left "one American battalion" in place to hold. "There is still enemy out there, but compared to everywhere else in the AO, Al Qa'im is the safest."[65] And that told the sheikhs they could count on RCT-2. Crowe intended to reinforce that message.

Having a lock on Al Qa'im, the RCT-2 chief planned to apply that model to the towns down the Euphrates corridor to include Rawah, Anah, Haditha, Baghdadi, and Hit. For each it would be the same COIN approach. Consider how RCT-7 took control of Anah, which lies on the right bank of the Euphrates along a bend in the river just before it turns south toward Hit: First, the Marines put a berm around the city to gain control of all points of entry. Next, they drove out the insurgents; RCT-7 left a company there to establish a COP to hold Anah. That provided security for the population and facilitated engagement. As a result, tips regarding AQI's clandestine cells poured in from the local population, and those cells were rolled up. The Al Qa'im model was established by RCT-7 in town after town down the Euphrates corridor to the Ramadi outskirts. This is what Colonel Crowe meant by "spreading that oil spot."

Responsibility for AO Raleigh in the spring of 2006 was assigned to the 5th Regimental Combat Team (RCT-5), commanded by Col. Larry Nicholson. It was the colonel's second time commanding a regiment in Anbar. In the summer of 2004 he relieved Col. John Toolan. That change of command, recalled Nicholson, took place on September 14, 2004. Later that evening he was sitting in his new office,

> just trying to get online . . . I asked the S-6 [communications officer] can you send me somebody . . . to get me online? . . . Maj. Kevin Shea walked in, said, "Hey, sir, I'll do it." "No, Kevin, just send me a Lance Corporal." He goes, "Nah, I got it." He's kind of leaning over me . . . typing. I say, "Hey, Kevin, let me get out of your way. Sit down." So Kevin sat down in the chair, and I walked over to that bulkhead and seconds later a 122 [mm] rocket came through what was the window. Kevin was killed immediately. I don't remember a whole lot, frankly. Things were burning . . . [and] the room was full of smoke.[66]

What followed was a medevac flight to Germany, seven operations at Bethesda Naval Hospital, months of rehab, and a return to Anbar. In February 2006 he returned as commander of the Fighting 5th—RCT-5—with responsibility for AO Raleigh. Nicholson was back, but the regimental mission had changed from what he had planned to execute in the fall of 2004. Then, the focus had been "actively kinetic." Now, "we all realized that we're not going to win this war by shooting. Marines are not going to win this war with a kinetic fight. It's just not going to happen."[67]

The model that Nicholson seized on for AO Raleigh was COIN in Fallujah. It was an outstanding illustration of clear-hold-build. Colonel Nicholson explained, "We've had significant success in the Fallujah AO. . . . When we took over from RCT-8 the seeds were already there . . . we inherited a better situation. We had more [local] security forces in this part of Al Anbar." The city had a robust Iraqi police force, and they helped make Fallujah, in the colonel's estimation, "without peer in terms of security" in any of Iraq's cities.[68] And that security and stability, empowered by engagement, opened the door for political progress and economic recovery. Fallujah had a functioning city council that was the envy of all of Anbar, and through this engagement efforts were under way to rebuild infrastructure and jumpstart business.

Nicholson thought if it worked in Fallujah, if that was the model, then build on it and spread it elsewhere in AO Raleigh. The goal he set for the Fighting 5th was to expand and take control of more and more territory employing counterinsurgency principles.

Col. Lawrence Nicholson, commander of RCT-5 in 2006

ESTES, *INTO THE FRAY*, 56

GRIM INTELLIGENCE

During the late summer, as Colonels MacFarland, Crowe, and Nicholson were executing Zilmer's OPLAN in each of their AOs, a devastating intelligence estimate on the situation in Anbar was completed by Col. Pete Devlin, the G-2 of I MEF. And when its conclusions hit the front page of the September 11, 2006, edition of the *Washington Post*—"Situation Called Dire in West Iraq"—they rocked the White House and Pentagon. Here was the opening salvo from its author, Tom Ricks: "The chief of intelligence for the Marine Corps in Iraq recently filed an unusual secret report concluding that the prospects for securing that country's Anbar province are dim and there is almost nothing the U.S. military can do."[69]

Ricks went on to write that he was told by one official familiar with the report that it "describes Anbar as beyond repair." And, another official said, "it concludes that the United States has lost in Anbar." Why? Because of a "lack of U.S. and Iraqi troops . . . [our] military operations are facing a stalemate, unable to extend and sustain security beyond the perimeters of their bases, but also local governments in the province have collapsed and the weak central government has almost no presence."[70]

In a January 2007 interview, Colonel Devlin explained how this shocking assessment came about. It is just "part of the intel job . . . so this was an absolutely natural, almost mandatory, intelligence product. . . . We were about six months into it, hadn't done an assessment yet, because we were still trying to gain mastery over what we thought was going on [in Anbar] and we were about at that point." Moreover, the G-2 added, the JCS chairperson, Gen. Pete Pace, was coming out to Anbar "at the beginning of August, and I knew I was going to have to brief him. And I just wanted to tell him precisely what's going on here in Anbar Province, regarding what the insurgency was and why our incident levels had increased."[71]

As noted earlier, those incident levels—violent attacks of various kinds—had not just increased, they had skyrocketed in Anbar. And Devlin's job was to tell the chairperson of the JCS why that had happened. "I get paid to look at the enemy. . . . This is what's difficult about making an assessment. So, anyway, I briefed him, and I think he was a little bit taken aback."[72]

Following the JCS chief, "General Odierno came through immediately afterwards and then there was a congressional delegation that came through."[73] They all received Devlin's briefing and had the same reactions.

In November the G-2 produced an update, and it was more of the same grim prognosis. Devlin recalled it this way: "That one had to get staffed carefully through the generals. But, again, the arguments and the conclusions in there were incontrovertible. If you looked at the statistics on what was going on, that's the way it was." The November assessment "said much of the same things" as its August antecedent.[74] And it also was leaked.

Statistics do not lie, goes the old saying. The G-2 could point to the numbers of violent attacks and the casualties. They all pointed in the same direction, and he said so. But how you interpret statistics, and the lens trough which you look at them, can change the conclusions you draw from the numbers. As we shall see later, if those November numbers are examined in a counterinsurgency context, the conclusion that Anbar was being lost is turned on its head. In other words, rather than being lost, General Zilmer and his I MEF forces were in the midst of establishing the conditions on the ground to prevail in Anbar.

THE WISE MEN SPEAK

When a major policy initiative goes seriously bad for Washington, the SOP is for the president or Congress to call in the wise men to figure out how to fix it. And sometimes, as in the case of the 9/11 Commission, it is a joint affair. Recall that

President George W. Bush and the United States Congress established that commission on November 27, 2002.

Therefore, it is not surprising that as the war in Iraq devolved into the grim sectarian bloodletting that followed the February 2006 bombing of the Shiite Askariyah Shrine in Samarra—the Golden Mosque—by Zarqawi's AQI organization, members of Congress called for an outside commission to take a fresh look and propose a way to resolve the conflict.

On March 15, 2006, a ten-member bipartisan panel was established to take this on: the Iraq Study Group (ISG). It was cochaired by former secretary of state James A. Baker and former Indiana Democratic representative Lee Hamilton, who also had cochaired the 9/11 Commission. In addition to the ten panel members, a supporting cast of forty-four academic, think tank, and public sector luminaries was engaged to provide advice on a range of issues to include reconstruction, development, and military options.

Over the next eight months the ISG and its advisers met with "hundreds of high-ranking current and former officials, most of them in the United States or Iraq, as well as senior military officers, nongovernmental organization leaders, and academics."[75] On December 6 the official *Iraq Study Group Report* was released. It painted a grim picture:

> The challenges in Iraq are complex. Violence is increasing in scope and lethality. It is fed by a Sunni Arab insurgency, Shiite militias and death squads, al Qaeda, and widespread criminality. Sectarian conflict is the principal challenge to stability. . . . Pessimism is pervasive.
>
> If the situation continues to deteriorate, the consequences could be severe.[76]

The ISG report made seventy-nine recommendations in what can only be described as a grand design. The report's external dimensions required nothing short of a grand bargain that, among other regional moves, would engage Iran and Syria as partners in a new "international consensus" aimed at establishing "stability in Iraq and the region."[77]

As for that part of the report focused inside Iraq, numerous recommendations dealt with all major parts of the Iraqi scene. But the key issue was security and the role of U.S. forces, with respect to which it stated, "There is no action the American military can take that, by itself, can bring about success in Iraq."[78]

The ISG proposal involved changing the "primary mission of U.S. forces in Iraq . . . to one of supporting the Iraqi army, which would take over primary responsibility for combat operations." If the United States took this course of action, then "by the first quarter of 2008, subject to unexpected developments in the security situation . . . all combat brigades not necessary for force protection could be out of Iraq."[79]

The proposal amounted to a plan for the phased withdrawal of U.S. troops. Recommendation 41 of the report left no doubt: "The United States must make it clear to the Iraqi government that the United States could carry out its plans, including planned redeployments, even if Iraq does not implement its planned changes."[80]

During the months the ISG was contemplating how to extricate the United States from Iraq, I MEF was implementing the strategy it had devised to establish stability and security in Anbar. That strategy did not seek to stand down, but rather to ramp up efforts to turn things around in Anbar. While the ISG wise men were contemplating grand designs and grand bargains with Iran and Syria as a way out of Iraq, I MEF was carrying out a much less grandiose way forward. Its plan was to take control of the ground and hold it, engage and integrate the sheikhs and their tribes into the fight, and send al Qaeda packing.

THE SHEIKHS AWAKEN—AGAIN

In the spring of 2006 al Qaeda sent the sheikhs running for cover with a ferocious murder and intimidation campaign against those who dared to stand up and challenge its authority in Anbar. Indeed, many fled both the province and the country. Consider the story of Sheikh Aifan Sadun al-Issawi. In 2005 he began publicly opposing AQI. He first did so by organizing a meeting at the main mosque in Fallujah. The session was attended by imams, sheikhs, and other important personalities from the city. At the meeting, he recounted, "I let the imams start to talk and tell the people that the insurgents who come from outside Iraq and cover their faces, they are not mujahideen. They are criminals. And they warned people that they were letting surrounding countries, like Iran, Saudi Arabia, and Syria, interfere inside Iraq."[81]

Among those who spoke out against AQI was Sheikh Hamza Abbas al-Issawi, head of the Religious Scholars Council in Fallujah. According to Sheikh Aifan, after Sheikh Hamza spoke out, he was murdered right in front of the mosque. AQI simply gunned him down. Others who came out against the insurgency, including Sheikh Shawkat al-Sa'ab, Sheikh Kamal al-Tikriti, and Sheikh Omar Sa'ed Horan, all prominent figures, suffered the same fate.

Sheikh Aifan was lucky and managed to dodge an attempted assassination when an ambush of his car failed. But members of his extended family were not so fortunate. As a result, the sheikh said, "I took my family to Amman, Jordan. I have

Sheikh Aifan Sadun al-Issawi, Fallujah Representative, Iraqi Awakening Political Party

MONTGOMERY AND MCWILLIAMS, EDS., AL-ANBAR AWAKENING, VOL. 2, 84

my own house in Amman, so I stayed there with my family—my wife and my children—in Amman." And he was joined by "Sheikh Hamis and Sheikh Khalid, my uncles, who also fled to Amman. They refused to fight al Qaeda. They came to Amman and lived with me in my house."[82]

Amazingly, AQI's brutality did not send all those who opposed it in Anbar "to ground," noted Tariq Yusif Mohammad al-Thiyabi, who would later become the director of police for Anbar. In May 2006 he helped open the first police station in the Ramadi area. Tariq al-Thiyabi recalled, "I received information right after we opened that al Qaeda was really shaken by the news of a police station opening. . . . They hit that police station with a VBIED [vehicle-borne IED] carrying, I think, a ton of explosives with gasoline and so forth. . . . Many policemen were burned . . . burned alive at the station. That was a very big blow against us, because that was our only police station."[83]

But the police station kept on functioning, said Tariq. "Fortunately, we had a couple of vehicles in the back of the police station that were not damaged. We were able to turn them on and use them again. . . . [We] were still defiant. We went and patrolled the area."[84]

Into the summer months al Qaeda, well aware of the potential consequences of a tribal uprising against it, gave no quarter in its efforts to crush any and all opposition from the sheikhs and tribes. Then, in August, it went too far when it murdered Sheikh Abu Ali Jassim, who had been encouraging members of his tribe to join the police and resist AQI. After killing him, his assassins hid the sheikh's body rather than returning it for a proper burial. This violated Islamic law and inflamed not only Sheikh Jassim's fellow tribesmen but also many other sheikhs from tribes across Al Anbar Province. It was a critical turning point.

One of those tribal leaders, Sheikh Abdul Sittar Albu Risha, decided that he had had enough. His father had been murdered by AQI, as had two of his brothers, all for opposing AQI's imposition of its interpretation of Sharia law. Their blood had to be avenged, and in 2006 he set out on a course to do so. Prior to the summer of 2006, it is not clear whether the sheikh had supported the nationalist elements of the insurgency in Anbar or was sitting on the fence waiting to see who prevailed. Sheikh Sittar did come from a family with a history of resisting occupation. His grandfather was a resistance leader against the British occupying forces in 1920, and his father fought against the British during the May 1941 Anglo-Iraqi War.

As for his own background, Sattar was said by some to be an import-export businessperson, with offices in the United Arab Emirates and Jordan. He also owned a construction company. Others said he ran a highway extortion enterprise and smuggled oil. In terms of his ranking among the sheikhs of Anbar, Sittar was younger and not considered a major player. But many of those who were more senior to him in the sheikhs' pecking order had fled to Jordan or elsewhere in the Gulf. Sittar stayed put, residing in his compound on the west side of Ramadi.

Considered to be a dynamic leader by Americans who would later engage with him, in August Sheikh Sittar began contacting his fellow sheikhs, encouraging them to resist AQI, work with I MEF forces, and send their tribesmen into their local police forces. This was the beginning of what would evolve into the Anbar Awakening, or Sahawat al-Anbar.

Sheikh Ahmed, Sheikh Sittar's brother and the paramount sheikh of the Albu Risha tribe, recalled in a 2009 interview how those August 2006 days unfolded. "We realized that the people had had it with the [al Qaeda] situation. . . . So Sheikh Sittar and I, we started thinking we've got to get in touch with the tribal sheikhs and their cousins, the ones who were active, so we could incite them to fight al Qaeda." Sheikh Sittar told his brother, "Leave it to me. I'll take care of it." And he began "talking with the tribal sheikhs, one by one. He told them that he was ready to do something, and he gathered them for a conference on the 14th of September, 2006."[85]

Sheikh Abdul Sittar Albu-Risha and Col. Sean MacFarland meet in 2006.
COURTESY OF SEAN MACFARLAND

One of those sheikhs receiving a call from Sittar was Wissam Abd al-Ibrahim al-Hardan al-Aeithawi, a senior figure from the paramount family of the Aeithawi tribe, one of the most respected families in Al Anbar Province.

> Sheikh Sittar called me by phone. He said, "Please, I want you to come to Anbar." I was living in a village. The name of the village is al-Mish Haniyah. That's where my grandfather lived. It's about seventy kilometers from Ramadi. I asked what he had in mind. He said there was a conference about to take place, and I told him I did not wish to attend any conferences, because they are to no avail. He insisted that I attend—or more likely he pleaded with me. His cousin is my wife, so he kind of used [family ties] to pressure me into attending.[86]

When Wissam arrived, Sittar got right down to business.

> When he saw me, when he laid his eyes on me at his house, he said, "We are victorious by the God of al-Kaaba." When I asked him what he had in mind, he said, "We have a huge undertaking, and nobody can take care of it, except you." Before he even said, "Hello," which is customary in the Arab world, he started telling me what he had in mind. . . . He said, "I want to fight al Qaeda." . . . So all night long, we sat down, and we were planning and plotting for this huge revolution we're about to undertake.[87]

Another sheikh who played a key role in the events of August and September was Ali Hatim Abd al-Razzaq Ali al-Sulayman, the paramount sheikh of the Dulaym tribal confederation. He recalled how they all met at Sittar's compound and agreed to "fight against al Qaeda." It was out of that initial meeting that "the Awakening Revolution" was to emerge. He noted, "When we started talking about this initiative, many of the sheikhs thought we were a little mad, because here we were trying to take on al Qaeda. They thought we were crazy."[88]

They may have seemed crazy to some of the sheikhs, but many others signed on. And that resistance to AQI began spreading across Anbar. Sheikh Sabah al-Sattam Effan Fahran al-Shurji al-Aziz, the sheikh general of the Albu Mahal tribe, explained why opposition grew so quickly in the fall of 2006. There were two reasons.

First, the methods that al Qaeda employed to maintain local control were draconian in the extreme. According to the sheikh, "They used two paths. The first path was by scaring people. . . . They dealt violently and toughly with all Iraqi citi-

Sheikh Wissam Abd al-Ibrahim al-Hardan al-Aethawi meets with Brig. Gen. John Allen in early 2007.

MONTGOMERY AND MCWILLIAMS, EDS., *AL-ANBAR AWAKENING*, VOL. 2, 52

zens. . . . The other path was financial. The families were in financial difficulties. None of them had any finances left." But al Qaeda had plenty of money, said the sheikh general of the Albu Mahal. "They were spending huge amounts of money by giving it to the people."[89]

The second reason, recounted Sheikh Sabah, was that the United States had finally decided to engage with the tribes. Not doing so in the early weeks and months following Saddam's ouster had been a big mistake. Rather than engaging, said the sheikh, U.S. forces employed "violence and toughness. I'm talking about the first two years after the invasion. And they didn't listen to us at all when we told them that the tribes are the keys to solving Iraqis' problems. After the weakening of the tribes, terrorists started entering our province—not only the province, but the whole of Iraq. We used to meet with the Americans . . . and we used to tell them frankly in our meetings that you will pay a high price for these mistakes. And it [turned into] a disaster when al Qaeda entered our country."[90]

The central importance of local tribal engagement in counterinsurgency operations was well understood by General Zilmer and the I MEF staff devising the OPLAN for Anbar in 2006. COIN precepts stressed the centrality of local engagement, in this case with the tribal sheikhs. So, when Sittar and more than fifty leading sheikhs and other important political figures met on September 14 in his compound on the west side of Ramadi to get the Anbar Awakening Council off the ground, I MEF was leaning forward to work with them. It was in the OPLAN.

About a week before the meeting was to take place, one of the battalion commanders from the 1st BCT learned about it. Lt. Col. Tony Deane was "making the rounds, visiting some of the sheikhs in his area of operations . . . and he happened to stop by Sheikh Sittar's house." During the mandatory tea drinking, "Sittar told him that he had been talking with some of the other sheikhs and that they want to pick up where Sheikh Abu Ali Jassim had left off before he was assassinated and that they wanted to meet with my brigade commander [to discuss the issue]. . . . Sure," Deane said, and he arranged for the commanding officer of the Ready First to attend the session.[91]

Colonel MacFarland did not know what to expect when he walked into the main room of Sittar's house and found it filled with sheikhs and "all kinds of other guys lining the walls." Sheikh Sittar came to the doorway to greet the brigade commander and brought him "up to sit down with him at the head chair at the head of the room and then proceeded to explain that they wanted to form this Awakening movement and that they had eleven planks in their platform."[92]

MacFarland found that "ten of them I would have written for them almost exactly the way they wrote them." But the eleventh had to go. It was "negative about the governor of Al Anbar, to the point where they kind of left open the implication that they might whack him." The colonel demurred, suggesting they "modify that plank and talk about working within the constitution." The sheikhs agreed to drop number eleven. In any case, the governor was not the issue they wanted to discuss with MacFarland.[93] The bottom line for those who gathered at Sittar's compound was the decision to align with I MEF to defeat AQI. To that end, they were willing to take what amounted to a blood oath.[94]

MacFarland explained the impact of tribal values on engagement: "They would treat any attack on Coalition forces as though it was an attack on their own tribesmen and that really meant something to them." And they stuck to that pledge: "Whenever a tribe 'flipped' and joined the Awakening, all the attacks on Coalition forces would stop in that area and all the caches of ammunition would come up out of the ground and, if there was ever an attack on us, the sheik would basically take responsibility for it and find whoever was responsible, and this happened time and again."[95]

All the pieces were coming together for a reversal of fortune in Anbar. And this was taking place in the shadow of those grim forecasts by the G-2 of I MEF and the ISG's wise men, each of whom said the end was near.

But it is one thing to be presented with an opportunity in war and quite another to seize that opening and exploit it successfully. War is an art, says Clausewitz, and it cannot be reduced to science. War is always characterized by uncertainty, friction, and surprise. But leadership by effective commanders can make a difference. In Anbar's AOs—Topeka, Raleigh, and Denver—there were two Marine Corps regimental commanders and their Army brigade counterpart who were poised to exploit that opportunity and make a difference.

AREA OF OPERATIONS TOPEKA—TAKING RAMADI

The 1st Armored Division (1st AD) has a storied history in twentieth-century conventional warfare. Nicknamed Old Ironsides, it stood up on July 15, 1940, at Fort Knox, one of the keystone units of the Army's new armored-division concept. It took part in Operation Torch, the Allied invasion of North Africa in 1942. In May 1943 the 1st AD joined the Fifth Army's invasion of mainland Italy. It landed at Anzio, helped liberate Rome, and fought in the Po Valley until German forces surrendered in May 1945.

During the Cold War the division relocated to the Bavarian city of Ansbach as part of American conventional forces committed to NATO's defense. With the Iraqi invasion of Kuwait the 1st AD deployed as one of four heavy divisions assigned to VII Corps. It led the attack on the flank of the Iraqi forces, destroying elite Republican Guard units. In 2003 the unit spearheaded the assault on Samawah and Karbala and then occupied the southern end of Baghdad.

As this précis illustrates, the 1st AD's fighting past is anchored in modern conventional warfare. But in January 2006 in Tal Afar the division's 1st Brigade—the Ready First—went through a metamorphosis. At heart a heavy Army brigade combat team (BCT), it adopted a counterinsurgency approach. What happened? Leadership. It made a difference.

Col. Sean MacFarland learned about population-centric warfare and COPs in Tal Afar. And he intended to establish COP look-alikes in Ramadi's most dangerous neighborhoods, places dominated by AQI. Marines and soldiers who served in AO Topeka often referred to Ramadi as "al Qaedastan," and with good reason. The place experienced a higher rate of attacks than anywhere else in Iraq. Al Qaeda controlled all of Ramadi except for the embattled Government Center, which was held by a company of Marines.

Dexter Filkins of the *New York Times* described that Marine outpost as resembling "a fortress on the wild edge of some frontier: sandbagged, barricaded, full of men ready to shoot, surrounded by rubble and enemies eager to get inside."[96] Step outside during the daylight, and AQI snipers started firing. At night, gun fights between Marines on patrol and insurgents were frequent.

Consider a July 2006 "midnight gun battle between a group of insurgents and American marines [that] lasted two hours and ended only when the Americans dropped a laser-guided bomb on an already half-destroyed building downtown. Six marines were wounded; it was unclear what happened to the insurgents [who were inside that building]." And like elsewhere in Anbar, Ramadi was thickly seeded with IEDs. Marines operating out of the Government Center told of how they often "spot bombs—covered in trash, made of metal and wires—in streets that are themselves covered in trash, metal and wires."[97]

On the mean streets of the capital, AQI insurgents ruled mercilessly. Tales of their cruelties were endless. If they decided they wanted a family's house, they just told them to get out. In the mosques they ordered imams to broadcast only their prepackaged propaganda, often at gunpoint. And they enforced their code of behavior on the local populace, much as they had in Fallujah. Men could not shave. Girls could not go to school. Music was verboten. Beauty parlors were closed. Get caught smoking, and you could be shot.

This was not the kind of war Army BCTs were prepared to fight. But MacFarland was an unusual Army colonel, able to get outside the conventional comfort zone of a brigade commander and to learn from Tal Afar. He also benefited from being part of I MEF. Everyone in that unit was on the same page when it came to the way forward in Anbar. Colonel MacFarland explained, "General Zilmer had a COIN plan for Ramadi, which was to roll from the West to the East to take control of the entire city." The goal was clear, hold, and build. And one of the key tactics for doing so, said the colonel, was to methodically establish COPs.[98]

Step one in that course of action was to isolate the city, ending AQI's freedom of movement. MacFarland told his commanders, "The first thing we do is we will complete the isolation of the city of Ramadi." That did not mean "isolation in the sense that nobody could get in or out." The objective was to "control access and be able to prevent the influx of weapons and fighters, at least in the numbers that had been [the case]. That was . . . step one."[99]

Step two entailed shutting down the principal rural bases that AQI used to feed forces and supplies into Ramadi. These also served as "enemy points of origin for indirect fire attacks" on the brigade's "forward operating bases and were enemy rat lines and cache locations."[100]

Those actions were the prelude. Next, "Looking at the map of the city," MacFarland asked his staff, "Okay, where is the enemy located and what will do them the most harm from our first operations [in the city]?" Noting that AQI "had a north-to-south orientation in the city, basically running from the train station at the southern end of the city up to the river banks along the Euphrates, which coincided with the Ramadi General Hospital," they concluded they would first "take away the train station." In doing that, the brigade would "seriously disrupt the enemy's operations in Ramadi as an opening gambit."[101]

A combat patrol in Ramadi in 2006

CONNABLE, *U.S. MARINES IN IRAQ, 2004–2008*, 194

So, MacFarland established two COPs—Iron and Spear—on the perimeter of the train station, right in the backyard of one of AQI's key emirs in southern Ramadi. He lived right next to a mosque, and MacFarland intended to take over the buildings he held and turn them into a COP that would dominate the approaches to the train station. The area had been a no-man's-land for the 2-28th ID (2nd Brigade Combat Team, 28th Infantry Division; 2/28 BCT) in 2005, and it took some tough fighting to secure it. But having done so, the second COP followed and the Ready First was set to push into Ramadi proper.

Next was the general hospital. In early July the 3/8 took control of it. Hospitals, according to the laws of war, are supposed to be off limits to military forces engaged in war. The 3/8 found that was not the case in Ramadi. AQI had made full use of the facility.

These actions began the methodical spreading of the oil spot across Ramadi. In neighborhood after neighborhood, the soldiers and Marines under MacFarland's command took control. And because AQI could not be sure where the next COP would spring up, said the colonel, "We found out pretty quickly that we were able to get in and set up . . . overnight and the enemy usually took about forty-eight hours to respond." But by then, "he was pretty severely weakened." The brigade "had to dedicate a fair amount of combat power to securing each COP and protecting the lines of communications [LOC]" between the COPs because "we knew AQI would try to come back in behind us and reseed our LOCs with IEDs." In effect, MacFarland's soldiers and Marines were beginning to network Ramadi with COPs that established "mutually supporting and interlocking fields of fire and observation along those LOCs [lines of communications] [that linked them together]. That was . . . the process."[102] And playing a key role in that campaign in central Ramadi—ground zero in the fight to oust al Qaeda—were the men of 1st

Battalion, 6th Marines (1/6), under the command of Lt. Col. Bill Jurney. At the end of the summer they relieved 3/8.

It was not too complicated, explained Jurney: "First and foremost" the objective was "to neutralize those criminal and terrorist threats that choose to do us harm. You do that by killing or capturing them. . . . It was one street, one block at a time," recounted the commanding officer of 1/6.[103] And more often than not it was bloody. Under Jurney's command, 1/6 started setting up COPs in September. There was no set rule for their size, but generally a company was assigned to each, under the command of a captain. The facility itself was a handful of buildings, the perimeter secured by concertina wire, huge thick bags of sand or dirt, and other barriers to make it impregnable.

Lt. Col. William Jurney, commander of 1/6 in Ramadi in 2006

McWilliams and Wheller, Eds., *Al-Anbar Awakening*, vol. 1, 186

Among the core duties for the forces assigned to a COP was to patrol the AO to eliminate AQI and protect the population. Generally, those patrols were conducted on foot, backed up by light armor and air support if needed. They also protected roads to facilitate movement of supplies through the network of COPs.

But, most important, the COPs sent a crucial message to the sheikhs and the population. Lieutenant Colonel Jurney explained, "The first question the people are going to ask you is, 'When are you leaving?' You got to show them you're not going to leave. . . . And so we started [to show them] by clearing areas, seizing terrain, and establishing a secure facility."[104]

MacFarland concurred. In 2005, he noted, "The sheikhs had been benignly neglected by the 2-28th [ID] and the strategic communications message that they were giving to the sheikhs was the same one that all Iraqis were being told by the Coalition at that time. . . . Don't worry, the Coalition forces aren't going to stay here forever. We are not an occupying force. We are here today but we will be gone tomorrow."[105]

Wrong message, explained the colonel. It was "what was worrying them . . . because al Qaeda was not telling them that. Al Qaeda was saying, 'We are going to stay here forever and this is going to be the capital of our new caliphate.' So, if you were an Iraqi . . . are you going to throw in with the Americans who say they are going to be gone, or mind your Ps and Qs so al Qaeda doesn't come and saw your head off?"[106]

To change that perception, words were not enough. The sheikhs and people of Anbar were looking for actions. The most visible action, said MacFarland, was to see one of "our combat outposts going up." What that said to them was "Don't worry. We are not leaving. We are going to stand by you, side by side, and fight al Qaeda until they are defeated."[107]

This was the signal the sheikhs organizing the Sahawat al-Anbar wanted to see. But COPs were only one side of COIN. The other side was to establish Iraqi police substations at or near the COPs. To do this, Iraqi police were needed, and in large numbers. To fill those police ranks the sheikhs began sending their tribesmen to help spread the oil spot.

When I MEF came back to Anbar it found the police system to be moribund. AQI had put it on its last legs. And when efforts were made to resuscitate the police, Zarqawi sent in a suicide bomber to shut the recruitment process down. "In June 2006, the Ramadi police force consisted of approximately 420 officers out of 3,386 authorized, and only about 140 ever showed up to work, with less than 100 present for duty on any given day."[108]

Engagement with the sheikhs changed those numbers in dramatic fashion. By the end of 2006 more than four thousand men had joined the police and received training, and many more were in the pipeline. And "90 percent of [those] police recruits came from tribes supporting the Awakening. . . . The sheiks [sic] knew whom to trust."[109]

It was a winning combination and had huge implications for the fight in Ramadi. MacFarland's battalion commanders now had the forces necessary to continue their steady and methodical campaign, clearing and securing the city from west to east, neighborhood by neighborhood. It was slow going, but very effective. By the beginning of 2007 the Ready First had made major headway in establishing control in Ramadi, and by mid-2007 their replacement would complete the pacification of the city.

As these developments were unfolding, al Qaeda well understood what they signaled for the fate of its caliphate, so it escalated the violence, increasing the number of daily attacks. This included attempting to use crude chemical weapons by combining chlorine gas with standard vehicle-borne explosives. The group succeeded for the first time on October 21, 2006, when a car carrying mortar shells and two chlorine tanks was detonated in Ramadi. It was poorly constructed, wounding only a handful. Nonetheless, it sent panic signals across the city.

Next, a major attack was carried out against the Albu Soda tribal area on the eastern edge of the capital. AQI had a key base there, and "intelligence indicated" that the area "harbored a large support network for the insurgents operating inside the city." But the sheikhs of the Albu Soda tribe had had enough of AQI and were joining the Sahawat al-Anbar. To put a stop to that, al Qaeda sent "30 to 40 gunmen" on November 25 to kill "members of the tribes. AQI forces took the tribal militiamen attempting to defend their homes by surprise, killing many while looting and burning those homes."[110]

When the BCT commanders learned of the assault, they reacted quickly, sending Marine Corps aircraft "overhead to perform show of force sorties . . . to intimidate the insurgents and convince them that an air attack was imminent." It worked, and AQI forces "started to withdraw" even before the "ground reaction force from Task Force 1-9 Infantry began . . . to move into the area and establish defenses for the Albu Soda tribe."[111]

The outcome of the battle was another setback for AQI. "Within two months, every tribe . . . had declared support for the Awakening, and four new combat outposts were constructed to secure the population. An area previously deemed high threat and a staging ground for AQI attacks became almost completely secure."[112]

Ironically, it was at this time that Colonel Devlin, I MEF's intelligence officer, produced his November intelligence update to the one that had shaken Washington at the end of the summer. It was more of the same doom-and-gloom predictions. AQI was escalating the number of attacks, using chemical weapons, and launching assaults like that in the Albu Soda region. Nothing had changed.

But when General Mattis, I MEF's commanding general, paid one of his frequent visits to the AO, he saw that change was taking place, recalled MacFarland. Mattis looked at the number of COPs that had been established, saw how that oil spot was spreading across Ramadi, securing the ground, and he told the colonel, "Keep pushing, you are doing real good."[113] What Mattis discerned was that while the number of attacks was the same, even higher, the area where they were taking place had shrunk considerably. Sure, AQI was fighting hard to stop that oil spot from spreading further; it understood the implications. But it was losing more and more ground with each new COP and police substation.

Colonel MacFarland recalled, "As my S-2 [intelligence officer] briefed General Mattis, he had one of those 'aha' moments."[114] The G-2 of I MEF had missed the key development of COP expansion and what that meant to AQI presence. But Mattis understood its implications for the fight in Ramadi. He would later characterize Devlin's update as "an unfortunate assessment, and inaccurate."[115]

Later, in interviews in December 2006 and 2007, the I MEF chief explained why "we are winning and the enemy is losing." In Ramadi, and elsewhere in Anbar, "the people turned [on al Qaeda] before the Americans were forced out," he said. "What you are seeing is al Qaeda being squeezed [out]. They use [sic] to own

Fallujah and they don't have it any more. They use [sic] to own Ramadi," but MacFarland was spreading COPs across the city and that showed Mattis that AQI was losing there as well.[116]

The G-2 was not alone in missing what was taking place on the ground in Ramadi and elsewhere in Anbar. The major media, which embraced the Devlin assessments and ran with his predictions, also could not see the forest for the trees. Recall how *Washington Post* reporter Tom Ricks characterized Devlin's August appraisal. And when its sequel appeared in November, Ricks reported it as further confirmation that the Marines had lost in Anbar: "The U.S. military is no longer able to defeat a bloody insurgency in western Iraq or counter al-Qaeda's rising popularity there."[117]

But on the ground MacFarland's soldiers and Marines were taking Ramadi. And, as discussed below, AQI was losing elsewhere in Anbar as well. Moreover, there was no detectable evidence of "al-Qaeda's rising popularity," as Ricks reported. To the contrary, sheikhs and their tribesmen were lining up in droves to kill the insurgents. But Ricks did not get it: "There is nothing U.S. troops can do to influence the insurgency," he and Linzer wrote.[118]

The numbers by the beginning of 2007 told the real story of what was taking place in Ramadi. By the spring, attacks by the insurgents "dropped almost 70 percent compared to the numbers in June 2006, and they had dramatically decreased in complexity and effect. The combination of tribal engagement and combat outposts had proved toxic to AQI's efforts to dominate Ramadi."[119]

The soldiers and Marines under Colonel MacFarland's command had cleared them out and were taking hold of Ramadi, with the help of rapidly growing numbers of police. They had initiated a process that their replacements in 2007 would complete: turning "what was once the capital of al Qaedastan" into "the safest city in all of Iraq."[120] And come September 2007 the runners in that 5K road race would gather at the starting line waiting for Mayor Latif Obaid to give the signal to start running.

AREA OF OPERATIONS RALEIGH—EXTENDING THE OIL SPOT OUT FROM FALLUJAH

Things were improving in AO Raleigh as well. Consider Fallujah. In 2004 it was the first al Qaedastan in Anbar, characterized in the press at that time as "the most dangerous city in the world."[121] No one in Fallujah wanted the Marines there, and cooperating with I MEF was out of the question. Marines were the enemy.

But in 2006, explained Colonel Nicholson, the commanding officer of RCT-5, things were different in Fallujah. On a daily basis, what you found in the city was cooperation and engagement: "Iraqi police, Iraqi army, Marine planners hovering over maps, looking at intelligence, looking at names, comparing notes, comparing intelligence. That in itself was a very rewarding aspect of where we've come from. I really think that's something," he stressed. "We've championed that. We've worked very hard in that regard." Nicholson called it "Team Fallujah." That had become RCT-5's "theme . . . our raison d'être for being here."[122]

In fact, as the sectarian killing in Baghdad spiraled out of control in the wake of the Golden Mosque bombing in Samarra in February, which had been orchestrated by Zarqawi, Sunnis were actually fleeing to Fallujah for refuge. Zarqawi had declared an "all-out war on the Shia," initiating a wave of killings, and Shia death squads reciprocated.[123] Even after joint Task Force 145, the combined U.S.–British Special Forces outfit tasked to hunt down high-value al Qaeda personnel, caught up with and killed the AQI chieftain on June 7, 2006, the sectarian violence he had set in motion continued in high gear.

But engagement had turned Fallujah into a relatively safe haven, explained the RCT-5 commander:

> I'm exceptionally proud of the police . . . of their ability to show up and do the job and stay engaged with us. I'm very proud of that, that's taken a lot of work. . . . They've had over twenty-five guys killed, assassinated [since we've been here]. . . . I am proud of the fact that a city like Fallujah is now considered a safe haven for Sunnis fleeing sectarian violence. If you could imagine two years ago saying that people will flee Baghdad to come to Fallujah [for safety], you would have been laughed out of the joint. And now, that's exactly what's happening.[124]

Nicholson was intent on spreading the conditions established in Fallujah elsewhere in AO Raleigh, providing stability and security to the rest of the population. It was the application of basic counterinsurgency principles. "You must go back to the people. You must engage the people." "Look," he exclaimed in a 2010 reflection on what RCT-5 had achieved in AO Raleigh, "It's the people, stupid."[125]

But engaging the population and gaining its support meant adapting to Iraqi ways of doing things, and being able to "deal with some very colorful Iraqis," noted Nicholson, "guys that are real dramatic in the way they do things."[126] To engage the Iraqis he gave the following guidance to all his commanders, right down to the platoon lieutenants. Be prepared to "eat plenty of goat, to drink plenty of tea, and to do a lot of man hugging. You have to spend time with the population, gaining their trust." And when you break through the cultural barriers, what you will find, he told all of them, is that "Iraqis are great to work with. They have great optimism. They fought back against al Qaeda at great costs to themselves."[127]

The way RCT-5 expanded its area of control into more and more of AO Raleigh was through team building with ISF. "We have almost doubled our battle space in terms of geography.... We now go all the way to damn near to Ramadi," said Colonel Nicholson in January 2007. "We've been able to do that because we've turned over a lot of existing battle space to Iraqis.... I have three Iraqi brigades, all of which are now independent brigades.... I'm incredibly pleased with our Iraqi police work.... I don't know of anybody who has had the kind of success we have had with the police."[128]

As a result of these developments, the regiment was rolling up al Qaeda cells at a rapid pace. Once RCT-5 established presence and secured an area with its Iraqi counterparts, local intelligence on the insurgents began rolling in. They were getting a treasure trove of it, intelligence that Marine regiments serving earlier in AO Raleigh could never have imagined receiving. In Fallujah and elsewhere in the AO the police had deep roots in the communities where they served because they were from those communities. The local population knew them, talked to them, and gave them information on the insurgents. AQI and its allies could no longer hide in plain sight. And once they were fingered, RCT-5 moved in and rolled them up.

Colonel Nicholson recounted one example—Operation Rapid Departure—of just how devastating this could be for AQI. "We did [that operation] three times, twenty-five targets each time." The intelligence on "all twenty-five targets was nontraditional, in the sense that it didn't come from higher headquarters, it didn't come down to us from I MEF and it didn't come up from Marine companies.... [Rather, the intelligence] all came from the police. All seventy-five targets came from the police. On three different occasions, we went out at one in the morning and hit, each time, twenty-five targets simultaneously. All twenty-five at the same time.... That's better than our special friends [Task Force 145]. We had very few dry holes. This would not have been possible.... This wouldn't happen if we didn't have that kind of trust and relationship with the police and the army."[129]

By the end of its deployment, RCT-5's mission was evolving, with nonkinetic activities on the increase. "We told our guys ... this is not a black and white fight. If you're a black and white kind of guy, if you're a cowboys and Indians guy, you better wait for Korea, you better wait for the next war, because this isn't your war," Nicholson said in plain words. "Yes, you are a gun-fighter and yes, you will still do those things, but you also have to worry about putting sewer lines in and if the schools are open and how can you help that clinic."[130]

The latter concerns are all part of successful counterinsurgency. They all seek to have a positive impact on the people. And Nicholson believed they were having that effect in AO Raleigh. "Schools were opening and families were sending their kids to them. They were, in effect, voting with their own flesh and blood." That was an important signal, in his estimation, "a big one." So too were the "large number of young men volunteering for service in the police and army."[131]

Another major sign that things were going in the right direction were tips. That is, the intelligence that local Iraqis were providing about "where the IEDs were placed, when bad actors moved into their neighborhood, where weapons were stored," and so on.[132] RCT-5 was receiving a large volume of this important local intelligence through the police. And it was using it to shut down insurgent networks and support systems.

As the commanding officer looked to the future in the waning days of RCT-5's deployment in Anbar, he believed the conditions were in place for his replacement to continue "battlespace expansion," but added that it was "not just battlespace, it is responsibility in that battlespace, that's what's key. Making sure that we have an Iraqi army and police that's equipped and manned to be able to handle the challenge. It's not a question of do they want it—they want it. It's a question of can they get the support from Baghdad that they need."[133]

That was another big challenge. And to meet it, the regimental leadership had become the "most vociferous proponents for the Sunni of Anbar." Nicholson put it this way: "We became the guys screaming at Baghdad that they're not getting enough money, that they're not getting enough resources, the allocation is insufficient to support governance and economic development. So we have inexplicably become the most ardent defenders of the Sunni."[134]

This was a most atypical position for a Marine commander to find himself in. But being a Marine, Colonel Nicholson turned it into an opportunity to increase his influence (*wasta*) with Sunni leadership in AO Raleigh. He did so by taking "General Mattis' old saying, 'no better friend, no worse enemy,' [and] morphed it into 'your only friend.'" Given the Sunni fear of a coming night of the long knives at the hands of the Shia, now in power in Baghdad, this further galvanized the decision of the sheikhs to line up with I MEF. "After the Samarra bombing, Marines were seen by the Sunnis as their protectors. We guarded them from attacks by those Shia death squads that they believed were headed for Anbar. I told the Fallujah City Council, Marines are at the gates so you can meet." And then the colonel wryly added, "We used that to our great advantage."[135]

AREA OF OPERATIONS DENVER—SECURING THE EUPHRATES CORRIDOR

General Zilmer described his 2006 counterinsurgency campaign plan for Anbar as a "book ends strategy." What this meant, he explained, was that I MEF would capitalize on the stability that had been established at the far ends of Anbar in Al Qa'im and Fallujah and extend that stability between those two book ends. It was an "outside-in strategy. The goal was to clear, hold, and build between Al Qa'im and Fallujah."[136]

In 2006 AO Denver belonged to RCT-7. One of its units, 3rd Battalion, 4th Marines (3/4), had responsibility for consolidating gains made in Al Qa'im as a result of Operation Steel Curtain. The commanding officer of 3/4, Lt. Col. Scott Shuster, described his mission as continuing what his predecessors had achieved: "If you recall, 3/6 participated in Operation Steel Curtain. . . . [It was] the genesis of the stabilization of the Al Qa'im region. Dale Alford, the former CO [commanding officer] of 3rd Battalion, 6th Marines [3/6], came up with the vision of putting pockets of Coalition forces in and among the population and then growing Iraqi security forces [police] from inside the population. . . . The idea was that the center of gravity is the population, not the terrain."[137]

Lt. Col. Nick Merano, commander of 1/7, "followed the template that Alford started and grew new positions—platoon-sized [combat outposts]—inside the population to add even more Iraqi security forces. I fell in on 1/7," said Shuster, and "we have transplanted coalition forces even more so throughout the area following that same template that was started by Alford. . . . I actually have autonomous zones now within my AO that are the responsibility of Iraqi security forces. I still have coalition forces with them," but they were only "token coalition forces," he explained, and this gave him "the combat power . . . [the] seed elements for further infusion [of 3/4 forces] inside the population."[138]

To accomplish this, Shuster had to engage with the local power brokers. It was only through them that he could grow the local police, one of the keys to expanding 3/4's footprint in that area. Here is what that engagement looked like on the ground through Shuster's eyes: "I've got three municipal mayors and three municipal councils. And then I have a regional mayor and a regional council. So I've got four governments I'm interacting with. Also there is the dynamic here between the tribes and the local government . . . [in which] the tribes decide what's going to happen. They're the executive agent. The municipal or civil government acts on the desires of the tribes."[139]

Shuster's role, as the battalion commander, "was to choose the right people from the tribes and the councils to interact with and to enable. . . . To identify those people and cultivate a relationship with them. . . . To teach them about the rule of law and the nature of government in this region, what they should be able to do for themselves and what they should seek to have their provincial government and their national government do for them. These are all new concepts."[140] It was all about maintaining those relationships with the tribal sheikhs, the mayors, and the members of the councils.

This paid dividends for 3/4 when it came to increasing the size of the local Iraqi police forces. By December 2006, Lieutenant Colonel Shuster noted,

> I've got 1,400 police . . . divided up into six police areas and substations with their own police chiefs that report to the district headquarters. And they're only trained as policemen. So one of the things that we've done to help that is we've developed . . . what we call [the] Iraqi Police Mid-Level Leaders Course. It's a week-long course teaching them how to be desk sergeants, shift supervisors, and watch commanders. We put them back into the police stations to add that NCO element. . . . [I also had] partnered with two Iraqi battalions . . . [in my AO and was] colocated with an Iraqi brigade headquarters that's partnered with my regiment.[141]

Col. Bill Crowe, the commander of RCT-2, intended to spread the Al Qa'im model to the hardscrabble towns down the Euphrates corridor all the way to Hit, at the southeastern end of AO Denver. AQI again was embedded in several of those localities and again would have to be cleared out. But after that was accomplished, as in Al Qa'im, Crowe intended this time around to hold those towns through COPs and Iraqi police.

Rawah was a good illustration. Two companies from the 3rd LAR initially moved into the town due east of Al Qa'im, and on the first day four of their Marines were killed at a traffic control point. In the next few days three more died from a pressure-plate mine. In the initial phase of the operation, said Colonel Crowe, his men "were on shaky ground trying to secure Rawah."[142]

Once two additional companies were added to the initial units things changed for the better. And then, as these forces spread control south of the town along the river, they found "over eight hundred IEDs." Crowe believed "that cache wasn't built just for AO Denver. It was probably to be sent throughout the country." They had "hit a major resupply point for the AIF [anti-Iraqi forces] north of the river. We found suicide belts. We found 120 mortars, 82s, seven SA-7s," recounted the commanding officer.[143]

Next, RCT-7 moved on Anah. It turned out to be an AQI command-and-control node. From here al Qaeda spread fighters and supplies into Anbar. It was a key transit point. To bring the town under control, RCT-7 built a berm around it, as they had in Al Qa'im. Moving into Anah, they found themselves in a protracted gun fight with AQI elements. They drove them out only to see them come back several times to counterattack. But eventually the oil spot encompassed Anah. And as in Al Qa'im and Rawah, tribal engagement led to the expansion of local police who, in conjunction with Marines who stayed in place, held Anah by maintaining a persistent security presence.

To clear AQI out of Rawah and Anah, RCT-7 had the help of high-speed counterterrorism units from what Colonel Crowe, in a January 1, 2007, interview, euphemistically called "the national task force." He was referring to the men from that combined U.S. and British Special Forces outfit—joint Task Force 145—that operated across Anbar against high-value AQI targets. In the Rawah-Anah area they had conducted several successful raids, including one that Crowe noted was "the culmination of about three months' worth of SIGINT [signals intelligence] and HUMINT [human intelligence] work coming together in that hit." The result was the capture of six AQI emirs, as well as thirty members of the rank and file. And RCT-7's number one al Qaeda target was also killed.[144]

South of Rawah and Anah the next critical place to clear and hold was Haditha, another AQI key command-and-control hub for fighters headed to Ramadi and Baghdad. In July, Crowe initiated Operation Majib. In the first six weeks, he reported, the 2nd Battalion, 3rd Marines (2/3), "lost 15 . . . killed, primarily by snipers and IEDs, and had over one hundred–plus wounded. They've taken the most casualties of any [of my] battalions."[145] To take control of Haditha, Crowe established platoon-sized COPs.

Farther down the corridor, the same strategy was implemented in Baghdad, Dubbah, and, as the deployment of RCT-7 neared its end, Hit. The oil spot that had started in the Al Qa'im region had continued to grow. AO Denver was a much more stable environment as Colonel Crowe prepared for his change of command in early 2007.

END-OF-YEAR SITUATION REPORT: THE TIPPING POINT

A situation report for Anbar Province in early 2006 would have had this ominous headline: *Surging Violence and Grim Prognoses*. But by December its end-of-year counterpart had a much different message to report: Anbar reached the security tipping point. The situation across this key province in the Sunni heartland had started to change dramatically, and it was tipping in favor of I MEF and against AQI.

I MEF's COIN-based OPLAN with its interrelated elements of clearing out insurgents, holding territory through COPs, engaging and aligning with the sheikhs and their tribes, and building local Iraqi police units drawn from those tribes had shifted the ground in Anbar. And when fused with what Ali Hatim Abd al-Razzaq Ali al-Sulayman, the paramount sheikh of the Dulaym tribal confederation, called "the Awakening Revolution," the conditions were in place to bring the insurgency that AQI had commandeered in 2005 to heel in 2007.

Several journalistic accounts have characterized the Sunni Awakening as a sudden flipping of the sheikhs from one side to the other. But what this account has made clear is that just the opposite was the case. The Awakening was, in fact, an incredibly painful and bloody process that began at the end of 2005 and passed through two phases in 2006. The first was the ill-fated effort in the early winter months that was snuffed out by AQI. The second came in the summer. It took root because of the successful execution of I MEF's OPLAN, in particular the linking of tribal engagement with the methodical establishment of COPs in the population centers of Anbar. In each of the AOs—Topeka, Raleigh, Denver—the forces of I MEF spread the oil spot, securing more and more ground.

The events of 2006 reveal that in war amongst the people holding territory is essential. It is the foundation for a successful counterinsurgency strategy. You must be able to secure the ground where the population lives. I MEF's COIN-based OPLAN cleared the insurgents out of the populated areas and then secured that territory through COPs. By doing this, I MEF demonstrated to the people of Anbar that engagement was for real. Territory is as important in counterinsurgency as it is in conventional operations, but for different reasons. In COIN, taking territory constrains the enemy's freedom of movement and gives the population a safe space to live and work. Once the sheikhs were convinced that I MEF intended to stay the course in Anbar, they opened the doors to the support of the population. And that population, in turn, swelled the ranks of the Anbar security forces and delivered a wealth of local intelligence on the whereabouts of the AQI network in the province.

Finally, 2006 demonstrated that the tipping point in counterinsurgency is not always self-evident. The year 2006 was an increasingly violent one in Anbar, as the statistics demonstrated. Understanding what that escalating violence signaled proved extremely tricky. Colonel Devlin's assessment of it was far off the mark, as were the conclusions drawn by the ISG. And the media got it wrong as well. In 2007 II MEF replaced I MEF. They saw opportunity and intended to capitalize on the tipping point that was reached in 2006. They intended to cash in in 2007, consolidating the gains made by I MEF to send AQI packing out of Anbar.

CHAPTER 6

2007

Cashing In

BACK TO ANBAR

THE YEAR 2005 HAD BEEN TOUGH for the Marines of II MEF. Recall that as they prepared to leave Iraq at the end of that bloody year, the situation in Anbar remained highly volatile. But there were also embryonic signs that change might be in the offing. Most observers of the war at that time, however, were not aware of those nascent indicators or of their potential implications. They viewed Anbar against the backdrop of the brutal and escalating fight that the Marines of II MEF and their Army counterparts had engaged in throughout 2005. Those clashes, described in chapter 4, were considerable in number, with the insurgents giving as good as they got.

But in November and December 2005, Governor Mamoon, II MEF's senior leadership, and a group of Anbar sheikhs had begun an engagement process that, to the surprise of many of the experts, would play an important part in the strategic defeat of AQI in Anbar by the summer of 2007. In 2005 the sheikhs had begun opening that door. The tribal leaders involved in those early discussions proposed that grassroots Sunni security forces recruited from among their tribesmen could provide the Marines with the added forces needed to hold and secure territory after the insurgents were pushed out.

During 2006 that tribal engagement initiative became both a key part of I MEF's counterinsurgency-based OPLAN for Anbar and a strategic target that AQI tried to obliterate. But by year's end it was I MEF that had gained the upper hand. Its COIN-based operations had been effective in clearing out insurgents, holding territory through COPs, engaging and aligning with the sheikhs and their tribes, and building local Iraqi police units made up of those tribesmen.

Consequently, II MEF found itself returning to an Anbar Province that was in the throes of change. But as the force prepared to deploy, it was hard to ascertain just how long it would take to capitalize on that opportunity. To be sure, II MEF's leaders understood the gains I MEF had made by the close of 2006, and they intended to piggyback on I MEF's strategy to exploit those gains.

To do so, said Maj. Gen. Walter Gaskin, the commanding general of II MEF (Forward), his men did not prepare a new campaign plan for 2007. I MEF "had [established] a tremendous foundation" to build on, he explained. "One thing, if you look back, and hindsight is always 20-20 . . . and there is one decision that you made that you're just glad you did, for me that was the decision not to start a new campaign plan." Instead, explained Gaskin, "I took his [General Zilmer's] campaign plan and I developed it."[1]

There was no need to reinvent the wheel. And so, as Gaskin went on to add, before deploying "we had a workup prior to coming here" that "was pretty much in sync with how Major General Zilmer was dealing with the threat, as well as the transition to Iraqi control. So when I arrived, I made one of my priorities transition. We put that under the umbrella of stability, meaning that we had to do security and we had to do governance, we had to do economics, but we also had to [be ready to] really delve into the tribal engagement part." Engagement was essential if II MEF was going to "in a COIN sense—a counterinsurgency sense—separate al Qaeda . . . from the population centers."[2]

Gaskin made clear why this was the key. "Anbar is such a large area, about the size of North Carolina [and] we were an economy of force." General Zilmer could not secure it because his forces were "stretched all the way from east of Fallujah . . . out to Al Qa'im and to the borders of Jordan and Syria and so there were vast areas that he just didn't have enough folks" to secure. The same would be true for his Marines and soldiers. And there were not sufficient Iraqi forces to make

Maj. Gen. Walter Gaskin, commander of II MEF in 2007, meets with a group of Anbar sheikhs.

McWilliams and Wheeler, Eds., *Al-Anbar Awakening*, vol. 1, 1 up the difference. "There was an assessment of how short we were on the Iraqi security forces." But there was a wild card on the table and Gaskin knew it. "There was the Awakening . . . of the tribes," and "it was very dynamic when I came in."[3]

In II MEF's workup for Anbar, preparing to take advantage of tribal engagement was front and center, explained then–Brig. Gen. John Allen, one of the unit's deputy commanding generals. He had been tasked at Camp Lejeune by General Gaskin with "putting together a PME [professional military education] program focused on tribal engagement, the history of Mesopotamia and Iraq into modern times and, in particular, about what we termed the human terrain in Anbar Province. So we spent a lot of time studying that."[4]

General Allen was uniquely qualified for the task. The holder of three master's degrees in national security and intelligence studies, he had developed a regional interest in the greater Middle East. In the late 1980s then-Major Allen taught courses on the region at the Naval Academy as a member of the faculty. More than a decade later he returned to Annapolis, first as deputy commandant and then as the first Marine Corps officer to serve as commandant. Through these and other schoolhouse assignments, Allen became the quintessential warrior scholar.

If effective tribal engagement was going to be the basis for building on what I MEF had accomplished, a keen understanding of the tribes of Anbar was indispensable. Equipped with that knowledge, "We intended not to operate around the tribes to win this insurgency. Rather, we had to operate inside the tribes. We had to penetrate the tribal membrane that excluded our influence. Our preparation to operate in this manner was vital, indeed crucial."[5] In July 2010 Allen noted that one of the Marines' difficulties earlier in Anbar, especially in 2004–2005, was that they "could not get inside the tribes. They operated among the people but were not inside the tribes. So, for us it was all about understanding the tribes. We spent a great deal of time studying culture, attempting to identify the means by which we could capitalize on the human terrain as circumstances changed."[6]

That meant, in the first place, doing a great deal of reading, which is SOP for Marines. Indeed, the Marine Corps stresses reading, and this starts with the commandant's "Official Reading List." Divided into sections ranging from books for privates to books for generals, the objective for all is the same: "to provide Marines with an intellectual framework to study warfare and enhance their thinking and decision making skills. . . . In a world characterized by rapid change and great uncertainty, our reading program will act as a combat multiplier by providing all Marines with a common frame of reference and historical perspective on warfare, human factors in combat and decision-making."[7]

To prepare II MEF Marines for Anbar, their reading list began with the history of the British experience in Iraq following World War I. The reason for this

Brig. Gen. John Allen, deputy commanding general of II MEF in 2007, meets with Sheikh Ahmed Bezia Fteikhan al-Risha.

McWilliams and Wheeler, Eds., *Al-Anbar Awakening*, vol. 1, 226

assignment, recounted Allen, was that "the British in the immediate post–World War I period faced nearly the same conditions in Mesopotamia as we did in late 2006 and early 2007 . . . and in nearly the same places. We became avid readers of the history of that period, and discovered value not only in the content of the history, but in the historians themselves."[8]

Among those writers considered most important for inclusion in the professional military education (PME) program for II MEF was Gertrude Bell, the remarkable British diplomat and intelligence officer who played a seminal role in the post–World War I founding of Iraq. The first woman to graduate with a degree in history from Oxford University, she became an outstanding scholar, archaeologist, and linguist and spent many years exploring the deserts of Arabia. In the process she became a great admirer of the Arabs and their culture, acquiring a deep understanding of them. Allen elaborated, "From Gertrude Bell and others we learned about the concepts of honor and shame, segmentation and aggregation, the concept of patronage, the role of Sheikh in tribal society, and tribal law and arbitration. And while nearly 90 years had passed from the British Mandate period, the central tenets of tribal society, especially in Anbar, had remained essentially unchanged. From Bell . . . and Lawrence and others, we came to truly appreciate this person called an Iraqi, and I personally came to admire a people called the Arabs."[9]

II MEF also brought to Camp Lejeune numerous specialists on these matters with much experience on the ground in the Arab world and with tribal societies. All of this was geared to preparing the officers and NCOs of II MEF to be able to work inside the tribes, to penetrate the tribal membrane. This was true not only for officers at the level of Generals Gaskin and Allen but also for those junior officers and NCOs of the MEF's companies and platoons. In fact, it was especially critical for the latter because counterinsurgency fights are won or lost by those small units.

Thus, as II MEF came together as a team in this predeployment phase at Lejeune, they put PME to work, said General Allen, "in shaping our minds, understanding that unless we went in fully understanding tribalism, understanding the personalities that we were going to face and the whole dynamic of this code of conduct associated with being a member of an Arab tribe in Mesopotamia, we were not going to fully grasp the opportunities in front of us."[10]

ADAPTING THE MARINE AIR-GROUND TASK FORCE

The MAGTF is the construct used by the Corps for organizing and employing Marine forces for a range of military operations. It is a standalone warfighting unit—in the vernacular of the Corps, an organic, integrated, combined arms force that is ready to respond quickly and to sustain itself without the assistance of the other military services. A MAGTF consists of a command element, a ground combat element, an aviation combat element, and a combat service support element (CSSE). Each of these has a highly specific set of established directions and objectives.

But also infusing each element and subelement of the MAGTF is that unofficial Marine Corps mantra to always be ready to improvise, adapt, and overcome in the face of ugly surprises. It is embedded in the Marine culture. And Marines like to tell you that they have demonstrated that facility for more than two centuries by clearing away the fog of war to find solutions to help win the nation's wars.

While General Gaskin opted not to draft a new campaign plan, deciding to stick with that of I MEF's, "The one thing that we did differently [from I MEF] as far as organization [goes]," he said, "is we went back to the MAGTF. We organized as a MAGTF: whereas the I MEF staff had one deputy for support and a deputy for maneuver, I had a GCE [ground combat element] commander. Gen. Mark Gurganus was the GCE commander. . . . And I had a general in charge of the ACE [aviation combat element] and a general in charge of the logistics department [CSSE]."[11]

The reason for this change had to do with counterinsurgency objectives and the associated lines of operations that were to guide II MEF once back in Anbar. The end state for II MEF was the transfer of its responsibility for security to provincial Iraqi control. This entailed meeting the following objectives: "PIC [provincial Iraqi control] is achieved when the Governor, the Provincial Chief of Police and the Iraqi Army Division Commanders can effectively plan, coordinate and conduct integrated COIN operations; the terrorist and insurgent threat level is within the capabilities of the ISF to neutralize; and the Provincial government provides basic services to its citizens, has a budget and a viable economic sector."[12]

The II MEF leadership intended to adapt the MAGTF to meet the objective of provincial Iraqi control, but adjustments had to be made to accommodate the COIN mission. General Allen described it this way: in a "conventional combined arms operation" the MAGTF is geared to "exploit a break-through against the enemy force," when it materializes. "As we began to see things change in front of us . . . you have a unit that applies firepower to achieve an effect on an enemy's frontage. A breakthrough force for us then holds the shoulders [each side of the opening], and an exploitation force penetrates into the depth of the enemy rear with the idea of tearing up the rear and creating despair and psychological dislocation."[13]

The same principles applied to irregular conflicts like the one in Anbar, said the general, but they had to be customized for COIN. The breakthrough was to be accomplished by the MAGTF's ground combat element, also called the ground force element. Those "security forces created a secure environment" and carried out "the training of the Iraqi army and the Iraqi police." The ground force element was the MAGTF's breakthrough force in a COIN environment.[14]

"The exploitation forces" were configured within the MAGTF's CSSE, explained Allen, who had responsibility for this element. They included "our civil affairs, our efforts at tribal engagement, economic opportunity, governance, the development of rule of law." But the security force mission came first, he stressed. Once "we got that right then everything else was possible. Without the security piece nothing else was possible."[15]

The ground force element of the MAGTF was commanded by Brig. Gen. Mark Gurganus. He had charge of the two Marine regiments deployed in AOs Denver and Raleigh and the Army brigade in AO Topeka. With those forces he intended to establish security and stability on the ground in Anbar, from one end of the province to the other. Gurganus had the breakthrough forces and the kinetic fight. He also had responsibility for training the ISF to expand the ranks of his breakthrough forces to hold the ground once it was cleared of AQI and its local counterparts.

The CSSE of the MAGTF, in a COIN environment, is the "exploitation force," and has responsibility for a broad set of nonkinetic activities. General Allen explained the task breakdown as follows: the MAGTF's "operations were organized along six Lines of Operations—LOOs—which were Security, Transition, Governance, Economic Development, Rule of Law, and Information. We planned and executed across these six LOOs and worked them in mutual support of each other." The ground force element, under General Gurganus, had responsibility for "Security and Transition, which were inextricably linked." Allen had "Governance and Economic Development, and the Rule of Law. Information touched them all."[16]

Moreover, Allen also had responsibility for "tribal engagement," which he described as "the critical enabler within and around all the Lines of Operation." This latter point is critical, for neither Gurganus nor Allen could successfully prosecute his lines of operations without it. Tribal engagement was the key to everything II MEF hoped to achieve in 2007.[17]

IT IS STILL WAR

Col. John Charlton took the 1st BCT of the Army's 3rd Infantry Division to central Al Anbar in February 2007, replacing Colonel MacFarland. He had been to the AO the previous November on a predeployment site survey. It had been a memorable visit. "It was a very, very violent place. Al Qaeda was entrenched there. In fact, I will never forget, one of the first events I went to during my recon was a memorial ceremony for a Marine that had been killed recently. It's a real eye-opener when you actually get there and as part of your PDSS [predeployment site survey] you are going to a memorial ceremony."[18]

So when he returned in February, Charlton thought he knew what the BCT would face. But then he visited one of those COPs held by a Marine company in downtown Ramadi, almost in the heart of the city, just east of the Government Center. "I remember going out there and the building itself looked like it had been subject to a lot of violence and fighting. It was near collapse and it was a four-story building and, of course, it had concrete barriers all around it and a lot of force protection."[19]

Once safely inside the COP, Colonel Charlton "met the Marine company commander and he took me on a tour of the outpost and I went up on the roof, where he had some security positions set up, and I noticed, when I got up there, that there was a bed of a dump truck on top of the roof. So, naturally, I had to ask how that dump truck bed had gotten on the roof, four stories up." A young Marine lance corporal recounted how it had landed there during a fight in December. AQI "launched a suicide attack against the combat outpost with a dump truck filled with explosives and the dump truck was able to penetrate the outer barriers of the combat outpost and detonate, nearly collapsing the building. The blast was so powerful that the bed of the truck landed on the roof. The roof was then set on fire, a lot of camouflage netting was on fire, and the Marines were continuing to fight while the building was on fire with the bed from this dump truck sitting there."[20]

The only thing more remarkable than the sight of that dump truck bed on the roof was the matter-of-fact way the Marine corporal told the story of that attack. It made crystal clear, said Charlton, that we "had our work cut out for us."[21] Ramadi remained the most dangerous place in Iraq. And the monthly enemy incident report for the city more than bore that out. In December 2006 there were more than 550 attacks of various kinds, and the first month of 2007 recorded 500, or approximately 125 per week.[22]

Moreover, there was plenty of violence elsewhere in the province, likewise borne out by the statistics. For example, the weekly average number of attacks for Anbar in January was four hundred.[23] II MEF faced a serious kinetic fight, said General Gaskin.[24] Each of Anbar's AO's still teemed with AQI fighters, and General Gurganus, in conjunction with his three battlespace regimental and brigade commanders, focused on driving them out of their territory and then securing that ground.

Area of Operations Topeka

In AO Topeka, Colonel Charlton knew the numbers:

> [The] 1-1 had been there eight months and lost eighty soldiers and Marines, just in eight months. So, they were averaging ten killed in action [KIA] per month in that city and I knew that we were going to be there for at least a year and we found out later that it was going to extend to fifteen months. So, I knew that there was no way we could sustain that [casualty rate] . . . for a full year, that we had to do something dramatic, something on a large scale, otherwise we would die from a thousand cuts. If my combat outposts were going to be subjected to those types of attacks on a daily basis, our casualty rates would just be off the charts.[25]

So the brigade commander decided he would clear AQI out of Ramadi en masse and take control of the city. MacFarland's brigade had made a "penetration, they had established a foothold" in Ramadi, noted Charlton. "The next logical step was to pour everything in there because we had the conditions set to do that. We had a nascent relationship now with the tribal leaders and that led to their greater support for the ISF. So, from a tactical standpoint, we were postured well."[26]

The colonel planned a six-week campaign. The first stage of that assault—Operation Murfreesboro—took place in the southeastern part of the city, known locally as the Ma'laab District. It was the part of Ramadi where al Qaeda was the most dug in. The Ready First had not gone there.

The 1/9 infantry battalion would kick off the campaign by moving against the Ma'laab on February 18, 2007. Charlton explained that the "techniques we used" mirrored the "clear, hold, build paradigm. . . . You have to do a physical separation of the population from the enemy and you do that through clearing . . . going in there house to house, street by street, and clearing the enemy out, killing or capturing them. . . . But there is another component to clearing as well: that is psychological separation so that the population is no longer threatened by the enemy and they are no longer supporting them psychologically."[27]

To prepare the battlefield, the high-speed boys from Task Force 145 went in over several nights to "cherry-pick the leadership" of AQI, to throw them off balance and mask what was coming. Charlton explained it this way: "We gathered as much intelligence as we could and did some very precise targeted operations to . . . hit their leadership, not giving them the indication that we were going to follow with a large-scale operation, and we were moderately successful at that. . . . It is really tough to get the level of intelligence necessary to actually go in and grab the key leaders; but we did get a few."[28]

Next came the assault, and it came fast. In the middle of the night Charlton's forces moved in and literally walled off the southeastern part of Ramadi, isolating it between a canal on one side and an "in the blink of an eye" barrier on the other: every street was blocked by some form of an obstruction that controlled traffic in and out of the southeast.

Isolation accomplished, the assault forces of 1/9 and the 1st Brigade of the Iraqi 1st Division moved in. They were backed up by the 3/69 Armor positioned in the west and 1/6 Marines in the north. The fight inside this part of Ramadi took three weeks, said Charlton, and it was "very intense. The enemy was dug in and they used IEDs in a defensive manner. They would position both individually placed IEDs and vehicle IEDs around the areas where they concentrated in a defensive manner and in large quantities. So, it was very, very difficult . . . exhausting work to try and reduce those obstacles. We took a lot of casualties and the EOD [explosive ordnance disposal] teams were going 24/7 trying to reduce the IED threat." Three weeks of this fight and the forces of 1/9 and their Iraqi counterparts were exhausted. To complete the clearing operation, "II MEF sent a Marine company."[29]

Now it was time to hold the southeast, to secure that separation of the population from AQI. For this Charlton's men started establishing COPs. The first was set up in an abandoned school; it went up in forty-eight hours. Charlton described the process as a "COP in a box, a prefabricated fighting position made out of steel and ballistic glass. We had trucks that were all packaged with these things and once we seized a building, we could have a fully functional combat outpost within about forty-eight hours. We had engineers standing by to go in there and establish power and wire the place up so you had lights and generators and radios. So, that was a key portion of the operation as well."[30]

An IED removal unit in Anbar
CONNABLE, *U.S. MARINES IN IRAQ, 2004–2008*, 128

And once the COP had secured the area, its forces began interacting with the local population to gain its support. They did so by providing humanitarian assistance including blankets, generators, food and potable water, and medical support. They even distributed damage payments on the spot, the day after a neighborhood had been cleared, to begin the rebuilding process. This was carried out through the deployment of more "COPs in a box." The result was that Operation Murfreesboro was able in three weeks to achieve the following objectives: One, it eliminated the insurgent safe havens while minimizing collateral damage to infrastructure. Two, U.S. forces and their ISF counterparts improved security in the Ma'laab District. Three, the empowerment of the Iraqi police enhanced the legitimacy of local government. Finally, public works projects improved the quality of life for the citizens of the Ma'laab.[31]

The next phase of the six-week campaign was Operation Okinawa. Having lost the southeastern part of Ramadi, AQI aimed to reposition itself in the northern part of the city and establish a new base of operations. Charlton intended to preempt that move.

Okinawa kicked off even before Murfreesboro came to an end. Charlton sent Lt. Col. Bill Jurney and the 1/6 Marines to cut off AQI. Jurney had been in Ramadi for some time, knew the ground, and was lauded by the BCT chief as "just a phenomenal commander." He "did just a phenomenal job," said Charlton, "using the same techniques that we used in Murfreesboro."[32]

The final phase of Charlton's campaign to clear and hold Ramadi was Operation Call to Freedom. But to finish the job he needed more boots on the ground in the city. Most of his forces were holding territory. He had to "try and figure out a way to hold these areas" while clearing the rest. But all he had left was a cavalry squadron. Charlton "went to II MEF and basically offered a proposal. They were looking to get a force south of Fallujah because there was some terrain down there, fairly open terrain, that had been a problem and they needed a force that was very mobile, that could cover a lot of ground, and . . . take care of the soft underbelly of Fallujah."[33] A Marine battalion—the 2/5—was due in AO Raleigh and had been earmarked for that mission.

Charlton thought he could make better use of those thousand Marines. They were made up of "a very high density of trigger pullers, exactly what I was looking for. So, the deal I made with II MEF was to offer up my cavalry squadron, which has a strength of five hundred to six hundred, but is tremendously mobile and is the perfect force to put south of Fallujah. And then I get 2/5 chopped [assigned] to me to allow me to hold the city which we had just cleared."[34]

Having struck the bargain, Charlton reset his battle plan. He secured the north with the 3/69 (Armor) and took the 1/9 Infantry, which had been given time to rest during Okinawa, and made them the main force for clearing the rest of Ramadi. And as they cleared, the 2/5 Marines would follow and hold the cleared area. It was an intricate operation with lots of moving parts, conceded Colonel Charlton. "I was essentially trying to chop a battalion, receive a new battalion, and reposition a battalion in the middle of a fight. Well, the way we did that probably would have received a no-go grade in tactics school because of the complexity, but it ended up working pretty well."[35]

By March 30 Operation Call to Freedom was over and Ramadi cleared. On that day Charlton surveyed the city from end to end and found that "the entire city is quiet. It is unbelievable. It is almost eerie it is so quiet. It is unnerving. But, there wasn't a single shot fired that day. There was not one single attack in my entire AO, to include downtown Ramadi."[36] In six weeks AQI had lost Ramadi, the capital of its self-styled Iraqi caliphate.

Now came the hold phase, and that meant COP proliferation. The initial COP in a box at the schoolhouse was to serve as the hub, out from which others would sprout. Charlton's men eventually established forty platoon- and company-sized joint security stations, COPs, and checkpoints throughout the city. And by the summer, he said, "You could safely go virtually anywhere in the city."[37] And in September would come the running of that Ramadi road race.

Area of Operations Raleigh

When he arrived in AO Raleigh to take command in January, 6th Regimental Combat Team (RCT-6) commander Col. Richard Simcock found that the security situation there was slipping backward. His mission was the same as that of the other regimental and brigade commanders in Anbar: "Conduct counterinsurgency operations to facilitate the standing up of Iraqi forces and establishing of provincial Iraqi control within AO Raleigh."[38] But the first order of business for the colonel and his Marines was to tackle the dogged and fierce insurgent attacks taking place in parts of their area of responsibility.

To illustrate the challenges the RCT faced, the colonel described a firefight he encountered near Fallujah as he was changing command: "When I first got here, there was a section of the battle space [that was a] very bad area. It was controlled by the terrorists, and during my turnover [of command] with my predecessor, he took me to a town that's about ten miles to the south of Fallujah in that section. We got into a big firefight. IEDs were all around, small-arms fire, RPGs [rocket-propelled grenades]. We were stopped."[39]

Parts of Fallujah were little better, said Lt. Col. Bill Mullen, who commanded the 2/6 Marines in 2007. His AO was inside Fallujah; when he arrived in the city he found the security situation there needed immediate attention. Mullen had heard that his good friend up in Ramadi, Bill Jurney, was having success in that toughest part of the Anbar fight, and so he decided to go look for himself. Mullen wanted to "figure out what the hell's different [in Ramadi], find out what they're doing there." He came back and "changed what we needed to put into place in the Fallujah situation." The result was Operation Alljah.[40]

Mullen intended to use swarming methods similar to what Jurney was employing in Ramadi. The tactic is straightforward: move rapidly into an area where the insurgents are ensconced with dispersed units, chase then out, and consolidate your forces to establish control through a permanent presence. Surprise would be the key element of the swarming tactics that Mullen intended to use in Operation Alljah. He provided these details of how 2/6 used swarming tactics to gain control of the city's precincts: "You go in here, you clear the enemy out. You hold it by putting the barriers around it, by putting in neighborhood watch, and with that comes the security of the precinct. You take measures within the population and they begin telling you where the enemy is, or the enemy's just gone because it's a nonpermissive environment for them because you've won that sector over. So . . . when we go in here [into a Fallujah precinct] we go in to stay."[41] And when 2/6 swarmed, it did so with speed, often catching the insurgents napping.

These measures were based on what 1/6 was doing up in Ramadi. "We used that general concept . . . making the specifics fit Fallujah. . . . Bill Jurney, if he were sitting here right now," observed Mullen, "he'd clearly recognize what we're doing as the same as what he did in Ramadi."[42] And the results were the same. By the end of spring, neighborhoods that 2/6 Marines had been unable to enter without getting into a gunfight in the winter months were now quiet.

Other parts of AO Raleigh also had some real hot spots. RCT-6 Marines learned quickly that when they went into those areas a gunfight would ensue. It was not a question of if but when it would break out. Consider the area covered by 3/6. It contained one of the most robust AQI bases in Raleigh, said its commanding officer, Lt. Col. Jim McGrath. It was located in the Habbaniyah region, west of Fallujah, "right in the center of my battle space, right across the river, up to the north. That was a true safe haven. . . . It had an IED belt on one side and an IED belt on the other side. You could not penetrate into that area without just getting blasted."[43]

On one occasion, recounted McGrath, when elements of 3/6 attempted to penetrate the area, the enemy response was especially potent:

> As soon as they saw us coming, all hell broke loose. They lit us up with a complex attack . . . SPG-9 rounds. They used two machine guns in a complex orientation, one direct and one from the flank. And they used sniper fire. They immediately killed one of my guys. We got the

> fires oriented to suppress the machine gun. Sniper fire knocked one of my guys to the ground, on his helmet. The helmet fortunately worked and saved his life. . . . It was twenty minutes before we gained fire supremacy over the enemy, we were able to suppress them, bring in air and dropping the houses that were firing on us. So, I got it. That's a significant and very ballsy enemy that's on the other side, with some skill to have that degree of tactical patience and to set up that degree of fire to take on a force that was prepared for it, and still they brought it to us. That's pretty good.[44]

McGrath put the area under surveillance and found it was a major logistics and operations base for the insurgents in his AO.

> That became my focus, because I knew that's where all the caches were being supplied from. That's where the arms were coming from. And we had JSTARs [joint surveillance and target attack radar system]—our ISR [intelligence, surveillance, and reconnaissance]—that was showing us that this stuff was coming across the river. It was being pulled out of caches there, moved down the road, and then pushed across at night. So we watched, we used all of the intelligence that we could fuse together to build a total picture.[45]

What it revealed was a major safe haven where AQI forces could "rest and refit, and rearm and train."

To take that AQI base, the commanding officer of the 3/6 planned to use the same tactics that Mullen was employing inside Fallujah. His forces went straight into the enemy's lair, through "an amphibious landing right across from our battle space into their battle space in the middle of the night. We just bypassed all of the IED belts. . . . The next morning, [AQI] woke up and we were there." It was a big surprise. And then the 3/6 "began cracking [their base] from the inside out."[46]

AQI did not stay around for the fight. In fact, said McGrath, "Somehow, [AQI] got word that we were coming" and scooted. He believed that happened because 3/6

> coordinated the operation with the Iraqi army. It was their battle space and most of that information leaked out. But what they couldn't move was these monster caches. We found a tremendous amount of caches. The two most important caches were electronics caches. . . . It was enough [for] radio-controlled IEDs to match what you'd find in a month and a half in all of Al Anbar. So a sizable electronics cache,

with all of the other components, your circuitry boards, your washing machine timers, your wire, everything and then some. In terms of ordnance, we found enough to fill a seven-ton and a half, so much that we could not blow it up.[47]

Once in control of the ground, 3/6 continued to follow the Jurney blueprint. That meant that it took root where AQI once roamed freely and with impunity. Lieutenant Colonel McGrath's forces established a "permanent, persistent presence there. That made all the difference in the world," he said, and then went on to explain how 3/6 connected the clear-hold-build dots:

> Once we got in there, all [enemy activities] stopped completely. Now, simultaneous with that, with the decrease in significant AQI actions, the people were really excited. They pushed and said, "We want to establish a neighborhood watch." And I said, "Well, I think it's a great idea," and they did. I didn't tell them how, where, when. I asked the mayor, "What do you think?" And the mayor said, "Yes, under local governance, I think it's good." "Bravo to you, Mr. Mayor." What does the district police chief think? He says, "I think it's good. They'll operate under me." So you have this group that has now decided they want to operate and provide security for their area. . . . They essentially created a gated community.[48]

Yet another hot spot in AO Raleigh that RCT-6 had to tamp down was in al-Karmah. Located sixteen kilometers northeast of Fallujah, it had long been an enemy stronghold. The early months of 2007 brutally illustrated that reality. In early February a Marine CH-46E Sea Knight was shot down by a shoulder-fired missile. The attack killed seven Marines. Then three Army engineers sent to secure the wreckage were also killed. They hit an IED. Later in the month RCT-6 forces captured an IED factory run by AQI in al-Karmah and found a number of vehicles, three fifty-five-gallon barrels of chlorine, three barrels of nitroglycerine, and enormous amounts of assorted munitions. The factory could produce IEDs with massive killing power.

These kinds of enemy attacks and Marine counteroperations continued through the spring months. And then in June Colonel Simcock initiated Operation Black Diamond, a series of major attacks on al-Karmah to bring AQI to heel there. Having taken control of the ground in the town, his forces established permanent outposts, which in turn led to the establishment of a permanent Iraqi police presence in al-Karmah. And that "empowered the citizens of al-Karmah to counter

AQI's murder and intimidation campaign." The terrorists could no longer hide in plain sight. Finally, all of these developments "facilitated the return of Sheikh Meshan of the influential Jumayli tribe from Jordan."[49]

By June major kinetic operations were over in AO Raleigh, said the executive officer of RCT-7. They were largely done. The mission was now to transfer control to the ISF, training its police and army to assume control. And that took time, he added.[50]

But RCT-7 could only get to this point by clearing, holding, and establishing permanent presence. It was a point that Simcock, the regimental commander, underscored. Through "permanent presence the people know that you're there to stay, you build those relationships, they start talking to you, and it just all rolls in your favor." Clearing is "the first step, and then the things that follow along afterwards are really what get you your ultimate success. It truly is about the people that live here," added the regimental commander, "winning them over . . . ultimately leads to success."[51]

Area of Operations Denver

In AO Denver, Col. Herman Clardy and RCT-2 initiated a series of operations to consolidate the security gains made there in 2006 in order to move into the nonkinetic stages of counterinsurgency. Recall how the commanding officer of RCT-7, Col. Bill Crowe, and his Marines built on Operation Steel Curtain by spreading the oil spot in AO Denver. What started in the Al Qa'im region continued to expand through 2006. And by the end of that year, AO Denver was a much more stable place when Colonel Crowe turned over command to RCT-2 in early 2007.

But there was still some kinetic work to be done. As detailed in chapter 3, insurgents in Haditha had been a potent force and had sought to take over municipal government, establish courts, and control other local institutions. They enforced all of these activities through murder and intimidation. RCT-7 rolled them back in 2006.

Operation Majid aimed to finish the job in the Haditha area by neutralizing what was left of AQI and other anti-Iraqi forces. The change in I MEF strategy in 2006 had resulted in significant improvements there, and the goal of Majid was to complete that effort. Marines from RCT-2 and their Iraqi allies began in February; by the end of the spring, violence in the Haditha Triad had dropped precipitously as AQI exited.

Also in February, RCT-2 initiated Operation Bulrush II. This was a continuation of operations began by the 15th Marine Expeditionary Unit (MEU) that aimed to deny the insurgents sanctuary in Rutbah, located in the far west of the AO, and to establish and maintain a presence in the city. They completed that mission in the spring and then helped launch a functioning city council in Rutbah that began engaging the provincial government on such key city issues as power, water, and fuel. To facilitate that process, the MEU coordinated through II MEF headquarters the visit of the Anbar governor to Rutbah on March 22.

In March, Colonel Clardy focused on interdicting, disrupting, and clearing out insurgent remnants holed up across AO Denver. He did so through Operation Harris Ba'sil, which exploited expanding local knowledge coming from the population on enemy hideouts. RCT-2 was able to gain that local knowledge because along with their ISF partners, the Marines demonstrated to the population that RCT-2 was going to ensure their security, isolate them from AQI, and facilitate reconstruction and the governance process. By the fall of 2007 these and other security consolidating operations made possible the handoff of multiple RCT-2 fixed positions to the ISF, particularly in the Al Qa'im area, increasing the ISF's responsibility and visibility with the populace.

IT TAKES A NETWORK

Implementing counterinsurgency was II MEF's main effort in Anbar in 2007. As illustrated above, this entailed securing the ground in the province by spreading that COIN oil spot. But there was a natural complement to those counterinsurgency operations. And that was the counterterrorist program carried out by the special mission units of the JSOC.

While COIN isolated the population from AQI, it did not eliminate the organization's operational apparatus or infrastructure. The reason for this had to do with its character and makeup. AQI maintained a highly clandestine iceberg-like structure—a secret underground composed of a complex and secretive array of below-the-waterline operational, command, and support units.[52] These surreptitious capabilities provided AQI with a broad assortment of means to conduct irregular warfare in Anbar and elsewhere in Iraq.

Furthermore, the units of that apparatus were networked. In other words, while AQI had a senior leadership in Anbar, the apparatus itself was not hierarchical. Rather, it was a horizontal collection of sometimes connected but often autonomous nodes. A node is the basic unit of a networked organization, which is linked through some means of communication. Modern networks are often joined together through information technology, which facilitates network undertakings. At the time of the insurgency in Anbar, off-the-shelf information technology available to AQI included cellular phones and Internet communications through email and websites. All of this made AQI's secret underground different from the secret underground organizations of armed groups that challenged states during the Cold

War. Outfits like AQI had transformed how armed groups fought in the twenty-first-century security environment.

To disrupt and degrade AQI's secret infrastructure in Anbar, the United States employed its own below-the-waterline organization that likewise operated in the shadows and consisted of highly trained special mission units. Their forte is offensive, highly lethal counterterrorism measures that are directly targeted at the enemy's clandestine iceberg-like apparatus.

In Iraq that high-speed outfit was put together by Lt. Gen. Stan McChrystal, who had spent a good part of his Army career in the special mission units of JSOC. And from September 2003 until June 2008 he commanded JSOC and deployed with units to Iraq. Once there he built a special task force made up of the Army's Delta Force; the Navy's SEAL Team 6; the Army's 160th Special Operations Aviation Regiment, or Night Stalkers; elements of the Army's 75th Ranger Regiment; and the 24th Special Tactics Squadron of the Air Force. Additionally, men from Britain's Special Air Service were part of this team, which came to be known as Task Force 145.

In Iraq, Task Force 145 was located at Balad, a Saddam-era airbase sixty-eight kilometers north of Baghdad. McChrystal had it up and running by June 2004; as noted earlier, it was operating in Anbar in 2005–2006. The Balad facility included a state-of-the-art joint operations center (JOC), whose daily activities were directed by the commander of Delta Force. Task Force 145 was subdivided into geographically targeted units: Task Force West was assigned to the greater Anbar area. The Baghdad area was assigned to Task Force Central. Task Force North focused on the Kurdish region, while the Special Air Service men of Task Force Black were in the south of Iraq.

In putting together Task Force 145, McChrystal started with the premise that he needed a networked organization to defeat the al Qaeda network in Iraq. He probably got the idea from the work of John Arquilla and David Ronfeldt, both analysts with the RAND Corporation. In 2001 they first argued that in the new era of "netwar," armed nonstate actors would wage irregular conflict through flexible social-network structures that constituted the core of their organization. In the Middle East, in particular, they found that terrorist groups like al Qaeda had shifted from formally organized hierarchical systems to flexible, decentralized network structures of loosely connected individuals and subgroups that operated with considerable tactical independence.[53]

For Task Force 145 to function at peak efficiency, McChrystal knew its operational units must have "actionable intelligence." This meant they had to gain real-time information on the whereabouts of AQI's mid-level commanders and managers, not just its top leadership. Without actionable intelligence, Task Force 145 units could not track them down. To acquire this intelligence, the JOC zeroed in on how AQI communicated through its networked system.

At the time, Iraq was experiencing an explosion in the use of cell phones. Unlike during Saddam's time, when no cell phone system was permitted, in the years since his removal cellular service had swept over Iraq. By the time Task Force 145 was up and running, several million Iraqis were on the phone, and that included AQI and other insurgent elements. It was a more convenient and much faster way of communicating than the old-fashioned courier system. To be sure, the latter was more secure, but it was also much slower. AQI and other anti-Coalition elements became addicted to the tools of the information age. And that turned out to be an opportunity for the intelligence specialists that supported Task Force 145 operations.

Of course, the managers of the AQI network knew of the National Security Agency and its signals intelligence collection systems, and they took many precautions to elude them. But they still had to communicate. It was an essential element of a networked system, and their reliance on it provided an opening for the signals intelligence specialists supporting McChrystal's outfit at Balad. This group had a bag full of tools for sifting through the intake of the signals intelligence vacuum cleaners collecting every phone call in Iraq, along with the header information of all email messages.

The tools that scoured those huge databases included link and nodal analysis. These data-mining programs extracted implicit and actionable knowledge from large data sets by discovering nonobvious patterns between a subject and other people, addresses, locations, and so on. This pattern-based inquiry used predictive models of behavior, in this case those of AQI midlevel managers. Searches in the cell phone and email databases collected in Iraq and the identification of patterns of behavior provided clues that intelligence specialists in the JOC followed up on.

To do this they made use of yet other information-age intelligence capabilities, including the unblinking eye of 24/7 drone air platforms. These pilotless craft, also known as unmanned aerial vehicles, can provide persistent observation once they are over a target. They are the information-age version of the age-old police stakeout. Images from drones of the movements of AQI managers were relayed instantly to the JOC, where imagery analysts were watching.

The combination of these signals and imagery tools, in conjunction with other sources of intelligence that included interrogation and human source collection, were all fused together at the JOC. A case study of how these tools came together and were employed in a synergistic manner can be built from reports of the operation that killed Zarqawi in 2006. That story has been told by several journalists, including Bill Roggio, Sean Naylor, and Mark Bowden.[54] Other reports include a pseudonymous first-hand account by the head of the interrogation team who make a key breakthrough in the hunt for Zarqawi.[55]

But Task Force 145 did much more than kill Zarqawi. Its operational tempo, set by McChrystal, was to hit them every night. And that resulted in the elimination of a large number of AQI's mid-level managers who ran the operational, command, and support units. How many did they remove? In the covert world of outfits like Task Force 145, such numbers are hard to come by.

But in his book *Task Force Black*, the story of the British Special Air Service element assigned to McChrystal, the well-connected journalist Mark Urban provides some startling figures. If he is to be believed, Task Force 145 became an AQI killing machine. "Between 2005 and early 2007," he reports, Task Force 145 "killed two thousand members of the Sunni jihadist groups as well as detaining many more.... McChrystal's high-tempo onslaught had begun in earnest" in 2005. And "JSOC's intelligence database had grown with each network it rolled up."[56]

The reason for success against AQI had to do with the fact that McChrystal placed a high premium on the "exploitation and analysis of each raid." And that "meant that intelligence gathering became [a key] point of each strike."[57] Everything found at the location of an attack on an AQI target was brought back to the JOC and mined for information that could lead to the next target. Consider those cell phones and laptops found by Task Force 145 teams: Deleting items from these devices is not so easy. In fact, data are retained on them even after the user deletes them. The ability to retrieve those data can be critical to the collection of actionable intelligence, as was the case for Task Force 145 specialists in such activities.

The operational units of Task Force 145 that served in Anbar were an important complement to the counterinsurgency strategy initiated in 2006, and that continued in 2007. RCT-2, RCT-6, and the 1st BCT isolated the population from AQI and secured the ground. But they did not eliminate all of AQI's operational apparatus or infrastructure. They got some of it, to be sure, but not all of it.

On more than a few occasions, AQI was able to redeploy as the forces of I MEF in 2006 and II MEF in 2007 moved into one of its sanctuaries. Those remaining secretive below-the-waterline units were left to Task Force 145. When asked whether counterinsurgency and counterterrorism worked well together in Anbar, General Allen replied, "That's correct. Actually, one is the component of the other. Counterterrorism is a component of counterinsurgency."[58]

The general went on to explain that there were three different kinds of forces focused on the midlevel commanders and managers in AQI's clandestine infrastructure and operational units. First, there was Task Force West from Task Force 145. He described it as "Stan McChrystal's outfit that came roaring out of Balad on a regular basis and would conduct operations in the region. The vast majority of the time black SOF [as the forces of Task Force 145 were called] worked well with us. We coordinated operations with them, we were the cordon force or might provide other support. They were the counterterrorism strike force. That would work out very well."[59]

II MEF also had "very close coordination with white SOF and our conventional operations and our security operations. When I say that I mean transition operations with the police. That worked out very well. We sought to combine their capabilities with ours." The police played an important part in finding insurgents embedded at the local level, and Allen knew it. He had a researcher at the Center for Naval Analysis study the British COIN campaign in Malaysia and the contributions made by indigenous police. The researcher found, "when the numbers of police were at a certain point the initiative shifted" in favor of the COIN effort. So, white SOF—the traditional Special Forces mission of working with indigenous peoples—was just as important as the contributions of the task force to rolling up AQI in Anbar.[60]

A final special capability that General Allen highlighted was that of "Marine reconnaissance fighting as a traditional recon force at very local levels."[61] What he meant by that was explained by Lt. Col. Jim Higgins, who commanded the 1st Recon Battalion in Anbar in 2007. On certain occasions, he noted, "We did coordinate with 'other Coalition Forces-Iraq,' Task Force [West] would be a better term. . . . We worked closely with them, because we were going into zones that had the highest enemy concentration. Those are the same zones that those folks are working, as well. Early on there were some hiccups," he explained. They both were trying to hit the same targets, he said, but "we hadn't been talking."[62]

Eventually they worked it out, as the following example illustrates: "We found out about five hours before we were going to do a raid that the 'Other Coalition Forces-Iraq' folks were also planning on doing a raid in that same area that night. We told them we were coming up there. They said, 'You're going to be up there already, you take it.' We did the raid, captured eighteen . . . flew in Black Hawks and pulled them away. . . . They didn't have to go do the hit. It worked out very well." But most of his recon operations were not focused on the AQI targets of Task Force 145. "That's not our bread and butter, by any means," said the 1st Recon commander.[63] That belonged to Task Force 145. And what the available evidence reveals is that they were quite effective in either killing or capturing many of those who managed AQI's operational apparatus or infrastructure.

EXPANDING THE BREAKTHROUGH FORCE

Earlier in this chapter, General Allen described the forces controlled by his II MEF counterpart, General Gurganus, as the breakthrough force for the kinetic fight against the insurgents. But Gurganus also had responsibility for training the ISF in order to expand the ranks of that breakthrough force to hold the ground cleared of AQI and its local counterparts. Of II MEF's six lines of operations, Gurganus had responsibility for security and transition, each of which was dependent on the other.

But when II MEF arrived in February, recalled General Gaskin, several parts of the province lacked the "persistent presence of Iraqi police." We found we were "very short on police," and that was a barrier in terms of transitioning to COIN's nonkinetic lines of operations. "So, even though we had acknowledged that the police were the solution, we were still having a difficult time recruiting."[64]

Gaskin also found that he had a similar shortfall in the ranks of the Iraqi army forces deployed in Anbar. Both the "1st and the 7th Divisions out here in Anbar were at a very low force level," he explained in the summer of 2007. "One was at about 50 percent, the other about 35 percent." Moreover, "the preponderance of those forces were from the Shia."[65]

Gaskin, Gurganus, and II MEF set out to grow the police and change the composition of the army units in the province. And as II MEF's commanding general knew, the key to accomplishing those objectives was tribal engagement. "What I soon discovered," said Gaskin, "is that there is a direct correlation between tribal engagement and recruiting. So that ability to connect the tribes with the cause that both of us had in common, getting rid of al Qaeda, and connecting them with their government, meant that they needed to be participants in that, both from a government standpoint, as well as from the military and police standpoint."[66]

That engagement policy, which was launched at the end of 2005 and expanded during 2006, came to fruition under II MEF in 2007. (The story of how that came about follows shortly.) The remarkable growth in Anbar of the police and Iraqi army in 2007 is evidence that II MEF capitalized on engagement.

General Allen was at the center of facilitating tribal engagement and tying the tribes into the emerging civil government in Anbar. At the end of II MEF's deployment, he highlighted the changes engagement brought about in the ISF in Anbar.

> We had access to the tribal leadership. We had access to the tribes themselves and the people in ways that others had not, and that was really how we operationalized our tribal engagement strategy. The benefit of that to us was that . . . hundreds, thousands of the sons of Anbar came forward and began to volunteer, initially for the police and ulti-

mately for the army. The numbers shot up very dramatically . . . [and] untold numbers of Sunni Anbaris threw down their weapons—some of them were fighting for al Qaeda, some of them were fighting for Ansar Al-Sunnah, some of them were fighting for Jaysh Islami or Jaysh Muhammad—and then joined the local police.[67]

The size of Iraqi police in Anbar grew from approximately 9,000 in December 2006 to roughly 25,000 a year later. This increase gave II MEF the capacity to dominate the physical and human terrain of the province, and the incidence of recidivism was very low among those reintegrated.

Recruiting Sunni tribesmen to the police was the first step. The second step was training them. To that end, General Gurganus established an Iraqi training center and police academy. This made a big difference, explained Allen, and you could see it on the street. The Iraqi police were accepted by the population. He gave the following illustration of the impact of these changes:

When I got to Anbar there wasn't a policeman at any checkpoint who didn't have a ski mask on. When I left you never saw a ski mask, not one. These guys became so comfortable in the operating environment and the population accepted them. Al Qaeda was beaten down. So, the police didn't have to go home and stay up and defend their families from al Qaeda attacks in the middle of the night for retribution. Mark Gurganus created that security environment, and he created the security forces—the Iraqi police forces . . . as the persistent presence which enabled us to go after the enemy in other places.[68]

Police expansion made a big difference in AO Topeka, said Colonel Charlton. "I watched the evolution of this police force over fifteen months and it was absolutely amazing. They formed into precincts and a district and another key thing was finding the right kind of police chiefs, guys that were capable and experienced. And once we had that in place this thing was really starting to look pretty good and it amazed me how far they came in a short period of time." And in once-malevolent Ramadi, Charlton was able to "reduce my combat power steadily inside the city to the point where I only had one battalion in there when I left as opposed to five when I got there and we had police primacy. The Iraqi police were largely in charge of the city."[69] The same progression could be seen in AO Denver and AO Raleigh.

By the summer the breakthrough forces of General Gurganus had been filled out by the Iraqi police, and local security was transforming apace. As Gurganus explained in a June 2007 interview, "We've seen a lot of success in security. The security situation is a whole lot better now and the beauty of that is it is opening up opportunities to connect the municipalities with the provincial government in Ramadi." The reason for these developments was "growing confidence in our police.... The numbers have grown and a lot."⁷⁰ The same was true for the Iraqi army, which had grown not only in absolute numbers but also in the number of indigenous recruits. The 1st Iraqi army division went from about 50 percent strength and mostly Shiite to 107 percent strength and at least 50 percent Sunni. The 7th Iraqi army division grew from about 30 percent strength and half Shia to 107 percent strength and mostly Sunnis from Anbar.⁷¹

This expansion of local security forces was a key to deescalating the insurgency in Anbar, explained Allen in a 2008 discussion. It was based on

> one of the central tenets of COIN doctrine: that indigenous police bring insurgencies to an end.... The Iraqi cop on the beat in his neighborhood denied the enemy access to the population and left AQ [al Qaeda] no place to go, no place to plot, and no place to rest.... Central to this police capability was the formation of special police intelligence units to quickly act on information collected at the local level to seize opportunity. And here perhaps was one of the most innovative approaches

Iraqi police and Marines on a training exercise in Fallujah in 2007.

LT. COL. DAVID A. BENHOFF, *AMONG THE PEOPLE*, 71

in preparing the IP [Iraqi police] for self-reliance. We hired a large number of retired Royal Ulster Constabulary police and embedded them in the IP district HQs. Leveraging their decades of experience fighting the IRA [Irish Republican Army], these reinforcements made an immediate difference in Anbar and gave the IP the same kind of special branch capabilities that had purchased victory in Malaya in the 1950s and later on the streets of Belfast and Londonderry. This program, called Legacy, has been expanded in Iraq and is en route to be fielded in Afghanistan.[72]

Legacy was based on the concept of local intelligence dominance. And the British were not the only ones to discover and employ this approach. According to research carried out by Roy Godson, this "model of local, or what some call tactical intelligence dominance, has been developed through trial and error over decades by several 20th-century democracies in diverse theaters and cultures." Its objective is straightforward: "degrading, disrupting, and neutralizing the challenge of armed groups to the government's authority—both its capacity and legitimacy—within the confines of the rule of law."[73]

The key is the creation of local intelligence units that collect "systematic local knowledge" on the secret underground or "covert armed infrastructure of armed groups." This local knowledge allows "police, military, and other elements of law enforcement to identify and target . . . those armed groups, while interfering with the local population as little as possible, which is vitally important if community support is to be maintained for the security forces."[74] The retired Royal Ulster Constabulary police that Allen referenced above, in conjunction with personnel from Marine Corps Intelligence Activity, began assisting the Iraqi police to develop these units in 2007. It was yet another tool for neutralizing the insurgency in Anbar.

SEA CHANGE

Once an armed insurrection takes root, as happened in Anbar in 2004–2006, considerable time and great effort are required to degrade and neutralize it. Insurgencies are protracted struggles—long and drawn-out affairs—and are not easily reversed. At least that is what the counterinsurgency classics say.

This is due, according to Galula, to the "asymmetry between the insurgents and the counterinsurgents." Because of the "disproportion of strength between the opponents," insurgents rely on subversion and irregular tactics. "Insurgencies are short only if the counterinsurgency collapses it at an early stage." Otherwise, they last for many years because of the asymmetry in fighting styles. Galula explains, "The insurgent blows up a bridge, so every bridge has to be guarded; he throws a grenade in a movie theater, so every person entering a public place has to be searched. When an insurgent burns a farm, all the farmers clamor for protection; if they do not receive it, they may be tempted to deal privately with the insurgents."[75]

Moreover, once the insurgents embed their secret below-the-waterline operational, command, and support units within the population, rooting them out is an arduous and lengthy process. The classics argue this, as do present-day students of COIN. For instance, one scholar has recently written, "Wars characterized by the use of insurgency tend to be longer, as insurgents are dispersed within the population. The medium length of insurgency appears to be between six and ten years."[76]

When II MEF deployed to Anbar in early 2007, it expected no immediate drop-off in insurgent violence. The situation it inherited from I MEF gave little hint that the ferocity of fighting in the province would dissipate any time soon; no near-term sea change was expected in Anbar.

In the week of January 19, 2007, just as II MEF was arriving, nearly 450 enemy actions took place. But four months later that number dropped to roughly 150 incidents weekly. And by the beginning of July it was less than 100 a week, and stayed there through mid-September, with a low of just over 50 the first week of August, and again the first week in September. In retrospect it is clear that I MEF had set the stage for many of the advances II MEF would leverage.[77]

"It was a striking drop off," said General Allen. "Within ninety days of coming over here, virtually the entire situation turned around."[78] It took II MEF by surprise. "We truly believed we were going to have hundreds of dead. And I remember . . . when we embarked for Iraq that Walt Gaskin or I, one of us said, 'We don't know if we'll see provincial Iraqi control in our deployment or even the next deployment,' because the violence was getting worse as we were leaving [for Anbar]." However, Allen added, "While we hadn't planned specifically for it [the sharp drop-off in violence] what we did plan for was to recognize it."[79]

What he meant by this was that II MEF's intelligence shop was looking for indicators that might signal change was coming and to capitalize on it. And in March, one of those indicators appeared. "Sometime around March we had a meeting . . . where Sheikh Sattar and the Awakening sheikhs were going to meet with the governor. They were going to meet with the governor and begin to talk about . . . giving the Awakening additional seating on the Provincial Council."[80]

At the end of that session, one of II MEF's liaison officers took Allen aside and said to him, "I want you to listen to what I'm going to say because I think this is pretty important." He then asked the general if he realized that during the "meeting there was never any conversation about security or fighting? The entire conversation was about postconflict power sharing and economic development. These guys are entering their postconflict period right now," said the liaison officer. The intelligence officer for II MEF came to the same conclusion—"things were profoundly changing."[81]

For all the reasons given above, the crossover point from the kinetic fight to the postconflict phase of COIN came up fast. The insurgency in Anbar was not conforming to the COIN classics. Once more, war—in this case irregular war— proved to be unpredictable. It did not follow a pattern. For II MEF this presented a strategic opportunity. The breakthrough force had achieved its missions. It was now time for the exploitation force to take over and consolidate those gains. Allen told the II MEF commanders,

> We were faced suddenly with the reality that if we didn't do something quickly about governance and reconstruction . . . we were going to face a pretty serious difficulty, because the people were throwing off al Qaeda and yearned for some kind of change. They yearned immediately for a new future, which would be defined largely in economic development. . . . The one sound we can't afford is . . . to have the kinetic phase suddenly be followed by a large, pregnant silence, where there's no governing and nothing being built and no money coming into the province.[82]

The MAGTF's CSSE had been organized for this moment, for that crossover from conflict to postconflict. "Once the population got security," said General Gaskin, "they immediately wanted services—electricity, water, sewerage, trash, rubble removal. All of those items were very meaningful to them."[83] And out in AO Denver, AO Topeka, and AO Raleigh, the local RCT and BCT commanders were hearing the same demands.

ADVISERS

In an essay titled "Political Capabilities to Stabilize Fragile or Post-Conflict States," the former U.S. ambassador to Afghanistan and Iraq, Zalmay Khalilzad, asserted that in situations like the one unfolding in Anbar in the spring of 2007, U.S. political and military advisers must be able to "take a 'hands-on' approach to shape the local political context." This mediation role seeks not to impose American-made solutions but to use American influence to persuade "local leaders to agree on local solutions to meet local challenges." Ambassador Khalilzad added that the United States "must develop cadres of officials and officers with . . . talent for political action to shape the orientation and conduct of local leaders and communities." Such advisers have to be entrepreneurial in outlook and capable of catalyzing "constructive internal political development" in settings where "political power is typically personalized and factionalized." They need the skills to "jump-start local institution building and economic development."[84]

However, when II MEF arrived in Anbar it had no such formally trained advisory personnel. In 2007 they did not exist within the military services, the Department of State, or the operational arms of intelligence agencies. None of these institutions had officers trained in the skill sets needed to shape the orientation and conduct of local leaders and communities in ways that facilitated post-conflict success.

Ironically, examples do exist in American history of politically skilled entrepreneurial advisers, but their appearance has always been serendipity, by a twist of fate, and not by design. In Anbar the commanding general of the MEF's CSSE had the skills listed by Khalilzad. As sketched out earlier, John Allen was uniquely qualified for that mediation task. And he had a major hand in organizing CSSE as an exploitation force able to capitalize on the security gains made by General Gurganus.

The counterinsurgency goals of CSSE as an exploitation force were to execute a range of nonkinetic lines of operations, including governance, economic development, rule of law, and information. Central to each of these tasks was tribal engagement. The CSSE, said Allen, was "organized to recognize change and then to exploit it. And that really is what made the difference. We were able to take advantage of that moment."[85]

CSSE had the tools for postconflict management, which could be used to exploit engagement with the sheikhs. Here is how Allen explained it: "When a sheikh came over . . . we were poised and able to instantly help him, to flow substantial resources to the tribe. The sheikh got credit for all of it and his people's quality of life was turned around all because we were organized as an exploitation force."[86]

Consider the case of Sheikh Hatem al Gaoud Albu Nimr. The sheikh sent his cousin to invite General Allen "to come with all dispatch to his guest house near the city of Hit. He wanted to talk about building a relationship." They met in the traditional tribal council for several hours. The sheikhs of the ancient and warlike Albu Nimr tribe assessed the general to determine his "suitability as an ally." The "council ended abruptly" and was followed by an enormous traditional feast to celebrate the meeting and the occasion. During the feast Sheikh Hatem took Allen into a separate room and, sitting alone, told Allen it appeared the meeting had gone very well and the Nimrs would want to participate in a security relationship with the Marines.[87] Allen had passed muster with Sheikh Hatem and his tribal council.

The next day the sheikh solidified the new alliance. He sent a message to Allen committing "350 of his tribal sons to the Iraqi police and 750 to the Army. The Nimrs were 'in' and AQ [al Qaeda] was out." For his support, II MEF hardened the sheikh's house, trained his personal security men, initiated a series of road-building projects in Nimr tribal areas, built an electric transformer to distribute power for the tribe, restored water treatment facilities destroyed by al Qaeda so there was fresh drinking water from the Euphrates River, and refurbished a number of schools.[88]

It was important that the sheikh and his tribe realize immediate benefits from the strategic decision to side with the Coalition against al Qaeda. The Nimr tribesmen benefited: the sheikh brought a better, more secure life to his people, and al Qaeda was now deprived of a substantial portion of the population within which it could hide. It was also important that other sheikhs and their tribes saw and understood the wisdom and benefits of this decision.

Allen had the advisory skills needed to convince Sheikh Hatem to cross the bridge. And later, he was able to persuade other senior sheikhs to support and enter Anbar's provincial government. In this he was supported by some superb warrior diplomats who served as his G-5s, such as colonels John Koenig, Dave Close, and Shawn Murphy. Even with these leaders, Allen needed help: others were required to shape the postconflict orientation and actions of local Anbari leaders and communities. But the ranks of II MEF lacked such individuals in sufficient numbers.

To fill that gap, II MEF instituted a PME program in the field. It was shaped by specialists like William McCallister, a tribal engagement expert who was already in Iraq. A retired Army officer, McCallister had a Special Forces background and field experience in the Middle East and Asia. He was a student of counterinsurgency and how tribal culture and tribal mediation processes fit into it.[89] He had lectured and published widely on these issues. In Iraq McCallister helped II MEF develop a tribal engagement model that was instilled into its officers and NCOs in Anbar. It provided an understanding of how to appreciate tribal institutions and how to operate within them to facilitate change.[90]

What the leadership of II MEF had in mind was providing its officers and NCOs with an advisory skill set that would help them carry out engagement up and down the tribal hierarchy. While Allen operated at the top with the senior sheikhs, the same kind of interaction needed to take place down the tribal structure. Marine commanders at the battalion, company, and platoon levels, explained Lt. Col. Jim McGrath, "had to mirror Allen." In 2007 McGrath commanded battalion 3/6 in Anbar. Engagement for the colonel and his company and platoon leaders started with coming to "understand the tribal structure, finding out who the key players were within the tribe, engaging with them, working to tie them back into the government of Anbar." The tribal leaders had been at odds with the governor and provincial and local government officials. Part of engagement at the local level, recounted McGrath, was for his company and platoon leaders to foster bonds between these adversarial groups.[91]

But to do so those company and platoon leaders had to "create their own bonds with each [of these groups] and to create bonds with others, showing that they could work with just about anybody in Anbar. This included being able to work with the Iraqi army, to work with the Iraqi police, to convince those two to work together, which was a significant challenge, because they are primarily a Shia army . . . [and] a primarily Sunni police force. When you get them in the same room and you force them over time to work with one another, they recognize—okay—there are advantages to working together."[92]

ENGAGEMENT IN ACTION: THE AWAKENING

To succeed in Anbar, the Marines had to be able to engage the tribal leaders of the province on their terms. And that involved developing a strategy that reflected a sound grasp of Bedouin tribal traditions, Islamic principles, and Arab cultural values. I MEF in 2006 and II MEF the following year embedded that knowledge in their shared campaign plan.

This was indispensable, asserted the II MEF leadership, because in an irregular war, engagement is a strategic tool. And when employed successfully, said General Allen, it can have strategic consequences. He put it this way: "When a sheikh came over he took his entire tribal AO off the map to the disadvantage of AQI. So, tribal engagement became in essence a strategic vulnerability for the enemy and a strategic strength for us." When Sheikh Hatem aligned with II MEF, that "meant that a huge piece of Anbar Province was no longer available to al Qaeda. Now, if you expand that . . . along the Euphrates River, with every tribal alliance . . . comes another big chunk of the map. And where does al Qaeda end up going? They have to go out into the desert and that was perfect for us."[93] They could no longer hide in plain sight within the population.

Engagement was a key facilitator and a major contributor to solidifying security. General Gurganus could not have consolidated the gains of his forces without it. The sheikhs provided the men to fill out the ranks of the police and army, which was a prerequisite for holding territory and denying it to the insurgents. Engagement was equally vital to facilitating the initiation of the postconflict phase of the war. Each of the nonkinetic lines of operation was dependent on buy-in from the tribal leadership and its willingness to take part in the governance process.

For these reasons, General Gaskin made tribal engagement a responsibility at all levels of II MEF. That was true whether it was General Allen dealing with the senior sheikh of a tribe or battalion, company, and platoon commanders partnering with lower-ranking sheikhs and neighborhood leaders. Gaskin was intent on consolidating the hard-won engagement gains made by I MEF in 2006. During that year, as described earlier, this took place in each AO—Denver, Topeka, and Raleigh. Sheikhs were coming off the fence and aligning with the Marines.

However, although engagement and tribal realignment was under way when II MEF arrived, it was very much a work in progress. Many sheikhs were still on the fence, unsure about whether to line up with the Americans. "They had not made a final decision," said Allen, "with respect to aligning themselves with the Coalition. There were isolated large tribal areas that had made that decision to come with us, but there were other substantial segments of the tribes that had not.... At the time we got to Anbar, there were still a lot of folks who were undecided."[94]

The Anbar Awakening (or Sahawat al-Anbar) at the time that II MEF took command was still developing. It had been nurtured by I MEF. It was a call to action that several sheikhs answered. But the movement had yet to reach its full potential. II MEF follow-through was needed to help the sheikhs who had initiated the Awakening bring it to fruition.

In 2006 Sheikh Sattar began mobilizing his fellow sheikhs to resist AQI and align with I MEF. He became the driving force behind the Awakening and quickly emerged as its leader. At that time and later, there was much fault-finding among senior sheikhs with Sattar.[95] He was an insignificant sheikh and a usurper, they said. Moreover, his tribe was a minor player in the Dulaym tribal confederation. Finally, these sheikhs would say, he was nothing more than a common criminal, a major smuggler of oil across the Syrian border.

While there is, perhaps, some truth to all of these allegations, and while in normal times they would have confined Sattar to secondary or lower status in the pecking order of the tribal system of Anbar, these were not normal times. It was wartime, and AQI was intent on breaking the authority of the sheikhs and taking control of the province. Its brutal murder and intimidation campaign was geared at doing exactly that.

Watching AQI cut down one after another of their compatriots, many top-tier sheikhs fled to the safety of Amman and Dubai. In some instances the tribes sent their tribal leaders away for safe-keeping. The tribes and sheikhs were not willing to take on al Qaeda and ruthless killers like Zarqawi. But Sheikh Sattar was.

Sattar was a surprise. No one expected him to play the role he played. But wartime knows no class status or sheikh pecking order. In conflicts like the one in Anbar, a person's status is achieved by actions and not by lineage. War brings forth exceptional people at all levels of command—strategic, operational, and tactical. But before the war begins they often are not prominent figures. Military history is replete with examples.

In the armed struggle that took place in Anbar, Sheikh Sattar's initiative, risk taking, and audacity catapulted him from obscurity into the leadership of the Awakening and a strategic partnership with the MEF. He started locally, organizing the smaller tribes of the northwest Ramadi area into a collective self-defense organization to stand up to AQI's bloody attacks. He convinced their sheikhs to pool their militias, weapons, and intelligence to fight back night after night.

As Sattar and his compatriots gained the upper hand over AQI in northwest Ramadi, the sheikhs of Anbar came to see that the terrorists could be stopped and the soldiers and Marines of I MEF could help them accomplish that mission. Sattar swiftly became a folk hero; through his message the tribes saw the possibility of eliminating AQI from the province. This was the beginning of the Awakening movement, born in Ramadi.

II MEF capitalized on these developments and worked with Sattar to spread the Awakening across Anbar. Sattar had the leadership skills and the charisma to make that happen, said Colonel Charlton in a 2009 interview: "When you met [Sheikh] Sattar, you immediately saw that this guy has a vision, he is charismatic, and you hear the words he is saying and it gives you tremendous hope and enthusiasm." Charlton recalled traveling with Sattar to meet with the tribal leaders west of Ramadi to bring them into the Awakening. Charlton thought it was going to be a tough sell. But the colonel "was just absolutely amazed . . . [at] how he was received. Sattar was like royalty. He was like a rock star. I had never seen anything like this, the impact, the effect he had. . . . Sattar's charisma and his appeal to win people over did the trick."[96]

Once in theater General Allen moved to expand tribal engagement. The first thing he did was make it a separate line of operation within II MEF. It had been part of governance, but Allen realized engagement was going to be central to everything II MEF hoped to accomplish, and therefore it needed to be separated from governance. This proved to be an astute decision for the kinetic fight and for managing the initial phase of the postconflict period.

Engagement by RCT-6, RCT-2, and the 1st BCT was crucial to clear-and-hold operations. It provided the force multiplier needed to win the kinetic fight, and it brought that fight to an end much more quickly than II MEF had anticipated.

To manage the transition to postconflict reconstruction and governance was going to require II MEF to be fully tied in with Anbar's tribal leadership. The changeover from armed struggle to the hard work of reconstruction was going to mean that Marines and soldiers were still going to have to be able to work inside the tribes.

The XO of RCT-6, Lt. Col. John Reeve, explained what that entailed for him and the regiment in AO Raleigh: "The key is to train and help emergent Iraqi [institutions] . . . arrive at tolerable Iraqi solutions for the various challenges that they face in the postconflict phase. 'It is an education process,' requiring the 'development of relationships that serve as the vehicle . . . for explaining to them what they need to accomplish. . . . Everything is a collaborative process.'"[97]

A typical week for the executive officer found him involved in governance and political engagement with tribal leaders from across the AO. Bringing the Awakening sheikhs into the political process was a major postconflict line of operation for II MEF. And it was reflected in Reeve's weekly activities: "My typical week will show me . . . doing various leadership engagements or attending meetings, Iraqi government meetings or engaging tribal leaders, four times a week, probably. And in the execution of that I go all over the area. Recently, it's been on the peninsula . . . immediately northeast of Fallujah . . . but I've been all over the area of operation on these kinds of things."[98]

POSTCONFLICT OPERATIONS

The transition from kinetic operations to governance, reconstruction, and rule of law transpired without much warning in the late spring. To manage that changeover required a broader array of capabilities than those employed in counterinsurgency's clear and hold phases. II MEF now confronted the challenges of COIN's build period.

In the years following 9/11, postconflict stabilization and reconstruction tasks generated a flurry of new doctrine, operational concepts, and interagency constructs. Both the Department of Defense and the Department of State paid increased attention to what came to be dubbed stabilization, security, transition, and reconstruction operations (SSTRO). This was set in motion at the Pentagon with the 2005 issuance of Department of Defense Directive 3000.0. This directive put forward guidelines for the military's role in SSTRO; it also stipulated that the Department of Defense was to work closely with other U.S. civilian departments and agencies that not only were involved in SSTRO missions but also would take charge of them once they were under way.

To prepare for this, the Department of State in 2006 instituted the Interagency Counterinsurgency Initiative. This initiative was intended to introduce counterinsurgency concepts across the U.S. government's civilian agencies and to increase their capacity to contribute to whole-of-government campaigns to manage SSTRO situations.

A whole-of-government approach looks to integrate civilian and military capabilities to assist indigenous governments revitalize their institutions and economy once the kinetic fight against armed groups has dissipated. As this postconflict phase unfolds, a transition from U.S. military to civilian control is supposed to take place. While the U.S. military has limited capabilities to begin this transition, according to the whole-of-government construct, once the transition is under way, civilian agencies are to take control and bring it to completion.

But in the spring of 2007 the whole-of-government construct was nothing more than a vision devised inside the Washington Beltway. There were no whole-of-government capabilities from across the U.S. government's interagency institutions to deploy to Anbar. Consequently, it was left to II MEF to jumpstart the build stage of COIN. According to General Gaskin, what "we've seen in cities like Hit and Al Qa'im, Ramadi, Baghdadi, Fallujah is once they [the sheikhs and their people] have seen peace and what it can be like, that's the way they want it."[99] In other words, once they have crossed the bridge from armed struggle to postconflict reconstruction, they do not want to go back.

But peace had to be more than an end to the carnage that had savaged Anbar for three blood-soaked years. And General Gaskin knew it, as he explained in June 2007. To keep the peace meant convincing the sheikhs to join the political process. Gaskin elaborated: "By placing the sheikhs in a position of authority and responsibility, it maintains what they're used to, so they don't feel threatened and they're participating in the political process."[100] To set that in motion across Anbar was the mission of those executing II MEF's governance line of operations.

Through governance and other nonkinetic operations, said General Allen, II MEF "employed a number of innovative engagement techniques including something called Helicopter Governance. We also pursued extensive expatriate engagement throughout the Middle East in places like Amman, Doha, and Dubai. Directly related to Governance was . . . a program of reconstruction and rehabilitation. Rule of Law was as paramount to the return to a stable society as governance and economic development, but it was completely broken."[101]

In 2007 Col. John Koenig was II MEF's assistant chief of staff for governance, economic development, and rule of law. His staff was organized to oversee each of these nonkinetic lines of operations. After arriving in Anbar, it marshaled resources for these civil-military operations, and coordinated them with the activities of three civil affairs detachments assigned to II MEF to execute these missions. Civil affairs forces support and facilitate the activities and functions that are normally the responsibility of local, regional, or national government. The skill sets and background that they bring to these responsibilities include public administration, public welfare, safety, education and health, government and legal systems, labor management, finance, communications, transportation, logistics, food and agricultural services, cultural affairs and information, and management of dislocated persons.

Each civil affairs detachment was assigned to one of the three RCT or BCT commanders, each of whom had responsibility for executing governance, economic reconstruction, and rule of law operations in his AO. These organizational developments illustrate how II MEF moved to capitalize on the new conditions in Anbar to jumpstart postconflict activities.

Koenig's staff also hoped to bring in the Department of State's provincial reconstruction teams (PRT) assigned to Anbar. Established by State to help facilitate reconstruction and development, the first PRTs were introduced in Afghanistan in 2002. They were tasked to assist indigenous government extend its authority, and to support reconstruction activities.

PRTs were to carry out nonmilitary development activities that fell within the purview of the Interagency Counterinsurgency Initiative. They consist of a military element (for civil affairs and force protection), civilian police advisers, and civilian representatives from the U.S. Agency for International Development (USAID), the Department of State, and the Department of Agriculture.

In Anbar a PRT was embedded with each RCT and BCT, as well as at MEF headquarters. Koenig and his staff sought to assimilate the embedded PRTs (ePRTs) when they arrived in the spring of 2007. His goal in this opening phase was to ensure unity of effort along all the nonkinetic lines of operations and to prepare the way to cede responsibility for the postconflict mission to U.S. civilian agencies.

These organizational developments illustrate how II MEF was poised to manage the transition opportunity that appeared in the late spring with the dramatic decline in enemy violence. It is important to note, however, that from this point its role was to be limited. II MEF could jumpstart the build process, but seeing the process through to completion was beyond its responsibility. Also, in each of these nonkinetic lines of operations—governance, rule of law, and development—II MEF was beginning at ground zero.

Governance

The initial governance challenges for II MEF in the late spring were twofold. First, the provincial government institutions had to be quite literally resuscitated and put on a path to gain legitimacy with the population. Second, the sheikhs of the Awakening had to be brought into the governance process and become political partners.

The provincial government in Anbar comprises three main institutions. The first is the governor, whose headquarters is located at the Government Center in Ramadi, which since 2005 had been under an insurgent state of siege. Governor Mamoon Sami Rashid al-Alwani was able to hole up there thanks to the 24/7 protection provided by a Marine infantry company. Mamoon, who dodged more than thirty assassination attempts, had little authority or legitimacy in the province. Elected as part of the Provincial Council in January 2005 when only 2 percent of the population voted because of the Sunni election boycott, few in Anbar actually knew who Mamoon was.

The second institution is the Provincial Council. Made up of civic leaders, businesspersons, and sheikhs from across Anbar, it likewise was in a moribund state. In early 2006 its members fled to Baghdad to avoid AQI assassination attempts; they were still there in the spring of 2007. Like the governor, the Provincial Council had little legitimacy.

The third provincial institution was the directors general, who represented the different national ministries at the provincial level. Here, as well, the II MEF leadership found, "the directors general—who represented the ministries on a day-to-day basis to the governor and the Provincial Council—had either been killed, had been coopted by al Qaeda, or had gone to ground. So you didn't really have effective ministerial representation on the ground in the province."[102] The situation at the provincial level was repeated at the local level in Anbar's cities and town—there was little governance.

Gaskin described the state of Anbar's government in the spring of 2007 as "in hiding because of the murder and intimidation campaign that al Qaeda took against anybody expected to be in leadership other than the implanted emirs that they put up."[103] But with AQI now out of the picture, those officials could come out of hiding, said the II MEF commanding general.

However, that was not going to be enough. The governance process was broken and II MEF had to start from scratch. What this meant, Gaskin recounted, was getting "the Anbar leadership sitting down and doing Government 101" with them. This included such basics as "how you plan a budget. Here's your budget . . . and this is how you've got to administer it, how you expend that money, and the cost of that expenditure."[104] Budget planning and execution would be one of the most daunting challenges the new provincial government would face. But it was simply a provincial reflection of the larger national problem in Baghdad.

It is beyond the scope of this study to go into all of the different Government 101 initiatives that II MEF carried out to jumpstart the governance process in Anbar. It was a startup effort in many respects that went from the provincial to the district to the local level. A few examples illustrate what it entailed, beginning with Governor Mamoon and the Provincial Council.

The governor was unknown in most parts of Anbar. Consequently, he had little legitimacy with the population. The same was true for the Provincial Council. To address this problem, explained General Allen in 2008, his civil-military operations team came up with the idea of helicopter governance. Here is how it worked:

> To every major municipality and district in the province we would fly the governor, Provincial Council chairman, provincial chief of police, [and] relevant members of the directors general. . . . We would go to some towns where the governor had never been seen in anyone's living memory. . . . We wanted to create both the appearance and the reality of participatory government. And, because it was too hard for the people to come to Ramadi, we came to them. . . . [Once on the ground] the governor would get off the bird and go see the mayor. The Provincial Council chairman would get off the bird and go with the town council. The director general would typically go with the council chairman. The provincial chief of police would meet with all the police officials of the area. They'd all meet separately. . . . [After these individual sessions] they'd all come together for a plenary session where the sheikhs would join in. The governor would come with a suitcase full of money and would fund on the spot a couple of important local projects; create a wish list of things that would be necessary, ultimately, to address within this municipality or this district, and take them back to Ramadi.[105]

The governor's on-the-spot funding of several local projects was important. It demonstrated a responsiveness of the provincial government, connecting it to that municipality. It brought credibility to the local political leaders by enhancing their people's lives, while creating personal patronage with the governor. Follow-up with the other requirements was critical and was an area where the Coalition played an important role.

This was the beginning of reviving and reorienting these provincial institutions and establishing government legitimacy in Anbar. It was part of a program of activities, said Gaskin, to get these officials to understand that government works through a set of legal rules and procedures. He put it this way with respect to how the governor handled appropriations: "He is still rough around the edges on the governance part, and he has to be explained to that this is not your money in your budget. It is the people's money, and you can't just use it for your tribe."[106]

Facilitating governance was also taking place in the cities and towns that ran up the Euphrates from Fallujah to Al Qa'im. Recall that in each of Anbar's AOs—Denver, Topeka, Raleigh—II MEF deployed a civil affairs detachment. Among its duties was governance. How this worked in Fallujah illustrates what these detachments were doing to (re)introduce governance across the province at the local level.

In early 2007 Fallujah experienced an upsurge in violence aimed at city officials. Three city council chairmen had been assassinated by al Qaeda in successive months, and the government was coming apart. RCT-6 Marines and their Iraqi counterparts engaged every day in tamping down the insurgents, and, as noted earlier, their efforts were having results.

Local government, not military forces, needed to sustain those security gains, but governance was on the decline in Fallujah. That is, until RCT-6 and its civil affairs detachment took action. They brought the governor and the Provincial Council chairperson to Fallujah to help reorganize the city council and to establish a democratically elected government, a government that "would hold and would prosper and," noted General Allen, become "a model in Iraq."[107]

Fallujah became an example of what II MEF's postconflict initiatives could help start. The city bore the signs of success across all the nonkinetic lines of operations. "The city council became a permanent, viable fixture connected to the provincial government in Ramadi. It became one of the first locations for our micro-loan program and several private bank branches opened. . . . A criminal court opened in the renovated court house, and the Iraqi Police in Fallujah are known throughout Iraq for their abilities to conduct both COIN operations and law enforcement."[108] The developments that unfolded in Fallujah spread to Anbar's other cities.

In summary, from the provincial to the local levels, II MEF revived governance in Anbar. Government institutions reemerged, and new authority concepts based on legal rules and procedures were introduced. These opening gambits set the stage for the whole government process to kick in and for U.S. civilian agencies to take it over from II MEF.

The other major governance challenge for II MEF was bringing the sheikhs of the Awakening into the provincial governance process. This was a major challenge, said Colonel Koenig, II MEF's assistant chief of staff for governance, economic development, and rule of law. The sheikhs had to be convinced of the value of working with provincial officials and come to see how they and their tribes could benefit from that involvement.[109]

Here again, Sheikh Sattar led the way. He was right out of central casting, a warrior sheikh. Sattar had been shot several times but was fearless. On more than one occasion he called AQI out during press conferences. For example, as he was returning from a trip out of the country during the emergence of the Awakening, al Jazeera caught up with him. He used the opportunity to announce, "To the terrorists I say I will be back in Anbar in five days. . . . If they want to see me I'm ready for them."[110]

However, the situation was changing in Anbar. Politics were emerging as the means for settling differences and advancing interests. Sattar, the warrior sheikh, recognized this and began adapting to capitalize on this change. General Allen, who was the senior II MEF officer working with the Awakening, met with its members as well as with other sheikhs several times a week as part of tribal engagement. He had a close working relationship with Sattar and saw him shift his focus to politics.

In fact, Allen recalled, by the summer months Sattar

> was rapidly leaping into a position where he was going to unify the tribes of the whole province. It was the darndest thing I'd ever seen. . . . Late August he held a gathering of the sheikhs of Al Anbar. He invited the sheikhs of the tribes throughout the province to come to his compound in Ramadi to meet about the creation of a tribal council— for the entire province. . . . Five committees were proposed—security, governance (intended to create power sharing with the emerging civil governance), external relations (aimed at connectivity with the Coalition), economic development, and religious affairs, to include taking care of the Christians in the province, rebuilding churches that had been destroyed. He had it all worked out."[111]

Sattar was transforming the Awakening into a political movement and a political party. The August meeting was remarkable for its size and composition. Nearly every sheikh of consequence from across Al Anbar came to this event. Even the paramount sheikhs of the largest, oldest, and most prominent tribes attended. The point is that nearly every tribal leader in the province was recognizing the ascendancy of Sheikh Sattar. In this one gathering, it was clear the future of Al Anbar had been wrested from the hands of al Qaeda and other insurgent elements.

Other sheikhs followed him. And, like Sattar, they were proving to be more than warriors, as they often are portrayed in Arab legend.[112] They also were businesspeople and political entrepreneurs. To capitalize on this evolving transition, Allen and the leadership of II MEF fostered the creation of the Anbar Higher Committee in December 2007. It consisted of the governor, the Provincial Council chairperson, the chairperson of the Tribal Council, other government officials, and several of Anbar's leading sheikhs. The purpose of the Anbar Higher Committee was important. Several sheikhs had gone to Baghdad on their own to create separate relationships with the emerging Maliki government, usually to the distinct disadvantage of the provincial government and the tribes. The Anbar Higher Committee was a face of solidarity of the political and tribal forces in Anbar with the government in Baghdad, and the message was clear: Anbar stands united.

But by that time, December, Sheikh Sattar had been murdered by al Qaeda. On the first day of Ramadan, while visiting his horses near his compound, he stopped to talk with a local farmer. Outside the secured part of his property, an IED was detonated as he stepped down from his unarmored SUV. The vehicle was torn apart and he was killed instantly. In his place his brother, Sheikh Ahmed Abu Risha, became president of the Awakening. He carried forward Sheikh Sattar's vision of turning the Awakening into a political movement. He became a founding member of the Anbar Higher Committee, which came to include all of Anbar's principal political and tribal stakeholders.

Reconstruction and Development

If resuscitating governance was a knotty challenge for II MEF, reconstruction and development were even more challenging. The industrial base of the province—the state-owned enterprises—all were shut down. The transportation networks were in disarray, having received little maintenance since they had been built in the 1970s. This was because of a lack of resources caused by eight years of war with Iran and then thirteen years of sanctions. The war since 2004 had further damaged the road system, in particular the bridges, a favorite target of the insurgents. The railroad running through Anbar likewise did not function. Consequently, any commercial enterprises that were working had a very difficult time transporting goods.

In addition to transportation challenges, reconstruction and economic revival suffered from a serious electricity shortage. Anbar required between 400 and 450 megawatts per day to light the province and provide reliable electricity for industry to get under way again. Those state-owned enterprises that were capable of restarting were all underpowered. The entire province was underpowered, because barely more than 100 megawatts per day were being generated. II MEF brought in generators and dispersed them throughout the province to boost the output but they needed fuel, which created another problem.

All of the stimulators of private business—opportunity, entrepreneurial access, and employment—also had suffered considerably since 2003. The banking system was in shambles, so there was little loan capital for small businesses and individual entrepreneurs.

To address these reconstruction and development challenges, II MEF needed civilian agency partners. To be sure, within its civil affairs detachments some expertise for addressing these issues existed. But here is where the concept of whole of government had a major role to play. And that meant the PRTs.

But the PRT (and there was only one PRT at this point) assigned to Anbar in 2007 was not ready for these missions. Its members came late to the province because of the dangerous security situation, noted Jim Soriano, the team leader of the PRTs.[113] A twenty-five-year veteran of the Foreign Service, he arrived at the height of the fighting in September 2006. But most of his Department of State and USAID colleagues arrived only in the spring of 2007. The provincial PRT was augmented in late spring of 2007, by the creation of three ePRTs, smaller but still capable of PRT operations. These ePRTs were aligned with the principal battle space owners in AO Denver, Topeka, and Raleigh.

The key missions of the PRTs, explained Soriano, rested on three legs. The first, he recalled in a 2009 interview,

> is capacity building with the provincial government. . . . That's our job. And my Iraqi counterparts . . . are the governor, the Provincial Council chairman, the Provincial Council as such, and then my staff engages the directors general of the various departments—sewerage, water, electricity and so forth. . . . [Second] is encouraging the private sector. We've got some activities there. And the third would be civil society, trying to encourage civil society organizations, such as a farmers' co-op we're trying to set up, and so on.[114]

Soriano was in charge of the PRT that partnered with II MEF headquarters at Camp Fallujah. He also had responsibility for the three ePRTs that were assigned to AOs Denver, Topeka, and Raleigh in the spring of 2007. However, at that critical juncture in Anbar, they did not have the organizational means or personnel to carry out their capacity-building mission. In order to stand up the three ePRTs, Soriano had to rely on Marine and Army reservists on active duty or on long-serving Department of Defense officials to fill out their ranks.

Since the PRT was a relatively new creation, it also faced a steep learning curve to account for the conditions found in Anbar. This was apparent at the operational level out in the province, said Colonel Koenig, the II MEF's assistant chief of staff. He worked with the PRTs on a daily basis and observed that those in charge of them were not used to managing such complex operations; their career experiences did not expose them to leading such ventures under these conditions. Moreover, they did not have the experience or background in the three missions identified by Soriano. For example, the PRT attached to the MEF headquarters needed a rule-of-law coordinator. Neither the Department of State nor USAID had anyone to assign. The Department of Justice likewise came up short. Therefore, a contractor was brought in. But he had none of the organizational contacts needed with Baghdad to facilitate this aspect of capacity building.[115]

Nevertheless, the ePRTs did seek to adapt and align closely with their military counterparts to advance the postconflict agenda as best they could. In AO Topeka, Colonel Charlton noted in a 2009 interview, "When we left Fort Stewart, we didn't know we were getting an ePRT. We got a briefing. It was explained to us what this was, but there was no textbook on how to use these guys. So, we kind of had to figure it out along the way." What the PRT gave his brigade was at least some "expertise in developing governance, rule of law, finance, banking, and agriculture, all things that you don't have a lot of within a BCT." The PRT, Charlton went on, "filled a niche. I had some holes. I had Army civil affairs and they had some pretty good skill sets, but I didn't have a banking expert or . . . an agriculture expert."[116]

Beyond learning how to make the most of the PRTs' expertise, a major challenge was to figure out how to integrate the ePRT and the BCT at the operational level. Charlton convinced the ePRT leadership to adopt the partnering concept the BCT was using with the ISF. "I remember talking to Kristin Hagerstrom, who was the ePRT leader, [and saying] I understand your charter but this is brand new to both of us. So, let me tell you how we do it with the Iraqi security forces. We learned, through trial and error . . . that the best way to develop the Iraqi security forces is by building a relationship with them and the best way to build a relationship with them is to partner with them, to spend time with them. You have to be there, shoulder-to-shoulder with them."[117]

The ePRT chief agreed, said Charlton: "What we did was we established a small municipal government center downtown and she developed a template where she took her ePRT and partnered them with the municipal government. So, the person in charge of the water department, that person had a corresponding ePRT adviser. The head of the municipal department had somebody from the ePRT that was an adviser. They paired up all across the functional areas within the municipal government. And Kristin [Hagerstrom], the ePRT leader, was partnered with the mayor. . . . It worked very, very well." To help the ePRT, the BCT commander "took 50 percent of my civil affairs force, since I had two civil affairs teams, one Army and one Marine Corps, I took the Army one, and essentially [assigned them] . . . to Kristin's ePRT so that they would have the support to get their operation going."[118]

Progress in reviving government created opportunities for reconstruction and economic revival. To get this under way, II MEF focused on three initiatives: restarting several of the old state-owned enterprises, establishing a microfinance system to provide small business loans, and reopening the banking system. While it is beyond the scope of this book to go into the details of each of these initiatives, it is sufficient to note that II MEF and the PRTs were able to begin to prime the economic pump in 2007 at the local level.

General Allen summed it up this way:

> Work creates jobs, jobs create money, and money creates a willingness to risk that money and to create small business. In the meantime, we created small business associations. We created vocational technology training centers. We created a fair, impartial and transparent contracting process, so this becomes an upward spiral, rather than a downward spiral, and that's our hope. It's like maneuver warfare. It seems counterintuitive. You've just got to understand that if you do these things in the right kind of combination and don't get too nervous on any given day, let it go for a while, chances are you won't be disappointed. That's kind of where we are. We're in the hope and faith phase."[119]

These reconstruction and economic measures fostered by II MEF in conjunction with the PRTs were baby steps that primed the pump. To advance them further was beyond what II MEF could muster.

A school renovation project takes place outside al-Karmah in 2007.

LT. COL. DAVID A. BENHOFF, *AMONG THE PEOPLE*, 25

Rule of Law

Of the postconflict operations initiated by II MEF in 2007, the most challenging was rule of law. Initially, this was assigned to the G-5, but they did not have sufficient expertise, so it was moved to the Multi-National Force–West staff judge advocate to align like functions. The staff judge advocate and rule-of-law initiatives for the province were the responsibilities of General Allen.

What General Allen found in 2007 was that there was no provincial rule-of-law system, there was no court operating in Anbar, and criminals were not being tried. Instead, tribal law was all that existed, and justice was in the hands of the security forces. The police were not operating as a law enforcement organization one would find in a functioning political environment. Perhaps most important, without the rule of law businesses were unwilling to invest in the province and there was little to spark economic growth.

The rule-of-law challenges facing II MEF and the PRTs included judicial engagement, restoration of judicial infrastructure, and the establishment of a criminal court system. Furthermore, they had to introduce rule-of-law training into the police forces as they transitioned from counterinsurgency police operations to democratic law enforcement.

As with the other nonkinetic lines of operations, II MEF was in the initiation phase. In conjunction with the PRTs, it sought to launch these rule-of-law initiatives and then hand them off to U.S. civilian agencies that as part of a whole-of-government strategy could advance them toward fulfillment. What follows is a brief description of some of the initiatives taken in 2007 to jumpstart the legal process.

At the basic level, the criminal justice system was revived and judges and lawyers were able to go back to work in a safe environment. Investigative judges, felony trial courts, and terrorism courts were all standing up. To secure these elements of the legal system, the Judicial Facility Protective Service was established. Rule-of-law procedures were introduced into the judicial process, including, for example, the review by judges of Iraqi police arrests to certify evidence for trial, conduct hearings, and submit cases for adjudication.

Court facilities across Anbar were being opened. For example, the criminal court facility in Ramadi began hearing cases in August with eleven trials in 2007. Courthouse renovations took place in Fallujah, al-Karmah, Khalidiyah, and Anah, and a new prison was scheduled for construction in 2008. Al Qaeda took particular interest in destroying the courthouses and judicial infrastructure.

The police were also supposed to start receiving training to make the transition to function under traditional law enforcement procedures. However, there is little evidence to suggest that the PRTs were able to muster specialists with the expertise to implement this kind of training. What was needed was a deployable rule-of-law training capability that either the PRTs or civil affairs detachments could use to provide integrity training and security sector reform to Anbar's law enforcement and security agencies. In 2007 they were unable to do so.

While each of these steps was small, they were all steps in the right direction and part of the transition from the kinetic fight to postconflict governance, reconstruction, and rule of law. It was a fragile foundation, to be sure. Transforming Anbar into a peaceful, democratically governed, rule-of-law-based, and prosperous part of a unified Iraq was well beyond the capacity of II MEF. But what it could do—and did—was to set the stage to begin the process.

FROM ARMED STRUGGLE TO POLITICAL COMPETITION

In 2007 Anbar changed dramatically, from being the setting of a bloody armed struggle to one of postconflict political competition and the beginning of reconstruction. As the leadership of II MEF prepared for a change of command with I MEF, it believed the transformation was going to be irrevocable. Consider General Gaskin's response in January 2008 to the question of whether al Qaeda could make a comeback in Anbar. The commanding general of II MEF did not think so because there now were "two Iraqi divisions out here, the 1st and the 7th, and we've got 24,000 police and we've got the border patrol and we've got the Iraqi highway patrol, all of them developing in their capacity." And these "Iraqi forces will have the capacity to stand up on their own."[120]

Among Gaskin's reasons for this optimism was that the ISF in Anbar "now know and understand the COIN fight. . . . These guys are good. There's no doubt in my mind. And I think the more that they are able to do these things, the better they become. We just can't buy experience. You have to earn it, live it, and do it. And so my greatest concern as I hand off command is that General Kelly will be able to hold on to and continue the timeline of development of the ISF."[121]

However, it was more than the ISF that stood in the way of an AQI comeback. The tribes and people of Anbar had had enough of its murder and intimidation tactics. The people had moved beyond the armed struggle and into postconflict reconstruction and political competition. That is what Colonel Charlton saw in Ramadi, which had once been ground zero for the insurgency. The people of Ramadi and its leadership were into rebuilding the city, not destroying it further. They had "completely rejected al Qaeda. You could see that was complete and they even held this massive parade in October to memorialize [Sheikh] Sattar and to show defiance toward al Qaeda. We knew then that Anbar was going to be good from then on out because the people had completely rejected al Qaeda and had united against them. When you have that going on, then everything else is not so hard."[122]

What Colonel Charlton saw transpiring in AO Topeka was likewise taking place in AO Raleigh, according to the executive officer of RCT-6, Lt. Col. John Reeve. The population there, explained the colonel, was "done with this war. They're done fighting terrorists. That is now probably tertiary in their level of concern. They are more concerned about how they're going to deal with each other in postconflict Iraq. They are far more concerned about how the political guys are going to stack up against the tribal guys, and how which political group is going to be in charge." As was the case in the other AOs of Anbar, the sheikhs and tribes in AO Raleigh had crossed the bridge from armed struggle to political struggle. Reeve saw this transition as "part and parcel of success. . . . They have already left this war and moved on to the next one."[123]

Of all of II MEF's senior leadership, no one was closer to the pulse of the province than John Allen. His tribal engagement responsibilities put him inside Anbar's most important institution. And what he observed only confirmed the conclusions drawn by Gaskin, Charlton, and Reeve. With respect to security, he asserted in early 2008, "I have no reason to believe that the security situation will deteriorate." In 2008 the Iraqis were scheduled to take over responsibility for security, and he expected that to take place. While it might not occur in March, Allen cautioned, it would take place under I MEF's watch. And it did, in September.[124]

But it was not just the ISF that led Allen to conclude Anbar had "achieved irreversible momentum." It was the mindset of the people. Successful counterinsurgency campaigns "create conditions where the people will buy into whatever it is you've done and seek to push it to the next level, so that the momentum created ultimately is irreversible. . . . It goes part and parcel with the winning of a counterinsurgency."[125]

The population of Anbar had made the transition and no longer was supporting armed struggle, said Allen. "We detected this in the late spring, early summer, that they had concluded in their own minds that they had emerged from the conflict, that the war was over in their minds and they were now transitioning into a postconflict era." And that resulted in a "common vision. The absolute laser-like focus that everyone had on beating AQI has now been replaced by the various political entities that are starting to emerge, jockeying for relative position of advantage to dominate the human terrain and ultimately to have a say or a hand in the spending of resources in the province. No surprise."[126]

Thus, as II MEF prepared to turn over command to I MEF in the early spring of 2008, the situation in Anbar had undergone quite a metamorphosis. Al Qaeda had been driven from all its strongholds. To be sure, it could still carry out random suicide attacks, and it continued to do so. But it had to commute to the province to initiate an operation. No longer did al Qaeda hold territory as it had at the height of the insurgency.

For I MEF the focus in 2008 was on (1) completing the professionalization of the ISF and handing off the security mission to it; (2) advancing those nonkinetic lines of operations that foster reconstruction, economic development, and the ascendance of the rule of law; (3) turning over responsibility for advancing the postconflict agenda to I MEF's civilian agency counterparts; and (4) exiting Anbar.

THUNDER OUT OF ANBAR

What the Marine Corps pulled off in Anbar was nothing short of a major turning point in the Iraq War. Many had declared the fight there lost at the very time I MEF was launching a strategy in 2006 that during 2007 culminated in the strategic defeat for AQI and those insurgents aligned with it. And that triumph took place before the success of the Surge and the counterinsurgency strategy on which it was based. The timelines between these two decisive points in the Iraq War are important to grasp.

Like the Surge, the Marine campaign plan for 2006 was based on counterinsurgency principles. And those precepts were being applied across the province before *FM 3-24 Counterinsurgency*, which served as the strategic basis for the Surge, was finalized at Fort Leavenworth and officially released on December 15, 2006. By that time, I MEF was well on its way to putting AQI out of business in Anbar.

In February 2007 General Petraeus succeeded General Casey as commanding general of MNF-I. The month before, during a televised speech, President Bush had announced his decision to order the deployment of more than 20,000 soldiers to Iraq, mainly in the greater Baghdad region. Petraeus intended to use those forces as part of a new strategy based on *FM 3-24*.

As chronicled in this account, I MEF had been executing its own counterinsurgency strategy well before February 2007. The OPLAN it initiated once back in Anbar in March 2006 was based on COIN principles. By the time General Petraeus took command in February 2007, the execution of that I MEF plan, now being advanced by II MEF, was reaching the crossover point in Anbar. Recall that in the late spring the level of violence fell precipitously in the province. And with that decline in violence, II MEF had started the transition to postconflict operations.

In effect, as the Surge forces were arriving in the spring of 2007 to begin to execute COIN operations in the greater Baghdad region, the fight in Anbar was ending. For General Petraeus, the months that followed were bloody. But in September 2007, when he reported to Congress on the situation in Iraq, there were important signs of progress. The number of weekly insurgent attacks had fallen to fewer than a thousand a week, from a high of sixteen hundred. And U.S. casualties were also dropping noticeably.

But contrast that situation with the state of affairs in Anbar. During the same month of September, the mayor of Ramadi was giving the signal for the start of the city's annual 5K road race. From being the most dangerous city in Iraq, Ramadi had become safe enough for its city fathers to again sponsor that 5K race. Anbar, including its once blood-soaked capital, was advancing into postconflict operations.

On July 30, 2009, General Petraeus gave the keynote speech to the Marine Corps Association's annual dinner. He extolled the Anbar campaign as illustrative of the Marines' "ready embrace of innovation," a long-established practice that allows the Corps to readily "adapt to the environments in which they operate and to the enemies they face. Unchanging, unyielding, bedrock principles are thus joined by an equally strong ability to innovate and adapt."[127]

And, observed the commanding general of Central Command, "Nowhere was this more evident than during the extraordinary turnaround led by the Marines in Anbar Province. . . . It is not an exaggeration to say that Anbar helped alter the course of events in Iraq, and I believe that generations from now, historians will continue to view it as a great example of the principled application of longstanding counterinsurgency principles, which are rooted in Marine Corps history."[128]

Through engagement with the sheikhs and tribes of the Awakening movement, in conjunction with a COIN strategy, explained Petraeus, the Marines had built trust by "living among, and sharing the risks with, those whose trust they sought. . . . From Ramadi, Marines worked to spread the movement across Anbar Province. Then it spread into Baghdad and elsewhere in Iraq. Violence went down steadily and civic life sprung anew from what were often quite literally ashes."[129]

"The battle for Anbar Province," concluded the Army general, again demonstrated the Marine Corps' "capacity to innovate, to learn, and to think deeply about complex and very difficult problems . . . while holding firm to the bedrock principles of loyalty and devotion among skilled, hardened warriors." Once more, the "Marines have proven that they possess this capacity and that they are more than up to the task."[130]

Conclusion

CLOSE THE DOOR AND TURN OUT THE LIGHTS

IN EARLY 2008 THE MARINES OF I MEF deployed back to Anbar. It was their third round in the Sunni heartland. In command this time was Maj. Gen. John Kelly. The province was remarkably different from the one he left after his initial deployment. Kelly first arrived in Anbar in March 2004 as the assistant commander of the 1st Marine Division—Blue Diamond. At that time the division found itself in a rapidly escalating and bloody fight.

But it was unclear who those people were who were responsible for killing a growing number of Marines. None of the senior civilian or military leadership warned them to expect an organized resistance. This was just not imaginable to the decision makers operating inside the Washington Beltway. Moreover, nothing in the classified intelligence databases that I MEF scoured before deploying to Anbar suggested they would be facing an insurgency.

Maj. Gen. John F. Kelly, commander of I MEF in 2008

MCWILLIAMS AND WHEELER, EDS., *AL-ANBAR AWAKENING*, VOL. 1, 240

Kelly kept hearing statements by Secretary Rumsfeld asserting that this faceless enemy was made up of just "pockets of dead-enders," only "small elements of ten to twenty people, not large military formations or networks of attackers."[1] Increasingly, it did not look that way to Blue Diamond's assistant division commander. Recall Kelly's rhetorical query during those early days in the province: "When do a bunch of guys that are trying to kill you turn into an insurgency?"[2]

By the end of 2004, the Marines of I MEF had no doubt that they were in a nasty and protracted test of wills with a mushrooming insurgency—a network of attackers—that AQI increasingly dominated. Reflecting on those days, Major General Kelly recalled that when he left Iraq in early 2005 "there were roughly 400 violent events a week in Anbar Province." But "when I returned in February 2008 that number was down to 50 attacks per week."[3]

Anbar was a very different place. Kelly found he was engaged with sheikhs who, in 2004, he had sent Marines to track down and either capture or kill. Now they were working together to advance through the postconflict phase to normalcy.

I MEF's challenge in 2008, he said, was to build on what II MEF had accomplished the previous year and "accelerate the situation toward normalcy." The goal was to continue to convince the people of the province that the fight was over and it was not going to reignite. By the end of 2008, Kelly believed that Anbar had reached that point. Violent actions "were down to, at the most, eight or nine a week." And that number "held for the last five–six months" of the year. "The frequency to which people would walk up to a Marine patrol and say there are some out-of-towners living in this house and they are not from around here was high."[4]

As a result, "AQI had to commute into Anbar to blow something up. . . . If they tried to set up and stay in a city the people very quickly would identify them." That told the general it was now "appropriate to use the term 'victory' in Anbar." The Marines, said Kelly, had proven to be "the most powerful tribe."[5]

At this point, many in the senior leadership of the Corps believed it was time to move on. In fact, in a June 2009 speech at the National Press Club the commandant, General Conway, said the moment had come to "close the door, turn out the lights and end the Marine Corps presence in Iraq," adding that the Corps was "coming out under a victory pennant. We have done essentially what the country asked us to do . . . we have crushed al Qaeda in the nation of Iraq." It was now time to shift their efforts to Afghanistan. The Marines in Iraq had "become a garrison force focused on reconstruction," he said, and "that's not our role."[6]

But the Marine Corps was to retain the mission through 2009, finally departing in January 2010. During that last year, as one news report put it, "Leathernecks are spending a lot of time on comparatively quiet duty."[7]

ADAPTING AND MAKING HISTORY

In the opening pages of this account of yet another historic Marine struggle against an implacable enemy it was noted how those hoping to become new Marines learn of the storied history of the Corps through the cadences of their DIs. As new enlistees run and train, the DIs of Parris Island employ lyrics, the content of which constitutes a short course in the long annals of such renowned clashes as Belleau Woods, Guadalcanal, Tarawa, Peleliu, Saipan, Iwo Jima, Okinawa, Inchon, Chosin, Khe Sanh, and Hue City.

From each of those campaigns, young Marine hopefuls learned about the Corps culture of adapting and overcoming relentless enemies. The DIs of Parris Island—no doubt—will be adding Anbar to those cadences. After all, that four-year test of wills is a textbook example of how Marines—true to their organizational culture—learned, adapted, and prevailed over a murderous, cold-blooded foe.

The four-year fight in the Sunni heartland is an outstanding illustration of that Marine mantra—improvise, adapt, overcome—that is infused into the Corps training and warrior ethos. Marines are taught to be prepared to rise above those unexpected obstacles always present in combat—what the great military theorist Carl von Clausewitz called the fog of war.

The history of war, as well as many tomes on organizational learning, tells us that in the midst of combat adapting is no easy task. Those volumes identify many factors that inhibit military learning, even in the face of dramatic changes in the operational environment.

John Nagl posits that the capacity of a military to learn lies in its organizational culture. He writes that while "military organizations are alike in many ways, different militaries have different organizational cultures." And those differences can "play a critical role in the organizations' ability to adapt their structure and functions to the demands placed on them."[8]

Military organizations that learn and adapt, maintains Richard Downie, are those flexible enough to "use new knowledge or understanding gained from experience or study to adjust institutional norms, doctrine and procedures in ways designed to minimize previous gaps in performance and maximize future successes."[9] An essential ingredient in this capacity to learn, adds John Nagl, is "institutional memory." It sustains "behaviors, mental maps, norms, and values over time."[10]

The Corps has an organizational culture that embeds in Marines a method of operating that embraces learning and memory. Its history is rife with examples of Marines at first being caught in the fog of war. But then, having learned from knowledge gained in the fight, the Corps shows itself to be flexible enough to make adjustments, overcome gaps in performance, and triumph. The Marine Corps has demonstrated this over and over throughout its history; it is adroit at embracing change.

Memory lies at the heart of Marine adaptability. The institutional memory of why and how those past victories came about reiterates operational principles that make for an agile fighting force.

The campaign in Anbar illustrates the enduring cultural norms of learning, memory, and adaptability. In 2004 I MEF found itself in the fog of war. While it prepared for this deployment by studying past experiences in the small wars fought from 1900 through the early 1930s, as well as by examining COIN practices in Vietnam, the situation in the Sunni heartland was not what the leadership expected.[11]

I MEF, in 2004, was not ready for the kind of insurgency emerging in Anbar and, subsequently, suffered ugly surprises. The OPLAN was not able to survive first contact, and I MEF spent considerable time trying to figure out, to paraphrase General Kelly, whether or not "those guys" trying to kill Marines had turned into an insurgency. I MEF lacked local intelligence necessary to produce a profile of the enemy.

In 2005 the situation in Anbar became increasingly violent as al Qaeda made Iraq the main front, the forward edge of the global battle with the United States. In doing so, AQI pulled out all the stops to inflict a defeat of strategic proportions on America. But at the same time, the Marines were learning and gaining ground knowledge from that fight.

This knowledge of the conflict was plowed into the development of I MEF's 2006 campaign plan. The pages of this narrative detail how I MEF designed and implemented a COIN approach that culminated by the end of 2008 in General Kelly's pronouncement that it was now "appropriate to use the term 'victory' in Anbar."[12] In achieving that state of affairs, the Marines were well served by their organizational culture.

TWENTY-FIRST-CENTURY CONFLICT

A decade into the twenty-first century reveals that the conflict in Iraq is not an anachronism. Rather, a persistent and prevalent pattern of irregular conflict has emerged, and the trend is here to stay for the foreseeable future. The conditions that lead to or foster irregular conflicts in various parts of the world—conditions found in weak and failing states—are not easily reversed. More than half the world's states are weak, failing, or failed, and are unable to control their territory, maintain a monopoly over the use of force, or perform core functions.

These situations provide opportunities for armed groups to pursue their objectives from the local, to the regional, and even to the global level, often causing major geopolitical damage. These iceberg-like secret organizations maintain an array of below-the-waterline operational units that employ protracted irregular tactics to gain control over territory and populations. These clandestine infrastructures are difficult for security forces to detect and disrupt.

Over the past two decades, armed groups have multiplied in number, and their capacity has ballooned. Moreover, they are made up of diverse subtypes—terrorists, insurgents, criminals, militias—that vary in vision, mission, and means. Each of these subtypes has more than one variant; there is no generic or single type of each.

Armed groups evolve and transform themselves, so while dividing them into four subtypes is useful for analytic purposes, these distinctions are not static or long lasting in the real world. Just the opposite. Armed groups can and do morph and transform from one subtype to another. Finally, insurgents, terrorists, militias, and criminal organizations are increasingly interacting and forming linkages with each other, as well as with other state and nonstate actors. Each of these characteristics was on full display in Al Anbar.

In the coming years, in more than a few cases where weak states are under attack from increasingly powerful armed groups, sometimes aided by authoritarian regimes, the United States will have interests at stake. Consequently, Washington will be confronted with the challenge of deploying military forces, in conjunction with its civilian-agency partners, to assist host nations establish security and stability.

In some cases, as Iraq and Afghanistan illustrate, this will entail major deployments of U.S. forces to irregular war zones to serve as the initial main security and stability forces. In other situations limited U.S. security capabilities will be sent to assist weak states in forestalling incipient armed group violence before it intensifies into a survival threat.

Regardless of the scenario, Marines will be a key component of those U.S. forces sent to meet twenty-first-century challenges and establish security and stability in irregular conflict zones. In preparing to do so, they should draw on important lessons from the Anbar campaign.

LESSONS FROM ANBAR

The lessons from Anbar are not unique to that four-year battle, and they are not only for the Marines to study. Given the persistence of irregular conflict challenges, those lessons will likely have an enduring applicability in the years ahead for all U.S. military and civilian security institutions. Therefore, they should be assiduously examined, dissected, and, where appropriate, institutionalized into training, organization, and preparation for future irregular challenges.

What follows is not the final word on those lessons. That is beyond the scope of this study. Rather, what follows are closing reflections, drawn from the narrative. They are presented not as definitive lessons but as informed observations taken from the Anbar campaign that relate to the future conflict environment, the nature of armed groups, and the efficacy of counterinsurgency as a strategy for managing these challenges.

Population-Centric Conflict Is Different

Anbar illustrates the changing conflict environment that Rupert Smith was among the first to document in *The Utility of Force: The Art of War in the Modern Age*. The former deputy SACEUR explained "that a paradigm shift in war has undoubtedly occurred. . . . The old paradigm was that of interstate industrialized war. The new one is the paradigm of war amongst the people."[13]

In the old paradigm the enemy was known, as was the conventional concept of operations to defeat him. The enemy's military was the center of gravity. In twenty-first-century irregular conflict, this is no longer the case. Now the center of gravity is the population. Providing security to the population and protecting it from armed groups is the casus belli in "war amongst the people."

War amongst the people is population-centric warfare, and it will necessitate institutional changes in how Marines and the other armed services approach operations. New concepts and capabilities are needed to manage these irregular fights, as the Anbar campaign displayed. Moreover, there is no one-size-fits-all in responding to wars amongst the people. The operational concepts for succeeding in Anbar were anchored in counterinsurgency doctrine. But the COIN plan had to be contextualized for that environment.

Understanding the Cultural Context Is Essential

To operate successfully in irregular conflict zones, Marines will need deep cultural understanding of the local population, the way the people perceive and think about their world, and the ways in which they organize social and political relations to survive. Without this understanding, it will be impossible to successfully prosecute population-centric warfare. To gain that local knowledge, Marine forces should be equipped with practical methods for decoding complex traditional cultures.

In Anbar, these took time to develop. They did not exist for I MEF to employ when it arrived there in March 2004. As a result, each successive MEF that served there had to learn from the unit that preceded it. Cumulatively, over time, the forces came to gain that understanding and integrated it into their operations.

To succeed, the Marines had to be able to engage the Sunni tribes and their leaders on their terms. That necessitated a sound grasp of Bedouin and Arabic tribal traditions, Islamic principles, and Arab cultural values. This knowledge came to serve as the foundation on which to build a tribal engagement strategy. I MEF in 2006 and II MEF the following year embedded that knowledge in their shared campaign plan.

Recall how II MEF prepared for 2007. A keen understanding of the tribes of Anbar was indispensable to engaging them in order to build on what I MEF had accomplished the previous year. Equipped with that knowledge, wrote General

Allen, "We intended not to operate around the tribes to win this insurgency. Rather, we had to operate inside the tribes. We had to penetrate the tribal membrane that excluded our influence. Our preparation to operate in this manner was vital, indeed crucial."[14] One of the difficulties that Marines faced in 2004–2005, Allen said in a 2010 interview, was that they "could not get inside the tribes. They operated among the people but were not inside the tribes."[15]

To achieve that objective, II MEF developed tribal engagement skills and instilled them in its officers and NCOs down to the platoon level. This provided an understanding of how to appreciate tribal institutions and to operate within them to facilitate change. Officers and NCOs could now carry out engagement up and down the tribal hierarchy. As a result, not only generals like Allen but also junior officers came to understand the tribal structure, to realize who the key players were, and to learn how to engage with them.

Armed Groups Are Complex and Diverse

Remember Sun Tzu. His advice was simple and yet timeless: "Know your enemy." Centuries later this maxim is still a basic principle for all who engage in armed conflict. But to know your enemy in irregular fights is more difficult than Sun Tzu could ever have envisioned. This is because of the complex and diverse nature of today's armed groups.

The Marines found that out in 2004. The armed groups comprising the insurgency did not look like the Iraqi army the Coalition forces had defeated in short order in the spring of 2003. The characteristics of these armed groups were very different from a conventional army.

First, the insurgency consisted of several clandestine organizations. Each maintained a secret infrastructure with varying levels of cohesion and complexity. Their subunits included intelligence and counterintelligence capabilities, as well as fighting units and financial, logistical, and communications networks. They used a wide range of violent and nonviolent tactics.

Armed groups in Anbar resembled icebergs, with below-the-waterline command, operational, and support units that were difficult to detect and disrupt. Recall the comments of Col. James Howcroft, the G-2 of I MEF in 2004. Once in Anbar he needed to know who the "bad guys" were, who the "good guys" were, and how to deal with each. But even by the late summer as he prepared to leave the province he did not have that kind of knowledge: "We didn't develop that [during my tour]," he said in a 2008 interview.[16]

To know this kind of enemy, who will surely be present in future irregular conflicts, Marines and soldiers will require new methods for profiling the organizational and operational capabilities of these diverse nonstate actors. New frameworks need to be conceptualized to provide commanders with detailed knowledge that encompasses the key characteristics of armed groups. By gaining understanding of these characteristics, comprehensive depictions can be generated and assembled.

Armed Groups Have Exploitable Cleavages

The insurgency in Anbar took hold in 2004 when different factions came together in an informal alliance. But the key elements of that partnership—the Sunni tribes and al Qaeda—were far from natural allies. Just the opposite. They had real differences that by 2005 had turned into deep rifts ripe for exploitation. II MEF recognized this opening in the fall of that year, and in 2006 I MEF sought to make the most of it.

The situation at that time was highly fluid, because the insurgent alliance was fragmenting. Tribal sheikhs, who were either part of the insurgency or giving tacit support to it, began changing sides. This proved to have strategic implications for the fight in Anbar.

As al Qaeda overplayed its hand, the Marines saw its missteps as an opening and took advantage of it, as this narrative records. In 2006 I MEF made this a key objective of its counterinsurgency plan and II MEF carried it to fruition in 2007.

The fragmentation of the insurgency was not atypical. Irregular conflicts in the future, in most instances, will feature more than one armed group challenging weak states where the United States has interests at stake. Those armed groups will have differences that, if acted upon, can undermine their cohesion and capacity to operate.

Counterinsurgency Works but It Must Be Adapted

Adopting a counterinsurgency strategy based on the standard COIN tenets of clear-hold-build-transfer and spreading that oil spot was very effective in Anbar. Remember, as General Zilmer prepared to take I MEF back to the province in March 2006, his staff devised a plan built around classic COIN precepts. And they employed them well before General Petraeus' *FM 3-24* reached completion.

What the Marine Corps achieved in Anbar by the summer of 2007 brought about nothing short of a major turning point in the Iraq War. The Marines in Anbar were the first to demonstrate that comprehensive counterinsurgency strategy works, as General Petraeus amplified in 2009: "It is not an exaggeration to say that Anbar helped alter the course of events in Iraq." It is "a great example of the principled application of longstanding counterinsurgency principles."[17]

COIN has a place in future irregular conflict where the objective is to influence and secure the population. To do this, counterinsurgency will include military, paramilitary, political, cultural, economic, psychological, and civic actions to defeat armed groups. And there are basic COIN tenets found in the classics and in the new *FM 3-24* that provide guidelines for future operations. For example, establishing security for the population must come first. It is the table setter for COIN operations. It creates opportunities for progress in the critical economic and governance lines of COIN operations. Likewise, clear-hold-build-transfer and spreading the oil spot will be SOP for future counterinsurgency efforts.

But COIN cannot be applied following a cookie-cutter approach. In Anbar the Marines adapted those classic precepts to a cultural context in which there were a number of different armed groups with dissimilar values and objectives. Anbar did not fit the classic insurgency model as it is spelled out in *FM 3-24*.

There is no "COIN in a box," no master plan to take off the shelf and implement. COIN principles must be customized for the context in which irregular war takes place. The counterinsurgency classics and *FM 3-24* can take you only so far. They provide a framework but not a blueprint for action. Anbar demonstrated that counterinsurgency has to be tailored to the fight.

It May Be Counterinsurgency, but It Is Still War

The new counterinsurgency literature devotes considerable attention to the nonkinetic lines of operations and the whole-of-government approach, with its emphasis on civil agencies carrying out humanitarian and developmental activities. To be sure, these measures are important.

But counterinsurgency is still war and involves combat. Success in Anbar began with Marine and Army units sweeping the insurgents from the cities and towns spread along the Euphrates from Fallujah to the Syrian border. Those operations were carried out by what General Allen described as "the breakthrough force." Their objective was to use fire and maneuver to attack enemy strongholds, drive them out, and then hold that ground after it was cleared. The breakthrough force carried out the kinetic part of counterinsurgency operations, setting the conditions for the exploitation force.

What's more, these were not the only forces carrying out combat operations in Anbar: special mission units of JSOC and theater special operators were also on the ground. While the MEF's breakthrough force isolated the population from AQI, it did not eliminate its clandestine infrastructure or secret underground. To root out this underground, the United States employed JSOC units, euphemistically called "task force units" in Iraq. Their forte, lethal counterterrorism operations, directly targeted the personnel that constituted AQI's clandestine apparatus. In Anbar those operations were carried out by Task Force 145. This task force established an operational tempo that hit AQI's network every night, killing or capturing a large number of its midlevel managers and operational commanders.

In Anbar these counterterrorism operations were an important complement and made a vital contribution to the overall success of the Marines' counterinsurgency campaign. So while Marine and Army forces conducted security-related operations and trained the emerging ISF, task force units systematically attacked and dismantled the command and control network of the enemy.

Counterinsurgency Requires Skilled Advisers

To execute successful counterinsurgency programs in future conflict environments such as the one in Anbar, the United States will need a contingent of political and military advisers who can take a hands-on approach and, through effective mediation, help shape the orientation and conduct of diverse local leaders and communities. Such advisers must be able to serve as political entrepreneurs, fostering constructive local and national interaction and cooperation in conflict and postconflict settings where political power is characteristically personalized and factionalized. As Zalmay Khalilzad explained, these advisers need mentoring skills to help "jump-start local institution building and economic development."[18]

An examination of successful counterinsurgency efforts in the past shows that individuals with these skills have often played key roles. But as we saw in Iraq as late as 2006, the military services, the Department of State, and the operational arms of intelligence agencies had few such individuals formally trained with the skills needed to shape the orientation and conduct of local leaders and communities in ways that facilitated successful postconflict developments.

As the narrative illustrates, the Marines—not by design but through on-the-job learning—began to develop this advisory capability. And when it became apparent how important it was to managing postconflict transition, II MEF initiated a training effort to instill advisory skills in officers and NCOs down to the company and platoon levels.

While this was a serendipitous effort, it paid off. In the future, the United States will need a capacity to shape political transition in irregular conflicts. Therefore, steps should be taken to institutionalize the training of diplomats, military, and intelligence officers to serve as trusted political intermediaries who can foster negotiations and forge compacts among key actors and communities to share power and make the transition from armed conflict to participatory politics.

Indigenous Police Are a Key Force Multiplier

Holding territory once it is cleared requires indigenous forces, as Anbar illustrated. When they were not available in 2004–2005, MEF units were mired in a deadly version of the arcade game whack-a-mole. They could hit the insurgents hard in one location only to have them withdraw and pop up somewhere else. Hit them there and they would return to a location that had been previously cleared but not secured. There were just not enough Marines and soldiers.

The key to holding territory was the expansion of the ISF, especially the police, because they presented a persistent presence within the local population. Recall the COIN classics: they all stressed indigenous police as a key counterinsurgency capability. Al Qaeda also understood this fact and the dangers it posed to its hold on the province. If the ranks of the police came to be filled with local tribesmen they would no longer be able to "hide in plain sight" and soon would be out of business.

In 2004 and 2005 the MEF commanding generals were well aware of this requirement. To their credit, they tried to expand the police forces, but to no avail. Increasing the size of the police as a part of COIN strategy cannot take place in a vacuum. It has to be facilitated by engagement.

The synergy between police expansion and engagement can be seen in the Anbar experience. Recall the words of General Gaskin, the II MEF chief in 2007: "What I soon discovered is that there is a direct correlation between tribal engagement and recruiting. So that ability to connect the tribes with the cause that both of us had in common, getting rid of al Qaeda . . . meant that the tribes needed to be participants in that."[19] Engagement opened the door for the remarkable growth of police, which in turn gave II MEF the capacity it needed to dominate the physical and human terrain of Anbar. That was step one. Step two was training the Anbar police, along with Iraqi army units, to take over the security mission.

Counterinsurgency Is an Intelligence-Led Fight

That COIN is an intelligence-led fight is one of those other maxims that dominate classic and current counterinsurgency thought. Moreover, a review of case histories confirms the centrality of local intelligence.

All successful COIN campaigns have had effective methods for amassing and disseminating timely and accurate local intelligence, gathered primarily through human collection methods and not by way of signals, imagery, or other national technical intelligence means. While technical intelligence can support human collection, it is not a substitute for it. Human intelligence activities are designed to gather, collate, and disseminate data to expose the clandestine apparatus of insurgent groups. Closely connected to this intelligence requirement are two other COIN prerequisites discussed above: a physical presence capable of holding territory and a strong indigenous police force.

In Anbar these three COIN requirements were symbiotically connected. Territory once cleared had to be held. But that could only happen if MEF forces could grow the police and change the composition of the army units in the province. That engagement policy, which was launched at the end of 2005, brought about a huge expansion of the indigenous security force expansion in 2006–2007. This resulted in the remarkable growth of the police and Iraqi army units.

The expansion of police forces was a key to de-escalating the insurgency in Anbar. With the expansion came local intelligence, which was needed to expose the underground insurgent organizations. No longer could AQI members hide among the population. To further exploit this opportunity, II MEF fostered the formation of special police intelligence units in the same vein as Special Branch units seen during the emergency in Malaya and in Northern Ireland. Though it came late in the game, this was one of the most innovative approaches developed to enhance the capacity of the Iraqi police to roll up AQI.

This program, known as Legacy, was based on the concept of local intelligence dominance. As noted earlier by leading intelligence scholar Roy Godson and colleagues, this "model of local, or what some call tactical intelligence dominance, has been developed through trial and error over decades by several 20th-century democracies in diverse theaters and cultures." Its objective is straightforward: "degrading, disrupting, and neutralizing the challenge of armed groups to the government's authority—both its capacity and legitimacy—within the confines of the rule of law."[20]

In Anbar the Marine Corps' Intelligence Activity arm began assisting the Iraqi police in developing this capability in 2007. It was yet another of those innovative tools that are available for neutralizing armed groups. Significantly, these innovations came from young Marine and Army officers who could see the need for change and understood history well enough to seek and adapt improvement from the past. In this, for example, Maj. Drew Cukor, a Marine intelligence officer, played a significant role in the key program enhancement of Iraqi police intelligence capabilities not just in Anbar but across Iraq as well.

It would seem sensible for the United States to institutionalize the skills and equipment needed to assist host nations threatened by armed groups to develop intelligence dominance capabilities, given the persistence of irregular conflict foreseen in the years ahead. To do so, according to Godson and colleagues, "would require a specialized U.S. unit capable of collaborating with host nation police, military, or intelligence services. The U.S. unit could be housed in State, Defense, or DoJ [Department of Justice], or in a nongovernmental entity designed or adapted for this purpose."[21]

The Nonkinetic Lines of Operations Are the Way Forward

The transition from kinetic operations to postconflict governance, reconstruction, and rule of law is a critical juncture in all counterinsurgency campaigns. Once it begins, managing COIN's build period requires a broader array of capabilities than those employed in the clear and hold phases. Moreover, as was illustrated in Anbar, once the bridge from armed struggle to postconflict reconstruction has been crossed, the population expects change to start taking place. Remember what General Allen told his commanders: "The one sound we can't afford is . . . to have the kinetic phase suddenly be followed by a large, pregnant silence, where there's no governing and nothing being built and no money coming into the province."[22]

II MEF was ready for that changeover. It had organized to jumpstart the processes of governance, economic development, and rule of law. To oversee each of these nonkinetic lines of operations, General Gaskin and his staff marshaled resources that included three civil affairs detachments assigned to help execute these missions. As the narrative details, through these steps II MEF was poised to manage the postconflict opportunities that appeared in the late spring of 2007 with the dramatic decline in enemy violence. And it did so effectively but within limitations. II MEF's role was restricted: it was able to get the build process started, but the completion of that process was beyond II MEF's responsibility and capabilities.

An important lesson from the Anbar campaign is that postconflict operations, whether they are a part of counterinsurgency missions or of other contingencies, are not the primary responsibility of the military services. To be sure, as II MEF demonstrated, they have a role to play. But postconflict activities are more the responsibility of the civil agencies of the U.S. government. Consequently, they require a whole-of-government approach that integrates civilian and military capabilities to assist indigenous governments to revitalize institutions and the economy once the kinetic fight has ended. While the U.S. military can help initiate this phase, once it is under way the civilian agencies have to develop the means to take control of it and bring it to completion. In the long decade of the two wars in Afghanistan and Iraq, the relationship of the military to civilian governmental and NGO development entities has matured dramatically. And while there is ground still to be covered, the habitual relationship among the Department of Defense, the Department of State, and USAID has grown to fill that unacceptable pregnant silence on the COIN battlefield with coordinated development to better facilitate the transition from the hold to build phase of counterinsurgency operations.

Be Prepared for the Unexpected in Counterinsurgency Fights

Finally, in counterinsurgency warfare, as with its conventional counterpart, the only constant is that the unexpected will always be present in the fight. The unforeseen will challenge COIN campaign plans. As Clausewitz warned, the fog of war is ever present. To deal effectively with the unexpected, military organizations, systems of command and control, and campaign planners must all be schooled to expect surprise and be predisposed to adapt when unprepared-for events cause friction, undermining preexisting plans and operations.

During the spring months of 2007 the unexpected happened in Anbar, and it happened fast. The course of the fight abruptly changed. When II MEF returned to the province in the beginning of that year, it anticipated no sharp dropoff in insurgent violence any time soon. The conflict had settled into a bloody protracted struggle, and according to the COIN classics, it would take considerable time and effort to root the insurgents out and defeat them. No sea change was likely. That is how the leaders of II MEF saw the situation as they deployed.

But a sea change is precisely what happened. Within a hundred days of arriving, II MEF saw the situation virtually turned on its head as insurgent violence dropped precipitously. It was unexpected. The crossover point from the kinetic fight to the postconflict phase of COIN was not by the book.

Rather, as Clausewitz warned, war proved unpredictable. However, to the credit of II MEF, its planners had prepared to exploit that turn of events, even though it happened well ahead of schedule. Waiting in the wings were those exploitation forces needed to take advantage of the situation. And they did. The result, as General Kelly noted in 2010, was that by the end of 2008 it was "appropriate to use the term 'victory' in Anbar."[23] The Marines had successfully adapted and improvised, and in doing so provided those Parris Island DI's with a new entry—Anbar—to add to the annals of renowned historical triumphs they recount in the cadences used to train future Marine warriors.

Notes

INTRODUCTION

1. Brig. Gen. Joseph Dunford, oral history interview conducted by Dr. Fred Allison of the U.S. Marine Corps History Division, December 18, 2006, transcript, 15.
2. Maj. Gen. John Kelly, presentation at the Fletcher School (Tufts University) roundtable "Marine Generals Discuss Anbar 2006," May 2, 2010, http://fletcher.tufts.edu/ISSP/Events/Video.
3. Learning: See Richard Downie, *Learning From Conflict: The U.S. Military in Vietnam, El Salvador, and the Drug War* (Westport, CT: Praeger, 1998); John Nagl, *Learning to Eat Soup with a Knife* (Chicago: University of Chicago Press, 2002); Janine Davidson, *Lifting the Fog of Peace* (Ann Arbor: University of Michigan Press, 2010); and Gordon Sullivan and Michael Harper, *Hope Is Not a Method: What Business Leaders can Learn from America's Army* (New York: Random House, 1996).
   Innovation: See Barry Posen, *The Sources of Military Doctrine: France, Britain, and Germany between the World Wars* (Ithaca, NY: Cornell University Press, 1984); Stephen Rosen, *Winning the Next War: Innovation and the Modern Military* (Ithaca, NY: Cornell University Press, 1984); Deborah Avant, "The Institutional Sources of Military Doctrine: Hegemons in Peripheral Wars," *International Studies Quarterly* 37, no. 4 (December 1993); and Elizabeth Kier, *Imagining War: French and British Military Doctrine between the Wars* (Princeton, NJ: Princeton University Press, 1997).
4. Davidson summarizes the organizational theory in Davidson, *Lifting the Fog of Peace*, chap. 1.
5. These theories have their origins in Graham Allison's classic study of decision making and his utilization of the texts on organizational behavior to explain the Cuban missile crisis. Graham Allison, *Essence of Decision: Explaining the Cuban Missile Crisis,* 2nd ed. (New York: Longman, 1999).
6. Davidson, *Lifting the Fog of Peace*, 11.

7. Ibid., 13. Also, see Anthony Downs, *Inside Bureaucracy* (Boston: Little, Brown, 1967); and James Q. Wilson, *Bureaucracy* (New York: Basic Books, 1989).
8. Downie, *Learning From Conflict*, 23–24.
9. Davidson, *Lifting the Fog of Peace*, 12, 18–19.
10. Victor Krulak, *First to Fight: An Inside View of the U.S. Marine Corps* (Annnapolis, MD: Naval Institute Press, 1999).
11. Ibid., 5.
12. See, for example, Chris Argyris, *On Organizational Learning* (Malden, MA: Blackwell, 1999); Peter Senge, *The Fifth Discipline: The Art and Practice of the Learning Organization* (New York: Doubleday, 1990); and the classics by James March, *Decisions and Organizations* (Oxford: Blackwell, 1991) and *Organizations*, 2nd ed. (Oxford: Blackwell, 1993).
13. Krulak, *First to Fight*, 137.
14. James Warren, *American Spartans* (New York: Free Press, 2005), 20.
15. Barbara Levitt and James March, "Organizational Learning," *Annual Review of Sociology* (1988), 319.
16. Davidson notes that "some organizations actively promote the collection and dissemination of new information, while others rigidly adhere to standard operating procedures and ignore new information—especially if that information challenges existing paradigms and norms" (*Lifting the Fog of Peace*, 19–20).
17. Downie, *Learning From Conflict*, 34–35.
18. Lt. Gen. John Allen, "Anbar Dawn: The Defeat of Al Qaeda," text of a lecture given at the Fletcher School, Tufts University, March 11, 2009, 28.

CHAPTER 1. This Is Al Anbar

1. Warren, *American Spartans*, dust cover.
2. *Culture matters* is the title of a book edited by Lawrence Harrison and Samuel Huntington. The study seeks to determine why some countries and ethnic groups are better off than others. The authors in this controversial collection argue that the answer lies in different cultural values that shape political and economic performance. Harrison and Huntington, *Culture Matters: How Values Shape Human Progress* (New York: Basic Books, 2000).
3. Brig. Gen. John R. Allen, oral history interview conducted by Chris Wilk at Camp Lejeune, NC, March 27, 2008, transcript, 56.

4. Ibid., 9.
5. Dafna Linzer and Thomas E. Ricks, "Anbar Picture Grows Clearer, and Bleaker," *Washington Post,* November 28, 2006.
6. Allen, Wilk interview, March 27, 2008, transcript, 5.
7. Paula Holmes-Eber and Barak Salmoni, "Operational Culture for Marines," *Marine Corps Gazette,* May 2008, 72.
8. Barak Salmoni and Paula Holmes-Eber, *Operational Culture for the War Fighter: Principles and Applications* (Quantico, VA: Marine Corps University, 2008), 15.
9. Lin Todd, R. Alan King, Andrea V. Jackson, Montgomery McFate, Ahmed S. Hashim, and Jeremy S. Harrington, *Iraq Tribal Study: Al-Anbar Governorate: The Albu Fahd Tribe, the Albu Mahal Tribe and the Albu Issa Tribe* (Alexandria, VA: Quantum Research International, 2006), ES-1.
10. Ibid.
11. Walter Pincus, "A Potentially Winning Tactic, With a Warning," *Washington Post,* August 27, 2007.
12. Todd et al., *Iraq Tribal Study,* chap. 2, 3.
13. Raphael Patai, *The Arab Mind* (New York: Charles Scribner's Sons, 1983), 78.
14. Todd et al., *Iraq Tribal Study,* chap. 2, 36.
15. Shelagh Weir, *The Bedouin* (London: British Museum Publications, 1990).
16. Michael Meeker, *Literature and Violence in North Arabia* (Cambridge, UK: Cambridge University Press, 1979).
17. Todd et al., *Iraq Tribal Study,* chap. 2, 37.
18. Ibid.
19. For a detailed discussion, see Joseph Ginat, *Blood Revenge: Family Honor, Mediation, and Outcasting* (Brighton, UK: Sussex Academic Press, 1997).
20. Todd et al., *Iraq Tribal Study,* chap. 2, 34.
21. Phebe Marr, *The History of Modern Iraq,* 2nd ed. (Boulder, CO: Westview, 2004), 4.
22. The teaching of al-Wahhab was founded on that of Ibn Taimiyya, who was a member of the school of Ahmad ibn Hanbal. Ibn Taimiyya claimed the power of one who can give independent decisions (*mujtahid*). His decisions were based on the Quran, which he understood in a literal sense. He rejected all innovations such as the visiting of the sacred shrines, and he viewed the invocation of the saints as idolatry.
23. According to al-Wahhab, a Muslim must give an oath of allegiance to a Muslim ruler during his lifetime to ensure his redemption after death. The

ruler is owed unquestioned allegiance from his people as long as he leads in conformity to the laws of God. The purpose of the Muslim community is to become the living embodiment of God's laws, and it is the duty of the ruler to ensure people know God's laws and live by them.

24. For a detailed assessment of the Salafi movement and its different factions, see Quintan Wiktorowicz, "Anatomy of the Salafi Movement," *Studies in Conflict & Terrorism,* no. 3 (2006), 207–239. The author divides Salafis into three major Salafi factions: purists, politicos, and jihadis. In the article he explains the sources of unity among these factions, as well as those factors that separate them. The latter center on issues related to politics and violence. He notes, "although Salafis share a common religious creed, they differ over their assessment of contemporary problems and thus how this creed should be applied" (Wiktorowicz, 208).

25. The five pillars of Islam constitute the basis, or foundation, of faith for Muslims. They are (1) belief in only one god and in Muhammad as his prophet, (2) the reciting of daily prayers, (3) almsgiving to the poor, (4) fasting during the holy month of Ramadan, and (5) for those who are able to do so, making a pilgrimage to Mecca.

26. Mark Sedgwick, "Al-Qaeda and the Nature of Religious Terrorism," *Terrorism &Political Violence* (October–December 2004); also Wiktorowicz, "Anatomy of the Salafi Movement."

27. See Richard H. Shultz, *Global Insurgency Strategy and the Salafi Jihad Movement,* INSS Occasional Paper 66 (CO: USAF Institute for National Security Studies, 2008); Norman Cigar, trans. and analyzed, *Al-Qa'ida's Doctrine for Insurgency* (Washington, DC: Potomac Books, 2009); and Jim Lacey, ed., *The Canons of Jihad: Terrorists' Strategy for Defeating America* (Annapolis, MD: Naval Institute Press, 2008).

28. See Colin Turner, *Islam: The Basics* (London: Routledge, 2006); John Alden Williams, *The Word of Islam* (Austin, TX: University of Texas Press, 1994); Annemarie Schimmel, *Islam: An Introduction* (Albany, NY: State University of New York Press, 1992); John L. Esposito, *Islam: The Straight Path* (Oxford, UK: Oxford University Press, 1991); John L. Esposito, ed., *The Oxford History of Islam* (Oxford, UK: Oxford University Press, 1999); and Ira Marvin Lapidus, *A History of Islamic Societies* (Cambridge, UK: Cambridge University Press, 2002).

29. Here is a more technical explanation, drawn from the World Religions Project:

> The Hanafi School is the first of the four orthodox Sunni schools of law. It is distinguished from the other schools

through its placing less reliance on mass oral traditions as a source of legal knowledge. It developed the exegesis of the Qur'an through a method of analogical reasoning known as *Qiyas*. It also established the principle that the universal concurrence of the Ummah (community) of Islam on a point of law, as represented by legal and religious scholars, constituted evidence of the will of God. This process is called *Ijma,* which means the consensus of the scholars. Thus, the school definitively established the Qur'an, the Traditions of the Prophet, *Ijma* and *Qiyas* as the basis of Islamic law. In addition to these, Hanafi accepted local customs as a secondary source of the law.

For the project's website, see http://www.philtar.ac.uk/encyclopedia/.
30. Amatzi Baram, "Who Are the Insurgents? Sunni Arab Rebels in Iraq," United States Institute of Peace Special Report, April 2005, 10.
31. Philip Hitti, *The Arabs: A Short History* (Washington, DC: Regnery, 1970), 260–261.
32. For the text of Maude's remarks, see Philip Willard, *Iraq: A Study in Political Development* (London: Jonathan Cape, 1937).
33. For a detailed discussion of the role of tribes in the formation of states in the Middle East, see Philip Khoury and Joseph Kostiner, *Tribes and State Formation in the Middle East* (Berkeley: University of California Press, 1990).
34. Amatzia Baram, "Neo-Tribalism in Iraq," *International Journal of Middle East Studies* 29, no. 1 (February 1997), 1; quotes are on p. 1.
35. Ibid., 13.
36. Todd et al., *Iraq Tribal Study,* chap. 4, 9.
37. Ibid., chap. 4, 6.
38. Montgomery McFate, "The Memory of War: Tribes and the Legitimate Use of Force in Iraq," in *Armed Groups: Studies in National Security, Counterterrorism, and Counterinsurgency*, ed. Jeffrey Norwitz, (Newport, RI: Naval War College, 2008), 300.
39. Baram, "Neo-Tribalism in Iraq," 13.
40. Ibid.
41. Hannah Allam, "Fallujah's Real Boss: Omar the Electrician," *Seattle Times*, November 22, 2004.
42. Carl von Clausewitz, *On War,* ed. and trans. by Michael Howard and Peter Paret (Princeton, NJ: Princeton University Press, 1976), 595–596.

43. Ibid.
44. Rupert Smith, *The Utility of Force: The Art of War in the Modern World* (New York: Penquin, 2006).
45. W. Patrick Lang, "Understanding How to Live and Work with Tribesmen," in Todd et al., *Iraq Tribal Study,* A1–1. Emphasis in original.
46. McFate, "The Memory of War," 318–319.
47. Arab tribal customary law quoted in ibid., 318.
48. Lang, "Understanding How to Live," A1–2. Emphasis in original.
49. McFate, "The Memory of War," 319.
50. Michael Hirsh, "Blood and Honor," *Newsweek,* February 2, 2004, 38.
51. Quote found in McFate, "The Memory of War," 317.
52. On these warfighting traditions, see John Jandora, *Militarism in Arab Society: An Historiographical and Bibliographical Sourcebook* (Westport, CT: Greenwood Press, 1997).
53. Lang, "Understanding How to Live," A1–4.
54. Ibid.
55. Ibid., A1–1.

Chapter 2. 2003: All the Wrong Moves

1. Kelly, presentation at the Fletcher School roundtable, May 2, 2010.
2. President George Bush quoted in George Packer, *The Assassin's Gate* (New York: Farrar, Straus and Giroux, 2005), 111. http://fletcher.tufts.edu/ISSP/Events/Video
3. Michael Gordon, "The Lost Year in Iraq," *Frontline* interview, July 18, 2006, transcript, http://www.pbs.org/wgbh/pages/frontline/yeariniraq/analysis/prewar.html; and August 10 and August 11, 2006, http://www.pbs.org/wgbh/pages/frontline/yeariniraq/interviews/gordon.html.
4. For a recounting of these debates, see Thomas Ricks, *Fiasco: The American Military Adventure in Iraq* (New York: Penguin Press, 2006), 4.
5. Michael Gordon and Bernard Trainor, *Cobra II: The Inside Story of the Invasion and Occupation of Iraq* (New York: Random House, 2007), 166–167.
6. Gordon, "The Lost Year in Iraq," *Frontline* interview, July 18, 2006.
7. The Future of Iraq project, National Security Archive, http://www.gwu.edu/~nsarchiv/NSAEBB/NSAEBB198/index.htm.
8. David Phillips, *Losing Iraq: Inside the Postwar Reconstruction Fiasco* (Boulder, CO: Westview Press, 2006), 90.

9. See, for example, Bob Woodward, *State of Denial: Bush at War Part 3* (New York: Simon and Schuster, 2006), 127–128.
10. Larry Jay Diamond, *Squandered Victory: The American Occupation and the Bungled Effort to Bring Democracy to Iraq* (New York: Henry Holt, 2005), 29.
11. Packer, *The Assassin's Gate*, 120.
12. Willson, quoted in ibid., 147.
13. Packer, *The Assassin's Gate*, 58–59.
14. Phillips, *Losing Iraq*, 67–76; Jay Garner, "Truth, War and Consequences," *Frontline* interview, July 17, 2003, transcript, http://www.pbs.org/wgbh/pages/frontline/shows/truth/interviews/garner.html.
15. Packer, *The Assassin's Gate*, 97.
16. Ibid., 125; Diamond, *Squandered Victory*, 31.
17. Rajiv Chandrasekaran, *Imperial Life in the Emerald City* (New York: Alfred A. Knopf, 2006), 129–140.
18. Rumsfeld quoted in Diamond, *Squandered Victory*, 31.
19. Douglas Feith, *War and Decision: Inside the Pentagon at the Dawn of the War on Terrorism* (New York: Harper, 2008), 143–144, 249–250.
20. Packer, *The Assassin's Gate*, 112.
21. Ibid.
22. Feith, *War and Decision*, 402–413.
23. Ibid., 413.
24. James Dobbins, Seth Jones, Benjamin Runkle, Siddharth Mohandas, *Occupying Iraq: A History of the Coalition Provisional Authority* (Arlington, VA: RAND, 2009), 39–40.
25. Gordon and Trainor, *Cobra II*, 159–160.
26. Michael Gordon, "A Prewar Slide Show Cast Iraq in Rosy Hues," *New York Times*, February 15, 2007, http://www.nytimes.com/2007/02/15/washington/15military.html.
27. Agoglia quoted in Gordon and Trainor, *Cobra II*, 160.
28. James Dobbins, "The Lost Year in Iraq," *Frontline* interview, June 27, 2006, transcript, http://www.pbs.org/wgbh/pages/frontline/yeariniraq/interviews/dobbins.html; and James Dobbins et al., *America's Role in Nation-Building: From Germany to Iraq* (Santa Monica, CA: RAND, 2005).
29. Ricks, *Fiasco*, 117.
30. Chandrasekaran, *Imperial Life in the Emerald City*, 46.

31. Jay Garner, "The Lost Year in Iraq," *Frontline* interview, August 11, 2006, transcript, http://www.pbs.org/wgbh/pages/frontline/yeariniraq/interviews/garner.html.
32. Packer, *The Assassin's Gate*, 139.
33. Phillips, *Losing Iraq*, 245.
34. Ibid., 138.
35. Packer, *The Assassin's Gate*, 142.
36. Garner, "The Lost Year in Iraq," *Frontline* interview, August 11, 2006.
37. Ambassador L. Paul Bremer and Malcolm McConnell, *My Year in Iraq: The Struggle to Build a Future of Hope* (New York: Threshold Editions, 2006), 107.
38. A captain in the U.S. Army, in Packer, *The Asssassin's Gate*, 223.
39. Thomas Ricks, "'It Looked Weird and Felt Wrong,'" *Washington Post*, July 24, 2006.
40. Packer, *The Assassin's Gate*, 122.
41. Dr. Thamer Ibrahim Tahir al-Assafi, interview, in *Al-Anbar Awakening: From Insurgency to Counterinsurgency in Iraq, 2004–2009*, vol. 2, *Iraqi Perspectives,* ed. Gary W. Montgomery and Timothy S. McWilliams (Quantico, VA: Marine Corps University Press, 2009), 33.
42. Sheikh Sabah al-Sattam Effan Fahran al-Shurji al-Aziz, interview, in Montgomery and McWilliams, *Al-Anbar Awakening*, vol. 2, 139.
43. Arnold Bray quoted in Ricks, *Fiasco,* 139.
44. "U.S. Troops Shoot Iraqi Protesters," *Online NewsHour,* April 29, 2003, http://www.pbs.org/newshour/updates/shooting_04–29–03.html.
45. Human Rights Watch, *Iraq: Violent Response: The U.S. Army in al-Fallujah,* June 17, 2003, http://www.unhcr.org/refworld/docid/3f4f59573.html.
46. Human Rights Watch, *Iraq: Violent Response*.
47. Ricks, *Fiasco,* 139.
48. Human Rights Watch, *Iraq: Violent Response*.
49. Rajiv Chandrasekaran, "Iraqis Vow Revenge for Killings by U.S. Soldiers; Apology Does Little to Placate Anger," *Washington Post,* September 14, 2003.
50. Bobby Ghosh, "In Fallujah, Where the Dead Have Become Martyrs," *Time,* October 8, 2010, http://www.time.com/time/world/article/0,8599,2024179,00.html.
51. Ibid.; Lt. Gen. John F. Kelly, "Foreword," in *Al-Anbar Awakening: U.S. Marines and Counterinsurgency in Iraq, 2004–2009* vol. 1, *American*

Perspectives, ed. Timothy S. McWilliams and Kurtis P. Wheeler (Quantico, VA: Marine Corps University Press, 2009), vi; vol. 2, *Iraqi Perspectives,* vii.
52. Jane Perlez, "A Nation at War: The Postwar Task; U.S. Overseer Set to Remake Iraq," *New York Times,* April 15, 2003, http://www.nytimes.com/2003/04/15/world/a-nation-at-war-the-postwar-task-us-overseer-set-to-remake-iraq.html.
53. Packer, *The Assassin's Gate,* 140. Also, Nora Bensahel et al., *After Saddam: Prewar Planning and the Occupation of Iraq* (Arlington, VA: RAND, 2008), 53.
54. Phillips, *Losing Iraq,* 8, 126.
55. Garner, "The Lost Year in Iraq," *Frontline* interview, August 11, 2006.
56. Bensahel et al., *After Saddam,* 54–58.
57. Eric Schmitt and David Sanger, "Aftereffects: Reconstruction Policy; Looting Disrupts Detailed U.S. Plan to Restore Iraq," *New York Times,* May 19, 2003, http://www.nytimes.com/2003/05/19/world/aftereffects-reconstruction-policy-looting-disrupts-detailed-us-plan-restore.html.
58. Tommy Franks, *American Soldier* (New York: HarperCollins, 2004), 524.
59. Packer, *The Assassin's Gate,* 133.
60. Garner, "Truth, War and Consequences," *Frontline* interview, July 17, 2003.
61. "The Lost Year in Iraq," *Frontline* interview, posted October 17, 2006, transcript, http://www.pbs.org/wgbh/pages/frontline/yeariniraq/etc/script.html.
62. Garner, "The Lost Year in Iraq," *Frontline* interview, August 11, 2006.
63. Perlez, "A Nation at War."
64. Jay Garner quoted in Carol Morello, "'Nucleus' of Iraqi Leaders Emerges; Occupation Chief Outlines Plan for Interim Authority," *Washington Post,* May 6, 2003.
65. Packer, *The Assassin's Gate,* 140–41.
66. Garner, "The Lost Year in Iraq," *Frontline* interview, August 11, 2006.
67. Woodward, *State of Denial,* 148.
68. Bremer and McConnell, *My Year in Iraq,* 12.
69. Ibid., 4, 12.
70. James Dao, "Aftereffects: The Overseer—Man in the News: At the Helm in Shattered Iraq: Lewis Paul Bremer III," *New York Times,* May 8, 2003, http://www.nytimes.com/2003/05/08/world/aftereffects-overseer-man-helm-shattered-iraq-lewis-paul-bremer-iii.html?ref=lpauliiibremer.

71. L. Paul Bremer, "The Lost Year in Iraq," *Frontline* interview, June 26 and August 18, 2006, transcript, http://www.pbs.org/wgbh/pages/frontline/yeariniraq/interviews/bremer.html.
72. Bremer and McConnell, *My Year in Iraq*, 5.
73. Ibid.,11; Gordon and Trainor, *Cobra II,* 560–561.
74. Phillips, *Losing Iraq,* 164.
75. Packer, *The Assassin's Gate,* 212; Chandrasekaran, *Imperial Life in the Emerald City,* 185.
76. Phillips, *Losing Iraq,* 172.
77. Chandrasekaran, *Imperial Life in the Emerald City,* 266.
78. Ibid., 268–272.
79. Ibid., 272.
80. Bremer and McConnell, *My Year in Iraq,* 20–21.
81. Ibid., 17.
82. Ibid., 29.
83. Woodward, *State of Denial,* 193.
84. Chandrasekaran, *Imperial Life in the Emerald City,* 83; Lawrence E. Howard, "Lessons Learned from Denazification and De-Ba'athification" (Carlisle Barracks, PA: U.S. Army War College, 2007), 12.
85. Bremer and McConnell, *My Year in Iraq,* 40–41.
86. Ibid., 42.
87. Anthony Cordesman, "The Lost Year in Iraq," *Frontline* interview, July 18, 2006, transcript, http://www.pbs.org/wgbh/pages/frontline/yeariniraq/interviews/cordesman.html.
88. Chalabi op-ed quoted in Mark Perry, *Talking to Terrorists: Why America Must Engage with Its Enemies* (New York: Basic Books, 2010), 11.
89. Bremer, "The Lost Year in Iraq," *Frontline* interview, June 26 and August 18, 2006.
90. Packer, *The Assassin's Gate,* 49–50.
91. Dobbins, "The Lost Year in Iraq," *Frontline* interview, June 27, 2006.
92. Volker Rolf Berghahn, *Modern Germany: Society, Economy and Politics in the Twentieth Century* (New York: Cambridge University Press, 1987), 186.
93. Chandrasekaran, *Imperial Life in the Emerald City,* 79.
94. Ibid.
95. Ricks, *Fiasco,* 105.
96. Bremer and McConnell, *My Year in Iraq,* 39.

97. Chandrasekaran, *Imperial Life in the Emerald City,* 80.
98. Garner, "The Lost Year in Iraq," *Frontline* interview, August 11, 2006.
99. Tim Carney quoted in Chandrasekaran, *Imperial Life in the Emerald City,* 82.
100. Packer, *The Assassin's Gate,* 191; Chandrasekaran, *Imperial Life in the Emerald City,* 83; "The Lost Year in Iraq," *Frontline* interview, posted October 17, 2006.
101. Packer, *The Assassin's Gate,* 193.
102. Ricks, *Fiasco,* 163.
103. Dobbins et al., *Occupying Iraq,* 116–117.
104. Bremer, "The Lost Year in Iraq," *Frontline* interview, June 26 and August 18, 2006.
105. Ibid.
106. Doug Struck, "'My Hands Are Not Stained with Blood,'" *Washington Post,* February 3, 2005, http://www.washingtonpost.com/wp-dyn/articles/A59279-2005Feb3.html.
107. Chandrasekaran, *Imperial Life in the Emerald City,* 83.
108. Packer, *The Assassin's Gate,* 191.
109. Chandrasekaran, *Imperial Life in the Emerald City,* 85.
110. Bremer and McConnell, *My Year in Iraq,* 54–55; quote on p. 55.
111. Packer, *The Assassin's Gate,* 193.
112. Bremer and McConnell, *My Year in Iraq,* 53, 56; quote on p. 56.
113. Chandrasekaran, *Imperial Life in the Emerald City,* 85.
114. Anthony Zinni quoted in Ricks, *Fiasco,* 164.
115. Gordon, "The Lost Year in Iraq," *Frontline* interview, August 10–11, 2006.
116. Ibid.; Williamson Murray and Robert Scales, *The Iraq War: A Military History* (Cambridge, MA: Harvard University Press, 2003), 82–84.
117. Dobbins, "The Lost Year in Iraq," *Frontline* interview, June 27, 2006.
118. Packer, *The Assassin's Gate,* 194.
119. Ricks, *Fiasco,* 164.
120. Gordon and Trainor, *Cobra II,* 556.
121. Feith, *War and Decision,* 433–434.
122. Franks, *American Soldier,* 419.
123. Paul Bremer, "Iraq's Path to Sovereignty," *Washington Post,* September 8, 2003, http://www.washingtonpost.com/ac2/wp-dyn/A39805-2003Sep7?language=printer.
124. Dobbins et al., *Occupying Iraq,* 267–268.

125. Feith, *War and Decision*, 453; Woodward, *State of Denial*, 249.
126. Dobbins et al., *Occupying Iraq*, 269–270.
127. Packer, *The Assassin's Gate*, 213.
128. Dobbins et al., *Occupying Iraq*, 268–269.
129. Woodward, *State of Denial*, 264; Dobbins et al., *Occupying Iraq*, 273.
130. Phillips, *Losing Iraq*, 180.
131. Dobbins et al., *Occupying Iraq*, 286–287; quote on p. 287.
132. Ibid., 288–289.
133. Bremer and McConnell, *My Year in Iraq*, 90.
134. Noah Feldman, "Sacrificed to the Surge," *Newsweek*, April 5, 2008, http://www.newsweek.com/2008/04/05/sacrificed-to-the-surge.print.html.
135. Officer quoted in Joe Klein, "Saddam's Revenge," *Time*, September 18, 2005, http://www.time.com/time/printout/0,8816,1106307,00.html.
136. Keith Mines quoted in Ricks, *Fiasco*, 241.
137. Ibid., 357.
138. Paul Bremer quoted in Joe Klein, "Is al-Qaeda on the Run in Iraq?" *Time*, May 23, 2007, http://www.time.com/time/printout/0,8816,1624697,00.html.
139. Keith Mines quoted in Ricks, *Fiasco*, 241.
140. Packer, *The Assassin's Gate*, 143.
141. Dobbins et al., *Occupying Iraq*, 109.
142. Special Inspector General for Iraq Reconstruction, Quarterly Report to Congress, March 30, 2004, 25. Available at http://psm.du.edu/media/documents/us_research_and_oversight/sigir/quarterly_reports_eng/us_sigir__report_to_congress_march_2004.pdf.
143. Chandrasekaran, *Imperial Life in the Emerald City*, 326.
144. Ibid., 170.
145. Dobbins et al., *Occupying Iraq*, 120.
146. Chandrasekaran, *Imperial Life in the Emerald City*, 170; Rajiv Chandrasekaran, "Blackouts Return, Deepening Iraq's Dark Days," *Washington Post*, July 3, 2003, http://www.washingtonpost.com/ac2/wp-dyn/A1629-2003Jul2?language=printer.
147. Chandrasekaran, *Imperial Life in the Emerald City*, 173.
148. Chandrasekaran, "Blackouts Return."
149. Special Inspector General for Iraq Reconstruction, Quarterly Report to Congress, March 30, 2004, appendix.
150. David Teeples quoted in Dobbins et al., *Occupying Iraq*, 121.

151. Ibid., 231.
152. Phillips, *Losing Iraq,* 164.
153. Packer, *The Assassin's Gate,* 168.
154. Garner, "The Lost Year in Iraq," *Frontline* interview, August 11, 2006.
155. Chandrasekaran, *Imperial Life in the Emerald City,* 320.
156. Bremer and McConnell, *My Year in Iraq,* 56; Feith, *War and Decision,* 431.
157. Chandrasekaran, *Imperial Life in the Emerald City,* 221.
158. Ibid., 221–222.
159. Bremer and McConnell, *My Year in Iraq,* 189.
160. Dobbins et al., *Occupying Iraq,* 284.
161. Allen, "Anbar Dawn," 28.

Chapter 3. 2004: Ugly Surprises

1. Darrin Mortenson, "Pendleton Warrior Conway Moves to Top Pentagon Spot," *North County* [CA] *Times,* October 3, 2004.
2. Tony Perry, "Marines' Mad Dog Mattis Battles for Iraqis' Support," *Los Angles Times,* April 16, 2004.
3. Michael Groen, *With the 1st Marine Division in Iraq, 2003* (Quantico, VA: History Division, Marine Corps University, 2006), 133.
4. Ibid. Emphasis in original.
5. Jim Mattis quoted in Pamela Hess, "An American in Sparta," United Press International, August 1, 2004. In several other instances, General Mattis displayed no reservations in taking uncompromising measures against Marines who did not keep their honor clean. As commanding general of the Marine Forces Central Command, he brought charges in late 2006 against eight Marines (four of them officers) for the November 2005 deaths of twenty-four Iraqis in Haditha.
6. For a first-hand account of the campaign by two former Marines who were embedded as journalists with the 1st Marine Division, see Bing West and Ray Smith, *The March Up: Taking Baghdad with the 1st Marine Division* (New York: Random House, 2004).
7. Joint Publication 1–02, *Department of Defense Dictionary of Military and Associated Terms.* This can be accessed at http://www.dtic.mil/doctrine.
8. Nicholas Reynolds, *U.S. Marines in Iraq, 2003: Basrah, Baghdad, and Beyond* (Quantico, VA: History Division, Marine Corps University, 2007), 131.

9. Brig. Gen. John Kelly, oral history interview conducted by John Piedmont of the U.S. Marine Corps History Division, March 31, 2004, transcript, 6.
10. Ibid., 5–6.
11. Ibid., 5.
12. Ibid., 6–7.
13. Dunford, interview, December 18, 2006, transcript, 3.
14. Ibid.
15. Ibid.
16. Col. James Howcroft, interview conducted by the author, December 3, 2008, transcript, 3.
17. Ibid., 4.
18. Christopher Cooper, "How a Marine Lost His Command in Race to Baghdad," *Wall Street Journal,* April 5, 2004.
19. Col. John Toolan, oral history interview conducted by Dr. Fred Allison of the U.S. Marine Corps History Division, February 4, 2005, transcript, 1.
20. Ibid., 2.
21. Ibid., 2–3.
22. Gen. James Conway, oral history interview conducted by John Piedmont of the U.S. Marine Corps History Division, June 21, 2005, transcript, 1.
23. Ibid., 2–3.
24. *Quadrennial Defense Review* (Washington, DC: Department of Defense, 2006), 1–19.
25. 1st Marine Division, "Narrative Summary 01 January–30 June 2004," 9. This and subsequent documents used in the chapters of this volume, unless otherwise noted, are from the official records and working papers held by the Marine Corps Archives, Gray Research Center, Marine Corps University, located at Marine Corps Base Quantico, Virginia. In addition, certain reference materials located at the Marine Corps History Division, Marine Corps University, have been used. Most important are its extensive oral history interviews.
26. Unnamed Marine officer quoted in Thomas Ricks, "Marines to Offer New Tactics in Iraq: Reduced Use of Force Planned after Takeover from Army," *Washington Post,* January 7, 2004.
27. Dunford, interview, December 18, 2006, transcript, 15.
28. 1st Marine Division, "Narrative Summary 01 January–30 June 2004," 9.
29. Speech to USMC Association, January 18, 2004, cited in Kenneth Estes, *Into the Fray: U.S. Marines in the Global War on Terrorism* (Washington, DC: USMC History Division, 2011), 11–12.

30. Dunford, interview, December 18, 2006, transcript, 5.
31. 1st Marine Division, "Narrative Summary 01 January–30 June 2004," 9.
32. Toolan, interview, February 4, 2005, transcript, 3.
33. Ibid., 2.
34. "Iraq's Most Dangerous City," *CBS Evening News,* June 9, 2003, www.cbsnews.com/stories/2003/06/09/eveningnews/main557758.shtml.
35. Toolan, interview, February 4, 2005, transcript, 4.
36. Kelly, interview, March 31, 2004, transcript, 17.
37. "Rumsfeld Blames Iraq Problems on 'Pockets of Dead-Enders,'" *USA Today,* June 18, 2003, www.usatoday.com/news/world/iraq/2003-06-18-rumsfeld_x.htm.
38. Richard Shultz and Andrea Dew, *Insurgents, Terrorists, and Militias: The Warriors of Contemporary Combat* (New York: Columbia University Press, 2006), 230.
39. "The CIA's Insurgency: The Agency's Political Disinformation Campaign," *Wall Street Journal,* September 29, 2004; Suzanne Goldenberg, "Bush Ignored Warnings on Iraq Insurgency Threat before Invasion," *Guardian,* September 29, 2004, www.guardian.co.uk/world/2004/sep/29/iraq.usa; and Douglas Jehl and David E. Sanger, "Prewar Assessment on Iraq Saw Chance of Strong Divisions," *New York Times,* September 28, 2004, www.nytimes.com/2004/09/28/politics/28intel.html.
40. "National Intelligence Council: Principal Challenges in Post-Saddam Iraq," appendix B in United States Senate Select Committee on Intelligence, *Report of the Select Committee on Intelligence on Pre-War Intelligence Assessments of Post-War Iraq,* February 2004, http://intelligence.senate.gov/prewar.pdf.
41. Howcroft, interview, December 3, 2008, transcript, 4.
42. Ibid., 10.
43. Ibid., 19.
44. Ibid., 18.
45. Ibid., 23.
46. Dunford, interview, December 18, 2006, transcript, 8–9.
47. Ibid., 5.
48. Conway, interview, June 21, 2005, transcript, 6.
49. Toolan, interview, February 4, 2005, transcript, 4–5.
50. Ibid., 7.
51. RCT-7, "Command Chronology for 14 February to 31 March 2004," Marine Corps History Division, 10.

52. Howcroft, interview, December 3, 2008.
53. Dunford, interview, December 18, 2006, transcript, 9.
54. Bing West, *No True Glory: A Frontline Account of the Battle for Fallujah* (New York: Random House, 2005), 3.
55. Ibid. Also, see "Bodies Mutilated in Iraq Attack," *BBC News,* March 31, 2004, http://news.bbc.co.uk/2/hi/middle_east/3585765.stm.
56. West, *No True Glory,* 58.
57. 1st Marine Division, "Narrative Summary 01 January–30 June 2004," 11.
58. Conway, interview, June 21, 2005, transcript, 10.
59. West, *No True Glory,* 59, 60.
60. Toolan, interview, February 4, 2005, transcript, 7.
61. *Military Operations on Urbanized Terrain,* Marine Corps Warfighting Publication (MCWP) 3–35.3 (Washington, DC: Headquarters United States Marine Corps, April 26, 1998).
62. Shultz and Dew, *Insurgents, Terrorists, and Militias,* 103–106; quote is on p. 64.
63. Carlotta Gall and Thomas de Waal, *Chechnya: Calamity in the Caucasus* (New York: New York University Press, 1998), 18.
64. Dunford, interview, December 18, 2006, transcript, 8–9. See also Gen. Charles C. Krulak, "The Strategic Corporal: Leadership in the Three Block War," *Marines Magazine* 28, no. 1 (January 1999), 28–34. Also, see "Cultivating Intuitive Decisionmaking," *Marine Corps Gazette* [online] (May 1999).
65. Dunford, interview, December 18, 2006, transcript, 18.
66. Toolan, interview, February 4, 2005, transcript, 8.
67. Ibid., 11.
68. Ibid., 12.
69. Ibid., 10.
70. Conway, interview, June 21, 2005, transcript, 10–11.
71. Ibid.
72. Alice Hills, "Fear and Loathing in Fallujah," *Armed Forces & Society,* no. 4 (2006).
73. West, *No True Glory,* 93.
74. Conway, interview, June 21, 2005, transcript, 11.
75. Ibid.
76. Gen. James Conway, oral history interview conducted by John Piedmont of the U.S. Marine Corps History Division, July 7, 2005, transcript, 5.

77. Howcroft, interview, December 3, 2008, transcript, 24.
78. Toolan, interview, February 4, 2005, transcript, 24.
79. Dunford, interview, December 18, 2006, transcript, 57.
80. Conway, interview, July 7, 2005, transcript, 5.
81. Maj. Gen. Richard Natonski, oral history interview conducted by John Way of the U.S. Marine Corps History Division, March 16, 2005, transcript, 22.
82. Ibid., 25.
83. Col. Michael Regner, oral history interview conducted by John Way of the U.S. Marine Corps History Division, March 25, 2005, transcript, 28.
84. RCT-1, "Narrative Summary: Command, Operations, Training," October 25, 2004, 11.
85. Ibid.
86. Cited in Brynjar Lia and Thomas Hegghammer, "Jihadi Strategic Studies: The Alleged Al Qaida Policy Study Preceding the Madrid Bombings," *Studies in Conflict & Terrorism* (Spring 2004), 361.
87. The notion that there exists a jihadi strategic studies discipline that addresses the same subjects found in the strategic studies departments of a modern nation's war college or command and staff school was first proposed by Lia and Hegghammer in their article "Jihadi Strategic Studies."
88. See William S. Lind et al., "The Changing Face of War: Into the Fourth Generation," *Marine Corps Gazette,* October 1989, 22–26; and Thomas X. Hammes, "The Evolution of War: The Fourth Generation," *Marine Corps Gazette,* September 1994, 35–44. For a later and more detailed elaboration of the concept, see Thomas X. Hammes, *The Sling and the Stone: On War in the 21st Century* (St. Paul, MN: Zenith, 2004). Also, see Martin van Creveld, *The Transformation of War* (New York: Free Press, 1991), for his insights into this changing context of war.
89. Lia and Hegghammer, "Jihadi Strategic Studies," 361.
90. Natonski, interview, March 16, 2005, transcript, 24.
91. Regner, interview, March 25, 2005, transcript, 46.
92. Howcroft, interview, December 3, 2008, transcript, 21.
93. Conway, interview, July 7, 2005, transcript, 1.
94. Dunford, interview, December 18, 2006, transcript, 86.
95. West, *No True Glory,* 246.
96. Lt. Col. Nicholas Vukovich, recorded interview conducted by the author, February 12, 2009.

97. Ibid.
98. Ibid.
99. Lt. Col. Christopher Woodridge, oral history interview conducted by William Hutson of the U.S. Marine Corps History Division, October 24, 2004, transcript, 9.
100. Ibid.
101. Ibid., 14.
102. Lt. Col. Garth Brandl, oral history interview conducted by William Hutson of the U.S. Marine Corps History Division, November 18, 2004, transcript, 11.
103. Toolan, interview, February 4, 2005, transcript, 35.
104. RCT-1, "Command Chronology for 1 July to 31 July 2004," 7.
105. RCT-1, "Command Chronology for 1 August to 31 August 2004," 11.
106. RCT-1, "Command Chronology for 1 September to 30 September 2004," 6.
107. Ibid., 7.
108. RCT-1, "Command Chronology for 1 August to 31 August 2004," 12.
109. Ibid., 13.
110. RCT-1, "Command Chronology for 1 September to 30 September 2004," 15.
111. Vukovich, recorded interview, February 12, 2009.
112. RCT-7, "Command Chronology for 1 October to 31 October 2004," 20.
113. Ibid., 18.
114. Francis X. Kozlowski, *U.S. Marines in Battle: An-Najaf* (Quantico, VA: U.S. Marine Corps History Division, 2004).
115. Lt. Gen. John Sattler, oral history interview conducted by John Way of the U.S. Marine Corps History Division, April 8, 2005, transcript, 6.
116. Kelly, interview, March 31, 2004, transcript, 22.
117. Col. John Toolan, oral history interview conducted by Dr. Fred Allison of the U.S. Marine Corps History Division, February 11, 2005, transcript, 14–15.
118. For a detailed account, see West, *No True Glory,* chap. 22.
119. Dunford, interview, December 18, 2006, transcript, 56.
120. Ibid., 56–57.
121. Ibid.
122. Natonski, interview, March 16, 2005, transcript, 14.
123. Conway, interview, July 7, 2005, transcript, 7.
124. Dunford, interview, December 18, 2006, transcript, 31.

125. RCT-1, "Command Chronology for 1 October to 31 October 2004," 16.
126. Natonski, interview, March 16, 2005, transcript, 19.
127. Ibid.
128. For an examination of these developments in vigilant resolve, see Maj. Alfred B. Connable, *U.S. Marines in Iraq, 2004–2008: Anthology and Annotated Bibliography* (Washington, DC: USMC History Division, 2010).
129. Dunford, interview, December 18, 2006, transcript, 36.
130. Ibid.
131. Natonski, interview, March 16, 2005, transcript, 18.
132. RCT-1, "Command Chronology for 1 October to 31 October 2004," 15.
133. Natonski, interview, March 16, 2005, transcript, 19.
134. Dunford, interview, December 18, 2006, transcript, 13.
135. Ibid., 70.
136. Prime Minister Allawi quoted in Dick Camp, *Operation Phantom Fury: The Assault and Capture of Fallujah* (Minneapolis, MN: Zenith Press, 2009), 153.
137. Dunford, interview, December 18, 2006, transcript, 82–83.
138. Sattler, interview, April 8, 2005, transcript, 6.
139. Howcroft, interview, December 3, 2008, transcript, 22.
140. Bing West, "The Road to Haditha," *Atlantic,* October 2006, http://www.theatlantic.com/magazine/archive/2006/10/the-road-to-haditha/305230/.
141. Quoted in Estes, *Into The Fray,* 75.
142. "Rumsfeld's war-on-terror memo," *USA Today,* October 16, 2003, http://www.usatoday.com/news/washington/executive/rumsfeld-memo.
143. Dunford, interview, December 18, 2006, transcript, 59.
144. Col. James Howcroft, interview conducted by the author, December 28, 2008, transcript, 28–29.

Chapter 4. 2005: Stalemate

1. David Walker, *Rebuilding Iraq: Governance, Security, Reconstruction, and Financial Challenges* (Washington, DC: U.S. Government Accountability Office, April 2006), 3.
2. Abu Musab Zarqawi quoted in Fawaz A. Gerges, "Zarqawi and the D-Word," *Washington Post,* January 30, 2005.
3. Thomas Mowle, "The Primacy of Politics: The First Election," in *Hope Is Not a Plan: The War in Iraq from Inside the Green Zone,* ed. Thomas Mowle (Westport, CT: Praeger Security International), 103.

4. Mowle, "The Primacy of Politics," 104.
5. Col. James Howcroft, interview conducted by the author, December 11, 2008.
6. U.S. Government Accounting Office, *Rebuilding Iraq, Governance, Security, Reconstruction, and Financing Challenges* (April 2006) 3. http://www.gao.gov/new.items/d06697t.pdf
7. Ibid., 14, 15.
8. Ibid., 13.
9. Bin Laden quoted in Gilles Kepel and Jean-Pierre Milelli, ed., *Al Qaeda in its own Words* (Cambridge, MA: Harvard University Press, 2008), 67–70.
10. Sheikh Sabah al-Sattam Effan Fahran al-Shurji al-Aziz, interview conducted by Col. Gary W. Montgomery and CWO Tim S. McWilliams of the U.S. Marine Corps History Division, February 25, 2009, transcript, 2–4.
11. Sheikh Aifan Sadun al-Issawi, Fallujah representative to the Iraqi Awakening Political Party, interview conducted by Col. Gary W. Montgomery and CWO Tim S. McWilliams of the U.S. Marine Corps History Division, February 14, 2009, transcript, 6.
12. Sheikh Ahmad Bezia Fteikhan al-Rishawi, oral history interview conducted by Col. Gary W. Montgomery and CWO Tim S. McWilliams of the U.S. Marine Corps History Division, February 18, 2009, transcript, 2.
13. Dr. Thamer Ibrahim Tahir al-Assafi, Anbar's Muslim Ulema Council [Council of Muslim Scholars] and professor of religious studies, Al Anbar University, interview conducted by Col. Gary W. Montgomery and CWO Tim S. McWilliams of the U.S. Marine Corps History Division, February 12, 2009, transcript, 5.
14. Ibid., 4.
15. Joe Dunford quoted in Bing West, *The Strongest Tribe* (New York: Random House, 2008), 96.
16. For a discussion of this issue, see Klein, "Is al-Qaeda on the Run in Iraq?" For a discussion of the problem of excluding traditional groups from a place in post-Saddam Iraq, see Mary Kaldor, "Iraq: The Democratic Option," *Open Democracy,* November 13, 2003.
17. "Armed Forces and Militia Agreement Announced," Coalition Provisional Authority News Release, June 5, 2004, http://govinfo.library.unt.edu/cpa-iraq/pressreleases/20040604a_MNFI.html.
18. Paul Wolfowitz quoted in Eric Schmitt, "Pentagon Contradicts General on Iraq Occupation Force's Size," *New York Times,* February 28, 2003.
19. Multi-National Force Iraq, MNF-I Framework OPORD Rev 01 Nov 05 Link Index, 2005. (No longer available online.)

20. Department of Defense Press Briefing, September 30, 2005, transcript, www.globalsecurity.org/military/ops/iraqi-freedom_briefs2005.htm.
21. James Fallows cites Gen. Peter Pace as making this claim. See Fallows, "Why Iraq Has No Army," *Atlantic,* December 2005, http://www.theatlantic.com/magazine/archive/2005/12/why-iraq-has-no-army/304428/. For a much less sanguine assessment, see William Thomas, "Creating the Iraqi Security Force," in Mowle, *Hope Is Not a Plan,* chap. 5.
22. Jeremy M. Sharp, "Iraq's New Security Forces: The Challenge of Sectarian and Ethnic Influences,"*CRS Report for Congress,* January 12, 2006, 3.
23. Ibid.
24. Sharp, "Iraq's New Security Forces," 4.
25. Natonski, interview, March 16, 2005, transcript, 10.
26. Maj. Gen. Stephen T. Johnson, oral history interview conducted by Craig Covert of the U.S. Marine Corps History Division, January 26, 2006, 7–8.
27. Maj. Gen. James Williams, oral history interview conducted by Jeffery Acosta of the U.S. Marine Corps History Division, February 20, 2006, transcript, 4.
28. Ibid.
29. Col. Stephen Davis, oral history interview conducted by David Benhoff of the U.S. Marine Corps History Division, June 20, 2005, transcript, 6.
30. Ibid.
31. Ibid., 8, 11–12.
32. Ibid., 14.
33. Ibid., 22.
34. Lt. Col. Julian Alford, oral history interview conducted by Craig Covert of the U.S. Marine Corps History Division, November 22, 2005, transcript, 6.
35. West, "The Road to Haditha."
36. Lt. Col. William Mullen, oral history interview conducted by David Benhoff of the U.S. Marine Corps History Division, June 11, 2005, transcript, 3.
37. Ibid.
38. Ibid.
39. Ibid., 13.
40. Ibid., 9.
41. Lt. Col. William Jurney, oral history interview conducted by Kurtis Wheeler of the U.S. Marine Corps History Division, February 17, 2007, transcript, 7.

42. Maj. David Barnes, oral history interview conducted by Craig Covert of the U.S. Marine Corps History Division, September 30, 2005, transcript, 28.
43. Ibid., 19–20.
44. Todd et al., *Iraq Tribal Study*, 4.
45. Brian Fishman, *Dysfunction and Decline: Lessons Learned from Inside Al Qa'ida in Iraq* (West Point, NY: Combating Terrorism Center at West Point, 2009), 17.
46. Hirsh, "Blood and Honor," 38.
47. Fishman, *Dysfunction and Decline,* 18.
48. Governor Mamoon Sami Rashid al-Alwani, oral history interview conducted by Col. Gary W. Montgomery and CWO Tim S. McWilliams of the U.S. Marine Corps History Division, February 16, 2009, transcript, 3–4.
49. Al-Assafi, interview, February 12, 2009, transcript, 5.
50. Ibid.
51. Williams, interview, February 20, 2006, transcript, 19–20.
52. Ibid., 19.
53. Todd et al., *Iraq Tribal Study,* 24.
54. Gerges, "Zarqawi and the D-Word," B1.
55. Williams, interview, February 20, 2006, transcript, 30.
56. International Mission for Iraqi Elections, www.elections.ca/imie/.

Chapter 5. 2006: The TIpping Point

1. Michael Ware, "The Most Dangerous Place," *Time,* May 21, 2006, http://www.time.com/time/magazine/article/0,9171,1196401,00.html.
2. Ibid.
3. Ibid.
4. IRIN, "Iraq: Anbar Province Plagued by Violence," January 15, 2007, www.irinnews.org/report.aspx?reportid=64374.
5. Ibid.
6. Quoted in ibid.
7. See "OIF-Iraq Significant Activities," http://www.globalsecurity.org/military/ops/iraq_sigacts.htm.
8. U.S. Government Accountability Office (GAO), *Securing, Stabilizing and Rebuilding Iraq* (Washington, DC: Author, June 2008), 20.
9. Maj. Alfred B. Connable, oral history interview contained in McWilliams and Wheeler, *Al-Anbar Awakening,* vol. 1, 125–126.

10. Ibid., 126.
11. Ambassador Zalmay Khalilzad, "Political Capabilities to Stabilize Fragile or Post-Conflict States," *Adapting America's Security Paradigm and Security Agenda* (Washington, DC: National Strategy Information Center, 2010), 25. Italics in original.
12. Connable, interview, in McWilliams and Wheeler, *Al-Anbar Awakening,* vol. 1, 127–128.
13. Hala Jabar, "Sunni Leader Killed for Joining Ceasefire Talks," *Times Online,* February 5, 2005, http://freerepublic.com/focus/f-news/1571952/posts.http://www.timesonline.co.uk/tol/news/world/article727041.ece
14. Connable, interview, in McWilliams and Wheeler, *Al-Anbar Awakening,* vol 1, 129.
15. Col. Peter Devlin, oral history interview conducted by Kurtis Wheeler of the U.S. Marine Corps History Division, January 31, 2007, transcript, 17.
16. Maj. Gen. Tariq Yusif Mohammad al-Thiyabi, oral history interview conducted by Col. Gary Montgomery of the U.S. Marine Corps History Division, February 17, 2009, transcript, 2–3.
17. Ibid., 4–5.
18. Smith, *The Utility of Force,* 5.
19. In the past five years different research organizations have established databases on armed groups. For example, the International Institute for Strategic Studies' Armed Conflict Database contains information on the composition, growth, and activities of more than 270 armed groups; see www.iiss.org. Databases have also been compiled by Jane's Information Group/Sentinel Security Assessments, at www.janes.com; Global Security, at www.globalsecurity.org; and the Federation of American Scientists' Intelligence Resource Program, at www.fas.org/irp.
20. Each of the following chronicles and assesses OIF and its immediate aftermath: Gordon and Trainor, *Cobra II;* John Keegan, *The Iraq War* (New York: Vintage Books, 2005); and Ricks, *Fiasco.*
21. Shultz and Dew, *Insurgents, Terrorists, and Militias,* chap. 7; Ian F. W. Beckett, *Insurgency in Iraq: A Historical Perspective* (Carlisle, PA: Strategic Studies Institute of the U.S. Army War College, March 2005).
22. Eliot Cohen and John Gooch, *Military Misfortune: The Anatomy of Failure in War* (New York: Simon and Schuster, 2005).
23. Nagl, *Learning to Eat Soup with a Knife;* quote on p. xiii.
24. Those experiences were expunged from the Army's collective memory. Furthermore, the considerable counterinsurgency capabilities built up

during the 1960s were drastically downsized. The paltry number of Special Forces remaining in the Army by the end of the 1970s illustrated this COIN cleansing. See Richard Hunt and Richard Shultz, *Lessons from an Unconventional War* (New York: Pergammon Press, 1982).
25. Nagl, *Learning to Eat Soup with a Knife*, x.
26. See Charles C. Krulak, "Ne Cras: Not Like Yesterday," in *The Role of Naval Forces in 21st Century Operations,* ed. Richard H. Shultz Jr. and Robert L. Pfaltzgraff Jr. (Washington, DC: Brassey's, 2000), xi–xii.
27. Gen. Charles C. Krulak, "Operational Maneuver from the Sea," *Joint Forces Quarterly* (Spring 1999), 79.
28. Ibid.
29. Sarah Sewall et al., *The U.S. Army/Marine Corps Counterinsurgency Field Manual* (Chicago: University of Chicago Press, 2007).
30. David Cloud and Greg Jaffe, *The Fourth Star: Four Generals and the Epic Struggle for the Future of the United States Army* (New York: Crown, 2009).
31. Nagl, *Learning to Eat Soup with a Knife*, xiv, xvi.
32. Kalev Sepp, "Best Practices in Counterinsurgency," *Military Review,* May–June 2005, 9–10.
33. David Galula, *Counterinsurgency Warfare: Theory and Practice* (Westport, CT: Praeger Security International, 1964).
34. Sir Robert Thompson, *Defeating Communist Insurgency: The Lessons of Malaya and Vietnam* (New York: Frederick A. Praeger, 1966); Richard Clutterbuck, *The Long Long War: Counterinsurgency in Malaya and Vietnam* (New York: Frederick A. Praeger, 1966); and Frank Kitson, *Low Intensity Operations: Subversion, Insurgency and Peacekeeping* (Harrisburg, PA: Stackpole books, 1971).
35. This was true of serving military officers. See John McCuen, *The Art of Counter-Revolutionary War* (Harrisburg, PA: Stackpole Books, 1966). An outstanding group of civilian specialists at the RAND Corporation did the same. See Stephen T. Hosmer and Sibylle O. Crane, *Counterinsurgency: A Symposium, April 16–20, 1962* (Santa Monica, CA: RAND, 1963, republished 2006).
36. Nagl, *Learning to Eat Soup with a Knife*, xvii.
37. Sewall et al., *Counterinsurgency Field Manual.* For a summary of the field manual's key underlying tenets, see Eliot Cohen et al., "Principles, Imperatives, and Paradoxes of Counterinsurgency," *Military Review,* March–April 2006.

38. Kenneth Estes, *U.S. Marine Corps Operations in Iraq 2003–2006* (Washington, DC: USMC History Division, 2010), 116.
39. Maj. Gen. Richard Zilmer, oral history interview conducted by Kurtis Wheeler of the U.S. Marine Corps History Division, January 3, 2007, transcript, 2.
40. Brig. Gen. Robert Neller, oral history interview conducted by Kurtis Wheeler of the U.S. Marine Corps History Division, January 23, 2007, transcript, 6.
41. Maj. Gen. Robert Neller, "Lessons Learned: Some Thoughts on COIN," *Marine Corps Gazette*, February 2010, 11.
42. Maj. Gen. Richard Zilmer, presentation at the Fletcher School (Tufts University) roundtable "Marine Generals Discuss Anbar 2006," May 2, 2010, http://fletcher.tufts.edu/ISSP/Events/Video.
43. Neller, interview, January 23, 2007, transcript, 1.
44. Sepp, "Best Practices in Counterinsurgency," 9.
45. Connable, interview, in McWilliams and Wheeler, *Al-Anbar Awakening*, vol. 1, 128.
46. Ibid., 132.
47. Neller, "Lessons Learned," 11.
48. Ibid.
49. Zilmer, interview, January 3, 2007, transcript, 13.
50. Ibid., 11.
51. Lt. Col. Scott Shuster, oral history interview conducted by Kurtis Wheeler of the U.S. Marine Corps History Division, December 28, 2006, transcript, 12.
52. Col. H. R. McMaster, *Frontline* interview, www.pbs.org/wgbh/pages/frontline/insurgency/interviews/mcmaster.html. This interview was part of a program devoted to the Iraq insurgency that aired February 26, 2006.
53. McMaster, *Frontline* interview, aired February 26, 2006.
54. Ibid.
55. Ibid., 241.
56. Thomas E. Ricks, "The Lessons of Counterinsurgency: U.S. Unit Praised for Tactics against Iraqi Fighters, Treatment of Detainees," *Washington Post*, February 16, 2006.
57. Col. Sean MacFarland, interview conducted by the Contemporary Operations Study Team, Combat Studies Institute, Fort Leavenworth, January 17, 2008, transcript, 7.

58. Ibid., 10.
59. Ibid., 22.
60. Ibid., 25.
61. Ibid., 29.
62. Brig. Gen. Sean MacFarland, interview conducted by the author, February 16, 2010.
63. Neil Smith and Sean MacFarland, "Anbar Awakens: The Tipping Point," *Military Review,* March–April 2008, 43.
64. Col. William Crowe, oral history interview conducted by Kurtis Wheeler of the U.S. Marine Corps History Division, January 1, 2007, transcript, 8.
65. Ibid., 4.
66. Col. Lawrence Nicholson, oral history interview conducted by Kurtis Wheeler of the U.S. Marine Corps History Division, January 3, 2007, transcript, 2.
67. Ibid., 3.
68. Ibid.
69. Thomas Ricks, "Situation Called Dire in West Iraq," *Washington Post,* September 11, 2006.
70. Ibid.
71. Devlin, interview, January 31, 2007, transcript, 9.
72. Ibid.
73. Ibid.
74. Ibid., 11.
75. Council on Foreign Relations, "The Baker–Hamilton Commission (akaIraq Study Group)," *Backgrounder,* December 6, 2006, www.cfr.org/publication/12010/bakerhamilton_commission_aka_iraq_study_group.html.
76. James A. Baker III and Lee H. Hamilton, *The Iraq Study Group Report* (Washington, DC: United States Institute of Peace, 2006), 6.
77. Ibid., 32.
78. Ibid., 48.
79. Ibid., 7.
80. Ibid., 51.
81. Al-Issawi, interview, February 14, 2009, transcript, 6.
82. Ibid., 7.
83. Al-Thiyabi, interview, February 17, 2009, transcript, 7.

84. Ibid.
85. Sheikh Ahmad Bezia Fteikhan al-Rishawi, oral history interview conducted by Col. Gary W Montgomery and CWO Tim S. McWilliams of the U.S. Marine Corps History Division, February 17, 2009, transcript, 2.
86. Sheikh Wissam Abd al-Ibrahim al-Hardan al-Aeithawi, oral history interview conducted by Col. Gary Montgomery and CWO Tim McWilliams of the U.S. Marine Corps History Division, February 15, 2009, transcript, 2.
87. Ibid.
88. Sheikh Ali Hatim Abd al-Razzaq Ali al-Sulayman, oral history interview conducted by Col. Gary W Montgomery and CWO Tim S. McWilliams of the U.S. Marine Corps History Division, February 15, 2009, transcript, 2.
89. Al-Aziz, interview, February 25, 2009, transcript, 2.
90. Ibid.
91. MacFarland, interview, January 17, 2008, transcript, 35.
92. Ibid., 36.
93. Ibid.
94. Lang, "Understanding How to Live," A1–2.
95. MacFarland, interview, January 17, 2008, transcript, 35.
96. Dexter Filkins, "In Ramadi, Fetid Quarters and Unrelenting Battles," *New York Times,* July 5, 2006.
97. Ibid.
98. Brig. Gen. Sean MacFarland, interview conducted by the author, February 10, 2010.
99. MacFarland, interview, January 17, 2008, transcript, 30.
100. Ibid., 36.
101. Ibid.
102. Ibid.
103. Jurney, interview, February 17, 2007, transcript, 2.
104. Ibid., 11.
105. MacFarland, interview, January 17, 2008, transcript, 33.
106. Ibid., 34.
107. Ibid.
108. Smith and MacFarland, "Anbar Awakens," 44.
109. Ibid.
110. Ibid., 49.
111. Ibid., 50.
112. Ibid.

113. MacFarland, interview, February 10, 2010.
114. Ibid.
115. Lt. Gen. James Mattis, or al history interview conducted by Charles Neimeyer of the U.S. Marine Corps History Division, June 17, 2009, transcript, 11.
116. "Mattis Calls for a Consensus on the War on Terror," *North County Times,* June 22, 2007; and "Gen. Mattis on the Marines in Iraq," *North County Times,* June 24, 2007.
117. Linzer and Ricks, "Anbar Picture Grows Clearer, and Bleaker."
118. Ibid.
119. Smith and MacFarland, "Anbar Awakens," 51.
120. MacFarland, interview, January 17, 2008, transcript, 45.
121. Toolan, interview, February 4, 2005, transcript, 3.
122. Nicholson, interview, January 3, 2007, transcript, 3.
123. Ibid., 5.
124. Ibid., 8–9.
125. Brig. Gen. Lawrence Nicholson, presentation at the Fletcher School (Tufts University) roundtable "Marine Generals Discuss Anbar 2006," May 2, 2010, http://fletcher.tufts.edu/ISSP/Events/Video.
126. Nicholson, interview, January 3, 2007, transcript, 9.
127. Nicholson, presentation at the Fletcher School roundtable, May 2, 2010.
128. Nicholson, interview, January 3, 2007, transcript, 8.
129. Ibid., 6.
130. Ibid., 12, 11.
131. Nicholson, presentation at the Fletcher School roundtable, May 2, 2010.
132. Ibid.
133. Nicholson, interview, January 3, 2007, transcript, 14.
134. Ibid.
135. Ibid.
136. Zilmer, interview, January 3, 2007, transcript, 1.
137. Shuster, interview, December 28, 2006, transcript, 2.
138. Ibid.
139. Ibid.
140. Ibid., 5.
141. Ibid.
142. Crowe, interview, January 1, 2007, transcript, 4.
143. Ibid., 5.

144. Ibid., 9.
145. Ibid., 12.

Chapter 6. 2007: Cashing In

1. Maj. Gen. Walter Gaskin, oral history interview conducted by Michael Visconage of the U.S. Marine Corps History Division, June 26, 2007, transcript, 3.
2. Ibid., 1.
3. Ibid.
4. Brig. Gen. John Allen, oral history interview conducted by Michael Visconage of the U.S. Marine Corps History Division, June 27, 2007, transcript, 1.
5. Allen, "Anbar Dawn," 17–18.
6. Brig. Gen. John Allen, interview conducted by the author, July 29, 2010, transcript, 1–2.
7. "Commandant of the U.S. Marine Corps Official Reading List," http://home.comcast.net/~antaylor1/usmccommandant.html.
8. Allen, "Anbar Dawn," 18.
9. Ibid., 21.
10. Brig. Gen. John Allen, oral history interview conducted by CWO Tim McWilliams of the U.S. Marine Corps History Division, April 23, 2009, transcript, 12.
11. Gaskin, interview, June 26, 2007, transcript, 6.
12. Maj. Gen. W. E. Gaskin, commanding general, II MEF (Forward), "Stability in Al Anbar," PowerPoint presentation detailing how II MEF prepared for and operated in Anbar during its deployment.
13. Allen, interview conducted by the author, July 29, 2010, transcript, 2.
14. Ibid.
15. Ibid.
16. Allen, "Anbar Dawn," 5.
17. Ibid.
18. Col. John Charlton, U.S. Army, interview conducted by the Contemporary Operations Study Team, Combat Studies Institute, Fort Leavenworth, December 9, 2009, transcript, 5.
19. Ibid.
20. Ibid.

21. Ibid.
22. Gaskin, "Stability in Al Anbar."
23. Ibid.
24. Maj. Gen. Walter Gaskin, oral history interview conducted by Michael Visconage of the U.S. Marine Corps History Division, January 11, 2008, transcript, 3.
25. Charlton, interview, December 9, 2009, transcript, 6.
26. Ibid.
27. Ibid.
28. Ibid., 6–7.
29. Ibid., 7.
30. Ibid.
31. Gaskin, "Stability in Al Anbar."
32. Charlton, interview, December 9, 2009, transcript, 7–8.
33. Ibid., 9.
34. Ibid.
35. Ibid.
36. Ibid.
37. Ibid., 11.
38. Col. Richard Simcock, oral history interview conducted by Michael Sears of the U.S. Marine Corps History Division, June 9, 2007, transcript, 1.
39. Ibid., 9.
40. Lt. Col. William Mullen, oral history interview conducted by John Visconage of the U.S. Marine Corps History Division, June 26, 2007, transcript, 1.
41. Ibid., 8.
42. Ibid.
43. Lt. Col. James McGrath, oral history interview conducted by Michael Sears of the U.S. Marine Corps History Division, July 14, 2007, transcript, 1.
44. Ibid., 6–7.
45. Ibid., 7.
46. Ibid., 6, 8.
47. Ibid., 8.
48. Ibid., 10.
49. Gaskin, "Stability in Al Anbar," slide 129.
50. Simcock, interview, June 9, 2007, transcript, 4.

51. Ibid., 10.
52. This description comes from Roy Godson and the work of the National Strategy Information Center. See their DVD *Adapting America's Security Paradigm & Capabilities,* http://www.strategycenter.org/.
53. John Arquilla and David Ronfeldt, *Networks and Netwars: The Future of Terror, Crime, and Militancy* (Santa Monica, CA: RAND, 2001).
54. Bill Roggio, "Zarqawi and Task Force 145," *The Long War Journal,* April 29, 2006, http://www.longwarjournal.org/archives/2006/04/zarqawi_and_task_for.php; Sean Naylor, "Inside the Zarqawi Takedown," *Defense News,* June 12, 2006; and Mark Bowden, "The Ploy," *Atlantic,* May 2007.
55. Matthew Alexander, *How to Break a Terrorist,* with John Bruning (New York: Free Press, 2008).
56. Mark Urban, *Task Force Black* (London: Little, Brown, 2010), 243.
57. Ibid., 83.
58. Allen, interview conducted by the author, July 29, 2010.
59. Ibid., 27.
60. Ibid.
61. Ibid.
62. Lt. Col. James Higgins, oral history interview conducted by John Visconage of the U.S. Marine Corps History Division, June 27, 2007, transcript, 6.
63. Ibid., 19–20.
64. Gaskin, interview, June 26, 2007, transcript, 3.
65. Ibid., 2.
66. Ibid.
67. Allen, Wilk interview, March 27, 2008, transcript, 26.
68. Allen, interview conducted by the author, July 29, 2010, transcript, 17.
69. Charlton, interview, December 9, 2009, transcript, 17, 24–25.
70. Bill Roggio, "An Interview with Brigadier General Gurganus," *Weekly Standard,* June 26, 2007, http://www.weeklystandard.com/weblogs/TWSFP/2007/06/an_interview_with_brigadier_ge.asp.
71. Allen, Wilk interview, March 27, 2008, transcript, 26.
72. Ibid.
73. Roy Godson et al., "Intelligence Dominance Consistent with the Rule of Law," in *Adapting America's Security Paradigm and Security Agenda,* ed. Godson and Richard Shultz (Washington, DC: National Strategy Information Center, 2011), 27.

74. Ibid.
75. Galula, *Counterinsurgency Warfare*, 5–6, 11.
76. Austin Long, "Time," in *Understanding Counterinsurgency: Doctrine, Operations, and Challenges,* ed. Thomas Rid and Thomas Keaney (London: Routledge, 2010), 242.
77. These figures are drawn from Gaskin, "Stability in Al Anbar." This PowerPoint presentation contains the statistics and details of how the statistics and details of how II MEF prepared and operated in Anbar and the results it achieved.
78. Allen, Visconage interview, June 27, 2007, transcript, 5.
79. Allen, interview conducted by the author, July 29, 2010, transcript, 14.
80. Ibid.
81. Ibid., 15.
82. Allen, Visconage interview, June 27, 2007, transcript, 5.
83. Gaskin, interview, June 26, 2007, transcript, 2.
84. Khalilzad, "Political Capabilities to Stabilize Fragile or Post-Conflict States," 25.
85. Allen, interview conducted by the author, July 29, 2010, transcript, 16.
86. Ibid., 18.
87. Allen, "Anbar Dawn," 34–36.
88. Ibid., 38.
89. See William S. McCallister, *COIN and Irregular Warfare in Tribal Society,* 2007, smallwarsjournal.com/documents/coinandiwinatribalsociety.pdf.
90. William McCallister, *MNF-W Engagement: Engagement Model,* briefing slides, June 20, 2007, http://www.smallwarsjournal.com/documents/engagementmodel.pdf.
91. McGrath, interview, July 14, 2007, transcript, 20–21.
92. Ibid., 21.
93. Allen, interview conducted by the author, July 29, 2010, transcript, 26.
94. Allen, McWilliams interview, April 23, 2009, transcript, 4.
95. See Montgomery and McWilliams, eds., *Al-Anbar Awakening,* vol. 2.
96. Charlton, interview, December 9, 2009, transcript, 14–15.
97. Lt. Col. John Reeve, oral history interview conducted by Michael Sears of the U.S. Marine Corps History Division, June 9, 2007, transcript, 4.
98. Ibid., 4–5.
99. Gaskin, interview, June 26, 2007, transcript, 8.
100. Ibid.

101. Allen, "Anbar Dawn," 10–11.
102. Allen, Wilk interview, March 27, 2008, transcript, 40.
103. Gaskin, interview, January 11, 2008, transcript, 4.
104. Ibid., 5.
105. Allen, Wilk interview, March 27, 2008, transcript, 44–45.
106. Gaskin, interview, June 26, 2007, transcript, 16.
107. Allen, "Anbar Dawn," 48.
108. Ibid.
109. Col. John Koenig, interview conducted by Maj. Jennifer Anthis and Douglas Nash, Civil-Military Operations Branch, SCENTC, Quantico, VA, October 16, 2007, interview notes, 3.
110. Jim Michaels, *A Chance in Hell* (New York: St. Martin's Press, 2010), 151.
111. Allen, interview conducted by the author, July 29, 2010, transcript, 5.
112. See Shultz and Dew, *Insurgents, Terrorists, and Militias,* chap. 7.
113. James Soriano, oral history interview conducted by Col. Gary W Montgomery and CWO Tim S. McWilliams of the U.S. Marine Corps History Division, February 13, 2009, transcript, 2.
114. Ibid.
115. Koenig, interview, October 16, 2007, interview notes, 6–7.
116. Charlton, interview, December 9, 2009, transcript, 21–22.
117. Ibid.
118. Ibid.
119. Allen, Visconage interview, June 27, 2007, transcript, 18.
120. Gaskin, interview, January 11, 2008, transcript, 9–10.
121. Ibid.
122. Charlton, interview, December 9, 2009, transcript, 26.
123. Reeve, interview, June 9, 2007, transcript, 7.
124. Brig. Gen. John Allen, oral history interview conducted by Michael Visconage of the U.S. Marine Corps History Division, January 10, 2008, transcript, 4.
125. Ibid., 16–17.
126. Ibid., 4.
127. Gen. David Petraeus, "Commander's Speech to the Marine Corps Association Annual Dinner," July 30, 2009. http://centcom.ahp.us.army.mil/ar/from-the-commander/commanders-speech-to-marine-corps-association-annual-dinner.
128. Ibid.

278 | NOTES TO PAGES 230–244

129. Ibid.
130. Ibid.

CHAPTER 7. Conclusion

1. "Rumsfeld Blames Iraq Problems."
2. Kelly, interview, March 31, 2004, transcript, 17.
3. Kelly, presentation at the Fletcher School roundtable, May 2, 2010.
4. Ibid.
5. Ibid.
6. Gen. James Conway, "Future of Marine Corps Operations," luncheon address to the National Press Club, June 11, 2009, http://press.org/news-multimedia/videos/cspan/286975-1.
7. Phillip Ewing, "Marines Itching to Leave Once-Violent Anbar," *Navy Times,* August 15, 2009.
8. Nagl, *Learning to Eat Soup with a Knife,* 6.
9. Downie, *Learning from Conflict,* 22.
10. Nagl, *Learning to Eat Soup with a Knife,* 6–7.
11. See *Small Wars Manual: United States Marine Corps 1940* (Manhattan, KS: Sunflower University Press, 1996).
12. Kelly, presentation at the Fletcher School roundtable, May 2, 2010.
13. Smith, *The Utility of Force,* 5.
14. Allen, "Anbar Dawn," 17–18.
15. Allen, interview conducted by the author, July 29, 2010.
16. Howcroft, interview, December 3, 2008, transcript, 4.
17. Gen. David Petraeus, "Commander's Speech to the Marine Corps Association Annual Dinner," July 30, 2009, http://centcom.ahp.us.army.mil/ar/from-the-commander/commanders-speech-to-marine-corps-association-annual-dinner.
18. Khalilzad, "Political Capabilities to Stabilize Fragile or Post-Conflict States," 25.
19. Gaskin, interview, June 26, 2007, transcript, 2.
20. Godson et al., "Intelligence Dominance Consistent with the Rule of Law," 27.
21. Ibid.
22. Allen, Visconage interview, June 27, 2007, transcript, 5.
23. Kelly, presentation at the Fletcher School roundtable, May 2, 2010.

Index

A

Afghanistan, 17–18, 25, 108–9, 232
al Qaeda. *See* Qaeda, al, and al Qaeda in Iraq (AQI)
Alford, Julian, 124, 180
Allen, John R.: advisory skills, 210–11; breakthrough forces, success of use of, 239; counterterrorism operations, 202; exploitation force, 189, 209, 210; helicopter governance, 216, 219; indigenous security forces and deescalation of insurgency, 206–7; MAGTF use, 188–89; postconflict decisions and policies, opinion about, 4, 57; postconflict transitions, 189, 210–11, 216, 221, 225, 226; reconnaissance fighting, 203; sheikh, meeting with, 168, 210–11; transition from combat to SASO operations, 208–9, 243; tribal engagement, importance of, 8, 186–88, 189, 236–37; violent events in Anbar, changes in, 7, 208
Anah, 11–12, 145, 160, 181–82, 226
Anbar Province: election process and voter turnout, 104–6; insurgent operations and terrorist activity in, ix, 1, 17, 18, 84–90, 102–3, 231–32; insurgent operations, AQI control of, 107–13; local knowledge of actors in, 71; location of, 11; naming of, 11; "not winnable" characterization of, 7, 161–62; population centers and geography of region, 11–12; population statistics, 11; SASO mission plans, 63–69, 72–74, 234; SASO mission, transition to after combat operations, 40–42; securing the peace operations, role of tribes in, 54; security environment in, 67, 69–71, 72–74, 106–7, 231–32; success and victory in, ix, x, 7, 103, 229–230, 232, 234, 239, 244; violent events in, 1–2, 4, 7, 24–28, 106–7, 108, 144–45, 154, 161–62, 190–91, 207–8, 231–32
armed groups, subtypes and characteristics of, 149–151, 234–35, 237–38, 267n19
army, Iraqi. *See* security forces/Iraqi security forces (ISF)/Iraqi army
Army, U.S.: 82nd Airborne, 41, 64, 65–66, 67, 74; 101st Airborne, 64; cavalry units, 40, 95–96, 129, 157–58, 193–94; COIN doctrine, 151, 152–53, 158, 238–39, 267–68n24; SASO mission, transition to after combat operations, 40–42; V Corps, 58

| 279

Army Brigade Combat Teams: 1st BCT, 85, 202; 2-2 BCT, 117, 119–120, 129–130, 131; 2-28 BCT, 117, 129, 131

Awakening and Anbar Awakening Council, ix, 110, 135, 137–140, 164–69, 174–75, 183, 186, 212–15, 221–22

B

Ba'athist Party: de-Ba'athification order, 46–49, 57; dissolution of, 46; loss of power of, 22, 24; murder of leader of, 25; playing cards with pictures of officials, 40; sheikhs and tribalism, attitude toward, 21

Baghdad: combat operations, 60; counterinsurgency operations, 182; election process and security in, 104–5; fall of, 39; jihadi insurgent and terrorist activity in, 25; reconstruction and restoration of basic services, 55; reconstruction and restoration of basic services in, 56; selection of as capital, 10

Barnes, David, 132–33

battle dress uniform (BDU), 65–66

beliefs and value system: Arab culture, 19–20; Bedouin traditions, 13–15, 32; cultural understanding and, 9, 12–20; Islamic principles, 15–19, 31, 247–48nn22–25, 248–49n29; loyalty and commitment to tribes, 13–14, 31–32; operational do's and don'ts, 29–31

bin Laden, Osama, 18, 25, 109

Blackwater USA contractors, 74–76, 77, 78

Blue Diamond. *See* Marine Division, 1st (Blue Diamond)

breakthrough forces, 189, 204–7, 239

Bremer, L. Paul, III: Blackwater contractors, response to attack on, 76; constitution, writing and ratification of, 52–53; de-Ba'athification order, 46–49; decisiveness of, 45; education and experience of, 44; electricity and power system, 55; Fallujah cease-fire, 79; Iraqi army, disbanding of, 49–52; postwar government role of, 43–46; shoot-the-looters idea, 45–46; tribes, attitude toward and role in securing the peace, 53–54, 112; wrong moves by, 32

Bush administration and George W. Bush, 33–40, 47–48, 55, 76, 162–64

C

Carney, Tim, 48, 49

Casey, George, 114–15, 117, 143, 153, 159, 229

Central Command, U.S. (CENTCOM), 35, 38–39, 50, 51–52

Central Intelligence Agency (CIA), 12, 34, 48, 69–71

Chalabi, Ahmed, 36, 38, 43, 45, 46, 47, 49

Charlton, John, 190–94, 205, 214, 224, 227–28

Clardy, Herman, 198–99

Clausewitz, Carl von, 26, 151, 233, 243–44
clear, hold, build strategy, 4, 119, 158–59, 238
Coalition forces and tribes, alliances between, ix–x, 4, 8, 41, 112, 113–16, 137–140, 146–49, 209–15, 232, 236–37
Coalition Provisional Authority (CPA): Bremer role in, 44–45; constitution, writing and ratification of, 52–53; de-Ba'athification order, 46–49, 57; disdain for tribal traditions by, 29; Iraqi army, disbanding of, 49–52, 115; OHRA transition to, 44; reconstruction and restoration of basic services, plans and resources for, 54–56; tribes, attitude toward and role in securing the peace, 53–54, 112; wrong moves by, 32
Connable, Alfred B., 146–47, 148, 155–56
Conway, James "Jim": Anbar insurgents, battles against, 85; Blackwater contractors, response to attack on, 75; combat operations, 58–60; education and experience of, 58; end of Marine presence in Iraq, 232; Fallujah battles and taking control of city, 78–79, 80, 81–82, 92–102; Fallujah Brigade, 80, 91; I MEF command by, 58; photo of, 60; return to Iraq, 64; SASO, opinion about, 60; SASO mission plans, 66, 73
counterinsurgency (COIN) strategy and campaign, 230; advisors to manage postconflict transition and success of, 209–15, 240; breakthrough forces, 189, 204–7, 239; clear, hold, build strategy, 4, 119, 158–59, 238; design, development, and adaptation of strategies and tactics, ix, 4, 151–57, 238–240; *FM 3-24* manual and strategy, 152–53, 158, 229–230, 238–39; indigenous security forces and, 147–48, 154–56, 205–7, 240–41; intelligence and success of, 199–203, 241–42; kinetic operations and it's still war, 119, 190–99, 239–240; lessons learned, 238–244; Partnership campaign plan, 114–16, 117–131, 142–43; planning for, 1; popular support and success of, 65; security for population and, 118–19, 153, 154–56, 183, 189, 202, 239; success of, ix, x, 1–2, 4, 7, 182–83, 229–230; tipping point in, 182–83; transition from combat to SASO operations, 207–9, 242–43, 244; unexpected, preparations for, 243–44
counterterrorism operations, 202
Crowe, William "Bill," 159–160, 161, 181–82, 198
culture and traditions: Arab culture, 19–20; beliefs and value system, 9, 12–20, 29–31, 247–48nn22–25, 248–49n29; concept of culture, 8; economy and economic conditions, 9; ethnonationalist identity, 19–20, 29; foreign domination, resistance to, 20;

framework for understanding, 8–9; physical environment and geographical location, 9, 10–12; political and economic performance and, 246n2; political structures and power, 9, 26–28; social organizations, 9, 26–28; understanding of and operational do's and don'ts, 28–32, 156–57; understanding of, importance of, 4, 6–8, 26–28, 32, 157, 236–37

D

Davis, Stephen, 120–21, 122, 123, 124

Defense, Department of. *See* Pentagon and Department of Defense

Denver AO: area included in, 72; counterinsurgency operations, 119, 120–25, 159–160, 179–182, 183, 198–99; insurgent operations, 73–74, 86, 89, 97, 106, 110; relief in place, 106, 116–17; security and stability operations, 189; tribal resistance to AQI, 133–35

Devlin, Pete, 148, 161–62, 175, 176, 183

Dulaym Liwa, 11. *See also* Anbar Province

Dulaym tribal confederation: adoption of US ways, no interest in, 32; Bedouin traditions, 13–15; history of, 13, 22, 28; Islamic principles followed by, 18; power and status of under Saddam, 21–22, 24, 28; respect for, 29; Saddam, alliance with, 21–22; security obligations and functions, 21–22, 24, 30–32; size and power of, 11, 22–24; social and political power of, 26–28, 31–32; traditions, satisfaction of living in accord with, 32

Dunford, Joe: Anbar deployment planning, 1; Anbar insurgents, battles against, 85; battle dress uniform decision, 66; Fallujah battles and success of insurgents, 81; Fallujah battles and taking control of city, 92–93, 94, 96–97, 98; Iraqi security forces, intimidation of by insurgents, 91–92; photo of, 67; SASO mission in southern Iraq, 62–63; SASO mission plans, 66–69, 72–73, 74; test of wills against insurgents, 103; tribes and Coalition forces, alliances between, 112; urban warfare training, 77

E

economy and economic conditions, 9, 37, 118, 189, 222–25

ethnonationalist identity, 19–20, 29

Euphrates River, 10–12

exploitation force, 189, 209, 210, 239, 244

F

Fallujah: AQI control of, 110; battles to take control of city, 76–84, 92–102, 103; Blackwater contractors, attack on, 74–76, 77, 78; cease-fire orders, 79–80, 81–82; city council members, 21; counterinsurgency operations, 120, 125–26, 161, 176–79,

194–97; defeat of Marines, claims of, 81; election process in, 141; geography of region, 12; insurgent infrastructure in, 84, 87–88; insurgent operations and terrorist activity in, 7, 25–26, 73, 77–84, 85, 87–89; Jolan district, 25, 78, 98, 99; mosques as part of battlefield, 78, 84, 105; police officers in, 132–33; postconflict governance in, 220; protest outside school in, 41–42; RCT-1 deployment to, 68; rebuilding of, 126, 161; SASO mission, 73; SASO mission plans, 68–69; security environment in, 63, 68, 73, 176–79

Fallujah Brigade, 80, 90–92

Feith, Doug, 36, 38, 43, 47–48

"First, Do No Harm," 66, 74

five, rule of, 30

Franks, Tommy, 35, 36, 42, 51–52, 58, 69

Future of Iraq project, 34–35

G

Garner, Jay, 35, 37, 39–40, 42–43, 48, 56

Gaskin, Walter, 184–86, 187, 188, 191, 204, 208, 209, 213, 216, 218, 219, 227, 228, 241, 242, 243

geographical location and physical environment, 9, 10–12

Governing Council, 45, 49, 52–53, 57, 79

government in Iraq: advisors to manage postconflict transition, 189, 209–15, 240; Chalabi role in, 36, 38, 43, 45, 46, 47, 49; civil servants, paychecks for, 37; constitution, writing and ratification of, 52–53; de-Ba'athification order, 46–49, 57; democracy and role of tribes in, 53–54, 112; democracy and transformation of region, 35–37, 104–6; de-Saddamification, 48; elections, planning and timeline for, 42–43; elections and path to sovereignty, 52–53; elections for national assembly and council representatives, 104–6, 140–42; exiles, role of in, 38; government buildings, looting of, 39; helicopter governance, 216, 219; interim government, 39–46; Iraqi Interim Authority plan, 38; laws and rules compared to reality on the ground, 45; Partnership campaign plan, 118; postconflict institutions and functions, 189, 215–222; regime change, 22, 28, 33, 34–37; temporary government, timeline for, 42–44; whole-of-government campaign, 216

Great Britain, 19–20, 24, 186–87

Gurganus, Charles "Mark," 126, 188, 189, 191, 204, 205–6, 210, 212

H

Hadid, Umar Husayn, 25–26, 91, 99

Haditha: counterinsurgency operations, 119, 122, 123, 124, 125, 159–160, 198; deaths if Iraqis in, 257n5; insurgent operations in, 7, 85, 86, 87, 97, 145; population

centers and geography of region, 11–12; SASO mission, 72
Hanafi school, 15, 18, 248–49n29
Hanbali school, 15, 16–18, 247–48nn22–25
Hit: counterinsurgency operations, 119, 122, 123, 124, 159–160, 182; insurgent operations in, 7, 86, 87, 89, 97, 145; population centers and geography of region, 11–12; SASO mission, 72
honor, personal and group, 14, 29–30, 31
Howcroft, James "Jim," 63, 70–71, 74, 81, 84, 98–99, 103, 237
Humanitarian and Reconstruction Assistance, Office of (OHRA), 39–40, 42–43, 44, 54–55, 62
Husaybah, 72, 86, 87, 97, 119, 122, 124, 142, 159–160
Hussein, Saddam, 18, 21–22, 24, 28, 33, 46

I

improvised explosive device (IED), 73–74, 84, 88, 192
innovation and learning, 2–4, 151–57, 186–88, 230, 233–34, 245n5, 246n16
insurgent operations: armed groups involvement in, 149–151, 234–35, 237–38, 267n19; defeat of, 1–2, 7, 232, 234; fragmentation of insurgency, 238; increase in, 7; infrastructure for, 18, 84, 87–88, 199–203; intimidation and terrorist acts, 25–26, 27, 32, 84–90, 91–92, 102–3, 140, 147–49, 164–69, 174, 231–32; jihadi warfighting principles, 83–84, 261n87; Marine preparedness to fight, 4; mosques as part of battlefield, 78, 84, 99, 105; "not winnable" characterization of, 7, 161–62; organized insurgency, identification of, 69–71, 234, 237; sanctuaries for, 81; training bases, 86; transnational jihadi warriors, 17–18, 98–99, 136; tribes and insurgents, alliances between, ix, 24–28, 41–42, 57, 109–13, 146–49, 238
intelligence operations, 199–203, 241–42
Iraq (Mesopotamia): ethnic and religious population distribution, 27; foreign domination, resistance to, 20; global battle against US in, 1, 17, 18, 108–9, 234; history of and cradle-of-civilization role, 10–11; independence of, 19–20; mandate system, 19–20, 187; map of, 23; stability in, map of, 108; Sunni rule of, 20; UN sanctions against, 18, 21–22; violent events in, 107, 108; war with Iran, 21; withdrawal of US troops from, 163–64
Iraq Study Group, 162–64
Iraq Tribal Study, 12–13, 22
Iraq War/Operation Iraqi Freedom (OIF): combat operations, 58–60; conventional war and fighting, 26; execution and success of war plan, 39; humanitarian army and battalions of engineers and

specialists to rebuild following, 33; jihadi insurgent and terrorist activity in response to, 25, 32; loss of power by Saddam, 22; occupation, force strength needed for, 114; occupation plan, 37; planning and preparations for, 4, 26, 33–39, 114; postwar transition plans, 4, 33–40, 42–43, 207–9, 242–43; resistance to invasion and occupation, 4, 7, 26, 29, 40–42; Sunni population opinions about, 7; sweets and flowers, greeting troops with, 36; wrong moves in aftermath of, 26, 32. *See also* security and stability operations (SASO)

Iraqi Leadership Council, 43

Iraqi National Congress (INC), 36, 43, 47

Islam: conversion of region to, 13, 15; moderate interpretation of, 18, 248–49n29; outside influences on, corrupting nature of, 17; pillars of, 17, 248n25; principles of, 15–19, 31, 247–48nn22–25, 248–49n29; purity of, 16; Return to Faith campaign, 18; splitting along sectarian lines, 15

J

jihad (holy war): elevation of and justification for, 17; global battle against US in Anbar, 1, 17, 18, 108–9, 234; homegrown Salafi jihadists, 18, 108; killing of jihadists, 202; Salafi jihad ideology, 16–18; training camp for, 25; transnational jihadi warriors, 17–18, 98–99, 108–9, 136; warfighting principles, 83–84, 261n87

Johnson, Stephen, 116, 118–19

Joint Special Operations Command (JSOC), 129, 199–200, 202, 239–240

Jones, Grier, 144–45

Jurney, William "Bill," 132, 173, 193, 195, 197

justice system and methods, 30, 31–32

K

Kelly, John F.: Anbar, success and victory in, 232, 234, 244; I MEF command by, 231; Iraqi security forces, development of, 90; organized insurgency, identification of, 69, 234; photo of, 231; postwar transition plans, 33; resentment of Iraqi population toward US, 61–62; SASO mission in southern Iraq, 62; violent events in Anbar, changes in, 1–2, 4, 231–32

Khalilzad, Zalmay, 44, 147–48, 209–10, 240

kinetic operations: Army use of, 65, 67; concept of, 65; counterinsurgency operations and need for kinetic operations, 119, 190–99, 239–240; focus on and planning for, 35, 39, 40; ineffectiveness of, ix, 1; transition from combat to SASO operations, 40–42, 207–9, 242–43, 244

Koenig, John, 211, 216–17, 220, 223
Krulak, Charles C. "Chuck," 76, 77, 96, 151–52
Krulak, Victor, 3

L

Lang, W. Patrick, 29, 30, 32
League of Nations and mandate system, 19–20, 187
learning and innovation, 2–4, 151–57, 186–88, 230, 233–34, 245n5, 246n16
lessons learned, 235–244; armed groups, subtypes and characteristics of, 237–38; counterinsurgency is still war, 239–240; counterinsurgency strategy and skills, 238–244; cultural understanding, importance of, 236–37; population-centric conflict, 236; unexpected, preparations for, 243–44
looters and looting, 39, 45–46

M

MacFarland, Sean, 155, 158–59, 161, 166, 169, 170, 171–74, 175–76, 190
mandate system, 19–20, 187
Marine Air-Ground Task Force, 72–73, 188–89, 209
Marine Corps, U.S.: attributes, character, and identity of, ix, 3, 233; birthday of, 100; cadences of drill instructors, 5–6, 101, 232–33, 244; Center for Advanced Operational Culture, 8; culture and traditions, 233; culture and traditions of, 2–6; end of Marine presence in Iraq, 232; framework for understanding culture, development of, 8–9; history and legacy of, ix, 4–6, 232–33, 244; history and legacy of, study of and learning from, 3, 5–6, 232–34; History Division, Field History Branch interviews, x; learning and innovation in, 2–4, 151–57, 186–88, 230, 233–34; training and professional education, 3, 5–6, 186–88; urban warfare training, 76–77
Marine Division, 1st (Blue Diamond): Anbar insurgents, battles against, 85; battle dress uniform, 65–66; combat operations, 58–60; command of, 59, 82; decorations earned by, 58; force strength of, 58; honor to the Corps and moral integrity directive, 59, 66; return to Iraq, 63–64; return to US, 63; SASO in southern Iraq, 60–64; Task Force Scorpion, 61
Marine Division, 2nd, 116–17, 119, 121, 129, 137–38, 141
Marine Expeditionary Force, 1st (I MEF): Anbar insurgents, battles against, 84–90; battle dress uniform, 65–66; combat elements and force strength for SASO mission, 71–73; combat operations, 58–60; command of, 1, 58, 90, 152, 231; counterinsurgency operations, 153–162, 164; deployments of, 1, 64, 71–73, 152, 153–54, 231; Fallujah battles and taking control of city, 76–84, 92–102, 103; relief in

place, 106, 116–17; success of counterinsurgency campaign, ix, 1–2, 4, 229–230; tribal engagement skills, 156–57

Marine Expeditionary Force, 2nd (II MEF): command of, 7; conflict to SASO operations, transition to, 243, 244; counterinsurgency operations, 117–131, 154, 155, 184–86; deployments of, 106, 184; relief in place, 106, 116–17; success of counterinsurgency campaign, ix, 229–230; tribal engagement strategy and skills, 186–88, 189, 204–5, 212–15, 237, 241

Marine Light Armored Reconnaissance Battalions: 1st LAR, 72, 86; 3rd LAR, 98, 181; 4th LAR, 61

Marine Regimental Combat Team, 1st (RCT-1): Fallujah battles and taking control of city, 76, 77–79, 82, 87–89, 95–97, 98–101; Fallujah region deployment, 68, 71; relief in place, 117, 125; return to Iraq, 63–64, 68

Marine Regimental Combat Team, 2nd (RCT-2), 106, 117, 119, 120–25, 134, 159–160, 198–99, 202

Marine Regimental Combat Team, 5th (RCT-5), 67, 160–61, 176–79

Marine Regimental Combat Team, 6th (RCT-6), 194–98, 202

Marine Regimental Combat Team, 7th (RCT-7), 72, 73–74, 86, 89, 95–97, 98–101, 117, 159–160, 180–82, 198

Marine Regimental Combat Team, 8th (RCT-8), 106, 117, 120, 125–28

Mattis, James N.: Blackwater contractors, response to attack on, 75; Blue Diamond command by, 59; COIN doctrine, 152; combat operations, 59–60; experience and reputation of, 59; Fallujah battles and taking control of city, 77; "First, Do No Harm," 66, 74; honor to the Corps and moral integrity directive from, 59, 257n5; nickname for, 59; "No Better Friend, No Worse Enemy," 59, 66, 74; opinions about, 59; photo of, 60, 67; Ramadi attacks and taking control of city, 175; SASO mission plans, 66, 73

McChrystal, Stanley A. "Stan," 129, 200–203

McGrath, Jim, 195–97, 211–12

McMaster, H. R., 157–58

Mesopotamia. *See* Iraq (Mesopotamia)

military learning and innovation, 2–4, 151–57, 186–88, 230, 233–34, 245n5, 246n16

military operations on urban terrain (MOUT) doctrine, 76–77

Mullen, William "Bill," 126, 194–95, 196

N

Najaf, 86–87, 90

nation building, 33, 36, 37, 104–6

National Security Council (NSC), 37–38, 47–48

nationalism and ethnonationalist identity, 19–20, 29

Natonski, Richard, 82, 84, 92, 93–95, 116, 117
Nicholson, Larry, 160–61, 176–79
"No Better Friend, No Worse Enemy," 59, 66, 74
Norwood, Byron, 101

O

Operation Iraqi Freedom. *See* Iraq War/Operation Iraqi Freedom (OIF)
operational do's and don'ts, 28–32, 156–57
Ottoman invasion and occupation, 10, 12, 19, 24, 28

P

Pentagon and Department of Defense: de-Ba'athification order, 47–48; postconflict operations, 215; postwar decisions, disputes about, 38, 47–48; postwar transition plans, 33–34, 35–39, 42–43, 243; Rice and decision-making process, opinion about, 37
Petraeus, David: *FM 3-24* manual and strategy, 152–53, 158, 229–230, 238–39; Iraqi army, opinion about disbanding of, 51; Iraqi army, recruitment of Sunni to, 115; Surge forces, 229–230
police units. *See* security forces/Iraqi security forces (ISF)/Iraqi army
political structures and power: advisors to manage postconflict transition, 209–15, 240; cultural understanding and, 9, 26–28; Dulaym confederation, social and political power of, 26–28, 31–32; intimidation of tribal and political leaders, 140, 164–69; Sunni domination of, 20, 56; tribalism as basis for, 20–24

Q

Qaeda, al, and al Qaeda in Iraq (AQI): Anbar and global battle against US, 1, 17, 18, 108–9, 234; Anbar insurgency, control of, 107–13, 144–45; Fallujah operations, 82–84; infrastructure and network to support, 18, 84, 87–88, 199–203; leadership of, 17; tribal resistance to, 111–13, 133–37, 164–69, 174–75, 182–83
Qa'im, Al: AQI, resistance to, 111–12; AQI control of, 110, 112, 145; counterinsurgency operations, 119, 122, 124, 159–160, 180–82, 198; insurgent operations in, 7, 85, 86, 87, 97; population centers and geography of region, 11–12; SASO mission, 72; tribal resistance to AQI, 133–35

R

Raleigh AO: area included in, 71; counterinsurgency operations, 120, 125–28, 160–61, 176–79, 183, 194–98; insurgent operations, 87–88, 106; relief in place, 106, 116–17; security and stability operations, 189; tribal resistance to AQI, 135
Ramadi: aerial view of, 129; AQI, resistance to, 112–13, 135; AQI

control of, 110–11, 113, 144–45; counterinsurgency operations, 119–120, 128–131, 159, 170–79, 191–94; election process in, 141; insurgent operations in, 7, 80–81, 85–86, 128–131; physical environment and geographical location, 12; police force and station in, 165, 174; road race in, 145–46, 176, 230; SASO mission, transition to after combat operations, 40; security environment in, 155–56, 170–76; violent events in, 144–45, 190

Ramadi Liwa, 11. *See also* Anbar Province

Rawah, 7, 72, 87, 89, 119, 145, 160, 181–82

reconstruction and restoration of basic services: electricity and power system, 55; in Fallujah, 126, 161; jobs programs, 55–56, 225; planning for, 33–40, 42–43; resources for, 42–43, 54–56, 62, 222–25, 243; role of Marines in, 232; Shia area, condition of infrastructure in, 55, 60–61; transition from combat to SASO operations, 40–42, 207–9, 210, 242–43, 244

regime change, 22, 28, 33, 34–37

Republican Guards, 21–22, 49

respect, 29, 31, 41, 157

Rice, Condoleezza, 33, 37–38, 158

rule of law and criminal justice system, 189, 226–27

Rumsfeld, Donald, 35, 36, 37, 43, 69, 76, 102, 114

Rutbah, 12, 72, 86, 198–99

S

Salafi movement, 16–18, 27, 248n24

security and stability operations (SASO): Anbar SASO mission plans, 63–69, 72–74; Anbar security environment assessment, 67, 69–71, 72–74; Anbar security environment reality, 73–74; Blue Diamond operations in southern Iraq, 60–64; concept of and definition of, 60; doctrine for, 62, 235; First Fifteen Plays, 66–69, 72–73, 90; planning and preparations for, 4, 33–40, 42–43, 62, 234; postconflict operations, 189, 215–227; security for population and COIN operations, 118–19, 153, 154–56, 183, 189, 202, 239; success of in southern Iraq, 62–63; transition to after combat operations, 40–42, 207–9, 242–43, 244; troop strength for, 39

security forces/Iraqi security forces (ISF)/Iraqi army: AQI killing of police, 110; building ISF/indigenous forces, 90–92, 114–16, 118, 131–33, 143, 147–48, 154–56, 204–7, 240–41; capacity to stand on own, 205–7, 227–29; de-Ba'athification effort and strength of, 48; disbanding of, 34, 49–52, 115; Fallujah Brigade, 80, 90–92; force strength of, 205, 206; independent operation of militias and indigenous forces, 112; intimidation of by insurgents, 91–92, 147, 174; loyalty of, 50; Partnership campaign plan, forces for, 114–16;

recruitment of tribal members, x, 8, 21–22, 115–16, 147, 204–7, 240–41; role of in postwar Iraq, 38, 50, 51–52, 227–29

sheikhs: AQI, resistance to, 111–13, 133–37, 164–69, 174–75, 182–83; ascension of, 23–24; Ba'athist Party attitudes toward, 21; power structure of tribes and, 22–24, 32, 136; Saddam, alliance with, 21–22, 24; security and protection obligation of, 22–23, 112, 143; tribes and Coalition forces, alliances between, 41, 112, 148; tribes and insurgents, alliances between, 238; working with, important of, 32

Shia: civil war between Sunnis and, 25; election process and empowerment of, 105; empowerment of through US presence, 7, 56–57; infrastructure in population areas, 55, 60–61; intimidation and terrorist acts against, 177; as majority sect, 15; recruitment of members for security units, 115–16; resentment of population toward US, 61–62; revenge campaign against Sunni by, 28; social engineering efforts of US, 57; splitting of Islam along sectarian lines, 15; university system, control of, 56–57

Shuster, Scott, 157, 180–81
Simcock, Richard, 194, 197–98
Sistani, Ali Al-, 52–53
Smith, Rupert, 26, 149–151, 153, 236
social organizations: advisors to manage postconflict transition, 209–15, 240; cultural understanding and, 9, 26–28; Dulaym confederation, social and political power of, 26–28, 31–32; Sunni domination of, 20, 56; tribalism as basis for, 20–24

Soviet Union, 17–18, 108–9
Special Republican Guards, 21–22, 50
State, Department of: de-Ba'athification order, 47–48; Future of Iraq project, 34–35; postconflict operations, 215–17; postwar decisions, disputes about, 38, 47–48; postwar transition plans, 34–35, 243; Rice and decision-making process, opinion about, 37–38

Sunni Arabs: about OIF, opinions, 7; Anbar population of, 15; armed resistance and loss of status of, 20, 28, 40–42, 57; character and identity of, 9–10, 13 (*see also* beliefs and value system); civil war between Shia and, 25; de-Ba'athification order and status of, 46–49, 57; election process and loss of power of, 105–6; elections, participation in, 140–42; fears of, failure to manage, 56–57; Islamic schools of thought subscribed to by, 15–18, 31, 247–48nn22–25, 248–49n29; loss of power and status of, 20, 28, 40–42, 56–57; recruitment of members for security units, 115–16; Return to Faith campaign, 18; rule of Iraq by, 20; Shia revenge campaign against, 28; social and political power of, 20,

28, 56; splitting of Islam along sectarian lines, 15; superiority and status of, 15, 28. *See also* Dulaym tribal confederation

Sunni Triangle, 1, 20, 21–22, 24, 26, 56

Surge forces, 1–2, 229–230

Swannack, Charles, 41

T

Tal Afar, 157–59, 170, 171

Task Force 145 (Task Force 626), 93, 99, 128–29, 177, 178, 182, 191–92, 200–203, 239–240

Tawhid al-Jihad, 25

Tigris River, 10–11

Tikrit, 40, 55, 60

Toolan, John: Fallujah battles and taking control of city, 76, 77–79, 81, 87; Fallujah region deployment, 68, 71; Iraqi security forces, development of, 90–91; Nicholson as replacement, 160; photo of, 72; return to Iraq, 63–64, 68; SASO mission plans, 68–69

Topeka AO: area included in, 72; counterinsurgency operations, 119–120, 128–131, 170–79, 183, 191–94; insurgent operations, 85–86, 97; relief in place, 106, 117; security and stability operations, 189

traffic and traffic laws, 45

tribes: AQI, resistance to, 111–13, 133–37, 164–69, 174–75, 182–83; arming of, 22; Bedouin traditions, 13–15, 32; Bremer and CPA attitude toward, 53–54, 112; Coalition forces and tribes, alliances between, ix–x, 4, 8, 41, 112, 113–16, 137–140, 146–49, 209–15, 232, 236–37; concept of and definition of, 13; confederation structure, 22, 24; duty to fight, 29–30; engagement strategy and operational do's and don'ts, 28–32, 156–57; engagement strategy and skills, 147–48, 156–57, 186–88, 189, 204–5, 212–15, 237, 241; fighting methods and skills, 14–15, 24, 31–32; history of, 28; honor, personal and group, 14, 29–30, 31; individual responsibility toward, 14; insurgents and tribes, alliances between, ix, 24–28, 41–42, 57, 109–13, 146–49, 238; leadership of, importance of working with, 32; loyalty and commitment to, 13–14, 31–32; political structures and power, 20–24, 32, 136; recruitment of members for police and security units, x, 8, 21–22, 115–16, 147, 154–56, 204–7, 240–41; respect for, 29, 31, 41, 157; revenge as duty, 14, 30, 31–32, 41, 136; Saddam, alliance with, 21–22, 24, 28; securing the peace, role in, 53–54, 112; security obligations and functions, 21–22, 24, 30–32, 112, 143; sheikhs and power structure in, 22–24, 32; social organizations and, 20–24; understanding of importance

of, ix. *See also* Dulaym tribal confederation
Tucker, Mark, 95

U

United Nations (UN), 18, 21–22, 35
United States (US): adoption of US ways by tribes, 32; global battle against by AQI, 1, 17, 18, 108–9, 234; jihadi insurgent and terrorist activity against, 25, 27, 32; withdrawal of troops from Iraq, 163–64

V

value system. *See* beliefs and value system
Vukovich, Nick, 86, 89

W

Wahhabi movement, 16, 247–48nn22–23
war: armed groups, subtypes and characteristics of, 149–151, 234–35, 237–38, 267n19; center of gravity and, 26, 84, 236; conventional war and fighting, 26, 40; counterinsurgency is still war, 239–240; fog of war, 3–4, 188, 233–34, 243–44; fourth-generation warfare, 83, 102–3; generations of warfare, 83; irregular warfare and long war, 26, 65, 102–3; irregular warfare, concept of and preparations for, 31–32, 59, 65, 149–151, 234–35, 237–38; irregular warfare, cultural understanding and success in, 4, 6; irregular warfare, understanding of, 59; jihadi warfighting principles, 83–84, 261n87; know your enemy, 237–38; phases of, planning for, 35, 38–39; population-centric conflict, 149–151, 236; raids and raiding traditions, 32; tribal fighting methods and skills, 14–15, 24, 31–32; unexpected, preparations for, 169–170, 243–44; urban warfare training, 76–77
West, Bing, 74, 80, 86, 100–101, 125
Williams, James L., 119, 137–140, 141
Wolfowitz, Paul, 35, 36, 43, 114
Woodridge, Christopher, 86–87
World War I, 19, 32, 186–87

Z

Zarqawi, Abu Mussab al-: election, war declaration against, 104, 140–42; Fallujah insurgent operations, 77–78, 99; global battle against US in Anbar, 109; intimidation and terrorist acts under, 25, 140, 147, 149, 174, 177; jihadi training camp of, 25; killing of, 202; network to support jihadi movement, 18; Tawhid al-Jihad creation under, 25; tribes and insurgents, alliances between, 113
Zilmer, Richard, 152, 153–57, 159, 161, 162, 168, 171, 179–180, 185, 238

About the Author

DR. RICHARD H. SHULTZ JR. is professor of international politics at the Fletcher School, Tufts University, and the director of Fletcher's International Security Studies Program. For the last ten years Dr. Shultz has served as a Senior Fellow to the U.S. Special Operations Command's Joint Special Operations University. His many books include *Insurgents, Terrorists, and Militias: The Warriors of Contemporary Combat* and *The Secret War against Hanoi: Kennedy's and Johnson's Use of Spies, Saboteurs, and Covert Warriors in North Vietnam.*

The **Naval Institute Press** is the book-publishing arm of the U.S. Naval Institute, a private, nonprofit, membership society for sea service professionals and others who share an interest in naval and maritime affairs. Established in 1873 at the U.S. Naval Academy in Annapolis, Maryland, where its offices remain today, the Naval Institute has members worldwide.

Members of the Naval Institute support the education programs of the society and receive the influential monthly magazine *Proceedings* or the colorful bimonthly magazine *Naval History* and discounts on fine nautical prints and on ship and aircraft photos. They also have access to the transcripts of the Institute's Oral History Program and get discounted admission to any of the Institute-sponsored seminars offered around the country.

The Naval Institute's book-publishing program, begun in 1898 with basic guides to naval practices, has broadened its scope to include books of more general interest. Now the Naval Institute Press publishes about seventy titles each year, ranging from how-to books on boating and navigation to battle histories, biographies, ship and aircraft guides, and novels. Institute members receive significant discounts on the Press' more than eight hundred books in print.

Full-time students are eligible for special half-price membership rates. Life memberships are also available.

For more information about Naval Institute Press books that are currently available, visit www.usni.org/press/books. To learn about joining the U.S. Naval Institute, please write to:

Member Services
U.S. Naval Institute
291 Wood Road
Annapolis, MD 21402-5034
Telephone: (800) 233-8764
Fax: (410) 571-1703
Web address: www.usni.org